ASP.NET 4.0 in Practice

ASP.NET 4.0 in Practice

DANIELE BOCHICCHIO
STEFANO MOSTARDA
MARCO DE SANCTIS

MANNING

Shelter Island

For online information and ordering of this and other Manning books, please visit www.manning.com. The publisher offers discounts on this book when ordered in quantity. For more information, please contact

Special Sales Department
Manning Publications Co.
20 Baldwin Road
PO Box 261
Shelter Island, NY 11964
Email: orders@manning.com

Manning Publications Co.	Development editor:	Cynthia Kane
20 Baldwin Road	Copyeditor:	Joan Celmer
PO Box 261	Typesetter:	Gordan Salinovic
Shelter Island, NY 11964	Cover designer:	Marija Tudor

ISBN 9781935182467
Printed in the United States of America
1 2 3 4 5 6 7 8 9 10 – MAL – 16 15 14 13 12 11

brief contents

contents

preface

This has been a very long journey. We found that writing this book was a challenging task, a much harder one than we had anticipated, but there were also moments of joy and discovery along the way! The idea for the book first came to us 18 months ago, and many days and nights have come and gone between the first sentence we wrote and the final book you hold today.

This is not our first book—it is the ninth book for Daniele, the seventh for Stefano, and the fourth for Marco—but it is the most complex one we've attempted because of the Techniques format we implement in the book. In addition, we were coauthoring another book for Manning Publications, *Entity Framework 4 in Action*, at roughly the same time.

Our aim in writing this book was not to create a typical reference book: there are plenty of those around. We felt that because ASP.NET has now reached a high level of maturity, the time was ripe for a book of best practices, and that is what we set out to do. Instead of focusing on how a class is implemented or what members offer, this book shows you how to get tasks done, the right way.

If your days (and nights) are spent on implementing web applications, you know that the best way to learn is from experience. This book contains all the tips we have learned in more than 10 years of working with ASP.NET. Everything in this book comes from our own day-by-day experience working as consultants as well from ASP.NET community members. We learned a lot from other people's problems, and we are happy to now share the solutions and best practices with you.

In this book you will find everything you need to build your web applications using a Problem/Solution/Discussion approach. Each scenario is motivated, then resolved, and finally discussed and explained.

This is a book that we felt was missing from the market. We hope we have filled that need successfully and we invite you to send us your feedback and let us know if we have been successful in attaining our goal.

We hope that our efforts will help you in your daily work. Enjoy the read, get your hands dirty, and have some fun!

acknowledgments

We can't mention by name all the individuals who made contributions to this book, adding to its value in ways both large and small. All of them deserve our sincere thanks, but here we will mention only a few whose help was invaluable to us during the writing process.

Cynthia Kane—Cynthia is our development editor at Manning. She was there for us from the the beginning, providing support and guidance, and has proved a master at transforming a bunch of words and images into an appealing book. Thank you.

Scott Guthrie—Scott, also known as ScottGu, is the man behind a number of products in the Microsoft Developer Division, including ASP.NET. Scott was always willing to let us solve some of the problems that we encountered with a beta. Thank you.

The Developer Division at Microsoft—thanks to everyone for their help and for building such a great product.

All the folks at ASPItalia.com, our "mother ship"—if we managed to collect enough scenarios for your problem-solving enjoyment, part of the credit has to go to the members of our community.

Many individuals at Manning worked hard on this book to bring it to our readers. A big thank-you to Michael Stephens and Marjan Bace for believing in us, and to the production team of Mary Piergies, Joan Celmer, Susan Harkins, Gordan Salinovic, and Janet Vail for their efforts.

Our peer reviewers deserve special mention. Their suggestions and feedback were invaluable and made this a much better book. We thank Alex Thissen, Dave Corun, Anil Radhakrishna, Philippe Vialatte, Nikander Bruggeman, Margriet Bruggeman,

Jason Jung, David Barkol, Perga Massimo, Braj Panda, Alessandro Gallo, Gary Bushey, Eric Swanson, Amos Bannister, and Andrew Siemer. We would also like to thank the technical proofreader, Matteo Casati, for his outstanding job of reviewing the final manuscript during production.

Last but not least, thank you, dear reader, for your trust in this book. Our hope is that it will help you in your day-to-day work and make you more productive with ASP.NET!

In addition to the people mentioned above, there are others who are important in Daniele's, Stefano's, and Marco's private lives. Even if they didn't directly work on the book, they contributed in other important ways to keep the authors on track.

Daniele would like to thank his wife Noemi for her support and patience and for giving him his beautiful sons, Alessio and Matteo. A big thank-you to my parents for letting me play with computers when I was a kid, and to my family in general for supporting me. A special thank-you to my coauthors for helping me on this journey: you guys rock! And thanks to Alessio, Marco, Cristian, Matteo, and Riccardo at ASPItalia.com for all their help and support.

Stefano wants to thank his wife Sara for being supportive and extremely patient, and his family (yes, the book is finally finished!). Special thanks to my closest friends (in alphabetical order), Federico, Gabriele, Gianni, and Riccardo. Of course, I can't help mentioning Filippo, who already bought a copy of the book. Finally, a big thank-you to William and Annalisa for their friendship and their support. My last words are for Marco and Daniele: thanks guys!

Marco thanks Stefano and Daniele because it's always a privilege when you have the chance to work with such smart and funny guys. I would also like to thank the whole ASPItalia.com team: I'm so proud to be a part of it. Special thanks to my family, and to Barbara, for their support and for the patience they've shown me. You have all my love.

about this book

ASP.NET is a Microsoft technology for building web applications that leverages all the fantastic technologies you can find in .NET Framework.

The book will move you from apprentice to master of ASP.NET by giving you specific techniques to solve problems you are likely to encounter. Each technique has a problem, solution, and discussion section. You might think of this book as a guided tour through ASP.NET best practices; we'll introduce each scenario, solve the problem, and then discuss the results. Once you've read this book, you'll have a better understanding of the most important aspects of designing, building, and maintaining ASP.NET-based applications.

You're going to find many devices in this book that will help you in the learning process:

- Figures—Pictures that show a workflow or summarize concepts
- Listings and snippets—Pieces of code that show the solution to a problem
- Tables—Visuals that summarize a list of features or options

We hope these devices will help make concepts clearer and the learning process faster.

Who should read this book?

This book targets developers who are working on everything from the smallest home application to the largest enterprise application. ASP.NET can be useful in simple scenarios, where you can apply most of the RAD features provided by Visual Studio 2010, as well as in enterprise applications, where its roots in .NET Framework offer a wider range of possibilities.

Roadmap

This book is designed for you to improve your ASP.NET expertise and is organized into sixteen chapters divided into five parts and two appendixes.

Part 1: ASP.NET fundamentals

In part 1, we introduce ASP.NET fundamentals. For those of you who are already somewhat familiar with ASP.NET, this part serves as a refresher before moving forward.

Chapter 1 provides an introduction to ASP.NET, with a focus on the Web Form's model.

Chapters 2 and 3 cover data access strategies in web applications. You'll learn the best practices for data access and how to leverage them in your application.

Part 2: ASP.NET Web Forms

Part 2 covers how to use ASP.NET Web Forms, the original model provided in ASP.NET to build the user interface.

Chapter 4 takes a tour into ASP.NET Web Forms, covering the most common scenarios. You'll also learn about the new features offered by version 4.0, how to use master pages to their fullest extent, and how to leverage URL routing.

Chapter 5 deals with one of the most common activities for a developer: using data binding and how to fully integrate this feature into your applications.

Chapter 6 covers an important extensibility point in ASP.NET Web Forms and shows how to build custom controls. You'll start with the basics and analyze complex scenarios.

Finally, chapter 7 explains how to control the markup generated by ASP.NET. You'll learn how to produce better markup and how adaptive rendering works.

Part 3: ASP.NET MVC

In part 3, we investigate the option to build your UI with ASP.NET MVC; after all, Web Forms aren't the only model you can use to do that.

ASP.NET MVC is a new option added in ASP.NET 3.5 SP1 and directly integrated into ASP.NET 4.0 as ASP.NET MVC 2.0. It's not the new Web Forms, but rather a different approach to solve the same problem. ASP.NET MVC lets you use the Model-View-Controller (MVC) pattern, and is built with testability and great markup control in mind.

Chapter 8 contains an introduction to ASP.NET MVC and shows the potential that this new toolkit offers when you're building the UI. You'll learn how to perform the basic actions that you're already acquainted with in ASP.NET Web Forms.

Chapter 9 covers how to customize and extend ASP.NET MVC in order to unlock the full potential that it offers.

Part 4: Security

In part 4, we take a look at one of the most important concerns of every web application: how to protect and make your code secure.

In chapter 10, we analyze the most common issues when dealing with security. You'll learn how to build stronger applications, how to avoid common errors, and how to preserve your application's integrity. You'll find plenty of helpful suggestions throughout the chapter.

Chapter 11 covers authentication and authorization in ASP.NET. It will show you how to build a secure area, how to leverage ASP.NET's infrastructure, and how to build a custom provider to extend the existing features provided by ASP.NET's Membership and Roles APIs.

Part 5: Advanced topics

Finally, part 5 is dedicated to more advanced scenarios and combines many of the topics previously addressed in this book. These chapters cover both ASP.NET Web Forms and MVC.

Chapter 12 covers how to integrate an ASP.NET application into an Ajax-enabled application and RIAs (Rich Internet Applications). We'll also take a look at how to leverage jQuery and ASP.NET Ajax.

In chapter 13, you'll learn how to handle state in ASP.NET—from cookies, to ViewState, to new features introduced in version 4, like the ability to compress the `SessionState`.

Chapter 14 is dedicated to caching. You'll find plenty of tips on how to achieve better scalability by implementing a good caching strategy. You'll also learn how to build custom cache providers and how Microsoft AppFabric caching works.

Chapter 15 contains miscellaneous topics related to fully extending ASP.NET, from `HttpRuntime`, to logging, to building a virtual path provider.

Last, chapter 16 offers some tips on how to build applications that perform better, with topics like content minifying, multithreading, and ParallelFX.

Code conventions and downloads

All the code used in this book is in a `monospace font like this`. The .NET code is in both C# and Visual Basic so that you're comfortable with the code, regardless of the language you are using. The language is indicated immediately above the relevant code. For longer lines of code, a wrapping character might be used so the code is technically correct while conforming to the limitations of a printed page. Code annotations accompany many of the listings, highlighting important concepts. In some cases, numbered bullets link to explanations that follow the listing.

Source code for all working examples in this book is available for download from the publisher's website at www.manning.com/ASP.NET4.0inPractice.

Author Online

The purchase of *ASP.NET 4.0 in Practice* includes free access to a private forum run by Manning Publications where you can make comments about the book, ask technical questions, and receive help from the authors and other users. You can access and subscribe to the forum at www.manning.com/ASP.NET4.0inPractice. This page provides information on how to get on the forum after you're registered, what kind of help is available, and the rules of conduct in the forum.

Manning's commitment to our readers is to provide a venue where a meaningful dialogue between individual readers and between readers and the authors can take place. It isn't a commitment to any specific amount of participation on the part of the authors, whose contributions to the book's forum remain voluntary (and unpaid). We suggest you try asking the authors some challenging questions, lest their interest stray! The Author Online forum and the archives of previous discussions will be accessible from the publisher's website as long as the book is in print.

In addition to the Author Online forum available on Manning's website, you can also contact us regarding this book, or anything else, through one of the following avenues:

- Book website—http://www.aspnetinpractice.com/
- Daniele's blog—http://blogs.5dlabs.it/daniele/
- Stefano's blog—http://blogs.5dlabs.it/stefano/
- Marco's blog—http://blogs.5dlabs.it/marcodes/

All comments sent to these blogs are moderated. We post nearly all comments; but if you include your email address or phone number, we won't post the comment out of respect for your privacy.

about the authors

DANIELE BOCHICCHIO is the cofounder of 5DLabs.it, a consulting agency specializing in ASP.NET, Silverlight, Windows Phone 7, and .NET Framework. He has worked on a lot of cool projects with many different technologies. Daniele is a well-known speaker and author, and you can find him at the main developer-focused events worldwide. He has also written several books, in both Italian and English. He's the coauthor of Manning's *Entity Framework 4 in Action*. Daniele is the network manager of ASPItalia.com, the largest Italian .NET Framework community. He currently lives in southern Italy with his family. You can reach him via his personal website at www.bochicchio.com/. Daniele shares his thoughts in 140 characters or less at http://twitter.com/dbochicchio/.

STEFANO MOSTARDA is a Microsoft MVP in the Data Platform category. He's a software architect focused on web applications and the cofounder of 5DLabs.it, a consulting agency specialized in ASP.NET, Silverlight, Windows Phone 7, and .NET Framework. Stefano is a professional speaker at many important Italian conferences and a well-known author. He has written many books for the Italian market and is the lead author of Manning's *Entity Framework 4 in Action*. He's also one of the leaders of the ASPItalia.com Network and a content manager of the LINQItalia.com website dedicated to LINQ and Entity Framework. In addition to visiting his blog, you can read his technical deliriums at http://twitter.com/sm15455/.

MARCO DE SANCTIS is a Microsoft MVP who has been designing and developing enterprise applications in distributed scenarios for the last seven years. He started developing with ASP.NET when it was first released; since then, he's improved his skills to become an application architect. Over the years, he has specialized in building distrib-uted services and has widened his knowledge to encompass technologies like Work-flow Foundation, Windows Communication Foundation, LINQ, and ADO.NET Entity Framework. Today Marco is one of the members of 5DLabs.it and works as a senior software engineer for one of the biggest Italian companies in the IT market. In his spare time, he's a content manager at ASPItalia.com. He shares his tweets at http://twitter.com/crad77.

about the cover illustration

The figure on the cover of *ASP.NET 4.0 in Practice* is captioned "Young woman from Montenegro." The illustration is taken from a collection of hand-colored drawings of Dalmatian regional dress costumes from the nineteenth century titled *Dalmacja*. The historical region of Dalmatia was much larger than it is today, stretching from the Istrian Peninsula to Albania along the Adriatic coast. Today, the region is divided between Croatia and Montenergo, the latter administering a small southernmost section. The long, rugged Dalmatian coast, backed by high mountains with hundreds of offshore islands, is fast becoming one of Europe's most popular vacation spots.

The young woman on the cover is wearing a costume typical for the villages and small towns found in this region. Rich embroidery, handmade linens, and colorful woolen scarves and skirts are the traditional elements of a Dalmatian costume, with small, not easily discernible decorative details indicating the locality of origin.

Dress codes and lifestyles have changed over the last 200 years, and the diversity by region, so rich at the time, has faded away. It is now hard to tell apart the inhabitants of different continents, let alone of different hamlets or towns separated by only a few miles. Perhaps we have traded cultural diversity for a more varied personal life—certainly for a more varied and fast-paced technological life.

Manning celebrates the inventiveness and initiative of the computer business with book covers based on the rich diversity of regional life of two centuries ago, brought back to life by illustrations from old books and collections like this one.

Part 1

ASP.NET Fundamentals

Welcome to ASP.NET 4.0 In Practice, dear reader!

ASP.NET was first introduced in the early 2000s as an effort from Microsoft to bring the easy development typical of Windows applications to the web. From this first attempt, the web has changed a lot and so has ASP.NET. Now ASP.NET is a mature framework that lets you create powerful applications.

This book is divided into four parts. Part 1 is going to give you a jump start into the fundamentals of ASP.NET. If you're an average developer who wants to put things in context, consider this part a quick refresher course. If you're new to ASP.NET, you'll get all the basics you need.

Chapter 1 is a general introduction to ASP.NET, specifically to the Web Form's model.

Chapters 2 and 3 cover data access strategies in web applications. You'll learn best practices for data access and how to leverage them in your applications.

Getting acquainted with ASP.NET 4.0

This chapter covers

- An introduction to ASP.NET
- Understanding ASP.NET Web Forms
- What's new in ASP.NET 4.0

ASP.NET is used to build web applications, and it's the preferred choice when using Microsoft technologies. It was built by Microsoft in the early 2000s as part of the .NET Framework initiative, which offered a unified environment in which to build and run applications for Windows developers. If you think of .NET Framework as a house, then ASP.NET is the rooms.

As ASP.NET approaches its fifth version (counting minor and major releases), the community of developers around ASP.NET is much more mature than it was ten years ago. In the beginning, ASP.NET developers came from backgrounds in Active Server Pages (ASP) or Visual Basic (VB) 6, so topics like design, architecture, and patterns were often ignored. But this isn't the case today. We've found ways to build better web applications and how to overcome challenges we face daily when we're working in ASP.NET. This book will explore how to solve common problems in ASP.NET, but before we get to the prize, everyone needs to be on the same footing.

3

You picked up this book because you want to get to know ASP.NET, specifically ASP.NET 4.0. Well, ASP.NET 4.0 isn't a revolutionary release, but an evolutionary one. In this book, we'll focus on the new features you'll find in version 4.0, but we'll also cover material from the previous releases that's still used in the 4.0 version. In the beginning of this book, you'll see content that's valuable in ASP.NET 3.5 or 2.0, but as we move further along, version 4.0 will be the main focus.

In this chapter, we'll introduce you to what ASP.NET is, how it works, and how to get started. We'll look at the typical architecture of an ASP.NET application and then move into the new features you'll find in the 4.0 release. When that's all said and done, we'll introduce a problem-solution-discussion scenario that should make the technology your friend rather than just an acquaintance.

1.1   Meet ASP.NET

You use ASP.NET to build web applications. Because it's part of .NET Framework, you'll use the same tools and similar code as when you write Windows desktop applications or service-oriented ones. Isn't that great? So what's new about ASP.NET 4.0 that you can't get in previous versions? Before we get into the specifics, let's install ASP.NET and then take a quick look at ASP.NET fundamentals.

1.1.1   Installing ASP.NET

ASP.NET 4.0 can run on top of Internet Information Services (IIS) 6.0 (Windows Server 2003), IIS 7.0 (Windows Server 2008 and Windows Vista), or IIS 7.5 (Windows Server 2008 R2 and Windows 7). ASP.NET uses Visual Studio as the integrated development environment (IDE) that it uses to create applications. To start building applications based on ASP.NET, you first need to install its runtime and a developer tool:

1 If you have Visual Studio 2010, install it on your machine. If you need the free version of Visual Studio, you can download Visual Web Developer Express at http://www.asp.net/.

2 If you want to test your applications on a server, download and install the software development kit (SDK) from http://www.asp.net/.

3 Optionally, download and install SQL Server 2008 Express (or a Developer Edition, if you prefer). SQL Server is useful if you want to use a database engine for development purposes.

More information on these downloads is available at http://www.asp.net/.

Visual Web Developer Express and Visual Studio Express

Visual Web Developer Express is a subset of Visual Studio, the IDE used to build ASP.NET applications. It's free, even for commercial use, but it's limited in functionality. If you're a professional developer, you'll want to buy a license for Visual Studio. Discussing Visual Studio isn't within the scope of this book, so we encourage you to take a look at http://msdn.microsoft.com/vstudio/.

In reality, you need only the .NET Framework SDK and a text editor to build ASP.NET applications. But if you want professional results, Visual Studio is the preferred choice for professional software development because it offers a lot of built-in features.

This book doesn't cover much about Visual Studio, but rather focuses on the nuts and bolts of using it to build applications in ASP.NET. We assume that you already have an understanding of Visual Studio and ASP.NET. If you don't, take some time to get familiar with them.

1.1.2 How ASP.NET works

ASP.NET is part of .NET Framework, so it takes full advantage of the object-oriented programming (OOP) capabilities offered by the framework itself. OOP lets you think in terms of objects and program their interactions. Because we as humans think in terms of objects in real life, OOP is one of the easiest programming paradigms to understand. When you create a web page using ASP.NET, you're creating an object with behaviors (the page's events), commands (methods), and state (objects instantiated).

The original and most common approach used to develop with ASP.NET uses Web Forms, which is similar to what VB gave Windows developers years ago. Every single object on a page is programmable and has events. Figure 1.1 shows the Web Form model.

Let's imagine a common item that occurs on a page: a button that can handle the user's click and provide feedback. Using the ASP.NET Web Form model, all you need to do is add a *Button* object and intercept the *Click* event. This approach is about as clear as it gets. You place objects on a design surface and program them, using a method that's similar to classic desktop application development.

Unfortunately, things tend to be a little bit complicated in real-world applications, so some specific scenarios might force you to take more control of the output. In such cases, using this approach to define the page might result in low flexibility. That's why, starting with version 4.0, you can choose a new alternative to define your pages, using ASP.NET MVC.

We'll go into Web Forms in more detail in chapters 6 through 9, and we'll explain ASP.NET MVC in chapters 10 and 11. Although most of the concepts we'll talk about from this point on are necessary to leverage the ASP.NET Web Form model, you might also find them useful when you're using ASP.NET MVC. Okay, now you've seen how ASP.NET works, let's try it out.

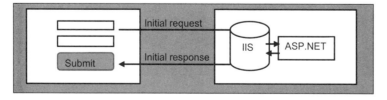

Figure 1.1   The Web Form model. Every interaction on the form causes a new request to go from the web browser to the server.

ASP.NET MVC versus Web Forms

There's a lot of debate in the ASP.NET community regarding MVC versus Web Forms. Each has different ambitions and serves different kinds of applications, so there's not a good choice and a bad choice. ASP.NET MVC implements the Model-View-Controller (MVC) pattern and was built to support testability. It gives you markup control, whereas Web Forms can increase your productivity. Keep both of them in mind and you'll be set.

MVC gives you flexibility, but you need to implement a lot of things that Web Forms give you out of the box. The rule here is not new: choose with your mind, not your heart!

1.1.3 Getting started

To start experiencing ASP.NET, all you have to do is open Visual Studio and create a new web project. In this first part, we're going to use Web Forms as our model.

Web Form really means "web page"; the term itself is a marketing name. The reason behind this name is that ASP.NET can have only one Web Form at a time on a single page. ASP.NET pages contain *server controls*, namely objects. A server control is a server-side programmable piece of a page. You typically add server controls in the markup part of the page, but you can add them via code too. A server control is a specific tag in the markup.

A Web Form is usually composed of two files, one with markup and one with code. The code file is commonly referred to as *code behind* or *code beside*, depending on your project type.

To run an ASP.NET application, you need a web browser for rendering (all you're doing is generating HTML) and a web server to run it. Figure 1.2 shows the typical flow associated with getting a request and producing a response.

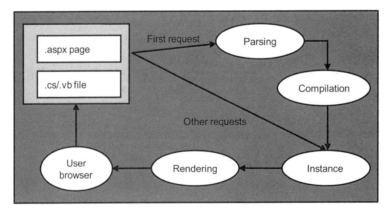

Figure 1.2 ASP.NET page compilation is performed on demand. The files are monitored for changes, and if modifications are made, the current compiled version is discarded.

NOTE Code behind is used when your project type is Web Project, and code beside (often referred to code file) is used for Web Site. The difference is in how ASP.NET and versus handle compilation and how you deploy the application. Web Site is commonly used for simple projects, whereas Web Project is more useful in complex ones.

It's possible to have both markup and code in the same page. A third option, called *code inline*, mixes markup and code in the same file. Even then, it's difficult to end up with *spaghetti code* because the blocks are separated.

ASP.NET provides a transparent mechanism to handle *page compilation*. The first time a user requests a page, if it's not yet compiled, both the page and its code are grouped and compiled to disk. What happens next is similar to what happens for other requests: the page is instantiated, rendered, and served in the browser as HTML. This process is completely transparent to the developer. ASP.NET continuously watches the file and, in case of modifications, automatically discards the old version. The new version is compiled instead, using the previously exposed flow.

Now you know what ASP.NET is in general, how to start it, and how it works. Now it's time to look at the typical architecture.

1.2 Typical architecture in ASP.NET applications

Inexperienced developers often think of a web site as a collage of code, so cut-and-paste is used as a pattern wherever possible. Using this method generates a lot of duplicate code, as well as inconsistency throughout the web site. Eventually, you might reach the point where maintenance is a nightmare because if you need to modify a functionality that's replicated in several places, you'll probably need to repeat the same work in different areas. This problem is particularly severe when the modification relates to a security bug. When that happens, the iteration necessary to accomplish a basic task will become extremely time consuming. Fortunately, you can avoid such complications by making use of ASP.NET's OOP support.

1.2.1 ASP.NET meets OOP

Having OOP support helps you build reusable components and avoid code redundancy. Architecture is important in your application and you should ensure that you provide a good one. To start using ASP.NET, you need to shape the big picture and understand how ASP.NET uses OOP concepts and architectural patterns in practice.

ASP.NET is organized into small components called pages. A page is typically the visual entry point for a given functionality, which is often an action.

THREE-LAYER ARCHITECTURE

Let's imagine that we want to build an application to manage a book library. One action associated with this application is "list the books", another is "give me details about a particular book", and so on. To display the results for these actions, we need a specific web page that extracts data from our storage system. The storage system is probably a database synchronized with our backend.

In this typical scenario, we need to design our application in layers so that we can better separate one from the others.

Let's try to write a simple list of components involved in creating the solution:

- A class to handle data retrieval
- A class to contain data in an object-oriented fashion
- A web page to display the objects loaded with data from the database

This list results in an architecture model called *three-layer*, where each layer is separated from the other, as show in figure 1.3.

Architectural considerations

Although it seems to be ubiquitous, three-layer architecture isn't the only available option, but it's certainly the most diffuse and well known. You can find more patterns at http://martinfowler.com/eaaCatalog/.

For example, to simplify data access, the *Repository pattern* is currently in vogue. It adds more abstraction and helps in using Object-Relational Mapping (ORM) (we'll talk about ORM in the next chapter). You can find more information about this pattern at http://martinfowler.com/eaaCatalog/repository.html.

The first layer is called the Data Access Layer, and the second layer is the Business Logic Layer. From our point of view, it's the last layer, the Presentation layer, that's the most interesting of the three. The other two layers remain the same, even if we decide

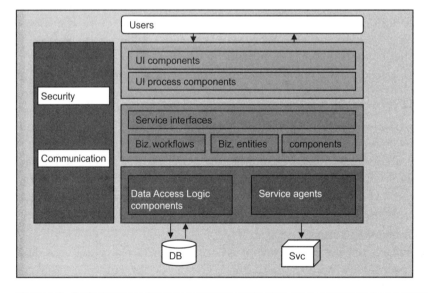

Figure 1.3 Typical schema for a three-layered application. Each component is separated from those above it, and each has no understanding of the inner capabilities of the others. Isolation provides the ability to change a layer implementation without affecting the other layers.

to build our application with a different user interface (UI), like a Windows Forms application. Before we get to the Presentation Layer though, we need to talk a bit about the first two layers.

DATA ACCESS AND BUSINESS LOGIC LAYERS

The *Data Access Layer* is responsible for data strategies. The *Business Logic Layer,* as its name suggests, contains the rules to be enforced with respect to the application business needs. This architecture isn't mandatory, but it's the most common one. Simplifications of this architecture exist in which a two-layer version is preferred, and more complex ones use an n-layer version. Keep in mind that you need different solutions to different problems, so the three-layer approach might not always work for you.

In a typical multilayer application, you need to exchange objects between different layers, so using objects that can contain data and be layer neutral is the best way to go. If you decide to go with a pure .NET Framework 4.0 solution, the best choice is the *Entity Framework*, which we'll discuss in detail in the following chapters.

At this point, we need to emphasize that you need to use different classes to handle different scenarios, and an *object model* to contain and present data in your application.

1.2.2 ASP.NET components

Let's go back to our library web page and assume that the rest of the code is already in place. When someone requests this page using a web browser, some magic happens under the hood; let's talk about that magic in detail.

ASP.NET is based on a class named `HttpRuntime`, which handles all the actions required to make the ASP.NET runtime communicate with the web server. `HttpRuntime` works with another important class, `HttpApplication`, which is responsible for processing the current request. This class is instantiated the first time you request a page and handles many future requests. You can have multiple instances of `HttpApplication`, but it can process only one request at a time. You can use this instance to store per-request data.

HttpApplication maximum number of instances

As of version 2.0, `HttpApplication` is automatically configured. You can change its default values by modifying machine.config in the .NET Framework Config directory.

Pool size indicates the maximum number of instances of `HttpApplication` for a given web application. The default value is 100 maximum instances per central processing unit (CPU). This doesn't mean that you'll have 100 instances available, but that ASP.NET regulates those instances using current demand from IIS. In many scenarios, you won't even get near this limit. `HttpApplication` instances are recycled and reused across different requests because it's difficult to have a lot of concurrent requests in common web applications.

This model gives you maximum flexibility; you could, in fact, intercept one of the events provided by this class and modify ASP.NET behavior at a particular point in the whole pipeline.

In addition to `HttpRuntime` and `HttpApplication`, there are a few other contributors to the magic. Let's look at those now.

HTTPHANDLERS

When a request hits `HttpApplication`, a couple of events are generated and consumed by the pipeline. One of these events is `BeginRequest`, which is used to handle the beginning of the request. This event is fired for every kind of resource that ASP.NET owns.

These events are useful when you need to extend ASP.NET features, for example, when you want to provide a different mechanism for authentication or to display errors. We're going to explain these scenarios in the next few chapters; for now, remember that ASP.NET is built for *extensibility* and that you can control most of its inner aspects.

When you request a resource, you typically want a web page with a fixed extension, commonly .aspx. Extensions in ASP.NET are handled by `HttpHandlers`, a set of classes that handle different kinds of request in different ways. If you're scratching your head, trying to understand this concept, imagine that `HttpHandlers` are the equivalent of what happens in Windows when you double click a file and the corresponding application opens.

`HttpHandlers` are in fact responsible for generating the output. You can map a complex pattern like /content/*.aspx, as well as a simple one like .aspx.

THE WEB FORM

The default `HttpHandler` associated with a Web Form is `System.Web.UI.Page-HandlerFactory`. This `HttpHandler` is a simple bridge between the page content and the ASP.NET *Page Parser*, an interesting piece of ASP.NET architecture in itself.

Page Parser is responsible for validating markup validation and converting code into classes. ASP.NET is part of .NET Framework, which runs on top of the Common Language Runtime (CLR). The CLR understands only objects, so some conversion has to occur to transform a Web Form into an object.

> **"PAGE" IN ASP.NET**   ASP.NET MVC uses a different concept of page from what you might be used to. You have a more restricted link to the actions performed under the hood, and a page (meaning what you see when you're browsing a site) is in fact called a view. We're going to discuss this topic in more detail in chapter 7.

The conversion from markup to code is transparent to the developer. In fact, it's much easier to write markup code for the Presentation Layer than for C# or VB code, so don't worry about having to learn a lot of new techniques. Page Parser will do the magic and convert the markup to code for you, as shown in figure 1.4.

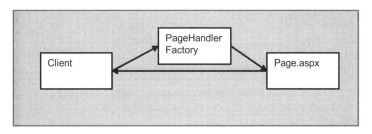

Figure 1.4
The simplified route for a page request. After the client request, a special `HttpHandler` called `PageHandlerFactory` gets the request and dynamically executes the given page.

We've simplified the picture in figure 1.4 for brevity's sake; in reality, between `Http-Application` and the designated `HttpHandler` are special objects, called `HttpModules`.

`HttpModules` are responsible for the majority of the features in ASP.NET and provide great flexibility when you have to add functionalities to an application. They work as filters for both the request and the response, and they register themselves for `Http-Application` events. Using `HttpModules`, ASP.NET offers mechanisms like authentication, authorization, session state, cache, and many others. You can write your own modules to modify the default behaviors and give yourself the flexibility you need.

1.2.3   *Global.asax and web.config*

If you're familiar with Classic ASP, you might remember a file named global.asa. ASP.NET has a similar file, named global.asax. This file functions similarly to an `Http-Module`, the difference being that it doesn't require registration. `HttpModules` are separate from the application, so you can reuse them in different projects; global.asax is pure code that you add to a specific web application.

> **NOTE** Global.asax and `HttpModules` are similar. The difference is that when you use `HttpModules` with IIS 7.x and Integrated Pipeline mode, they're called for every kind of request, but global.asax events fire only for pure ASP.NET requests.

Both `HttpHandlers` and `HttpModules` need to be registered to be used by your applications. ASP.NET provides a centralized mechanism for you to store configuration, based on *delegation*. The central configuration, for all applications, is in a special file called machine.config, in the .NET Framework Config directory (typically C:\Windows\Microsoft.NET\Framework\v4.0.30319\Config). This file includes configuration shared by every .NET Framework application, including ASP.NET applications.

An ASP.NET application might contain a file called web.config in every directory of the web site. When it's placed in the root, web.config has the ability to overwrite some special configuration options, such as `HttpHandler` and `HttpModules`, authentication, `SessionState`, and so on. If you place web.config in subdirectories, you can overwrite only selected features, like `HttpHandlers` and authorization.

If you specify a value for a given property in web.config, this value will be used by all the pages in that particular path. This feature helps delegation and enhances customization.

web.config is an XML file, composed of a special set of nodes. Don't worry—you don't have to learn them. You can use Visual Studio's Intellisense to explore different options, or just explore Microsoft Developer Network (MSDN) documentation.

The following snippet is an example of simple web.config content:

```
<configuration>
    <system.web>

      <pages enableViewState="false" />

      <customErrors mode="Off" />

    </system.web>
</configuration>
```

You access web.config nodes by using classes under the `System.Configuration` namespace, located in an assembly with the same name.

Now you know all the components of the ASP.NET pipeline architecture. Let's put it all together and see what it looks like.

1.2.4   *The ASP.NET pipeline*

Figure 1.5 shows the basic architecture of the ASP.NET pipeline, with the different steps involved in sending a request and generating a response.

The architecture shown in figure 1.5 is interesting because both `HttpHandlers` and `HttpModules` can be developed to increase application flexibility. Given this architecture, you can adapt ASP.NET to different scenarios.

Now that you have a clear understanding of what happens under the hood, let's move on to cover the basics behind the single most used object in ASP.NET development: the ASP.NET page, also known as a Web Form.

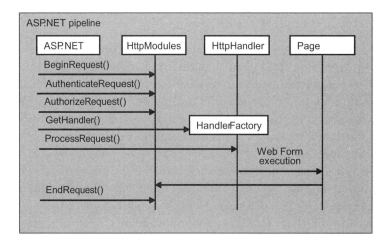

Figure 1.5   The ASP.NET pipeline for request and response (principal events only). `HttpModules` **and** `HttpHandlers` **are used by the developer to make the pipeline extensible.**

1.3 Your first ASP.NET Web Form

In this section, you'll discover the basics of how to build ASP.NET pages using a Web Form. The Web Form is the preferred paradigm for implementing an ASP.NET web page and is specially tailored for beginners. A Web Form is based on a simple concept: It's your design surface; all you need to do is insert your objects and program them.

Sticking to this vision leads to productivity and ease of use, but some developers who use other technologies look down on it. So, is it a good way to develop your view, or a not-so-good way? The truth, as always, is somewhere in the middle. It's a great boost for productivity, but you have to use it with caution.

At this point in the chapter, you're ready to implement your first Web Form and see how you can use ASP.NET to build rich pages. To that end, let's start looking at some common scenarios in building web applications, such as handling PostBack, validating form input, and styling. These tasks are the most typical that you, as a developer, will perform in your day-to-day work. Mastering them will let you spend less time on repetitive tasks, as you leverage the ASP.NET infrastructure.

We've analyzed the pipeline; the next step is to understand how a single Web Form works. Because Web Forms contain your UI logic, and you'll spend most of your development time working with them, understanding them is of utmost importance. The first step toward that understanding is knowing about server controls.

1.3.1 Server controls

A single page is composed of different objects that are all called controls. They're also called *server controls* because these objects run server side.

You've already met the ASP.NET Page Parser. The Page Parser transforms server controls in C# or VB code for you.

Let's take a look at some simple ASP.NET Web Form markup:

```
<html>
...
    <form runat="server">
        <asp:button runat="server" Text="Click Me" ID="ClickButton" />
    </form>
</html>
```

You'll notice a couple of XML/HTML tags with a strange attribute named `runat`. The value for this attribute is always set to `server`. This setting is what makes the server control usable in the server code.

> **FROM SERVER CONTROLS TO MARKUP** Every server control is transformed to an instance of an object, but normal markup is rendered using a special control, the `Literal`. In some cases, such as in Ajax scenarios, an HTML tag is preferable. You'll get true flexibility and have greater control over what you can do.

To programmatically access server controls, you can specify the optional `ID` attribute. For example, you could use an ID value to access a button's `Text` property for a `Button`.

If you're absolutely sure that your ASP.NET page won't perform any PostBacks and your controls don't need to be hosted by the Web Form, simply remove the `<form />` tag. This tag generates the infrastructure markup to enable PostBacks, but if your controls don't need it, then you don't need to include it. Removing this tag also removes ViewState rendering, so remember this tip to avoid generating markup code that no one's going to use.

Two different kinds of server controls provide different functionalities: HTML controls and web controls. Let's look at each one.

HTML CONTROLS

If you add the `runat` attribute to an arbitrary HTML tag, then you've created an HTML control. HTML controls are inside the namespace `System.Web.UI.HtmlControls` and are used for compatibility reasons.

The object model for an HTML control is similar to the corresponding HTML tag object model. These controls aren't special; you use them to avoid complexity and to better adapt existing HTML markup to ASP.NET.

WEB CONTROLS

XML tags that use a prefix followed by semicolon and a suffix (for example, `<asp:Button . . . />`) are called web controls and are grouped in the `System.Web.UI.WebControls` namespace. These controls produce HTML by generating the markup using a set of conditions, such as browser type and version. Generating markup this way is called *adaptive rendering*. We'll talk about adaptive rendering in chapter 10.

Now that you know how to interact with the page, let's return to the Web Form.

1.3.2   *Page events*

The page itself has events. When you need to program an object, you'll typically use one of the Web Form events. To program an event, you'll most likely use `OnLoad`. To simplify this task, ASP.NET defines special event handlers, where the `Page_` prefix is used. These methods are effectively called automatically.

To programmatically set the `Text` property of the `Button` we showed you in the previous snippet, you would use one of the following code examples:

C#:
```
void Page_Load()
{
    ClickButton.Text = "Please click me!";
}
```

VB:
```
Sub Page_Load()
{
    ClickButton.Text = "Please click me!"
}
```

This snippet is quite simple and lets you appreciate the Web Form approach: You have objects, you have events, and all you have to do is program them.

A Web Form has a lot of events, but you'll probably stick to the ones listed in table 1.1, presented in order of invocation.

Table 1.1 Main events exposed by the `Page` class through special event handlers

Event	Description
`Page_Init`	Called when the class associated with the page is loaded. This event is used to initialize values, not to modify controls' state (because the state isn't loaded).
`Page_Load`	Raised when the `Page` and its controls are ready to be used. This event is often used to modify control properties.
`Page_LoadComplete`	As the name suggests, this event occurs every time a `Page_Load` event is completed.
`Page_PreRender`	This event is the last event that you can use to modify the `Page` state before ASP.NET renders the content.

Your last chance to modify page controls is the `Page_PreRender` event. After this event, the Web Form content is rendered.

PAGE RENDERING

The ASP.NET Web Form is a special kind of control—the root one. Just like any other control, its output is generated using the `Render` method. This method is shared by every control and is called recursively, so every piece of content on the page is rendered. You have time to program controls prior to using `Render`; after you use that call, you can't modify their state any more.

The Web Form is based on this rendering mechanism. You need to keep this in mind as you develop your web pages. If you're new to this model, you'll need a different mindset to effectively organize your page using server controls. But don't worry. Most of the examples in this book will show you how to leverage this approach.

> **NOTE** A Web Form is the right model to use for common web page tasks. That said, keep in mind that it wasn't designed with testability and complete control over markup in mind, but for productivity. If you prefer to adopt a different approach, ASP.NET MVC implements the Model-View-Controller pattern in ASP.NET. We're going to talk more about that in chapter 8.

1.3.3 *Using server controls*

We introduced server controls in section 1.3.1. Now we're going to try to complicate the previous scenario. When you need to include user interaction in a page, things tend to be more complicated than in the example we presented in that section.

The following snippet contains a more common use of server controls.

```
<html>
...
    <form runat="server">
            <asp:literal id="ResponseText" runat="server" />
```

```
                Enter your name:
                <asp:textbox runat="server" ID="Name" />
                <br />
                <asp:button runat="server" Text="Click Me" ID="ClickButton"
        OnClick="HandleSubmit" />
        </form>
...
</html>
```

In this snippet, we've added two new controls, a Literal and a TextBox. The Literal doesn't correspond to an HTML tag (it's literal content), but the TextBox corresponds to the tag <input type="text" />. Remember that this is true with the most common scenarios, but adaptive rendering might produce different output.

One other difference is the presence of a new Click *event handler* for our button. This event handler will be invoked when the user submits the form; it's also used to add a code to handle the response.

POSTBACK AND VIEWSTATE

Our task for this example is to get the name in the form and display it on the page. Using ASP.NET, this task is pretty easy, as you can see if you analyze the following snippet:

C#:
```
void HandleSubmit(object sender, EventArgs e)
{
    ResponseText.Text = "Your name is: " + Name.Text;
}
```

VB:
```
Sub HandleSubmit(sender as Object, e as EventArgs)
    ResponseText.Text = "Your name is: " & Name.Text
End Sub
```

This code will intercept the Click event for the Button and modify the Text property on our Literal to show the corresponding value. The results are shown in figure 1.6.

ASP.NET handles the state for you, using a mechanism called ViewState. Both the page and the controls are able to persist their state during the iteration between client and server (called PostBack). A PostBack is a post of the form back to the server.

NOTE Complex pages might have a very large ViewState associated with it. A large ViewState can severely affect performance and give the user the impression that your application is slow.

Starting with version 4.0, you can tweak ViewState behavior. We'll discuss these new features in chapter 12.

Figure 1.6   The code snippet results in a Web Form that shows the TextBox and Literal control after the button is clicked. The code used to render this page takes advantages of OOP techniques to program objects during their lifecycle.

To give you these functionalities at no cost, ASP.NET uses ViewState to preserve the state of the controls and PostBack to leverage event-based development.

ViewState, by default, is saved in a hidden field in the Web Form. This field is sent back and forth between the client and server, so that ASP.NET can load the control states prior to the last PostBack, apply the necessary modifications to the controls associated with the code, and display the modification to the user.

Now that you've got a taste for what ASP.NET is, let's go back and look at the new features that make ASP.NET 4.0 the wonderful thing that it is.

1.4   What's new in ASP.NET 4.0

Let's assume this is your first time with .NET Framework version 4.0. As in the previous releases, .NET Framework 4.0 includes not only a new version of ASP.NET, but new technologies inside the framework itself. Even though the framework includes these technologies, you don't always have to use them in your ASP.NET applications.

Upgrading an existing application to this new version is painless. Version 4.0 includes all the features of the earlier versions. If you're planning to migrate an application from version 2.0 or 3.5, rest easy; you won't need to modify your code.

You can take full advantage of the new CLR, compilers, fixed bugs, and increased performance with no effort at all beyond a simple conversion. Visual Studio 2010 can handle projects for .NET Framework 2.0, 3.0, 3.5, and 4.0, but you can't convert the project file to a previous version. Upgrading your project is a one-way-only step.

When you build your ASP.NET applications, an intermediate language (IL), is produced at compilation time. This code will run inside a virtual machine that's created by the CLR and benefits from .NET Framework services, such as memory management, security, and garbage collection.

As we've previously noted, the runtime contains all the technologies inside the framework. You'll get out-of-the-box support not only for ASP.NET, but also for Windows Communication Foundation (WCF), which is the technology used to implement service-oriented scenarios, the Entity Framework (an Object-Relational Mapping [ORM] specifically built for .NET Framework), and so on.

1.4.1   .NET Framework 4.0

Using ASP.NET might help you leverage the other technologies inside the framework because they share a common background. Sharing a similar environment is a key aspect for you to consider when you're choosing a framework. .NET Framework offers consistency across the kinds of applications you might need to build, from web applications to services, from Windows applications to mobile ones.

Different technologies use different classes for the UI, but both the framework and the IDE remain the same, as shown in figure 1.7.

.NET Framework and its Base Class Library (BCL) are wide in scope, so it's virtually impossible to master every single aspect of them. You'll find that you learn what you need to know as you work.

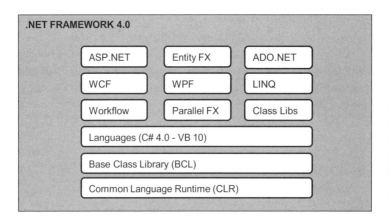

Figure 1.7
The main components of .NET Framework 4.0. Every piece is a separate technology available in the framework. You can combine any of them or use them separately.

ASP.NET is a subset of the framework. As you'll notice in figure 1.7, a lot of components are shared by different kinds of applications. You can leverage Language Integrated Query (LINQ) from both ASP.NET applications and Windows Presentation Foundation (WPF) desktop applications. The underlying compilers, runtime, and class library also share the components.

PROGRAMING LANGUAGES

An interesting aspect of .NET Framework 4.0 is that it includes new versions of programming languages; you can choose between C# 4.0 and VB 10. In this book, you'll find examples in both languages.

Both C# 4.0 and VB 10 are evolutions of preceding versions. VB 10 is more similar to C# in terms of functionalities, whereas C# has support for something similar to VB late binding, called *dynamic types.*

.NET Framework 4.0 includes a Dynamic Language Runtime (DLR) that calls dynamic languages (such as Ruby or IronPython) from managed code. C# 4.0 fully supports executing code at runtime, just like dynamic code does. On the other hand, VB has introduced support for multiline statements, as do languages like C# or Java, without using a special character (like the underscore).

No matter which language you program in, you'll have access to all the features of .NET Framework. You've decided on a specific style of programming; you haven't jeopardized performance.

Now you know about .NET Framework. Let's talk about all the new features that ASP.NET 4.0 has in store for you.

1.4.2   *A panoramic overview of ASP.NET 4.0 features*

ASP.NET 4.0 has significantly changed the controls rendering behavior. All the controls generate markup that's compliant with XHTML 1.1. If you have some specific client-side code that isn't compliant with XHTML 1.1, you should check that everything runs fine. Producing such markup isn't the default behavior, which makes migrations easier. (We're going to discuss this topic in more depth in chapter 6.)

Controls impacted by this change are ListView, FormView, Login, CheckboxList, and pretty much all the controls that previously generated HTML tables.

Both Visual Studio 2010 and ASP.NET 4.0 Web Controls are now compliant with Cascading Style Sheets (CSS) 2.1 specifications to ensure web standards compatibility. Additional libraries used as CSS control adapters are no longer required.

WEB.CONFIG MINIFICATION

ASP.NET 4.0 has a new web.config setting that minifies its content. You can include just the minimum required settings to load the application, using a specified .NET Framework version.

Speaking of new functionalities, ASP.NET 4.0 introduces a new set of features for both ViewState and ClientID generation.

THE FLEXIBLE VIEWSTATE

You can now activate ViewState on a per-control basis. This feature gives you both flexibility and some control over the ViewState size. In previous versions of ASP.NET, you could specify this behavior only for parent controls. If you had a child control inside a parent whose ViewState was off, the child controls inherited this behavior. In version 4.0, you can tweak this property and disable ViewState for the parent and enable it for a particular child control. You can do the same thing to Page, too, because it's a special control (the root one). You'll learn more about this topic in chapter 11.

CONTROL CLIENTID GENERATION

When you set the ID property of a server control, ASP.NET generates a corresponding ID attribute for the HTML tag at rendering time. This value is called ClientID and is generated automatically by ASP.NET. Automatic generation ensures that the ID is unique for each page. The problem is that automatic generation also results in a complex ID when a control is inside other controls. It's difficult to handle this kind of ID with JavaScript because you need to access the control ClientID property every time.

To mitigate this problem, ASP.NET 4.0 gives you the option to control ClientID generation. We're going to talk about this in detail in chapter 5, when we'll discuss all Web Forms 4.0 features.

DATA BINDING AND DYNAMIC DATA CONTROLS

In version 4.0, you also get better data binding support. *Data binding* is the action that displays data from the data source on the page. It's important to master because ASP.NET pages are dynamically generated and they quite often display data from a database.

You'll also find a new version of *Dynamic Data controls*, a technology introduced with ASP.NET 3.5 Service Pack 1. Dynamic Data controls help you build a rich data entry interface with less work. The new version has better template handling, more features, and supports .NET RIA Services. It uses the Entity Framework and LINQ to SQL to generate data models. A new search architecture that simplifies filtering and searching is also available.

IIS 7.5 INTEGRATION

Improvements have been made to URL routing and session state, and there's a new warm-up feature. You can specify that an ASP.NET application needs a specific warm-up through IIS 7.5, a feature introduced with Windows Server 2008 R2 and Windows 7 and detailed later in appendix A.

Using a special class, you can add tasks to the warm-up event, such as informing a load balancer that the current node is ready or performing data-intensive loads to be used in the whole application. ASP.NET accepts HTTP requests for the application after this method has completed.

ASP.NET AJAX 4.0

ASP.NET Ajax 4.0 has a new set of features and improves performance. Client-side templates enhance support for rich data-binding scenarios in Ajax applications, and the new `DataView` control adds support for binding JavaScript objects.

Last but not least, ASP.NET Ajax 4.0 gives you the ability to use only certain features by selecting which JavaScript file you want to include. This feature can help to increase performance because you can select which functionality you want to use and let ASP.NET generate only the file you need.

We're going to discuss every one of these features, and more, in its own chapter. In this section, we've just introduced you to the main features introduced in version 4.0. But now we're going to talk about Web Forms.

1.5   *ASP.NET Web Forms in practice*

This section uses the in-practice approach that we'll use in the rest of the book. We'll analyze every aspect of a topic using a problem-solution-discussion style. The first topic we'll discuss in this way is how to handle PostBack in a Web Form. Because the foundation of ASP.NET is the same for all versions, we've designed this scenario to help you understand a common challenge that you can solve using any version of ASP.NET.

TECHNIQUE 1   **Handling PostBack**

HTML forms consist of a series of input tags used to capture values when they're submitted. ASP.NET uses PostBack to implement a mechanism that lets the developer handle this behavior easily. Mastering PostBack is important because the ASP.NET model is based on this concept.

PROBLEM

As a user, you want to interact with the page in the easiest way possible. If you need to correct a value, it's easier to find it than to do some rewriting.

SOLUTION

The first time you request a page, ASP.NET renders its content and generates the correct markup. Let's suppose we have a page with a `Button`; this `Button` will be the control that causes a PostBack when it's clicked. A second request for the page is caused by the PostBack and is executed differently by ASP.NET. Every control on the page has its state restored; as the developer, you don't need to explicitly set the properties for every control.

Let's imagine you have a basic form with two `TextBox` controls that capture first name and last name and a `DropDownList` in which the user selects his country from a limited set of values. The code for this form is shown in the following listing.

Listing 1.1   Handling PostBack with the Web Form model

```html
<html>
...
    <form runat="server">
            Your first name:
            <asp:textbox runat="server" ID="FirstName" />
            <br />

            Your last name:
            <asp:textbox runat="server" ID="LastName" />
            <br />

            Your country:
            <asp:DropDownList runat="server" id="Country">
                    <asp:ListItem value="IT">Italy</asp:ListItem>
                    <asp:ListItem value="UK">UK</asp:ListItem>
                    <asp:ListItem value="USA">USA</asp:ListItem>
            </asp:DropDownList>
            <br />

            <asp:button runat="server" Text="Next" ID="ClickButton"
    OnClick="HandleSubmit" />
    </form>

</html>
```

Try to run this example and submit the form. Even though you have no code in place to handle the state logic, the page will be posted back to server and a response will be generated. You can see the results in figure 1.8.

What's interesting about this example is that we didn't specifically handle state maintenance across different requests. Automatically handling state is one of the services that a framework such as ASP.NET offers to you at no cost.

Now that you know the basics, let's improve the code.

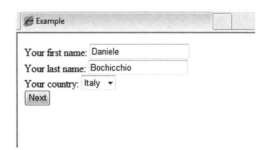

Figure 1.8   Web Form behavior resulting from the code shown in listing 1.1. After PostBack, the input boxes retain their values and new text that reflects the input is added at the top of the form.

Using container controls

You can use container controls to group controls together. Building on listing 1.1, let's add a simple container control and include the previous controls inside it, as shown in the following listing.

Listing 1.2   A complete Web Form with markup and code

Markup:

```
<html>
...
    <form runat="server">
            <asp:Placeholder id="FormContainer" runat="server">
                Your first name:
                <asp:textbox runat="server" ID="FirstName" />
                <br />
            </asp:Placeholder>
            <asp:Placeholder id="FormResponse" runat="server"
                             Visible="false">
            <asp:Literal id="ResponseText" runat="server" />
            </asp:Placeholder>
    </form>
...
</html>
```

C#:

```
void HandleSubmit(Object sender, EventArgs e)
{
    FormContainer.Visible = false;                          ◁────┐
    FormResponse.Visible = true;                                 │    ◁──┐
    ResponseText.Text = string.Format("Hello {0} {1} from {2}",  │       │
                              FirstName.Text,                    │       │
                              LastName.Text,                     │       │
                              Country.SelectedItem.Text);        │       │
}                                                   Form container        Response
```                                                 becomes invisible       text
                                                                         container
VB:                                                                      is shown

```
Sub HandleSubmit(sender as Object, e as EventArgs)
    FormContainer.Visible = False                          ◁────┘
    FormResponse.Visible = True
    ResponseText.Text = string.Format("Hello {0} {1} from {2}",  ◁──┘
                              FirstName.Text,
                              LastName.Text,
                              Country.SelectedItem.Text)
End Sub
```

We used two `Placeholder` controls to isolate data input and to show results. This simple control can include other controls, so it's useful when you need to group controls. For example, you could use the `Visible` property to tweak the visibility of some controls. This property is fundamental; it instructs the Page Parser to not produce the control content when it renders the Web Form.

> **NOTE** If you need to determine at runtime whether a page is in PostBack state or not, you can check the `IsPostBack` property of the `Page` class. `IsPostBack` is a boolean property whose value is `True` if the page is in PostBack state. It's often used to avoid loading data from a database after a PostBack, using the ViewState as storage.

Figure 1.9   The Web Form we created in listing 1.2, before and after PostBack. The first request contains the controls to add your input. The second request hides them and shows only the resulting text.

The technique shown in listing 1.2 is the preferred way to make a Web Form. You can have both data entry and response feedback in the same page, and show or hide blocks based on the state. In this example, we applied one of the most common patterns in ASP.NET applications. Both the first and the second requests are shown in figure 1.9.

DISCUSSION

PostBack is fundamental in ASP.NET applications based on Web Forms. Working with PostBack helps you to understand the magic behind this model. Like it or not, Web Forms boost productivity. If you're an experienced web developer, PostBack might seem restrictive. In reality, this model is flexible enough to let you add your own touch and implement your needs.

Now that you're ready to use the Web Form paradigm, it's time to move on and gain more control over ASP.NET infrastructure by using form validation. Form validation is one of the best examples of how to increase productivity with little effort. In common forms, you need some control over the user to ensure that she's inserting the right values into your form. That's when the ASP.NET validation infrastructure comes to the rescue.

TECHNIQUE 2   **Form validation**

By validating data on a form, you can guide your user to enter the correct values and, at the same time, enforce your application needs. Validation is a useful tool, especially when you use it at both client and server side.

To fully appreciate the content of this section, you should be familiar with the concepts presented in technique 1.

PROBLEM

Form validation is just another pain that web developers need to address. The average user isn't happy when he has to re-enter data into a form from scratch because he forgot to include a seemingly trivial piece of data, like a ZIP code. When the user makes a mistake and has to re-enter something, he expects to see the data he already entered on the form. This expectation probably derives from the classic Windows application, where, obviously, you have true state support.

SOLUTION

A Web Form has state support across PostBack. Form validation is built on top of this feature to simplify both client-side and server-side validation.

Let's imagine that we want to add a check to listing 1.2 that prevents one of the fields from being blank. In ASP.NET, you use a special class of web controls, called *validator controls* to make this check.

The validator controls are shown in table 1.2

Table 1.2 Validator controls offered by ASP.NET

Control	Description
CompareValidator	Compares the values of two controls (for example, a password to be repeated) or compares the value of a control to a fixed value.
CustomValidator	Lets you write your own server-side code, client-side code, or both, to validate the corresponding control.
RangeValidator	Checks that a value is within a given range.
RegularExpressionValidator	Checks for a complex value against a regular expression pattern.
RequiredFieldValidator	Ensures that a field is not left blank.
ValidationSummary	Provides a summary of validation results.

Table 1.3 lists the properties that are shared by the ASP.NET validator controls that are shown in table 1.2.

Table 1.3 Properties shared by ASP.NET validator controls

Property	Description
ControlToValidate	Contains the control ID that validation is performed against.
Display	Used to control the behavior of the alert message that's displayed when an error occurs. The value of Display can be Dynamic or Static.
ErrorMessage	This message is available if a ValidationSummary control is present on the page.
SetFocusOnError	A boolean value that gives focus to the corresponding validated control in case of error.
Text	The text to be displayed where the validator control is inserted.
ValidationGroup	A string that groups together different validator controls and separates them from another group (used in complex pages, with different logical forms).

On the simplest forms, you'll want to use RequiredFieldValidator because that's the kind of validation you need in a form. If you choose to use another control, keep in mind that they're activated only if a value is present in the field that the validator is associated with. Remember, you always need to include a `RequiredFieldValidator` if you want to make sure an empty value won't bypass your controls.

Validator controls use adaptive rendering, so they'll send client-side JavaScript code to recognized browsers. You need to access the `IsValid` property of the `Page` class to ensure that validation is also done server side, as shown in the following listing.

Listing 1.3   Validation controls at work

Markup:
```
...
Your first name:
<asp:textbox runat="server" ID="FirstName" />
<asp:RequiredFieldValidator runat="server" ID="FirstNameValidator"
    ControlToValidate="FirstName"
    ErrorMessage="First name is required"
    Text="*" />                                    ◁─┐ Control to
<br />                                                │ act against
...

<asp:ValidationSummary ID="MyValidationSummary" runat="server"
    HeaderText="You need to check:" />             ◁─┐ Summary of
...                                                  │ validation
                                                     │ errors
```

C#:
```
void HandleSubmit(Object sender, EventArgs e)      ─┐ Collection
{                                                   │ to bind to
    if (Page.IsValid)                          ◁───┘
    {

    }
}
```

VB:
```
Sub HandleSubmit(sender as Object, e as EventArgs)
    If Page.IsValid then#3

    End If
End Sub
```

Your code
logic here

`ValidationSummary` has a boolean property called `ShowMessageBox` that pops up an alert message when the validation isn't passed. If you set this property to `true` and `ShowSummary` to `false`, you can display only this alert. Default values are respectively `false` and `true`.

Figure 1.10 shows you the results of the code in listing 1.3 if the user has omitted the value for the field "Your first name" and PostBack has been invoked.

Other controls in this group do about the same thing; the difference is only in the property you will use. If you need more examples of validator controls, check out the ones included in the MSDN documentation at http://msdn.microsoft.com/en-us/library/aa310913(VS.71).aspx.

Figure 1.10   A Web Form with validator controls. As you can see, the validator generates a warning (displayed in red, by default) and blocks the form from being submitted.

DISCUSSION

Input validation is a key factor in today applications. Both the client-side and server-side validation offered by validator controls in Web Forms is a killer feature for web applications, and you get it by default. It's just one of the free services the ASP.NET infrastructure lets you use to enhance your UI.

Now that you've validated the form, the next step is to manipulate the page characteristics, such as the header (title, meta, or keywords), style, and CSS.

TECHNIQUE 3   **Page header, styling, and CSS**

Programmatic access to the page header can help when you need to set some properties via code. A common problem when dealing with a dynamic page is that often the page is composed of data coming from a database. In situations like this, you need to set the page headers programmatically. By manipulating page headers you can dynamically set the title, style sheets, or syndication feeds.

PROBLEM

You need to access the page headers from your code and programmatically set the values that correspond to the kind of header you're manipulating.

SOLUTION

Starting with ASP.NET 2.0, you can manipulate page headers if you add a `runat="server"` attribute to the `<head />` tag. If you need to set the page title, the `Title` property on the `Page` class lets you access `Page.Header.Title` and programmatically set this information.

Version 4.0 lets you set meta tags for search engines. You have to use the `Page.Keywords` and `Page.Description` properties to set the meta keywords and description respectively, as in the following listing.

Listing 1.4   Dynamically setting page headers

C#:
```
Page.Title = "My Page title";
Page.Keywords = "list separated by commas";
Page.Description = "Page description, shown by search engines.";
```

VB:

```
Page.Title = "My Page title"
Page.Keywords = "list separated by commas"
Page.Description = "Page description, shown by search engines."
```

The strongly typed model provided by the `Page` class is powerful. You can manipulate the corresponding headers using a simple approach, from anywhere in your page, before the whole page is rendered. This code is especially helpful when you're dealing with dynamic content coming from a database.

Styling and CSS

All web controls use a common approach to styling because they all derive from the `WebControl` class. You can modify some properties directly, using properties like `Back-Color`, `ForeColor`, `BorderColor`, or `Font`. When you need to apply styles to controls, it's always better to rely on a CSS for formatting from a centralized point.

`WebControl` (and derived controls, like `Label` and `TextBox`) offers a `CssClass` property, which is a string containing the CSS class that you're going to use. If you're using CSS IDs as a way to add style to your markup, you need to take a look at the new features for `ClientID` that are included in ASP.NET 4.0 (which we'll discuss in chapter 5). In any case, it's better to use CSS classes than CSS IDs; if multiple pieces of markup are being generated by iteration (such as data coming from a database into a page list), you'll probably end up with autogenerated IDs anyway.

Unfortunately, ASP.NET doesn't provide a mechanism to register an external CSS directly. You can always create an instance of the `HtmlLink` class and add the new control to the `Controls` collection of the `Page.Header` property, as shown in the following listing.

Listing 1.5   Registering a CSS

C#:

```
HtmlLink cssLink = new HtmlLink();
cssLink.Href = "/styles/styles.css";
cssLink.Attributes.Add("rel", "stylesheet");
cssLink.Attributes.Add("type", "text/css");
Page.Header.Controls.Add(cssLink);
```

VB:

```
Dim cssLink As New HtmlLink()
cssLink.Href = "/styles/styles.css"
cssLink.Attributes.Add("rel", "stylesheet")
cssLink.Attributes.Add("type", "text/css")
Page.Header.Controls.Add(cssLink)
```

As previously noted, this technique is useful when you don't know the path to the CSS file, and you have to determine it at runtime. An example is when you need to personalize a link based on user preference.

Registering RSS feeds

Remember that you can use the code shown in listing 1.5 to add other kinds of `HtmlLink` controls, such as a reference to Internet Explorer (IE) Web Slice or an RSS (Really Simple Syndication) feed.

RSS or Atom feeds are quite popular these days in web applications because they let users subscribe to updates and receive them in their news aggregator. This process is similar to what mail readers do. RSS differs from Atom in terms of format, but both are XML based. You can dynamically register the path to RSS or Atom feeds by using code similar to that shown in the following listing.

Listing 1.6   Programmatically adding an RSS feed to the current page

C#:

```
HtmlLink rssLink = new HtmlLink();
rssLink.Href = "/rss.aspx";
rssLink.Attributes.Add("rel", "alternate");
rssLink.Attributes.Add("type", "application/rss+xml");
Page.Header.Controls.Add(rssLink);
```

VB:

```
Dim cssLink As New HtmlLink()
rssLink.Href = "/rss.aspx"
rssLink.Attributes.Add("rel", "alternate")
rssLink.Attributes.Add("type", "application/rss+xml")
Page.Header.Controls.Add(rssLink)
```

application/atom+ xml for Atom

If you're using Web Slice, you need to set the `rel` attribute to `default-slice` and type to `application/x-hatom`. Web Slice is a special feature of IE 8.0+; for more information, go to http://www.ieaddons.com/.

DISCUSSION

You'll usually need to generate and add controls at runtime in the page header when you want to provide additional interactions to users visiting your pages. Syndication feeds, page title or page description, and dynamic CSS are used to leverage the dynamic nature of ASP.NET and let your user get what he needs to fully use your web application, but with his own personalization.

1.6   *Summary*

Almost everything we've talked about in this chapter applies to all versions of ASP.NET. That said, ASP.NET 4.0 does introduce some interesting features, but the pillars of this technology are the same as those that were used in the first version. If you're relatively new to ASP.NET, this chapter should have helped you visualize the big picture surrounding this technology.

ASP.NET is built on top of .NET Framework and gains a lot of its features from this base. .NET Framework is full of interesting technologies, such as the Entity Framework, WCF, and ADO.NET, and you can leverage them in your web application to enhance functionalities. If you don't know about these yet, you'll find specific examples of each of them in the upcoming chapters.

Keep in mind that ASP.NET is built with extensibility as a pillar, so the succeeding chapters will contain advanced implementations of what you've learned in this one.

You'll find concepts like Web Forms, PostBack, ViewState, `HttpRuntime`, and IIS integration in every new step you'll take.

This chapter didn't contain a lot of examples, but don't worry. In the following chapters, you'll find plenty of tips and code to implement the most common scenarios in web applications.

Now you're ready for chapter 2. We're going to delve into an analysis of the data access options available in .NET Framework 4.0 and specifically for ASP.NET 4.0.

Data access reloaded: Entity Framework

This chapter covers

- Designing an application
- Understanding an ORM
- Learning Entity Framework
- Reading and updating data with Entity Framework

When databases are in place, accessing data becomes a key concern. The way you communicate with the database and, more importantly, the way you represent data inside your application becomes one thing that can shift your application from one that works to a real success.

You have a lot of options. The first option is to use ADO.NET objects, like connections, adapters, readers, and datasets. This approach is easy to understand and enables you to immediately start writing code.

Another option is to use ADO.NET classes to interact with the database and then create your own classes (object model) to represent data inside the application. The initial learning curve with such a pattern is higher compared with the previous one, but in the long run, this pattern ensures higher maintainability.

The last option is to use an ORM tool, which hides the complexity of using ADO.NET classes and lets you work only with objects in your application. An ORM tool includes the best of the previous approaches because it offers immediate and sustained productivity. Microsoft has developed an ORM whose name is Entity Framework.

Microsoft touts Entity Framework as its best practice for data access. That's why we focus on Entity Framework only in this chapter. If you want to take a look at how to perform data access using the classic ADO.NET approach, take a look at appendix A.

Understanding data access using Entity Framework is vital because it lays the foundation for the next chapter and for the rest of the book. We'll be using Entity Framework in the chapters about data binding, authentication, authorization, and performance.

If you're an experienced Entity Framework developer, you can skip this chapter and go straight to chapter 3. If you're new to this topic, you'll find this chapter to be a good starting point to build on.

Before delving into the details of using Entity Framework, let's take a step back and analyze the pattern you should follow when you develop an application. By looking at the pattern up close, you'll clearly understand where Entity Framework stands in your application design.

2.1   *Designing an application*

In this chapter, you'll create an application that handles orders for the Northwind database (more information about it is in the sidebar). This database contains data about customers and products stored in several tables: Orders, Customers, Order Details, and Products. The tables that contain this data are Orders, Customers, Order Details, and Products.

You need to create an internal network of classes (the *object model*) that holds data that can be filled from a query in the database. These classes also need to handle data that updates the database. The classes are Order, Customer, Order_Detail, and Product. They contain properties that represent data on the database and that are useful for business.

These classes hide the complexity of the database structure from the business code (also known as the *Business Logic Layer* or *BLL*), letting the code communicate only with them and with a specific layer that will be responsible for interacting with the database (the *Data Access Layer* or *DAL*). The Business Logic Layer knows nothing about the database and interacts only with the four classes. The DAL is responsible for communicating with the database. With this nifty organization, the classes we create become the business Logic Layer database. Figure 2.1 shows an example of this design.

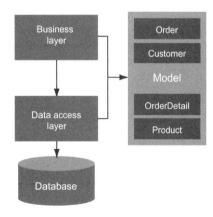

Figure 2.1   The Business Logic Layer uses classes in the model and then persists modifications through the Data Access Layer. The business code doesn't communicate with the database.

Why the Northwind database?

In this chapter and throughout the rest of the book, we'll use the Northwind database. Although it's a simple database, it has lots of useful characteristics. First of all, it represents a real-world scenario but exposes it in a manner that's pretty easy to understand. Secondly, it's been around for a long time, and it's probably the most used demo database in the world. We've attended countless conferences and courses and this database is always used.

With the advent of SQL Server 2005, Microsoft introduced the AdventureWorks database. This database represents a complex scenario and uses lots of SQL server features. It also has an online transaction processing (OLTP) database and a data warehouse so that every aspect of the business problem is covered.

Explaining SQL Server using AdventureWorks is wonderful, but we're talking about ASP.NET. We need a simpler model that allows us to focus on what matters so the complexity of the database doesn't bog us down.

Separating the code inside isolated layers is a technique that guarantees faster development and, maybe more important, easier maintenance.

So far, we've said that the model contains classes that in turn contain data that is persisted into the database. But how do you make a model? What techniques do you need to use to build it? The answer is: it *depends*.

2.1.1 *What's an object model?*

In many, possibly most, applications, a model can be a simple set of classes that contain data coming from a database and that have only a little *behavior*. This kind of model is known as an *object* model. Let's look at a few of the characteristics of the object model classes.

DATA VALIDATION

One of the behaviors that an object model class contains is data validation. For instance, the Customer class has the CustomerID property. Because it's the key of the class (and the primary key in the Customers table), this property can't be null or empty. Placing validation code in the property setter makes sense because it prevents the property from being set with an invalid value.

PROPERTY JOINING

Another behavior that is commonly added to an object model class is property joining. You often need the full customer address in a single string. Writing a piece of code that joins all address-related properties into a string every time you need the customer's full address is feasible, but it's repetitive and error prone. The Customer class contains an additional property, FullAddress, which internally joins the address properties and returns them as a string so you don't have to write the code to retrieve the full address every time you need it.

CONNECTING CLASSES TO EACH OTHER

Classes in an object model are not standalone; they're connected to each other. For instance, the `Order` class is connected to `Customer` and `Order_Detail` classes and `Order_Detail` is connected to `Product`.

In a database, tables are connected by foreign key columns. In an object model, referencing another class simply by using a property that acts as a foreign key isn't the optimal solution because you can directly reference another class using a property of the referenced class type. For example, the `Order` class keeps a reference to the `Customer` class by using the `Customer` property (we used the `Customer` name but you can use any name you like) whose type is `Customer`.

If an object must reference multiple objects, you can create an enumeration property whose type is `List<T>`, where `T` is the type of the objects in the collection. For instance, an order must reference a list of details. To do that, The `Order` class contains the `Order_Details` property, which is of type `List<Order_Detail>`.

> **NOTE** You don't have to use `List<T>`. You can use any other collection classes, like `Collection<T>`, `HashSet<T>`, or even the non generic `ArrayList`.

When you've completed the design process for the object model relationships, you end up with the model shown in figure 2.2.

As I said before, an object model works perfectly well in lots of applications, but its data-only nature is a limitation in complex scenarios. For some applications, you want a higher level of interaction between the object model and the environment. In other words, the object model must contain behavior.

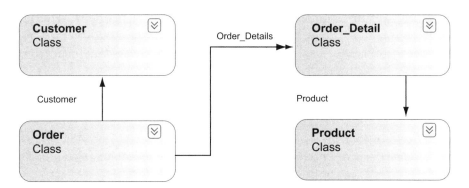

Figure 2.2 The `Order` class is connected to the `Customer` class by the `Customer` property. The `Order` class also contains details through the `Order_Details` property. Eventually, each detail is connected to the product via the `Product` property.

2.1.2 *The evolution of the object model: the domain model*

A *domain model* is an object model where classes have a lot more behavior. The behavior that's added to domain model classes creates a broad and rich integration between the classes and the environment.

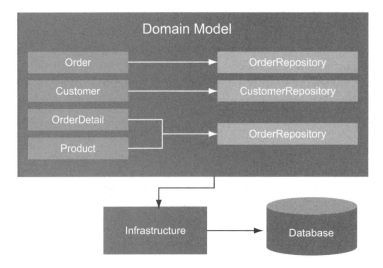

Figure 2.3   The domain model comprises the model classes and the repositories. The model uses the infrastructure layer to abstract the physical interaction with the database.

More exactly, a domain model doesn't involve just classes and their data. It introduces a new design for your application. The classes are integrated in the BLL and communicate with *repository* modules that are the new gateways to the database. All these classes and modules becomes a single layer: the domain model.

The domain model itself doesn't communicate directly with the database. An infrastructure layer that's underneath the model does the actual work. This layer hides database communication. The repositories deal with the infrastructure layer, which they use to send commands that retrieve data from a database or update data in it. Figure 2.3 shows the result of such a design.

You probably know that because classes are aware of the repositories, they can retrieve data from the database. Because the classes can do this, they offer a brand new range of services to the developers who use them. Not only that, the domain model pattern contains lots of other features that are outside the scope of this book. If you're interested in knowing more about the domain model, check out the book *Domain Driven Design* by Eric Evans.

Now you know how to effectively layer an application to create a better design and more maintainable code. Layering is the foundation of every successful application and the thing to keep in mind as you progress through the rest of the book.

All this discussion about object model and domain model includes a concept that has always remained the same: you have to deal with a database and with objects whose data must be persisted into it. Let's discover how you can do that using an ORM.

2.2 *Using an ORM to build a data layer*

An ORM is a framework that lets you build applications based on a paradigm that's completely different from the one you use when you work directly with ADO.NET. You can just work with objects and ignore the database.

An ORM lets you map your classes and properties against tables and columns in the database. You can design your classes and tables independently and then let the ORM do the dirty work of using the mapping information to generate SQL code to read data from a database, create objects with it, and persist data inside objects in the database. The SQL code is then executed through ADO.NET, which remains at the lowest layer.

Given this definition, you might think that an ORM is a mere code generator, but it's not. An ORM stores modifications made to objects, ensures that only one object with a given *identity* is in place, supports many optimization tweaks, and a lot more.

An ORM does another vital thing: it handles the differences between a relational database and the OOP paradigm (a.k.a the object/relational mismatch). The relational database and OOP paradigms are different in terms of data granularity, the way relationships are defined, inheritance, and available datatypes. Before we tell you how to use an ORM, let's examine the problems it solves so that you better understand how an ORM makes your life easier. In this section, we're going to analyze each problem separately, starting with the easiest one: data granularity.

2.2.1 *The granularity mismatch*

In the Northwind database, the customer's full address consists of the street address, city, region, Zip Code, and country. The shipping address for orders has the same information. In a database, you put the columns in each table, but when you're designing the classes in your model, you'll probably create an `AddressInfo` class that contains all the address-related properties. You'll reuse this class in the `Customer` and `Order` classes. This design gives you three classes and two tables, as shown in figure 2.4.

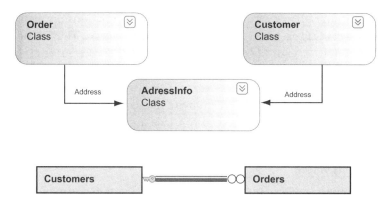

Figure 2.4 The `Customer` and `Order` classes have an `Address` property of the type `AddressInfo` that contains address information. Address-related columns are repeated in the `Customers` and `Orders` tables.

Because the number of classes is different from the number of tables in the database, you have a mismatch. This mismatch is known as the granularity problem.

2.2.2   *The relationship mismatch*

Another difference between the relational and OOP models is in the way they maintain relationships. Think about the order/customer relationship. In a database, you create a `CustomerId` foreign key column in the `Orders` table (*child* table) that points to the `CustomerId` primary key column of the `Customers` table (*parent* table). In the object model, you can reference the customer from the order using a property with the type `Customer`, so there's no need for a foreign key property.

In a database the associations are unidirectional from the child table to the parent table. In the object model, associations can be both unidirectional and bidirectional. You can have the `Customer` property in `Order`, but you can also have an `Orders` property in the `Customer` class. Figure 2.5 shows an example of this design.

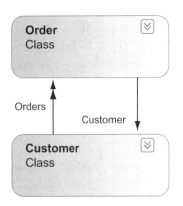
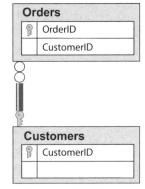

Figure 2.5   Orders are related to their customers using a foreign key in the database. The OOP model uses a reference to the object.

In the case of a many-to-many relationship, the differences between a relational database and OOP paradigms grow. Think about the relationship between the `Employees` and `Territories` tables in the Northwind database. They're not related to each other through foreign keys but via a third table: `EmployeeTerritories`. In the object model, you let the classes refer directly to each other without resorting to a middle class.

The differences we discussed in this section are known as the *relationship* mismatch. What's more, in the many-to-many scenario you face a granularity mismatch because you have three tables and two classes.

2.2.3   *The inheritance mismatch*

Suppose that customers in Germany require different data than customers from other countries. You could create a base class for all customers and then create a separate class for German customers and another class for all other customers. Both these customer classes inherit from the base class.

In the database, the concept of inheritance doesn't exist at all. What you can do is create an artifact to simulate inheritance. You can create inheritance in the database using one of three methods:

- *Table-per-hierarchy (TPH)*—One table contains the data for all the classes in the inheritance hierarchy and usually uses a discriminator column to determine the kind of object that's stored.
- *Table-per-type (TPT)*—Each class in the inheritance hierarchy has one table. Each table adds only the columns that are necessary for the type.
- *Table-per-concrete (TPC)*—Again, each class has a table, but each table contains all the columns mapped to all the properties of the mapped class.

Whatever approach you choose, you're bending the relational model to represent something it's not designed for. This mismatch is known as the *inheritance* problem.

THE DATATYPE MISMATCH

Last, but not least, there's the data type problem. In a database, you have `varchar`, `int`, `datetime`, and other datatypes that might or might not have a counterpart in .NET.

Let's use as an example the `int` datatype in SQL server. You can map it to an `Int32` property, and it works perfectly. Now, think about the `varchar` datatype, which can be easily mapped to a string. But if the column has a maximum length, you can't represent that in the .NET string type unless you write code to check the length. The situation worsens for datatypes like `RowVersion` or `Timestamp` that are represented as an array of bytes. This mismatch is known as the *datatype* problem.

When you write code using ADO.NET, you have to handle all these differences on your own. An ORM handles these differences for you so that you can focus on objects that demand database interaction.

> **NOTE** Never commit the suicide of ignoring the database. It might be masked by the ORM, but it's still there. *Always* measure the performance of SQL code generated by the ORM. Plenty of profiler tools can help you trace commands and measure performance.

You've learned *what* problems an ORM addresses and *why* it can ease your mind when you're developing data access. Now let's see *how* to use it. In the coming sections, we'll use Entity Framework, which is the ORM introduced by Microsoft in the .NET Framework 3.5 SP1. Entity Framework is now in its second version (named 4.0 only because its versioning has been aligned with that of the .NET Framework).

2.3 *Introducing Entity Framework*

The first step you take to introduce Entity Framework in an application is to generate the *Entity Data Model* (EDM). The EDM is the heart of the Entity Framework. It's where the mapping information between the classes and database is stored. The EDM is made up of three XML files. The first one describes the object model classes, the second one describes the tables in the database, and the last one stores their mapping. Let's see now how to handle these files.

TECHNIQUE 4 **Creating a model using Entity Framework**

Manually creating and maintaining EDM files is a time consuming operation. That's why the Entity Framework team has created a wizard and a designer inside Visual Studio that you can use to handle these files visually without worrying about their structure.

PROBLEM

Suppose you have to write an application that manages orders in the Northwind database. You have to work with the Orders, Order Details, Customers, and Products tables, and with the Order, Order_Detail, Customer, and Product classes. You also have to generate the EDM to map these classes and tables, and generate code for classes so that you're productive immediately.

SOLUTION

To create the EDM, add a new item of the type ADO.NET Entity Data Model to the project. In a three-layer application, the best place to put this item is in the model assembly. If you adopt the domain model way of designing, you'll probably create a separate assembly that references the repository.

After you've added the item, Visual Studio starts a wizard. The first step lets you choose whether you want to create a model starting from a database or from scratch and then create a database from it. Because we already have a database, we're opting for the first choice. Figure 2.6 shows the form where you make this choice.

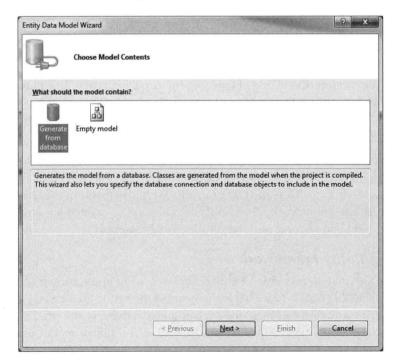

**Figure 2.6
The first form of the Visual Studio wizard lets you choose to create a model from a database (first option) or from scratch (second option).**

Choosing this design option means that at the end of the wizard, you'll have the tables described in the EDM and an automatically generated class for each of them. The properties and the columns will also be mapped one-to-one. What's more, the wizard inspects foreign keys on the database and reflects them in the classes. For example, it places the property Customer in the Order class and the property Orders in Customer.

On the second form, you first choose the database you want to connect to. Use the drop-down list that shows the database already configured inside Visual Studio (you can create a new connection on the fly by clicking the New Connection button). After you've chosen the database, you'll see the connection string that Entity Framework uses to connect to that database in the Entity connection string box. Use the check box at the bottom of the form to choose whether to store the connection string in the configuration file; if you select the check box, type the name of the key that the connection string has in the configuration file in the text box. All this is shown in figure 2.7.

The third, and last, form connects to the selected database; scans its tables, views, stored procedures, and functions; and shows them in a check box tree. Here you select the tables that you want to use (in this case, Orders, Order Details, Customers and Products).

Figure 2.7   In the second form of the wizard, you choose the database to connect to or create a new connection on the fly (by clicking the New Connection button). Finally, you choose the name of the connection string in the configuration file.

Below the tree are two options that deserve your attention. The first one lets you choose whether to pluralize or singularize the class names. If you select this check box, the Orders table generates a class named Order and vice versa. If you don't select this check box, the Orders table only generates a class named Orders. The second option lets you choose whether to create a foreign key property along with the property that references another object. For instance, in addition to the Customer property, you can decide to include the CustomerId property in the Order class. This last choice is enabled by default, and you should keep it. Using foreign key properties makes relationship management a whole lot easier. Figure 2.8 shows this last form.

When you've made your selections, click Finish. The wizard creates the classes and shows them in a designer.

TIP   The designer shows the classes, not the tables.

You can edit the classes to modify their names or the names of their properties to add relationships with other classes, to add inheritance, and so on. You have full control over your model.

If you look at the Solution Explorer window in Visual studio, the wizard has generated a file with the extension .edmx that's associated with the designer. It contains the three EDM files merged into one so that each time you modify an entity visually, its modifications are recorded inside that file.

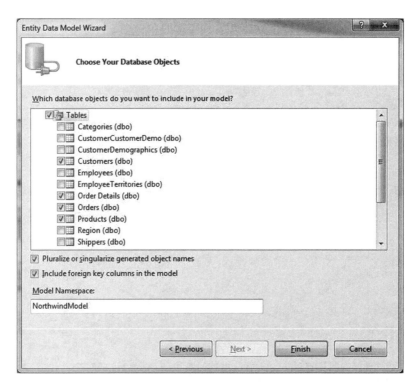

Figure 2.8   The last form lets you choose the tables to import into the EDM.

EDMX VERSUS EDM The EDMX file is not the EDM. The EDMX is an artifact for enabling the designer. It is not understood by Entity Framework. At compile time, the compiler splits the EDMX into the three EDM files and then embeds those files into the assembly or saves them in the output directory so that the runtime of Entity Framework can read them. What the compiler does depends on the value of the `Metadata Artifact Processing` property of the designer. Its possible values are `Embed in Output Assembly` and `Copy to Output Directory`.

In the Solution Explorer window, nested into the EDMX file, you see either a .cs file or a .vb file, depending on your programming language. This file contains the code for the classes described in the EDM and one important class: the *context* (we'll get back to this later).

The last step you have to take is to enable Entity Framework in your application is to copy the connection string generated by the wizard into the configuration file of the application. (The connection string is in the app.config file of the assembly in which you generated the EDMX file). Now Entity Framework is correctly set up, and you can start writing data access code.

DISCUSSION

When all's said and done, enabling Entity Framework is as easy as completing a wizard. Naturally, if you don't have a database and you need to start from the object model, the path is harder because you have to design classes from scratch. Fortunately, the designer is powerful enough to help you do that rather painlessly. It lets you create properties, associations, inheritance hierarchies, and so on.

Speaking of classes, if you take a look at their code, you'll see that it's cluttered by lots of uninteresting stuff. Attributes decorate the class definition, the property, and even the assembly. The getters and setters of the properties are full of infrastructure code. In other words, the classes are aware of Entity Framework, which is *wrong*. In a domain model design, classes can be aware of the data layer, but they must *not* be aware of the technology that it uses. Classes must be ignorant of persistence. Each must be a Plain Old CLR Object (*POCO*) and worry only about business code.

TECHNIQUE 5 Generating POCO code

The reason the generated code is not POCO is that the first version of Entity Framework didn't support POCO classes. One of the new features in the current version of Entity Framework is support for POCO classes. Developing with POCO classes is far better than developing with classes that are generated by default. POCO classes contain only business code and not persistence-related code. What's more, if you change the persistence tool (say, from pure ADO.NET to Entity Framework or vice versa), you don't have to change your model classes but only the layer that talks to the database.

To let you generate legacy classes, POCO classes and, more broadly speaking, any code you want, the Entity Framework team has leveraged a feature of Visual Studio called T4 templates. By using templates, you can fully customize the way classes are generated so that you can add your logic.

PROBLEM

For this example, our scenario is that before you start your development work, you want to change from default code generation and customize the process. You need POCO classes, and you want to both customize their generation and extend them.

SOLUTION

Templates are the key to custom code generation. A template is a markup file where you can dynamically add content. You can think of it as a Classic ASP page that creates C# or VB code instead of generating HTML. The syntax is only slightly different: classic ASP uses <% markers and templates use <#.

Fortunately, the Entity Framework team has already created a template that generates POCO code. Unfortunately, this template is not integrated in the .NET Framework and Visual Studio. You've got to download and install it using the Extension Manager tool inside Visual Studio.

This template is available for both C# and VB in two flavors: one for web site applications and one for others. Figure 2.9 shows how to search for the templates in the Extension Manager window.

After installing the templates, you can right-click on the designer and choose the Add Code Generation Item. Visual Studio opens the Add File wizard. Here's where you select the POCO template.

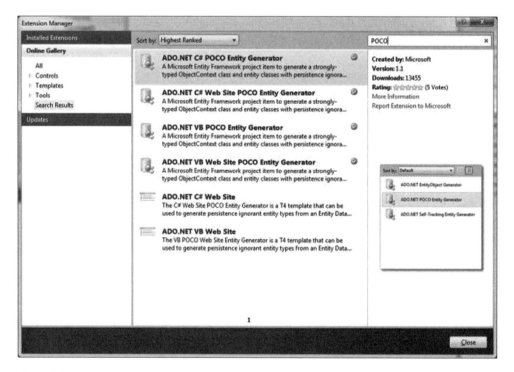

Figure 2.9 **The Extension Manager window lets you search for and install the templates in your Visual Studio.**

Now the project contains two new template files. One generates POCO classes and the other one creates the context class (we'll talk more about this in the next section). In the Solution Explorer window, The POCO template contains a nested file for each class in the model; the other template contains only one nested file.

Because we generated the EDMX file inside the model assembly, the POCO template must remain there because it generates classes. The other template generates the context that's required only by the real data access code, so you must move it into the assembly that's responsible for accessing data. Because it points to the EDMX file, you have to open it after you move it and change its reference to the file by modifying the `inputFile` variable.

DISCUSSION

With a few clicks, you've created a well-structured application. In fact, now you've got .NET classes, the database, the class mappings, and a data access gateway (the context). At last! You're ready to write real code. In the next section, you're going to see how to query with Entity Framework.

TECHNIQUE 6   Reading data using Entity Framework

Querying a database using the classic ADO.NET approach requires you to write SQL code and leverage several classes to execute it and read returned data. Querying with Entity Framework is different. Because you don't work directly with the database, the only structure you need to know about is the model. That's how the model becomes your database and why your queries are written against it. The burden of translating everything into SQL and executing it against the database is shifted to Entity Framework.

Entity Framework is a huge step towards development simplicity. Remember that in section 2.2.1, we discussed that the classes in the model can be different from the database tables that classes are mapped to. Classes have inheritance. The number of classes and tables does not have to match, and so on. You don't have to worry about any of these problems. You write queries against the model, and then Entity Framework generates SQL for you. What's more, classes express business better than database tables do, so writing queries against them is a more business oriented approach.

PROBLEM

Suppose you have to create a web page that shows orders in a grid. The user must be able to filter orders by customer name, shipping city, total amount, and the product sold. The user must also be able to sort the orders by any column, and data must be paged because we're in a web environment. Finally, the data shown in the list is the full shipping address, the customer name, and the amount of the order.

SOLUTION

For a single web page, that's a lot of requirements. For now, let's ignore the page and focus on the data access code you need to satisfy them. As we hinted before, the second template generates the context class. The context class is your gateway to the database. This class inherits from `ObjectContext` and has an *entity set* for each class that doesn't inherit from any other in the model. In our case, we have four classes and four entity sets, but if there were a `SpecialProduct` class that inherited from `Product`, we would have five classes and four entity sets.

If the context is your gateway to the database, the entity sets are your gateway to the data. Think of them as an in-memory representation of a table (data doesn't reside solely in memory). The context class exposes each entity set as a property whose name is the name of the table (identical, pluralized, or singularized, depending on your choice) and whose type is `ObjectSet<T>`, where `T` is the model class it exposes (you can modify the name of the entity set by using the designer). The following listing shows what the context class looks like.

Listing 2.1   The generated context class

C#:
```
public partial class NorthwindEntities : ObjectContext
{
  ...
  public ObjectSet<Customer> Customers { ... }
  public ObjectSet<Order_Detail> Order_Details { ... }
  public ObjectSet<Order> Orders { ... }
  public ObjectSet<Product> Products { ... }
}
```

VB:
```
Public Partial Class NorthwindEntities
  Inherits ObjectContext
  ...
  Public Property Customers() As ObjectSet(Of Customer)
  Public Property Order_Details() As ObjectSet(Of Order_Detail)
  Public Property Orders() As ObjectSet(Of Order)
  Public Property Products() As ObjectSet(Of Product)
End Class
```

To query the model, you have to perform a LINQ to Entities query against an entity set. LINQ to Entities is just a dialect of LINQ that triggers the process that transforms the LINQ query in SQL (instead of performing an in-memory search).

Now that you have the fundamentals, let's start writing the query that returns orders. The first search parameter is the shipping city. Applying this type of filter is extremely simple.

C#:
```
using (var ctx = new NorthwindEntities())
{
  return ctx.Orders.Where(o => o.ShipCity == shippingAddress);
}
```

VB:
```
Using ctx = New NorthwindEntities()
 Return ctx.Orders.Where(Function(o) o.ShipCity = shippingAddress)
End Using
```

Isn't that expressive? We love LINQ expressiveness when querying, and these snippets are proof of that power.

> **NOTE** From now on, we'll remove context instantiation and will always use the `ctx` name to identify it.

The second filtering parameter is the customer name. Here, the filtering is applied not on the order but on an entity that's associated with it. Because the order has a reference to the customer entity, we can navigate the model from the order to the customer and filter by its name.

C#:

```
ctx.Orders.Where(o => o.Customer.CompanyName == customerName);
```

VB:

```
ctx.Orders.Where(Function(o) o.Customer.CompanyName = customerName)
```

As you see, we don't need to specify joins as we would do in SQL code. Entity Framework reads relationships from the EDM and automatically generates correct joins for us. Thumbs up for Entity Framework.

The third search parameter is a bit harder. We have to calculate the total amount of an order and compare that with the user value. Performing such a query in SQL is challenging and requires a `GROUP BY` clause. In LINQ to Entities, we can do it with a couple of methods that are unbelievably simple.

C#:

```
ctx.Orders.Where(o =>
    o.Order_Details.Sum(d => (d.UnitPrice * d.Quantity)) > amount);
```

VB:

```
ctx.Orders.Where(Function(o) _
    o.Order_Details.Sum(Function(d) (d.UnitPrice * d.Quantity)) > amount)
```

These snippets navigate from the orders to their details and sum the total of each of them. Then they check that the sum is greater than the given input. Isn't that awesome?

The last search parameter is the product. The user searches for orders that include that product in the list of those sold. Here we have another type of search because we have to determine whether a product is included in the associated list of details. Once again, LINQ makes it simple.

C#:

```
ctx.Orders.Where(o =>
    o.Order_Details.Any(d => d.ProductID == productId));
```

VB:

```
ctx.Orders.Where(Function(o) _
    o.Order_Details.Any(Function(d) d.ProductID = productId))
```

The `Any` method checks whether a product with the same ID is in the details associated with the order and returns a boolean.

So far we've applied filters statically, but because the user can enter some and ignore others, we have to find a way to apply them dynamically. The solution is the IQueryable<T> interface. Take a look at the following listing.

Listing 2.2   Applying filters dynamically

C#:
```
IQueryable<Order> result = ctx.Orders;
if (!String.IsNullOrEmpty(shippingAddress))
  result = result.Where(o =>
    o.Order_Details.Any(d => d.ProductID == productId));
if (!String.IsNullOrEmpty(customerName))
  result = result.Where(o => o.Customer.CompanyName == customerName);
```

VB:
```
Dim result As IQueryable(Of Order) = ctx.Orders
If Not String.IsNullOrEmpty(shippingAddress) Then
  result = result.Where(Function(o) _
    o.Order_Details.Any(Function(d) d.ProductID = productId))
End If
If Not String.IsNullOrEmpty(customerName) Then
  result = result.Where(Function(o) _
    o.Customer.CompanyName = customerName)
End If
```

Each LINQ method returns an IQueryable<T> object, so you can add filters to it dynamically. Easy as pie, isn't it?

Another requirement is data paging. Doing it in SQL requires you to write a long statement. In LINQ to Entities, you can leverage the power of the Skip and Take methods. Skip ignores the first *n* rows, and Take takes only the following *n* rows.

C#:
```
  result = result.Skip(10).Take(10);
```

VB:
```
  result = result.Skip(10).Take(10)
```

This query skips the first 10 rows and returns the next 10 rows. If the grid you show data in shows 10 rows per page, this query retrieves rows from the second page. All the methods we've been discussing are reason enough for you to move to Entity Framework and LINQ.

Another important requirement is the ability to sort orders. Thanks to the OrderBy method, once again this is a simple task. Because the user decides what column to sort by, we have to check at runtime which column the user has selected and sort the data by that column. The following listing shows how to achieve this goal.

Listing 2.3   Sorting data dynamically

C#:
```
if (sortField == "shipcity")
  result = result.OrderBy(o => o.ShipCity);
else if (sortField == "shipaddress")
```

```
  result = result.OrderBy(o => o.ShipAddress);
else
  result = result.OrderBy(o => o.ShipCountry);
```

VB:
```
If sortField = "shipcity" Then
  result = result.OrderBy(Function(o) o.ShipCity)
ElseIf sortField = "shipaddress" Then
  result = result.OrderBy(Function(o) o.ShipAddress)
Else
  result = result.OrderBy(Function(o) o.ShipCountry)
End If
```

The final requirement has to do with data to be shown on the mask. We need only the full shipping address, the customer name, and the total amount, and we can optimize the query to retrieve only this data. This data contains properties about the order, plus its customer and its total amount. This kind of data is referred to as a *projection*.

In LINQ to Entities, you can perform a projection using the Select method. The result of a projection is an anonymous type. Now, you know that an anonymous type can be exposed outside a method only as an instance of type Object. Having the result of the query exposed as an Object instance isn't good from a design point of view.

You can optimize design by creating a Data Transfer Object (DTO) with the properties that match the result of the projection. In the query, you pour the result into the DTO. Finally, you let the method in the DAL expose and return the DTO class. The following listing shows the code for the query.

Listing 2.4   Returning a DTO with only necessary data

C#:
```
IQueryable<OrderDTO> finalResult = result.Select(o =>
  new OrderDTO
  {
    CustomerName = o.Customer.CompanyName,
    ShipAddress = o.ShipAddress,
    ShipCity = o.ShipCity,
    ShipCountry = o.ShipCountry,
    ShipPostalCode = o.ShipPostalCode,
    Total = o.Order_Details.Sum(d => (d.UnitPrice * d.Quantity)) );
  }
```

VB:
```
Dim finalResult As IQueryable(Of OrderDTO) = result.Select(Function(o) _
  New OrderDTO() With { _
    .CustomerName = o.Customer.CompanyName, _
    .ShipAddress = o.ShipAddress, _
    .ShipCity = o.ShipCity, _
    .ShipCountry = o.ShipCountry, _
    .ShipPostalCode = o.ShipPostalCode, _
    .Total = o.Order_Details.Sum(Function(d) (d.UnitPrice * d.Quantity))
```

The OrderDTO class is the class in the model assembly that acts as a DTO. Its only purpose is letting data flow to the GUI in a typed way.

DISCUSSION

Well, putting it all together uses about 21 lines of code (we're counting blank lines). Now think about how much SQL and .NET code you would have written to do this in classic ADO.NET style and ask yourself, isn't this a better way? In an ASP.NET environment, everything needs to be optimized and using Entity Framework is a great way to do that.

Before we get to the end of the chapter, let's look at the other side of the coin: data writing.

TECHNIQUE 7   **Writing data using Entity Framework**

Writing data on the database is as simple as reading it. In most cases, you just need to call the three basic methods of the entity set to add, modify, or delete data from the database.

PROBLEM

Suppose that you have to create a form to edit customers' data. You need to be able to create, modify, and delete customers.

SOLUTION

As before, we're not going to talk about the user interface here. We're going to focus on the data access code. The process of saving objects passes through two phases:

- *Tracking*—During this phase, the context tracks modifications made to objects that it references. The context references all objects that you read through it and objects that you *add* or *attach* to it. More generally, the tracking phase starts when you instantiate the context and ends when you trigger the next phase.
- *Persistence*—During this phase, the context gathers modifications made to objects during the tracking phase and persists them into the database.

Creating a customer is pretty simple. We need to create a `Customer` instance and pass it to the `AddObject` method of the customer's entity set (tracking phase). After that, we call the context `SaveChanges` method to trigger persistence to the database. The following listing puts this technique into practice.

Listing 2.5   Creating a new customer

C#:

```
var c = new Customer()
{
  Address = "address",
  City = "City",
  CompanyName = "CompanyName",
  ContactName = "ContactName",
  ContactTitle = "ContactTitle",
  Country = "Country",
  CustomerID = "15455",
  Fax = "222222",
  Phone = "2333333",
  PostalCode = "123445",
```

```
  Region = "Region"
};
ctx.Customers.AddObject(customer);
ctx.SaveChanges();
```

VB:

```
Dim c = New Customer() With _
{ _
  .Address = "address", _
  .City = "City", _
  .CompanyName = "CompanyName", _
  .ContactName = "ContactName", _
  .ContactTitle = "ContactTitle", _
  .Country = "Country", _
  .CustomerID = "15455", _
  .Fax = "222222", _
  .Phone = "2333333", _
  .PostalCode = "123445", _
  .Region = "Region" _
}
ctx.Customers.AddObject(customer)
ctx.SaveChanges()
```

The `AddObject` method adds the customer instance to the context and marks the instance as `Added`. `SaveChanges` transforms the added object into a new row in the database.

Updating the customer is equally simple. You can do it in one of two ways. You can retrieve the customer, update it, and then call `SaveChanges` to report modifications to the database. This scenario is defined as *connected* because you use the same context to read and update customer data.

C#:

```
var c = ctx.Customers.First(c => c.CustomerId == "15455");
c.Address = "newaddress";
ctx.SaveChanges();
```

VB:

```
Dim c = ctx.Customers.First(Function(c) c.CustomerId = "15455")
c.Address = "newaddress"
ctx.SaveChanges()
```

Another way to update an entity is to create a `Customer` instance, attach it to the context using the `Attach` method of the customer's entity set, and then mark it as `Modified`. This scenario is known as *disconnected* because the context you use to update customer data is not the same one you use to read customer data. The code required for the disconnected scenario is shown in the following listing.

Listing 2.6 Updating a customer

C#:

```
ctx.Customers.Attach(customer);
ctx.ObjectStateManager.GetObjectStateEntry(customer).
```

```
  ChangeState(EntityState.Modified);
ctx.SaveChanges();
```

VB:

```
ctx.Customers.Attach(customer)
ctx.ObjectStateManager.GetObjectStateEntry(customer).
  ChangeState(EntityState.Modified)
ctx.SaveChanges()
```

Whichever pattern you follow (connected or disconnected), the code is pretty easy.

The last requirement in this example is deleting a customer. This action also gives you a choice of a connected or disconnected pattern. In the first case, you retrieve the customer and then call the `DeleteObject` method of the customer's entity set. In the second case, instead of querying the database, you already have the object so you can attach it to the context and then invoke the `DeleteObject` method. For both patterns, the last step is to invoke the `SaveChanges` method. The following listing shows both scenarios.

Listing 2.7   Deleting a customer

C#:

Connected scenario:

```
var c = ctx.Customers.First(c => c.CustomerId == "15455");
ctx.DeleteObject(c);
ctx.SaveChanges();
```

Disconnected scenario:

```
ctx.Customers.Attach(customer);
ctx.Customers.DeleteObject(customer);
ctx.SaveChanges();
```

VB:

Connected scenario:

```
Dim c = ctx.Customers.First(Function(c) c.CustomerId = "15455")
ctx.DeleteObject(c)
ctx.SaveChanges()
```

Disconnected scenario:

```
ctx.Customers.Attach(customer)
ctx.Customers.DeleteObject(customer)
ctx.SaveChanges()
```

Deleting an object is pretty straightforward. Like object updates, it requires only a few lines of code.

DISCUSSION

As you've seen, not only does the ORM approach save many lines of code, but it also lets you write more readable code. `AddObject` and `DeleteObject` are self-explanatory, and `SaveChanges` does exactly what it says: it persists, in the database, modifications you make to objects. When you use an ORM, your productivity is going to increase dramatically.

2.4   *Summary*

Entity Framework is definitely worth a look if you want to ease your data access development. Working with ADO.NET is feasible, but the amount of code you have to write and maintain quickly becomes too large, especially in big projects.

Entity Framework is software that's built on top of ADO.NET, so it requires a bit more attention to be integrated in an application. Fortunately, it was designed to be as easy as possible, and it will work in any kind of design you choose for your application. If you opt for a three-layer design, you can easily isolate Entity Framework in the DAL; if you go for the domain model, it can be leveraged by the repository code.

Now that you know how to perform the basic stuff with Entity Framework, it's time to dig deeper into it and see how you can use it in ASP.NET applications.

Integrating Entity Framework and ASP.NET

3

This chapter covers

- Handling the context in ASP.NET applications
- Optimizing persistence in ASP.NET applications
- Managing concurrency
- Optimizing performance

In the previous chapter, we talked about the different ways you can design your application. We focused mainly on data access code, and you discovered how using Entity Framework might save your life.

In this chapter, we'll look at integrating Entity Framework and ASP.NET. You'll see some of the techniques you learned in the previous chapter and how to use them in this environment. You'll learn how to handle context instantiation and destruction to achieve the best performance and design. You'll also learn how to persist modifications made in an ASP.NET page in the database, and we'll give you a few tips about performance. To be in sync with the previous chapter, all examples use the Northwind database to show how to integrate Entity Framework and ASP.NET.

Do you remember the `ObjectContext` class (a.k.a context) from the previous chapter? It's the class where the Entity Framework magic begins. We'll start by talking about the most important concept of this class in ASP.NET applications: lifetime. We're starting with the basics because if you ignore the foundation, your applications might be slow or even crash.

3.1   Understanding context lifetime

By *context lifetime* we mean the way the context is generated, reused, and then destroyed by the application. Depending on what type of application you're developing, this behavior changes; windows applications require a lifecycle that's different from the one required by web applications which, in turn, are much like web service applications.

Because this book is about ASP.NET, we're going to focus on web applications in this section. In the previous chapter, we created a context for each method, but that's not the only way you can handle context lifetime. You'll discover that ASP.NET has features that can manage the context much better than that. Now it's time to get your hands dirty by modifying the sample we used in chapter 2 to learn better approaches.

TECHNIQUE 8   First approach: one context per method

In chapter 2, each time you had to execute a command, you created a context, executed the command, and then destroyed the context. All these operations were performed inside a method. This approach is surely the simplest, but also the least flexible and, in some fringe cases, dangerous. Let's discover why that's so and how you can improve things.

PROBLEM

Suppose you have a web page where the user is shown a list of orders that were placed on the current day. He selects some of them, clicks a button, and then sees the customer's name and billing address beside each selected order. You need to retrieve this additional data in the fastest and most reliable way possible.

SOLUTION

The code for retrieving orders is straightforward. We create the context, perform the query, return the result, and destroy the context:

C#
```
using (var ctx = new NorthwindEntities())
{
  return ctx.Orders.Where(o => o.OrderDate == DateTime.Now.Date);
}
```

VB
```
Using ctx = New NorthwindEntities()
  Return ctx.Orders.Where(Function(o) o.OrderDate = DateTime.Now.Date)
End Using
```

Querying for the customer who made the selected orders requires some more code. What you can do is iterate over the orders and, if the current one is selected, invoke a method that retrieves the customer. An example is shown in the following listing.

Listing 3.1 Retrieving customers who made the selected orders

C#:

```
private void RetrieveCustomersForOrders()
{
  for(var i=0; i<selectedOrders.Count; i++)
  {
    selectedOrders[i].Customer =
      _repository.RetrieveCustomer(selectedOrders[i].OrderId);
  }
}

private Customer GetCustomerByOrder(int orderId)
{
  using (var ctx = new NorthwindEntities())
  {
    return ctx.Orders.First(o => o.OrderId == orderId).Customer;
  }
}
```

VB:

```
Private Sub RetrieveCustomersForOrders()
  For i As var = 0 To selectedOrders.Count - 1
    selectedOrders(i).Customer =
      _repository.RetrieveCustomer(selectedOrders(i).OrderId)
  Next
End Sub

Private Function GetCustomerByOrder(orderId As Integer) As Customer
  Using ctx = New NorthwindEntities()
    Return ctx.Orders.First(Function(o) o.OrderId = orderId).Customer
  End Using
End Function
```

See how easy that was? With just a few lines of code, we've solved our problem.

DISCUSSION

What's great about the method approach is its simplicity. Even so, this approach suffers from a dangerous drawback. If two orders have the same customer, you obtain two Customer instances that refer to the same row in the database.

Suppose that the user selects two orders from the same customer. When the code iterates over the selected orders, it queries for the same customer twice. Suppose that between the first and the second read, the customer uses the application to change their address. The result is that the first read retrieves data before it was changed, and the second read retrieves it after it was changed. Figure 3.1 shows an example of such a flow.

The user will, at the least, be confused by this situation; he'll surely think it's a bug. If the name changes, instead of the address, he might even think that there are two separate customers. We definitely have to improve our solution to avoid this trap. In the next section, we'll investigate how to handle the context in a better way.

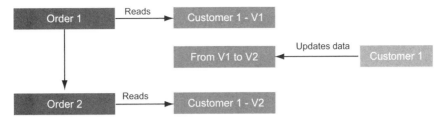

Figure 3.1   The code reads Customer 1 related to Order 1. Someone externally updates Customer 1, changing its data. The code reads once again, but now Customer 1 is also related to Order 2. The two reads return different data for the same customer.

TECHNIQUE 9   A better approach: one context per ASP.NET request

To overcome the limitation we exposed in the previous discussion, you can instruct the context to span for the entire lifetime of the web request. The context implements the *Identity Map* pattern, meaning that it enables only one instance of an entity for the same key properties. The result is that the second time the user reads the same customer, the user receives the same object as that of the first read. It's stale data, but without discrepancies.

PROBLEM

The problem we have to solve in this section is the same problem we had in technique 1. We have to ensure that only one instance of an object for the same row of the database is in place.

SOLUTION

The Identity Map logic is embedded in the `ObjectStateManager` component (*state manager* from now on) of the `ObjectContext` class. The state manager holds a reference to all objects that have been read and attached to the context.

> **NOTE**   Technically speaking, when we say we attach an object to the context, we're actually attaching it to the state manager. Because the state manager is an inner component of the context, it's perfectly correct (and more widely understood) to say that we attach an object to the context, not to the state manager.

When an object is read by the context, the context gets data from the database and then queries the state manager to see whether an object of the same type with the same key properties already exists. If this query returns true, the context returns the object that's already in the state manager, ignoring data coming from the query. If this query returns false, the context creates an instance of the object, attaches it to the state manager, and returns it to the caller. Figure 3.2 shows this process.

This logic ensures that only one object of the same type and with the same key properties is tracked by the state manager. The result is that the second time the user reads the same customer, he doesn't get data from the database, but rather he gets data that was read the first time. This process ensures that the data contains no discrepancies. Now, the next problem is, how can we switch from a method-based context lifetime to a request context lifetime?

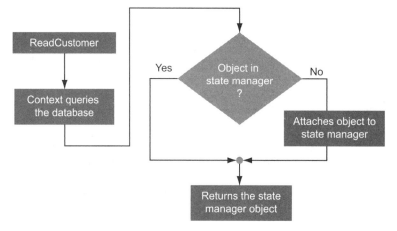

Figure 3.2   The context reads data from the database. If the object is already tracked by the state manager, the state manager object is returned. If not, the object created from the database query is attached to the state manager and then returned.

What you can do is create a couple of methods in your repository: one creates an instance of the context and the other one destroys it. The context instance is stored in the `HttpContext.Items` collection, which is a common place that's reachable by other repositories. The code is shown in the following listing.

Listing 3.2   Creating repository methods to handle context lifecycle

C#:
```
public class ContextHandler
{
  public void CreateContext()
  {
    HttpContext.Current.Items["__EFCONTEXT"] = new NorthwindEntities();
  }

  public void DestroyContext()
  {
    ((NorthwindEntities)HttpContext.Current.Items["__EFCONTEXT"]).Dispose();
  }
}
```

VB:
```
Public Class ContextHandler
  Public Sub CreateContext()
    HttpContext.Current.Items("__EFCONTEXT") = New NorthwindEntities()
  End Sub

  Public Sub DestroyContext()
    DirectCast(HttpContext.Current.Items("__EFCONTEXT"),
      NorthwindEntities).Dispose()
  End Sub
End Class
```

Now that we have a gateway to handle the context lifecycle, all we have to do is invoke the methods we just created in the repository. `CreateContext` can be invoked in the page's `Init` event and `DestroyContext` can be invoked in the page's `Unload` event. The following listing puts this concept into action.

Listing 3.3   Invoking a repository method to handle the context lifecycle

C#:
```
public partial class _default : Page
{
  protected override void OnInit(EventArgs e)
  {
    base.OnInit(e);
    new ContextHandler().CreateContext();
  }

  protected override void OnUnload(EventArgs e)
  {
    base.OnUnload(e);
    new ContextHandler().DestroyContext();
  }
}
```

VB:
```
Public Partial Class _default
    Inherits Page
    Protected Overrides Sub OnInit(e As EventArgs)
          MyBase.OnInit(e)
          New ContextHandler().CreateContext()
    End Sub

    Protected Overrides Sub OnUnload(e As EventArgs)
          MyBase.OnUnload(e)
          New ContextHandler().DestroyContext()
    End Sub
End Class
```

Placing this code in each page isn't ideal. What you can do is create a class and let it inherit from the `Page` class. You put the code in listing 3.3 in the class and let your pages inherit from it. Now all your pages can handle context without you having to do it each time. The following listing shows how this way makes things simpler.

Listing 3.4   Invoking repository methods via a base class

C#:
```
public partial class Base : Page
{
  //context management code
}

public partial class _default : BasePage
{
}
```

VB:
```
Public Partial Class Base
  Inherits Page
  'context management code
End Class

Public Partial Class _default
  Inherits BasePage
End Class
```

The code for each page is much shorter now. Don't you like it?

DISCUSSION

Having a single context for each ASP.NET request makes things easier and, more importantly, handles data correctly. But there's something we don't like here: the page is responsible for creating and destroying the context. Wouldn't it be better if the data access code could manage the context instantiation and destruction without us having to write anything in the page or in its base class? That's the subject of the next section.

TECHNIQUE 10   **Instantiating the context using modules**

Invoking context creation and disposal methods in the page creates dangerous circular dependencies. The page depends on the data access to retrieve data from the database and the data access depends on the page to invoke specific methods to create and destroy the context. No matter how you look at it, this situation is bad.

PROBLEM

The problem we have to solve is the same as what we had in the previous sections. This time, we want to eliminate the problem of circular dependencies by using a more elegant solution.

SOLUTION

The cleanest solution to the problem is the adoption of an HttpModule. An HttpModule is a class that lets you subscribe to the events of the ASP.NET execution pipeline so that you can plug in your logic. In our case, we can subscribe to the BeginRequest event to create the context and to the EndRequest event to destroy it.

You can place the module in the data access assembly, eliminating every circular dependency. The following listing shows the code for HttpModule.

Listing 3.5   Creating the module for handling context lifecycle

C#:
```
public class ContextModule : IHttpModule
{
  public void Dispose() { }                              Subscribe to begin ❶
                                                         and end of requests
  public void Init(HttpApplication context)
  {
    context.BeginRequest += new EventHandler(context_BeginRequest);
    context.EndRequest += new EventHandler(context_EndRequest);
  }
```

```
  void context_BeginRequest(object sender, EventArgs e)
  {
    new CustomerRepository().CreateContext();
  }

  void context_EndRequest(object sender, EventArgs e)
  {
    new CustomerRepository().DestroyContext();
  }
}
```

VB:

```
Public Class ContextModule
  Implements IHttpModule
  Public Sub Dispose()
  End Sub

  Public Sub Init(context As HttpApplication)
   context.BeginRequest +=
     New EventHandler(AddressOf context_BeginRequest)
   context.EndRequest += New EventHandler(AddressOf context_EndRequest)
  End Sub

  Private Sub context_BeginRequest(sender As Object, e As EventArgs)
    New CustomerRepository().CreateContext()
  End Sub

  Private Sub context_EndRequest(sender As Object, e As EventArgs)
    New CustomerRepository().DestroyContext()
  End Sub
End Class
```

**Subscribe to begin ❶
and end of requests**

The code is pretty simple. First, you subscribe to the events that are fired at the beginning and at the end of each request ❶. Later, in the handler for the begin request, you create the context, and in the handler for the end request, you destroy it. That's all you need to do.

DISCUSSION

At this point, the context is set up, the pages are no longer responsible for handling context lifecycle, and you no longer have multiple instances of the same entity. You achieved what you wanted!

Now we can leave context lifecycle management and move on to how to use the context the right way so that the application is lightweight and doesn't burden the database.

3.2   *Using the context the right way*

Now that the context is instantiated and destroyed in the best way possible, let's *use* it in the best way possible. In chapter 2, we worked with Entity Framework, using both the connected and the disconnected approach.

If you take the connected approach, you read and update an entity in the scope of the same context. The disconnected approach is the opposite: you read and update an entity using two different contexts.

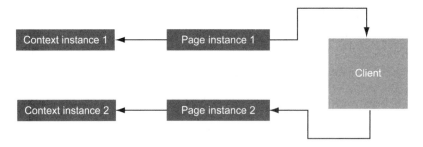

Figure 3.3 Each time a page is processed, a new instance of the page is created. Each instance uses a new context instance without reusing existing ones.

In this section, we want to emphasize the disconnected way of working because ASP.NET imposes, by nature, a disconnected model. In fact, most ASP.NET applications read data, show it in a page, let the user modify it, and finally save it into the database. In the previous section, you learned that when the page is sent to the client, the server destroys any reference to the context. This means that the context that's used to read data is different from the one that's used to update it. Figure 3.3 clearly shows this concept.

Working in the disconnected way is harder than the connected approach. But there are enormous benefits in terms of performance because you spare a query to the database. In some cases, you can spare even more.

Let's start analyzing the best practices to update an object.

TECHNIQUE 11 **Persisting entity modifications**

Persisting updates made to an entity in an ASP.NET environment is tricky. In this section, we're going to analyze the easiest approach. In subsequent sections, we'll look at more complex scenarios.

PROBLEM

A customer fills in a page with personal data. When they send it back, the personal data needs to be updated in the database.

SOLUTION

The solution to this problem is pretty easy. You can create a `Customer` entity and fill its properties with values that come from page text boxes. After you create the entity, you can attach it to the database, mark it as modified, and persist it. The code in the following listing shows you how it's done.

Listing 3.6 Persisting customer modifications using ChangeObjectState

C#:
```
var customer = new Customer()
{
  CustomerID = "15455",
  Address = "Address",
  City = "City",
  CompanyName = "CompanyName",
```

```
    ContactName = "ContactName",
    ContactTitle = "ContactTitle",
    Country = "Country",
    Fax = "11111",
    Phone = "222222",
    PostalCode = "00000",
    Region = "Region"
};
ctx.Customers.Attach(customer);
ctx.ObjectStateManager.ChangeObjectState(customer,
    EntityState.Modified);
ctx.SaveChanges();
```

VB:

```
Dim customer = New Customer() With {
    .CustomerID = "15455",
    .Address = "Address",
    .City = "City",
    .CompanyName = "CompanyName",
    .ContactName = "ContactName",
    .ContactTitle = "ContactTitle",
    .Country = "Country",
    .Fax = "11111",
    .Phone = "222222",
    .PostalCode = "00000",
    .Region = "Region"
}
ctx.Customers.Attach(customer)
ctx.ObjectStateManager.ChangeObjectState(customer,
    EntityState.Modified)
ctx.SaveChanges()
```

You're not going to learn anything new from this code. You're simply reusing your knowledge because attaching the entity, marking it as modified, and persisting it is something you've done before.

DISCUSSION

As usual, simplicity comes at a cost. When you use the ChangeObjectState method to mark an entity as modified, it marks *all* the properties as modified. The result is that all the properties are persisted in the database. You have to recreate the entity and then populate all its properties; otherwise, the empty ones will override the value in the database, and you'll lose data. In our example, this isn't a big problem because all customer properties are available in the form. But how do you handle cases where you can't correctly set all the properties of the entity before it's persisted?

TECHNIQUE 12 **Persisting only selected properties**

In situations where you don't have data to populate all an entity's properties, you have to find a mechanism that lets you update only the populated properties. With Entity Framework, you can do this in two ways:

- By selectively marking which properties must be persisted
- By creating a stub entity, attaching it to the context, and then setting the properties to persist

Let's explore both ways now.

PROBLEM

In the page, you want customers to be able to modify only the address information.

SOLUTION

As we said, you can use two approaches to accomplish this task. You can create the entity, fill the properties that must be persisted on the database, and then mark only those properties as modified. After you take these steps, the entity goes to modified state. When the SaveChanges method is invoked, only the properties that are marked as modified are persisted in the database. The following listing shows an example of this technique.

Listing 3.7 Explicitly marking modified properties for persistence

C#:

```csharp
var customer = new Customer()
{
  CustomerID = "15455",
  Address = "Address",
  Country = "Country",
  Fax = "11111",
  Phone = "222222",
  PostalCode = "00000",
  Region = "Region"
};
ctx.Customers.Attach(customer);
var entry = ctx.ObjectStateManager.GetObjectStateEntry(customer);
entry.SetModifiedProperty("Address");
entry.SetModifiedProperty("Country");
entry.SetModifiedProperty("Fax");
entry.SetModifiedProperty("Phone");
entry.SetModifiedProperty("PostalCode");
entry.SetModifiedProperty("Region");
ctx.SaveChanges();
```

VB:

```vb
Dim customer = New Customer() With {
  .CustomerID = "15455",
  .Address = "Address",
  .Country = "Country",
  .Fax = "11111",
  .Phone = "222222",
  .PostalCode = "00000",
  .Region = "Region"
}
ctx.Customers.Attach(customer)
Dim entry = ctx.ObjectStateManager.GetObjectStateEntry(customer)
entry.SetModifiedProperty("Address")
entry.SetModifiedProperty("Country")
entry.SetModifiedProperty("Fax")
entry.SetModifiedProperty("Phone")
entry.SetModifiedProperty("PostalCode")
entry.SetModifiedProperty("Region")
ctx.SaveChanges()
```

Mark entity ❶ as modified

The code is a bit longer than the code in listing 3.6, but it's extremely expressive. First, the `Attach` method attaches the entity to the context. Next, the entity is retrieved from the state manager, and then the `SetModifiedProperty` method marks the properties that must be persisted as modified ❶. When `SaveChanges` is reached, only marked properties are persisted.

What's good about this approach is that you can also create an extension method to cut some lines of code, like in the following listing.

Listing 3.8 An extension method to specify modified properties easily

C#:
```
public static void SetModifiedProperties(this ObjectStateEntry entry,
  params string[] properties)
{
  foreach (var p in properties)
    entry.SetModifiedProperty(p);
}

entry.SetModifiedProperties("Address", "Country", "Fax", "Phone",
  "PostalCode", "Region");
```

VB:
```
<System.Runtime.CompilerServices.Extension> _
Public Shared Sub SetModifiedProperties(entry As ObjectStateEntry,
  ParamArray properties As String())
  For Each p As var In properties
    entry.SetModifiedProperty(p)
  Next
End Sub

entry.SetModifiedProperties("Address", "Country", "Fax", "Phone",
  "PostalCode", "Region")
```

The extension method is quite simple. It accepts an array containing the name of the properties. Internally, the extension method calls the `SetModifiedProperty` method for each of the input properties. The last line of the snippet shows how to invoke the extension method. As you can see, you just need to pass the properties to be modified.

If you're a fan of strong typing, you can create a smarter extension method that accepts a *lambda* expression instead of a string to represent the property name. It's a bit more complicated to do, but it's effective. For brevity's sake, we won't show this method here, but you can find it in the source code at www.manning.com/ASP.NET4.0inPractice.

The drawback of updating data this way is that it requires several lines of code. Our next solution drastically reduces them. First, you recreate the `Customer` instance and set only the key properties (such an entity is usually referred to as *stub*). After that, you attach the entity to the context and then fill the properties that need to be persisted in the database. The context automatically marks the entity and those properties as modified and persists only them. Figure 3.4 shows this flow.

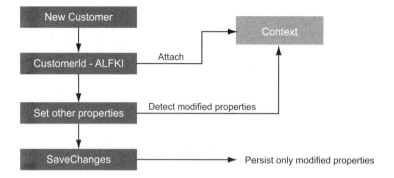

Figure 3.4 Create a customer instance and set its key property, and then attach the instance to the context, which tracks modifications to properties. When persistence is invoked, only the modified properties are persisted.

When you understand the flow, understanding the code in the following listing becomes even easier.

Listing 3.9 Persisting modifications of a customer through a stub

C#:

```
var customer = new Customer()
{
  CustomerID = "15455",
};
ctx.Customers.Attach(customer);
customer.Address = "Address";
customer.Country = "Country";
customer.Fax = "11111";
customer.Phone = "222222";
customer.PostalCode = "00000";
customer.Region = "Region";
ctx.SaveChanges();
```

VB:

```
Dim customer = New Customer() With {
  .CustomerID = "15455"
}
ctx.Customers.Attach(customer)
customer.Address = "Address"
customer.Country = "Country"
customer.Fax = "11111"
customer.Phone = "222222"
customer.PostalCode = "00000"
customer.Region = "Region"
ctx.SaveChanges()
```

Don't you think this path is easy to follow and, at the same time, effective? Try it next time you're in a similar situation.

DISCUSSION

Using the patterns shown in this section ensures that the application will perform quickly and well. The second option lets you write few lines of code and ensures readability. But in some situations, you need the full entity to perform a correct update. What do you do then?

Persisting an entity using ViewState

Several times during project development, we've had to hash the user password based on a *salt* stored in the entity. (A salt is a randomly generated string that is used to hash or encrypt another string.) When we created the form to change the password, we obviously couldn't show the salt in a form field. So how did we hash the password without the salt? In this section, we propose a solution to the problem.

PROBLEM

Suppose that the customer has a username and a password he uses to log into the system. You need to create a page where the customer can modify all their personal data, including their password. All these changes must be made in a secure way.

SOLUTION

What you can do is serialize the whole entity in the page's ViewState. You'll have a copy of the entity when it was originally read. When data comes back from the client, you retrieve the entity from the ViewState and attach it to the context.

After that's done, you use the salt in the entity to hash the password and populate the Password property. Then you use data from text boxes to modify only the properties editable by the customer, leaving the others unchanged. Entity Framework will try to persist only the modified properties and ignore the ones that haven't been touched. The following listing shows the code.

Listing 3.10 Persisting modifications using ASP.NET ViewState

C#:
```
var c = (Customer)ViewState["c"];
ctx.Customers.Attach(c);
c.Fax = fax.Text;
ctx.SaveChanges();
```

VB:
```
Dim c = DirectCast(ViewState("c"), Customer)
ctx.Customers.Attach(c)
c.Fax = fax.Text
ctx.SaveChanges()
```

This approach has one problem. By default, when you read an entity, Entity Framework doesn't return a plain instance, but returns a proxy that inherits from that entity. This proxy overrides property setters to add features like change tracking and lazy loading (which is why when you modify a property, the entity in the state manager becomes modified, even if there's no such code in the property setters).

The drawback is that proxy instances cannot be serialized into ViewState so you receive an error during the rendering phase. Fortunately, you can disable proxy creation and have the plain instance returned. You lose lazy loading and change tracking, but that's not a problem here. You can disable proxy creation by setting the Context-Options.ProxyCreationEnabled property of the context class to false.

C#:

```
ctx.ContextOptions.ProxyCreationEnabled = false;
```

VB:

```
ctx.ContextOptions.ProxyCreationEnabled = false
```

Now when you put the entity in the ViewState, you don't get an error. But, as always, there's one last caveat. By default, ViewState isn't encrypted; the salt reaches the client in the clear. To avoid that, just encrypt the ViewState using the following snippet:

```
<%@ Page ... ViewStateEncryptionMode="Always" %>
```

With this last snippet, persisting modification in an ASP.NET environment holds no more secrets for you.

DISCUSSION

Now you know how to store an entity retrieved using Entity Framework into ViewState. This solution is pretty easy and works fine in most scenarios, but unfortunately, it does have limitations. If the entity contains many properties, the ViewState becomes too large and slows network performance. What's worse, encrypting ViewState requires server resources, which causes further performance degradation. Even so, you'll probably use this solution often in your code.

So far we haven't talked about an important issue: concurrency. In a multiuser environment, concurrency must be carefully evaluated.

TECHNIQUE 14   **Keep concurrency in mind**

Imagine the following scenario: Two users retrieve the same customer information simultaneously. The first user changes the address and saves the data. The second user updates the customer's name and also saves the data. The result is that the second user overwrites the modifications made by the first one; the name is changed, but the address is overwritten with the old value. Overwriting happens because the second user initially read the data before it was updated by the first one. Figure 3.5 visually explains this series of events.

Handling this issue requires you to enable a mechanism to detect that something has changed in the interval between database read and database write. More exactly,

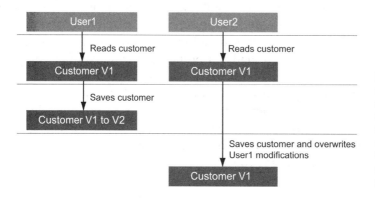

Figure 3.5 Two users read the customer data at the same time. User1 modifies some data and saves it. User2 modifies data that's now old. When User2 saves the data, he overwrites the modifications made by User1.

when the user submits data, he must be notified that something changed while he was editing it.

This mechanism has a performance cost (negligible in most cases), and code development and maintenance are more painful for you. Because of these disadvantages, concurrency isn't something you should account for in all your forms. It's fairly rare that two people in the same organization will modify the same data at the same time (we'll use the customer example here just for demo purposes). Worry about concurrency only for critical situations that have a high probability of concurrency and in which the loss of data will create serious problems.

PROBLEM

Two users are updating information about a customer at the same time. You have to ensure that the second user doesn't overwrite data modified by the first user. You also want the second user to receive a notification if he's worked on stale data.

SOLUTION

The solution is an optimistic concurrency check.

> **NOTE** A pessimistic concurrency check also exists, but it often creates more problems than it solves. Entity Framework doesn't support it and won't do so even in future releases.

The concurrency check technique is pretty simple. You create a *version* column (generally with the type `Timestamp/RowVersion`) in the `Customer` table. This column is updated each time the row is changed. When you perform the UPDATE, this column is included in the WHERE clause. If the version is different from what you initially read, the UPDATE statement doesn't affect any records because the rows were changed since you read the data (there's been concurrency on the data). If the version is the same as what you initially read, then there was no concurrency. You can see this technique explained visually in figure 3.6.

If you can't modify the table structure to add the Version column, you can configure Entity Framework to include *all* the columns in the WHERE clause. If at least one

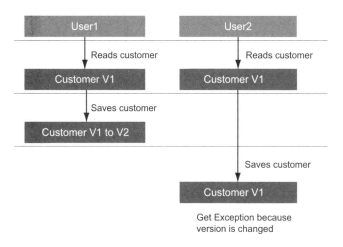

Figure 3.6 Two users read the same customer at the same time. User1 saves the customer and version changes. User2 saves the customer changes, but because this user initially read the old version, he gets an exception.

column changed since you read the data, the UPDATE affects zero records and the concurrency check has worked successfully.

The great thing is that Entity Framework does most of the work for you. All you have to do is specify which properties to include in the concurrency check and then handle the exception that's raised when a concurrency problem occurs.

Because the Northwind database doesn't have a Version column, we need to use all the properties for the concurrency check. To do that, open the designer, select all the properties of the entity, open the Properties window, and set the Concurrency Mode property to Fixed. Now, each time you update the Customer entity, the *original* value of all properties is included in the WHERE clause.

We say the original value because the state manager keeps the current value of the properties and what their values were at the moment the entity was attached to the context. The values of the properties when the entity is attached to the context are the original values. For our purposes, the best way to work is to implement the ViewState pattern that we discussed in technique 13. That pattern ensures that the state manager has the original values that it reads from the database and the new ones that come from the page.

If you have a Version column, you can set the mapped property as the only one to perform concurrency check on. You don't need to keep the entity in the ViewState but you need the version property value so you can follow the patterns that we talked about in techniques 11 and 12.

To understand whether there was a concurrency exception, you simply have to catch System.Data.OptimisticConcurrencyException, as in the following listing.

Listing 3.11 Handling concurrency exception

C#:
```
try
{
  ctx.SaveChanges();
}
catch (OptimisticConcurrencyException ex)
{
  //handle exception
}
```

VB:
```
Try
  ctx.SaveChanges()
Catch ex As OptimisticConcurrencyException
  'handle exception
End Try
```

Handling concurrency isn't difficult at all, is it?

DISCUSSION

Concurrency management is an important feature in many applications. Entity Framework was designed with this concept in mind and makes concurrency management easy.

The fact that you just need to mark the concurrency properties and handle an exception is a clear demonstration of its simplicity.

We want to point out one more thing: the methods we've described in this section are valid for deletions, too. Although deleting an entity requires you to set only key properties, the same update rules with respect to concurrency are followed.

You've now mastered another important piece of data access using Entity Framework and ASP.NET. You can correctly persist modifications made to objects in a single roundtrip to the database. You've taken a first step toward good performance, but just the first. Now let's take a few more steps down that road.

3.3   *Optimizing performance in an ASP.NET environment*

Data access performance is a key aspect of any application. This statement holds especially true for web applications where a single weakness can take down an entire site. We've seen countless applications that run slowly only because some pages don't respect basic rules about data access. In this section, we're going to show you some tricks to ensure the best performance for your data access code.

TECHNIQUE 15   **Optimizing fetching**

By default, when you query for an order, you get the `Order` entity without the details or the customer information. When you access the `Order_Details` property, a query is issued to the database to automatically retrieve the details without you having to do anything. This technique is known as *lazy loading*.

> **NOTE** Lazy loading works only if the context is still alive. If the context has been disposed of, accessing the `Order_Detail` property throws an exception.

If you don't know in advance whether you'll need to fetch details, lazy loading might be a good choice. If you already know you'll need them, you better load the details in the same query in which the order is loaded. That technique is known as *eager loading*.

Overanalyzing lazy loading is useless. It's automatically done when you access a navigation property without you needing to do anything else. For this reason, in this section, we'll talk about eager loading only.

PROBLEM

You have to create a form where orders are shown in a grid. Each order has a row in the grid. An inner grid that contains the details is inside the row. For this example, you already know that you'll need orders and details, so you need to extract them together.

SOLUTION

Retrieving a graph of entities from the database is simple, thanks to the `Include` method of the `ObjectSet<T>` class. It accepts the name of the property that must be loaded along with the main entity, and the game is done. The next snippet shows how to do that.

C#:

```
var orders = ctx.Orders.Include("Order_Details");
```

VB:

```
Dim orders = ctx.Orders.Include("Order_Details")
```

The best part is that the `Include` method returns an `ObjectQuery<T>` instance (which is the base class of `ObjectSet<T>`), so we can concatenate LINQ to Entities operators and other `Include` calls.

If you've loaded the details and the customer information for each order, you can write the following query:

C#:

```
var orders = ctx.Orders.Include("Order_Details").Include("Customer");
```

VB:

```
Dim orders = ctx.Orders.Include("Order_Details").Include("Customer")
```

In this case, we're retrieving only entities that are directly connected with the order. If you also need to retrieve the product linked to the details, you need to traverse the object model:

C#:

```
var orders = ctx.Orders.Include("Order_Details.Product");
```

VB:

```
Dim orders = ctx.Orders.Include("Order_Details.Product")
```

Using the `Include` method isn't difficult at all.

DISCUSSION

Eager loading data is one of the best ways to optimize performance. Suppose you have 100 orders. If you need their details and load them on demand, you end up triggering 100 queries. If you need related customer information too, retrieving the orders causes 100 more queries to execute. You end up with 201 queries to fetch data that you could get in a single request.

Eager loading isn't bulletproof. It pulls a lot of data out of the database and performs joins that might be heavy on the database. Always test your application carefully on a case-by-case basis to choose the best way to load data: lazy loading or eager loading.

Now let's examine how to avoid a common pitfall in query execution.

TECHNIQUE 16   **Avoiding multiple query execution**

Many times you'll create a LINQ to Entities query and then iterate over its result. The iteration causes the query to execute. If you iterate over the query twice, the second iteration triggers a new query to the database instead of reusing the previous query data.

PROBLEM

You have to iterate over the result of a query multiple times. Because you know such a query always returns the same data, you don't want the query to be executed each time.

SOLUTION

The solution to this problem is pretty easy. The first time you perform the query, you download data into a `List<T>` class. All the iterations use the in-memory list instead of the query result. The following listing shows how you can do this easily.

Listing 3.12 Avoiding multiple queries

C#:
```
var customers = ctx.Customers.ToList();
foreach (var c in customers) { ... }
foreach (var c in customers) { ... }
```

VB:
```
Dim customers = ctx.Customers.ToList()
For Each c As var In customers
Next
For Each c As var In customers
Next
```

This simple tweak really makes a difference. Unexpected query execution is one of the most common causes of slow performance that you'll encounter in applications.

DISCUSSION

Solving the problem of multiple query executions isn't difficult at all. Always remember that LINQ to Entities queries are executed only when data is actually used.

Now let's learn another trick and discover a way to optimize queries that look for a single entity.

TECHNIQUE 17 Optimizing queries that retrieve a single element

The easiest way to retrieve a single element is to search its key and use the LINQ to Entities `First` method. Even if the object has already been queried once and is in the state manager, Entity Framework reissues the query each time the `First` method is used. Data already exists in the state manager; because Entity Framework reuses the state manager entity, it discards the data from the database. This process is a waste of resources that you can avoid.

PROBLEM

A `GetCustomerById` method is called frequently in your code. This method uses the LINQ to Entities `First` method to access the customer. You have to optimize the performance of this method to avoid a query against the database.

SOLUTION

Even this problem has a relatively simple solution. The `ObjectContext` class has a `GetObjectByKey` method that lets you retrieve a single object by its key. Its peculiarity is that before going to the database, this method asks the state manager if an entity of that type with the given key is already in memory. If this query is true, the method returns the in-memory entity without going to the database; otherwise, it queries the database and puts the entity in the state manager. Figure 3.7 shows this pattern.

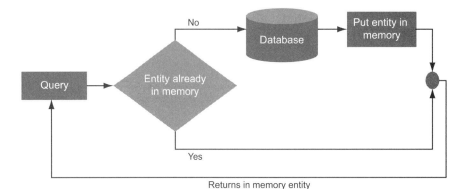

Figure 3.7 A query looks for an entity by its key. If the entity is in memory, it's returned immediately. If it's not in memory, the `GetObjectByKey` method retrieves it from the database and puts it in memory.

Invoking the `GetObjectByKey` method is a bit cumbersome. You have to create an `EntityKey` instance (a class that the state manager uses to represent the key of an entity) and pass in the entity set, the name of the primary key, and its value. After that, you pass the `EntityKey` object to the `GetObjectByKey` method, which returns an `object` instance that you have to manually cast to the real type. The following listing transforms this scenario into code.

Listing 3.13 Retrieving an entity using the `GetObjectByKey` method

C#:
```
var c = (Customer)ctx.GetObjectByKey(
  new EntityKey("NorthwindEntities.Customers", "CustomerID", "ALFKI"));
var c2 = (Customer)ctx.GetObjectByKey(
  new EntityKey("NorthwindEntities.Customers", "CustomerID", "ALFKI"));
```

VB:
```
Dim c = DirectCast(
  ctx.GetObjectByKey(
    New EntityKey("NorthwindEntities.Customers", "CustomerID",
      "ALFKI")),
    Customer)
Dim c2 = DirectCast(
  ctx.GetObjectByKey(
    New EntityKey("NorthwindEntities.Customers", "CustomerID", "ALFKI")),
    Customer)
```

The first statement retrieves the entity from the database, whereas the second statement retrieves the entity from the state manager, sparing a database roundtrip.

   If the object doesn't exist on the database, the `GetObjectByKey` method throws an exception. To keep that from happening, you can use the `TryGetObjectByKey` method. We encourage the use of `GetObjectByKey` and `TryGetObjectByKey` as another little precaution that, performance-wise, really makes the difference.

DISCUSSION

You've seen several little tricks that you can adopt to make your applications faster. Even though `GetObjectByKey` and `TryGetObjectByKey` are a bit cumbersome to use, their benefits are enormous and must not be ignored.

Next up, another big trick that boosts performance: disabling change tracking.

TECHNIQUE 18   **Disabling change tracking**

In chapter 2, we talked about the change tracking mechanism. In section 3.1, we discussed the Identity Map pattern. We also explained how an identity map can save your life in certain circumstances. Both mechanisms slow down performance, especially the identity map check. Let's see how you can make things better.

PROBLEM

You need to improve the performance of the pages. Specifically, you need to increase the performance of database reads.

SOLUTION

To improve query performance, you can disable the change tracking mechanism. Disabling it means that the state manager doesn't need to keep track of each object, and it doesn't perform the identity map check either. Although it's an important feature, sometimes it's useless, so disabling it won't cause a problem (for example, a page that shows all customers doesn't need change tracking or an identity map).

Disabling such features is extremely easy and improves performance to an incredible extent. To disable change tracking, you have to set the `MergeOption` property of the entity set being queried to the value `System.Data.Objects.MergeOption.NoTracking`, like in the following snippet:

C#:
```
ctx.Customers.MergeOption = MergeOption.NoTracking;
```

VB:
```
ctx.Customers.MergeOption = MergeOption.NoTracking
```

We've carried out a test and performed the same query 50 times in both configurations. The result is that by disabling change tracking and identity mapping, the code is 32% faster. This result is a *huge* leap in performance, don't you think?

DISCUSSION

Yet another brilliant way to improve performance. Aren't you falling in love with Entity Framework? You probably are. Even though it's wonderful, always keep in mind the three tricks you've learned in this section. When you're experiencing performance problems in your applications, these tricks are the most likely solution.

Entity Framework is a vast subject. What you have now is a strong base to start using it, but you've still got a lot to learn. If you want to deepen your knowledge of Entity Framework, read *Entity Framework 4.0 In Action*, published by Manning. We wrote that book too, and it's available at http://www.manning.com/mostarda.

3.4   *Summary*

It's been a long trip, but now you know how to get the best out of ASP.NET and Entity Framework. You have a deep knowledge of Entity Framework, and you know how to get the most out it in an ASP.NET environment. You learned how to handle the context lifecycle to avoid nasty surprises. You can handle the context to update entities in a disconnected environment without causing extra hits to the database. Finally, you discovered how to optimize performance in several ways.

Now that you have the knowledge to write better code to manipulate data, we can completely change the subject and move on to ASP.NET Web Forms development.

Part 2

ASP.NET Web Forms

Y ou've completed part 1, where you learned the fundamentals of ASP.NET. In part 2, we're going to take a deeper look at ASP.NET Web Forms, one of the preferred models among ASP.NET developers for building the UI. ASP.NET Web Forms is the original model provided by ASP.NET. It combines the ease of use of the traditional rapid application development (RAD) environment with the power of .NET Framework and its object-oriented nature.

Chapter 4 takes a tour of ASP.NET Web Forms, covering the most common scenarios. You'll also learn about the new features offered by version 4.0, how to fully use master pages, and how to leverage URL routing.

Chapter 5 deals with one of the most common activities for a developer: using data binding and how to fully integrate this feature in your applications.

Chapter 6 covers an important extensibility point in ASP.NET Web Forms and shows how to build custom controls. You'll start with the basics and end up analyzing complex scenarios.

Finally, chapter 7 explains how to control the markup generated by ASP.NET. You'll find out how to produce better markup and how adaptive rendering works.

Building the
user interface with
ASP.NET Web Forms

4

This chapter covers

- New features in Web Forms 4.0
- ClientID and markup generation
- Master pages
- URL rewriting
- URL routing

All the chapters before this one have been about fundamentals: how ASP.NET works and how to access data. Now that we've addressed the basics, it's time to focus on other matters. This chapter begins the part of the book dedicated to topics related to the user interface (UI).

The approach that's most used to build a user interface with ASP.NET is to use a Web Form. The Web Form was the first abstraction introduced to create the UI for the ASP.NET application and has its roots in its integration with Visual Studio.

As its name suggests, Web Forms are the result of some tentative steps made by Microsoft in the early 2000s to apply the typical Windows development paradigm to web applications. Windows developers are used to dragging objects on the UI surface and programming them accordingly. This approach is useful for implementing event-based development because each component on the design surface can be programmed that way. Event-based programming is common in a lot of development technologies; from VB 6 to Delphi, generations of developers had been programming this way to increase productivity.

So, what's a Web Form? It's an abstraction layer built on top of the ASP.NET core infrastructure that lets the developer build the UI without needing to understand HTTP (the transfer protocol used in the Internet for web pages) or HTML (the markup language).

The ASP.NET team tried to achieve a full abstraction; in reality, a full abstraction isn't so easy to achieve. It's important to understand both HTTP and HTML, and Web Forms can help you increase productivity, but productivity comes at the cost of less control on markup output. To give you back some of this control, ASP.NET 4.0 provides a better markup engine and the most advanced techniques to mitigate the issues of previous Web Form incarnations.

This chapter is dedicated mainly to the new features available in ASP.NET 4.0, with some mention of existing ones. Some features that were present in previous versions can be useful in your day-to-day work, so we want to touch on those as well. We should mention here that to preserve compatibility with previous versions, you have to opt in the new features.

If you're not familiar with Web Forms, go back and look at chapter 1 to get some background. This chapter is based on specific topics and doesn't include basic information.

4.1   *The UI and Web Forms*

Web Forms are the most common paradigm used to create ASP.NET pages. They've been available since version 1.0, and they're based totally on an event-driven approach. The name recalls the characteristic of an ASP.NET page: to be composed of a *maximum of one server form* at a time. You can embed non-server forms at your discretion, but only one of them is the server form. You can also have a page that doesn't have a server form. You need one only if you're planning to include a server control that needs PostBack (or that explicitly requires it). (If all this sounds strange to you, take some time and review chapter 1).

Most developers use Web Forms to build the GUI in a web application. Even if you decide to opt for MVC (outlined in chapter 8), many of the ideas we'll present here will still be valid. Remember, though, that the reason behind the success of ASP.NET is, without a doubt, Web Forms and their simplicity. ASP.NET MVC looks cool and promising (and it is), but it's relatively new. Although the Web Form model is fully extensible, it's not designed to be used in scenarios where you need 100% markup control or testability. In those cases, ASP.NET MVC is the better choice.

ASP.NET 4.0 includes new features related to Web Forms, especially in the area of markup. Beginning with this version, server controls can produce better markup—leading to better adherence to web standards—and they play nicely in environments where accessibility is a requirement (mostly in the public sector). This section focuses specifically on new features offered by ASP.NET 4.0.

4.1.1 New features in Web Forms 4.0

ASP.NET 4.0 isn't a revolutionary release, but it contains many innovations in the area of markup generation. Before we talk about these innovations, let's review how markup generation works.

When you place a server control in the page, the control markup is generated as part of the `Render` method, which is called recursively from the page, until the last nested server control has been reached. This action produces the final output, which is sent to the browser. You can see this process at work in figure 4.1.

You have little control over how a server control generates its output because generally you enter an XML fragment that isn't closed to the final HTML markup. Lack of control is the price you pay for the benefit of the abstraction provided by ASP.NET.

HTML vs XHTML and HTML 5.0.

Although they differ in some key ways, we tend to consider HTML and XHTML to be similar in meaning. XHTML is considered a stricter implementation, where the final markup composing the page must be a valid XML document. HTML is considered easier to deal with. Even though you have to produce a valid XML document in the latest versions, producing one requires only that you obey some simple rules (tags can't be nested and must be closed, special characters must be escaped, and so on).

HTML 5 promises to be a synthesis, combining the pros of the two. In this book, we'll generally use HTML to refer to the markup because much of our discussion can be applied to both HTML and XHTML. HTML 5 is not yet supported directly by ASP.NET.

You can find more information about HTML 5 at http://www.w3.org/TR/html5/.

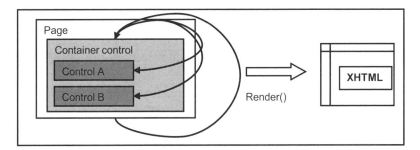

Figure 4.1 Markup generation is done by server controls. Each control has its own generation strategy; the page requests that each control generate its markup. If the page has inner controls, each one repeats this action with its own child controls.

ASP.NET 4.0 produces markup that's compatible with HTML 4.01 or XHTML 1.0 Strict, and markup that's mostly compatible with XHTML 1.1. ASP.NET 4.0 doesn't target HTML 5 directly, but it's possible to produce specific markup in some situations by writing custom controls or by writing the corresponding markup for a specific feature, like for the new <audio /> or <video /> tags.

Getting back to what's happening in figure 4.1, the rendering is controlled by a simple attribute that's set on the page section, in the web.config file:

```
<system.web>
  <pages
    controlRenderingCompatibilityVersion="4.0"/>
</system.web>
```

By default, the value of this attribute is 3.5, but if you set it to 4.0, the rendering engine behaves differently:

- XHTML 1.0 Strict markup is produced, and the xhtmlConformance section in web.config is ignored.
- The enabled attribute is rendered only by tags that support it (for example, <input />). When this attribute is applied to other controls, such as Label, it's not rendered in the markup (represented by a <span /> tag), but a CSS style attribute is added so that you can customize this behavior.
- The <div /> tags created inside hidden input fields that ASP.NET generates are output with <div class="aspNetHidden">...</div> around them. This output makes it easier to hide these types of controls by using a CSS.
- All the controls that inherit from Table or Image don't render the border attribute.
- Validation controls don't render any inline style. In previous versions, the red color was hard coded, and if you needed to specify another color, the CSS rules did take effect because the local value overrode the style definition.

The Menu and TreeView controls produce more correct markup, to better comply with accessibility and semantic markup. In general, a lot of other controls have taken minor steps in the same direction, to improve adherence to web standards. You'll find new features for ViewState handling, but we'll cover those in detail in chapter 13.

Since ASP.NET 3.5 Service Pack 1 (SP1), the action attribute on a Web Form is honored and is reflected in the generated markup. If you've skipped version 3.5 SP1, take a look at your pages to ensure that you don't include this attribute, unless you want to redirect the PostBack to another URL.

ASP.NET 4.0 introduces a new set of opt-in features, not available in version 3.5, that provide better markup generation. Let's look at those now.

Better markup generation in ASP.NET 4.0

In the previous section, we talked about the new features for markup generation. Other controls also benefit from this new effort, but to avoid conflicts with existing applications, you have to opt them in.

PROBLEM

You want to adhere to web standards. Maybe you want better accessibility or to produce correct markup. Your objective is to take advantage of the new feature offered by ASP.NET 4.0 and to opt-in for better markup generation.

SOLUTION

To improve site markup, part of the problem with certain controls in ASP.NET 3.5 is that `<table />` tags are rendered around them, which controls the visual style of the control. The truth is that you don't need tables to control appearance. You can use `<div />` tags to do that, and with good results.

Previous versions of ASP.NET weren't designed with control over markup in mind. If you needed real control over markup, you had to use basic controls or reproduce some of the advanced behavior of the controls by hand. This situation meant that useful controls with flexible features, like `Login` or `FormView`, weren't used often because they didn't generate good markup.

It's true that you can write a *control adapter* to modify the control output, but this isn't easy to do and has some drawbacks. Using a control adapter keeps you from using adaptive rendering in the way it was designed.

> **ADAPTIVE RENDERING IN ASP.NET** You can alter markup control, but it's not easy—you'll need advanced knowledge of building custom controls. We'll cover adaptive rendering control adapters in chapter 7.

Version 4.0 introduces a new attribute named `RenderOuterTable` that modifies the control output. The default value of `RenderOuterTable` is `true`. When it's set to `false`, a specific set of controls doesn't output a `<table />` tag, but a `<div />` tag instead (or it results in no container at all, depending on the control). The controls that implement this attribute are listed in table 4.1.

Table 4.1 Server controls that implement the new markup generation

Name	Description
ChangePassword	Used with the Membership API to change the user password (see chapter 11).
CreateUserWizard	Used with the Membership API to register a new user (see chapter 11).
FormView	Used to display data coming from a database (see chapter 5).
Login	Used with the Membership API to log in a user (see chapter 11).
PasswordRecovery	Used with the Membership API to recover the user password (see chapter 11).
Wizard	Displays a generic wizard, composed of steps and a final summary.

You can modify the control output by using code like this:

```
<asp:Wizard runat="server" RenderOuterTable="false">
</asp:Wizard>
```

We've used the Wizard control in this example. The Wizard control in version 4.0 gives you full control over markup that's generated for each step. You use a Layout-Template, which has been available in the ListView control since ASP.NET 3.5 SP1. The code is shown in the following listing. This approach is applicable to the Create-UserWizard control too, which inherits from Wizard.

Listing 4.1   Using the new Wizard control features to enhance markup

```
<asp:Wizard ID="MyWizard" runat="server"
     RenderOuterTable="false" DisplaySideBar="false">
  <LayoutTemplate>
    <asp:PlaceHolder ID="headerPlaceholder" runat="server" />
    <asp:PlaceHolder ID="sideBarPlaceholder" runat="server" />
    <asp:PlaceHolder ID="wizardStepPlaceholder" runat="server" />
    <asp:PlaceHolder ID="navigationPlaceholder" runat="server" />
  </LayoutTemplate>
  <StartNavigationTemplate>
      <p><asp:LinkButton ID="StartNextButton" runat="server"
             CommandName="MoveNext" Text="Next" /></p>
  </StartNavigationTemplate>
  <WizardSteps>
    <asp:WizardStep ID="WizardStep1" runat="server" Title="Step 1">
      Step 1
    </asp:WizardStep>
    <asp:WizardStep ID="WizardStep2" runat="server" Title="End">
      End!
    </asp:WizardStep>
  </WizardSteps>
</asp:Wizard>
```

If you browse the resulting page with one of the previous versions of ASP.NET, you'll see markup similar to this:

```
<table cellspacing="0" cellpadding="0" id="MyWizard"
    style="border-collapse:collapse;">
  <tr>
...
  </tr>
</table>
```

In version 4.0, literally no markup is generated by the control because only the templates are rendered. The visual result, using CSS, is similar to what you would see in previous versions, as shown in figure 4.2

This new feature is provided by a new LayoutTemplate property. You can specify the markup of the steps as in previous versions, but you can also indicate the template that's used by the common layout. The results are the exact reflection of the HTML fragment we wrote, and you've got great control over the generated markup.

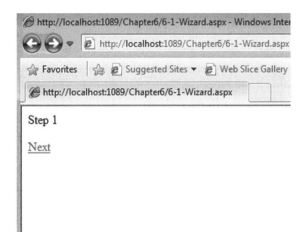

Figure 4.2   The appearance of the `Wizard` control markup is similar in ASP.NET versions 3.5 SP1 and 4.0. The 4.0 markup is much cleaner, though.

DISCUSSION

We picked `Wizard` to use in this scenario because in version 3.5 it provided probably one of the worst examples of generated markup. Now, in version 4.0, it shines with great flexibility and gives you tremendous control over the generated markup.

Keep in mind that many of the controls that we're not specifically discussing here have made minor tweaks in the current version and that every control has its own story in terms of flexibility. In the majority of cases, the new features presented here can help you achieve better adherence to web standards and accessibility.

The next scenario covers a different aspect of this problem, more related to combining ASP.NET with client-side JavaScript code: how to control the IDs that server controls generate. This issue is related to controlling markup, but is more specifically about working |with JavaScript.

TECHNIQUE 20   **Controlling ClientID generation**

Prior to ASP.NET 4.0, playing well with JavaScript wasn't easy. Server controls automatically generated the ID that's associated with tags. This autogenerated ID differed from the original one that was applied to the tag. Version 4.0 has a new feature specifically designed to take control over ID generation.

This feature is especially useful when you're dealing with container controls, which influence the child IDs. The generated ID is composed such that conflicts are avoided, much like what happens if you use `ContentPlaceHolder` in master pages.

PROBLEM

When you're referencing a server control in JavaScript, you can't use the designated server-side ID. Frequently, the corresponding `ClientID` that's generated at runtime is different than the server-side ID, depending on its containers. For generic JavaScript routines, you need a solution to simplify this behavior.

SOLUTION

This solution isn't limited specifically to JavaScript; it's applicable to CSS styles, too. Even though it's not always a good idea to apply a style directly to a control ID, it might be helpful in specific cases. Maybe you can't modify the CSS, or you want to reuse the same style in different kinds of applications (where ASP.NET ones are only part of the picture).

Here's a basic example of the problem:

```
<p><asp:Label ID="MyLabel" runat="server" /></p>

<p>ClientID of MyLabel is: <%=MyLabel.ClientID %></p>
```

In this situation (as in previous versions of ASP.NET) a control ID will be autogenerated by default and will be similar to this markup:

```
<span id="ctl00_Body_MyLabel"></span>
```

The ID is composed by concatenating the different container IDs: `ctl000` is the page ID, `Body` is the `ContentPlaceHolder` ID, and `MyLabel` is the real control ID.

> **TIP** You can read more about how the `ClientID` is composed on naming containers at http://mng.bz/397U.

It's clear that the ID will vary, depending on the final hierarchy of controls in the page. This behavior isn't flexible for our client-side code. To take care of this problem, ASP.NET 4.0 introduces a new property, called `ClientIDMode`. The different values it can take are listed in table 4.2.

Table 4.2   ClientIDMode property values

Value	Description
AutoID	The default value for a page. Indicates that the same generation algorithm as in ASP.NET 3.5 SP1 should be used.
Static	This value forces the control to use the specified ID, ignoring the containers. This value isn't intended for data-bound controls with multiple children because it will generate duplicated IDs.
Predictable	Useful in data-bound controls, the ID is generated by concatenating the `ClientID` value of the parent naming container with the ID value of the control.
	If the controls generate multiple children, you can specify a `ClientIDRowSuffix` property. This property specifies text that's appended at the end of the generated ID. If the property value is left blank, a sequential number is used.
Inherit	As the name suggests, this value causes the ID that is generated to inherit the behavior of the container. This value is the default for server controls (which continue to work as in ASP.NET 3.5 SP1).

Let's change our previous snippet to include the following one:

```
<p><asp:Label ID="MyLabel" runat="server" ClientIDMode="Static" /></p>
```

Now the value will be rendered differently:

```
<span id="MyLabel"></span>
```

As you can imagine, the `ClientIDMode` property is helpful when you're dealing with JavaScript code or you need to enforce CSS in specific scenarios. Note that the `name` attribute isn't influenced by this property and remains the same, as in this example of an `<input />` tag:

```
<input name="ctl00$Body$MyName"type="text" id="MyName" />
```

You can use the `ClientIDMode` property whenever you need to take full control of the real IDs that are generated at runtime, with no limitations. `AutoID` is the default value for pages and `Inherit` is the default for controls. Your pages and controls will behave as they did in ASP.NET 3.5 SP1 and you won't break your code. We're going to cover the `Predictable` value in chapter 5. This value is used in data-bound scenarios.

DISCUSSION

Being able to control the generation of the `ClientID` is one of the most anticipated—and useful—features in ASP.NET 4.0 Web Forms. It gives you, the developer, real control over markup. Another common pitfall of Web Forms has disappeared.

Not limited to ASP.NET Web Forms, but built for the first time for this architecture, master pages maintain a common look in a web application. We're going to explore their features in the next section.

4.2 Defining a common UI: using master pages

Master pages can be used by both Web Forms and ASP.NET MVC, and provide a common design surface for different pages. Their purpose is to simplify the sharing of a given UI across the same application by letting the developer compose different pages with a common base.

The magic behind master pages is performed by a set of entities:

- The master page file (.master)
- The `ContentPlaceHolder` control, used to represent the content placeholder in a master page
- The `Content` control, which contains the local page content that will be substituted in the generated page by combining the master page `ContentPlace-Holder` with the local `Content` controls

You can have multiple master pages in a given application. You can set them in the following ways:

- Directly in the `@Page` directive, using the `MasterPageFile` attribute
- Programmatically, in the `PreInit` event of `Page`
- In web.config, under configuration\system.web\pages

Figure 4.3 shows a schema of how master page substitution works against a page.

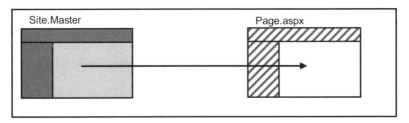

Figure 4.3   Master page behavior and architecture. The master page contains blocks of information that are substituted from the page. The result is a page that contains both the master page structure and the page content.

Most of the difficulties involved in master page substitution are taken care of by Visual Studio, so our focus will be on two more advanced and interesting techniques: using nested master pages and setting them programmatically.

TECHNIQUE 21   Using nested master pages

When you're dealing with a complex solution, you typically separate a site into different sections, where every section has specific features. Nested master pages come to the rescue in this kind of scenario. They let you componentize your solution, but at the same time maintain the exact look-and-feel across the various parts of your site.

Nested master pages have been supported in the runtime since ASP.NET 2.0 and by Visual Studio since version 2008 (with ASP.NET 3.5). Visual Studio 2010 increases the usability of nested master pages, and ASP.NET 4.0 provides the same features as previous versions did. Nesting master pages is a hot topic among developers, so we've decided to include this scenario in the book even though it's not entirely new to 4.0. Nested master pages componentize your application, differentiate the UI based on the section the user is in, and maintain the same behavior across sections.

PROBLEM

Our objective is to use a main master page that's shared by other master pages. Each master page will be specific to a different section. We also need to differentiate them in some way, across sections.

SOLUTION

If you want to nest a master page inside another one, you have to take care of some details. Let's take a deeper look to understand the possibilities.

First of all, a master page can itself have a master page. Practically speaking, you can assign the `MasterPageFile` property of the `@Master` directive to another master page, as you'll do for the `@Page` one.

To start, build a common master page. We'll call this master page the root master page. The root page is the lowest common denominator for all sections. Other pages can use it directly, so we'll keep it simple and usable.

The rule to obey is simple: you must give your `ContentPlaceHolder` controls inside the nested master page names that are identical to the names of the `ContentPlace-Holder` controls inside the root master page. You'll be able to switch easily from one master page to another and maintain the same features across them. The first master page is shown in the following listing.

Listing 4.2   Markup for Root.Master

```
<%@ Master %>
...
<head runat="server">
    <title></title>
    <link href="~/Styles/Site.css" rel="stylesheet" type="text/css" />
    <asp:ContentPlaceHolder ID="HeadContent" runat="server" />          ◁───┐
</head>
<body>
                                                    Header placeholder  ❶
...
    <div class="main">
      <asp:ContentPlaceHolder ID="MainContent" runat="server"/>         ◁───┐
      </div>
...
                                                    Body placeholder  ❷
 </body>
</html>
```

The idea behind this master page is to host as many entry points as possible ❶ ❷ to increase flexibility over specific nested master pages. Listing 4.3 contains a nested master page specifically designed for a hypothetical article section of a website, where the area on the right side of the layout is fixed across the application and the central part (the body) can be overwritten from the root master page.

Listing 4.3   Articles.Master enhances Root.Master layout

```
<%@ Master MasterPageFile="Root.master" %>

<asp:Content ContentPlaceHolderID="MainContent" runat="server">
    <h2>Articles</h2>

    <asp:ContentPlaceHolder ID="MainContent" runat="server" />

    <div class="rightCol">
        <h2>This is the right container</h2>
        <p>Some stuff here</p>
    </div>
</asp:Content>
```

In this master page, we're providing some specific content for the local master page (a menu and a header), but we're leaving the ContentPlaceHolder controls exactly the way they're defined in the root master page. This trick lets you change the master page more easily because the placeholders maintain the same name across different master pages. Notice that the ID and the ContentPlaceholderID are identical, as they must be.

Figure 4.4 shows what Visual Studio 2010 looks like at design time. As you can see, using master pages in this way is fully supported.

You can nest more than two master pages, using the same technique. Obviously, it's better to limit the total number of nested master pages so the Page Parser can avoid doing extra work.

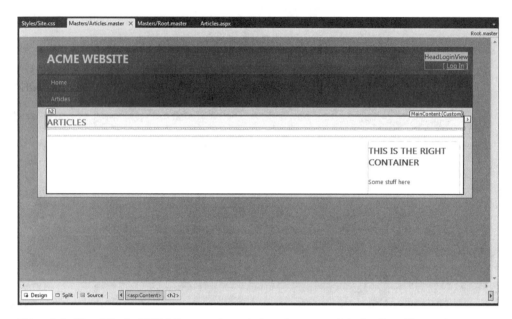

Figure 4.4   Visual Studio 2010 fully supports nested master pages at design time. The master page content is grayed, so you can visually identify the page content.

This feature is useful and has no limits except your own needs and creativity.

DISCUSSION

This solution isn't difficult to implement, but it shows you the power of master pages. You can easily apply a basic user interface design to the whole site, but differentiate it from section to section, with minimal effort. There's nothing more to add to complete this solution; the results are clear and the code is simple.

On a similar note, the next scenario is dedicated to a side issue you'll encounter when you're dealing with master pages: how to apply them programmatically, in response to specific needs.

TECHNIQUE 22   **Setting a master page programmatically**

One of the common problems in modern applications is that users demand more control over the application, typically using a control panel to manage the organization of the UI. Programmatically setting the master page can help you implement this feature.

PROBLEM

You want to implement a simple control panel to programmatically define the master page used at runtime by choosing from a list of available master pages.

SOLUTION

You can specify master pages programmatically by setting the `MasterPageFile` property of the `Page` class. Because the master page changes the page's control tree, you need to apply it before the `Init` event, using the `PreInit` event. This special event was added in ASP.NET 2.0 to perform this kind of action. Even though it's not new to ASP.NET 4.0, it is useful and we decided to include it here to complete the discussion.

To begin implementing this feature, define a base class to represent the common page behavior. The code is shown in the following listing.

Listing 4.4 The base page reads from .config of the master pages and applies it

C#:
```
public class BasePage: Page
{
  protected override void OnPreInit(EventArgs e)
  {
    string masterPage =
        File.ReadAllText(                                          ❶ Read path
        Server.MapPath("~/App_Data/MasterPage.config"));     ◁──    from file
    if (!string.IsNullOrEmpty(masterPage))
    {
      MasterPageFile = masterPage;                     ◁─┐ Assign
    }                                                    └ master page

  base.OnPreInit(e);
  }
}
```

VB:
```
Public Class BasePage
  Inherits Page
  Protected Overloads Overrides Sub OnPreInit(ByVal e As EventArgs)
    Dim masterPage As String =
        File.ReadAllText(                                          ❶ Read path
        Server.MapPath("~/App_Data/MasterPage.config"))      ◁──    from file
    If Not String.IsNullOrEmpty(masterPage) Then
      MasterPageFile = masterPage                       ◁─┐ Assign
    End If                                                └ master page

    MyBase.OnPreInit(e)
  End Sub
End Class
```

The MasterPage is read from the special .config file ❶, then it's assigned to the MasterPage (.Code in Text) property of the current Page (.Code in Text) instance. You'll associate this simple code with every page in the application by replacing the default inherited class `System.Web.UI.Page` with this one. In figure 4.5 you can see the running page.

To specify the master page, you need to write a simple page that can extract the file list. To simplify development, we're going to save the master pages under a common directory named Masters, which is under the root. To save the value, all you need is to get the path and save the file to a place from which the code in listing 4.4 will read it. In a production application, you can enhance this feature by saving the value in a database and adding a caching system. You'll learn how to do that in chapter 14.

Test Master Page

Page contents.

Figure 4.5   When you programmatically set the master page, the page automatically reads the correct value from the configuration and applies the master page at runtime.

The following listing shows you both the markup and the code used to programmatically change the master page.

Listing 4.5   Markup and code that saves the master page from the list

Markup:

```
<form runat="server">
  <div>
    <p>Select you Master Page from here:</p>
    <p><asp:DropDownList ID="MasterList" runat="server" /></p>
    <p><asp:Button ID="ConfirmButton" Text="Confirm" runat="server"
           OnClick="SaveMasterPage" /></p>
  </div>
</form>
```

C#:

```
protected void Page_Load(object sender, EventArgs e)
{
  if (!IsPostBack)
  {
    MasterList.DataSource =                               Get file list and
           Directory.GetFiles(Server.MapPath("~/Masters/"))  extract name
                 .Select(x => x.Substring(x.LastIndexOf("\\")+1));
    MasterList.DataBind();
                                                         Select current
    string currentMaster = File.ReadAllText(             master page
           Server.MapPath("~/App_Data/MasterPage.config"));
    MasterList.SelectedValue =
         currentMaster.Substring(currentMaster.LastIndexOf("/") + 1);
  }
}
                                                         Save selected
protected void SaveMasterPage(object sender, EventArgs e)  option
{
  File.WriteAllText(Server.MapPath("~/App_Data/MasterPage.config"),
                 "~/Masters/" + MasterList.SelectedValue);
}
```

VB:

```
Protected Sub Page_Load(ByVal sender As Object, ByVal e As EventArgs)
  If Not IsPostBack Then
      MasterList.DataSource =                                    ◁─┐ Get file list and
          Directory.GetFiles(Server.MapPath("~/Masters/"))         │ extract name
              .Select(Function(x) x.Substring(x.LastIndexOf("\") + 1))
      MasterList.DataBind()                                       ─┐ Select current
                                                                 ◁─┘ master page
      Dim currentMaster As String =
          File.ReadAllText(Server.MapPath("~/App_Data/MasterPage.config"))
      MasterList.SelectedValue = currentMaster.Substring(
                                  currentMaster.LastIndexOf("/") + 1)
  End If
End Sub                                                          Save selected
                                                                      option
Protected Sub SaveMasterPage(ByVal sender As Object, ByVal e As EventArgs)
  File.WriteAllText(Server.MapPath("~/App_Data/MasterPage.config"),   ◁─┐
                  "~/Masters/" & MasterList.SelectedValue)
End Sub
```

This solution is relatively simple, but it shows you how you can implement a common scenario (especially in content management systems [CMS] or community systems) with little effort. It also shows you how open ASP.NET is in terms of customization.

DISCUSSION

Master pages are fundamental in every application: they simplify the process of maintaining the same user interface across the whole application. The basics are simple, but the scenarios proposed in this chapter will cover your most advanced needs for everyday applications.

Moving right along, we're going to cover a relatively new feature of ASP.NET that was first introduced in ASP.NET 3.5 SP1 and further enhanced in the current release. URL routing, along with URL rewriting, is much diffused among modern web applications. They let you give vanity URLs to pages easily.

4.3   *URL rewriting and routing with ASP.NET*

Search engine optimization (SEO) techniques are quite popular in web applications these days because part of the traffic a public web site receives is based on search engines. How well a site performs against a search engine crawler can influence the success of a service or render it dead.

As a leading technology to build web applications, ASP.NET has several features related to SEO. One of the most important things to pay attention to is probably the URL of a page. The URL helps drive traffic by increasing your link value in a search engine index. It should also be easy for your users to remember. As you might have noticed, modern web browsers include a special search feature in the address bar: when you type something, the search history is searched, so a key word in the URL might help your site usability, too.

As an example of this issue, we'll use a basic CMS where articles are saved in a database for ease of use. In this kind of situation, typical URLs are something like this:

http://mysite/content.aspx?ID=15. For better results, our aim is to convert them to something like this: http://mysite/books/ASP.NET-4.0-in-practice/. Good-looking URLs like these can be supported in different ways, primarily using two techniques known as URL routing and URL rewriting.

ASP.NET 4.0 introduces full support to URL routing for Web Forms, too. Originally designed to be used by ASP.NET MVC, they officially became part of ASP.NET in version 3.5 SP1, under the `System.Web.Routing.dll` assembly. In ASP.NET 4.0, the classes have been moved from their previous location to `System.Web.dll`, the assembly where the ASP.NET core is contained.

To get the most from these two techniques, you need to understand their pros and cons by analyzing different implementations.

4.3.1   *URL rewriting versus URL routing*

Both rewriting and routing are devoted to presenting clean URLs to the clients, so what's the difference between these techniques? Both are invisible to the client. As far as the browser is concerned, the URL is the rewritten one, not the real executed URL.

URL rewriting

URL rewriting is simple. When a client makes a request to a given URL, the rewriting component intercepts this request, based on a predetermined pattern, and changes the flow to execute a different URL on the same server.

URL routing

URL routing is a dispatching mechanism. You can bind a different set of URLs with a specific handler (an ASP.NET page) that will process the requests made to these URLs. Routing is managed by registering the routes in the application, linking together the path to be handled, and invoking the `HttpHandler`.

Differences between URL rewriting and routing

From a technical point of view, the main difference between URL rewriting and routing is that rewriting generates a new, transparent, and invisible request to a different resource (with its own flow), whereas routing invokes the corresponding handler. ASP.NET URL routing is implemented as an `HttpModule` that plugs into the pipeline before the Map Handler stage. Generally, rewriting is performed by a module that intercepts the request in the Begin Request stage, well before any other event has taken place. In some applications, rewriting is also performed by implementing an `HttpHandler`. Implementing `HttpHandler` avoids the extra overhead associated with `HttpModules`, which are executed for every request.

Figure 4.6 shows the different behavior of routing and rewriting.

Rewriting can be used by every type of application and isn't limited to just ASP.NET ones. Thanks to the managed pipeline of IIS 7.x, you can easily use URL rewriting to rewrite PHP, ASP, or static pages. When you're using Classic mode, URL routing needs to be associated with specific file extensions already mapped to ASP.NET, unless wildcard mapping (*) exists.

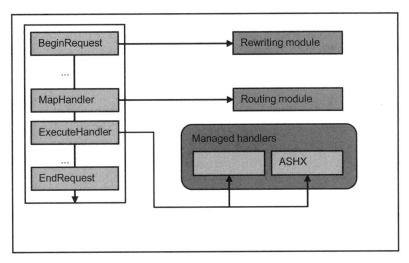

Figure 4.6 URL routing vs. rewriting, head-to-head. Rewriting takes place at the very beginning of a request. Routing is handled after the `MapHandler` event, at the Handler stage.

URL rewriting can be performed using advanced rules. You can base rewriting on the request status, the user status, the HTTP header, and so on; routing is less flexible.

> **USING EXTENSIONLESS URLS** Traditionally, extensionless URLs are used to represent rewritten or routed URLs. To maximize performance, ASP.NET 4.0 includes a new `*.` mapping, created for specific scenarios. You don't need to map `*.*`, as in previous versions, to use extensionless URLs. You also make gains in performance because static files won't be handled by these modules. You can find more information about IIS prerequisites at http://support .microsoft.com/kb/980368.

You'll use routing in new projects because it's fully supported by emerging technologies like ASP.NET MVC and Dynamic Data controls. You'll probably limit rewriting to existing ASP.NET applications. We decided to mention rewriting anyway because this book is focused on good advice for ASP.NET 4.0. Even though rewriting isn't new to this version, this information might help you take your application to a higher level.

TECHNIQUE 23 URL routing with Web Forms

The first scenario we're going to talk about deals with a new web application or an existing one where clean URLs weren't used previously. ASP.NET URL routing with Web Forms represents a great addition to ASP.NET because it's fully integrated in the runtime and is available for both ASP.NET Web Forms and MVC. In this scenario, we'll focus on Web Forms specifically, but the basic considerations are the same.

PROBLEM

An ugly URL isn't necessarily bad, but it's not useful to your users and to your site ranking in the search engines. To be clear: *bad URLs aren't a technical issue,* but an aesthetic one. A clean URL means that you care about your users to the same degree that you care about the site design: you want both to be simple and usable.

Our objective is to gain control over this relatively new feature in ASP.NET by implementing a simple routing mechanism for a fictitious content management web site.

SOLUTION

To understand ASP.NET URL routing, we'll take a deeper look at its implementation.

During the `PostMapRequestHandler` phase of `HttpApplication`, the routing module changes the `Handler` property of the current `HttpContext`. At execution time, ASP.NET executes the handler that was selected by this module. Consequently, if this information isn't set, the module doesn't interfere with the normal flow; a file from disk, if it exists, is served for non-routed requests.

> **USING URL ROUTING IN EXISTING APPLICATIONS** If you're migrating from ASP.NET 2.0 or 3.5, you can use URL routing with no modifications. This feature is available automatically when you run your application with the ASP.NET 4.0 runtime. In ASP.NET 3.5 SP1, you had to manually register the `HttpModule` in web.config.

To register a route, you have to add a new `RouteValueDictionary` to the `Routes` property of the `RouteTable` class from the `System.Web.Routing` namespace. Typically, you can do that in global.asax or, if you prefer, in an `HttpModule`. The code is shown in listing 4.6.

ASP.NET 4.0 differs from ASP.NET 3.5 SP1 with respect to registering routes. Version 4.0 includes a special route handler, `PageRouteHandler`, designed to work with Web Forms. You can find more information about this new class on MSDN at http://mng.bz/5ENS.

Listing 4.6   Registering a route in your application

C#:
```
using (RouteTable.Routes.GetWriteLock())          ◁──┐  Write-lock
  RouteTable.Routes.Add("ArticleRoute",                │  the collection
      new Route("articles/{id}/{description}",          │
      new PageRouteHandler("~/Articles.aspx")));    ◁──┤
```

VB:
```
Using RouteTable.Routes.GetWriteLock()            ◁──┤  Register
  RouteTable.Routes.Add("ArticleRoute",                │  route
      New Route("articles/{id}/{description}",          │
      New PageRouteHandler("~/Articles.aspx")))     ◁──┘
End Using
```

In this listing, a new route was registered for a path that contains `articles/`, text that represents the ID, and free text that represents the clean URL. You can also use a similar URL without specifying the ID. This example serves as a general footprint that you can modify to better suite your needs.

As you'll see in technique 24, you can modify the `RouteHandler` to manage additional details about the request. The new `PageRouteHandler` class hides some of the details to increase usability. In fact, you can simply retrieve the route parameter by accessing the new `RouteData` property on `Page`. The following listing shows you how to access the parameters in your pages.

Listing 4.7 Easily accessing the parameters in local pages

C#:

```csharp
protected int Id { get; set; }
protected string Description { get; set; }

protected void Page_Load(object sender, EventArgs e)
{
  Id = Convert.ToInt32(Page.RouteData.Values["id"]);
  Description = Page.RouteData.Values["description"] as string;
}
```

VB:

```vb
Protected Property Id() As Integer
Protected Property Description() As String

Protected Sub Page_Load(ByVal sender As Object, ByVal e As EventArgs)
    Id = Convert.ToInt32(Page.RouteData.Values("id"))
    Description = TryCast(Page.RouteData.Values("description"), String)
End Sub
```

You can access parameters easily in typical scenarios where you need to pass simple values. If you need to specify different parameters (like an ID and a page number), but the last one is not mandatory, you can do one of the following things:

- Define a default value for a parameter and register it with the route (using this method involves overloading
- Define multiple routes and check for null parameters in the page

If you opt for the last way, keep in mind that the more routes you have, the more time ASP.NET will consume to identify the right one. Registration order is also important because the first matching route will be used.

Some situations require you to have more control over the parameters. The following listing shows you a more advanced route registration.

Listing 4.8 Registering a route with advanced parameters

C#:

```csharp
Route articlesWithPageRoute =
   new Route("articles/{id}/{description}/page{page}",
       new PageRouteHandler("~/Articles.aspx"));

articlesWithPageRoute.Constraints = new RouteValueDictionary {
   { "id", @"\d{1,5}" },
   { "page", @"\d{1,5}" }
};

RouteTable.Routes.Add("ArticleRoutePaged", articlesWithPageRoute);
```

VB:

```
Dim articlesWithPageRoute As Route =
    New Route("articles/{id}/{description}/page{page}",
      New PageRouteHandler("~/Articles.aspx"))

articlesWithPageRoute.Constraints = New RouteValueDictionary
        From {{"id", "\d{1,5}"}, {"page", "\d{1,5}"}}

RouteTable.Routes.Add("ArticleRoutePaged", articlesWithPageRoute)
```

In this listing, a new route is created by adding a new pattern and registering two constraints on the id and page parameters to accept only integer values. We've chosen to implement a new route because the patterns aren't similar (there's a string [page] in the new one). After registering this new route, you can automatically pass the corresponding values to the page and read them in the same way. The advantage is that now non-numeric values won't be passed to the page, which restricts the allowed requests. You still can't forget to validate the parameters; it's always a best practice to do that.

If you run this example, you'll achieve a result similar to the one shown in figure 4.7.

Later on, we're going to discuss how you can define routes with granularity and precisely control their behavior.

DISCUSSION

URL routing in ASP.NET 4.0 introduces new features to the consolidated ones available since ASP.NET 3.5 SP1. Now routing is a more mature feature, with a new native integration with Web Forms, and more brand-new scenarios are accounted for.

Clean URLs are a hot topic these days among web developers, so it's important to understand how URL routing can help your application gain more accessibility and achieve better search-engine indexing.

So that you can fully appreciate URL routing, now we're going to cover some advanced situations that you might encounter during your work.

Figure 4.7   Notice the address bar on the browser: it's a sign that routing has been used. The real page that was requested is different from the one displayed in the address bar.

TECHNIQUE 24   Advanced URL routing scenarios

The URL routing mechanism in ASP.NET supports advanced scenarios, such as constraints, default values, and adding additional data to the route. URL routing isn't limited to just Web Forms and can generally be applied to `IHttpHandler`, too.

PROBLEM

URL routing is flexible enough to be applied to most of the common routing strategies. But how do you implement advanced routing scenarios like validating the route parameters or providing default values? We're going to address these problems in this section.

SOLUTION

Let's go back to listing 4.8 for a moment. In that example, we showed you how to add custom data while registering a route. We defined two constraints to limit the number of values that would be considered valid for the parameters. Listing 4.9 shows you more advanced options. This listing specifies a default value for the `description` parameter, defines a new constraint to limit requests to `GET` ones, and passes an arbitrary value with the route.

Listing 4.9   Using more advanced options when registering a route

C#:

```
RouteValueDictionary defaultValues = new RouteValueDictionary();    ◁──┐ Default
defaultValues.Add("description", "");                                    │ parameter
                                                                         │ value

RouteValueDictionary constraints = new RouteValueDictionary();
constraints.Add("httpMethod", "GET");                               ──┐ Constraints
constraints.Add("id", @"\d+");                                        │ on parameter

RouteValueDictionary dataTokens = new RouteValueDictionary();
dataTokens.Add("finalUrl", "~/articles.aspx");     ◁──┐ Custom value for
                                                       │ RouteHandlerst
using (RouteTable.Routes.GetWriteLock())
  RouteTable.Routes.Add("ArticleRoute",
    new Route("articles/{id}/{description}",
    defaultValues, constraints, dataTokens, new ArticleRouteHandler()));
```

VB:

```
Dim defaultValues As New RouteValueDictionary()     ◁──┐ Default
defaultValues.Add("description", "")                    │ parameter value

Dim constraints As New RouteValueDictionary()
constraints.Add("httpMethod", "GET")                ──┐ Constraints
constraints.Add("id", "\d+")                          │ on parameter

Dim dataTokens As New RouteValueDictionary()
dataTokens.Add("finalUrl", "~/articles.aspx")     ◁──┐ Custom value for
                                                      │ RouteHandlerst
Using RouteTable.Routes.GetWriteLock()
  RouteTable.Routes.Add("ArticleRoute",
    New Route("articles/{id}/{description}",
    defaultValues, constraints, dataTokens, New ArticleRouteHandler()))
End Using
```

In listing 4.9, we didn't use `PageRouteHandler`, but defined a new `RouteHandler` to handle the request. This new route handler is defined in listing 4.10; it receives the request and provides the effective response.

If you need a / character in the route name to specify multiple categories, you can define a route URL like `Categories/{*Category}`. The * character allows a / character in the route parameter so that you can further define your pattern.

During route registration, we provided additional information via a custom value, which is passed to the route handler. Using a custom value is especially useful if you want to use a single route handler to manage different behaviors. By defining a new route handler, you can implement custom logic, such as providing a custom authorization mechanism or validating user input, even before the page is requested. The following listing shows you how to do that.

Listing 4.10   A simple route handler to manage routing

C#:

```csharp
public class ArticleRouteHandler : IRouteHandler                  // Parameter from route
{                                                                 // configuration
  IHttpHandler IRouteHandler.GetHttpHandler(RequestContext requestContext)
  {
    string realUrl =
        requestContext.RouteData.DataTokens["finalUrl"].ToString();   // ◄─┐
    string virtualPath = VirtualPathUtility.ToAbsolute(realUrl);      // ◄─

    IArticlePage pp = BuildManager.CreateInstanceFromVirtualPath(
        virtualPath,
        typeof(Page)) as IArticlePage;                                // ◄─
    pp.Id = Convert.ToInt32(requestContext.RouteData.Values["id"]);
    pp.Description = requestContext.RouteData.Values["description"];
    return pp;                                                    // Create Web
  }                                                               // Form instance
}
```

VB:

```vb
Public Class ArticleRouteHandler
  Implements IRouteHandler
  Private Function GetHttpHandler(ByVal requestContext As RequestContext)
   As IHttpHandler Implements IRouteHandler.GetHttpHandler
      Dim realUrl As String =
      requestContext.RouteData.DataTokens("finalUrl").ToString()   ' ◄─ Parameter
                                                                   '    from route
      Dim virtualPath As String =                                  '    configuration
          VirtualPathUtility.ToAbsolute(realUrl)      ' ◄─┐ Converted to
                                                      '    absolute path
      Dim pp As IArticlePage = DirectCast(
        BuildManager.CreateInstanceFromVirtualPath(virtualPath,
            GetType(Page)), IArticlePage)                          ' ◄─

      pp.Id = Convert.ToInt32(requestContext.RouteData.Values("id"))
      pp.Description = requestContext.RouteData.Values("description")

      Return pp
  End Function                                                    ' Create Web
End Class                                                         ' Form instance
```

To use this new route handler, we created a new interface, `IArticlePage`. This interface will be used by the pages that execute the final request. You can also use this interface in scenarios where you prefer to have control over parameters. You won't directly access the `RouteData` property of `System.Web.Page`, but instead you'll rely on a strongly typed property. The next listing contains the code used in the Web Form.

Listing 4.11   A Web Form using the custom route handler

C#:
```
public partial class Articles : System.Web.UI.Page, IArticlePage
{
  public int Id { get; set; }
  public string Description { get; set; }

  protected void Page_Load(object sender, EventArgs e)
  {
    IDValue.Text = Id.ToString();
    DescriptionValue.Text = Description;
  }
}
```

VB:
```
Public Partial Class Articles
  Inherits System.Web.UI.Page
  Implements IArticlePage

  Protected Property Id() As Integer
          Implements IArticlePage.Id
  Protected Property Description() As String
          Implements IArticlePage.Description

  Protected Sub Page_Load(ByVal sender As Object, ByVal e As EventArgs)
    IDValue.Text = Id.ToString()
    DescriptionValue.Text = Description
  End Sub
End Class
```

You can use this approach with `IHttpHandler` in general, so it's applicable when you're dealing with non-HTML responses, such as images or documents.

One problem related to routing is how to generate URLs in markup without hardcoding them. ASP.NET 4.0 introduces a helper function that you can use to safely generate a routed URL, which internally calls the `GetVirtualPath` method from `Routes` in `RouteTable`:

C#:
```
string url = Page.GetRouteUrl ("ArticleRoute",
  new RouteValueDictionary {
                    { "Id", 5 },
            { "Description", "Test-URL" } });
```

VB:
```
Dim url As String = Page.GetRouteUrl("ArticleRoute",
      New RouteValueDictionary() From {
                    {"Id", "5"},
            {"Description", "Test-URL"}})
```

If you prefer to define the links in markup and not in code, a new *Expression Builder* is supported. Expression Builders are specially defined expressions that can use custom classes to generate code at runtime by using a markup expression. You can add a link in your page by simply using this snippet:

```
<asp:HyperLink
    NavigateUrl="<%$ RouteUrl:RouteName=ArticleRoute,id=5,
        Description=Test-Url %>" Text="View #5 article" runat="server" />
```

Note the <%$...%> syntax that's designated for the Expression Builder. This approach has the same results as the previous example in listing 4.11, but is more useful to include in markup. At runtime, both these snippets generate the correct routed URL. If you change part of the path, the results remain the same: the routing engine generates the correct routed URL for you.

You can also redirect by using `Response.RedirectToRoute`. Like the `Page.GetRouteUrl` method, this method accepts the same parameters and then redirects to the appropriate generated URL:

C#:
```
Response.RedirectToRoute("ArticleRoute",
        new RouteValueDictionary {
            { "Id", 5 },
            { "Description", "Test-URL" } });
```

VB:
```
Response.RedirectToRoute("ArticleRoute",
        new RouteValueDictionary from {
            { "Id", 5 },
            { "Description", "Test-URL" }
        })
```

If you need to use a 301 HTTP Status Code, use the equivalent `RedirectToRoutePermanent` method.

> **IMPLEMENTING CUSTOM ROUTE CONSTRAINTS**   You can implement custom constraints by writing a class that implements the `IRouteConstraint` interface. Using its `Match` method, you can validate complex parameters, such as date or email. You can find more information in the MSDN documentation at http://mng.bz/2BtB.

URL routing was built with customization in mind, so you can implement additional features if the default ones don't fit your needs. In this scenario, we took a look at the more common advanced features. For additional details about how to customize ASP.NET URL routing, consult the MSDN documentation at http://mng.bz/8DDI.

DISCUSSION

ASP.NET 4.0 URL routing offers interesting features, mixing some new and existing stuff together to simplify building nice-looking URLs in your applications. URL routing has a strong link with ASP.NET, and, because you can use it in both ASP.NET Web Forms and MVC, it's definitely a topic you want to follow.

To continue our examination of routing and rewriting, the next topic we'll address is probably the most diffused among ASP.NET developers coming from ASP.NET 2.0 or 3.5. UrlRewriting.NET is in fact considered the de-facto solution when dealing with URL rewriting in previous versions of ASP.NET.

TECHNIQUE 25   Rewriting in practice: UrlRewriting.NET

URL rewriting might be able to help you when you need to control access to resources, not just ASP.NET pages (in general, when we refer to rewriting, we're referring to both Web Form pages and MVC actions).

The de-facto class library used in ASP.NET applications is UrlRewriting.NET. You can freely download it at http://urlrewriting.net/. Using it is free, even in commercial projects. A similar alternative exists at http://www.urlrewriter.net/. They have similar features, but UrlRewriter.NET probably has more features that are similar to the Apache mod_rewrite module.

PROBLEM

URL routing is scoped to ASP.NET pages, so if you need to rewrite non-ASP.NET resources or perform redirections, you can't use routing. UrlRewriting.NET can help you solve these specific problems.

SOLUTION

UrlRewriting.NET contains an assembly that you can reference in your application. After you reference the assembly, you can start using its features.

The rules are mapped in the configuration files, using a regular expression. The following listing contains an image rewritten to the real path.

Listing 4.12   Rewriting an image to a real path

```
<configuration>
  <configSections>
    <section name="urlrewritingnet"
             restartOnExternalChanges="true"
             requirePermission ="false"
             type="UrlRewritingNet.Configuration.UrlRewriteSection,
                   UrlRewritingNet.UrlRewriter"  />
  </configSections>

  <system.web>                                    ◁——  IIS 6.0+
    <httpModules>                                       configuration
      <add name="UrlRewriteModule"
        type="UrlRewritingNet.Web.UrlRewriteModule,
              UrlRewritingNet.UrlRewriter" />
    </httpModules>
  </system.web>

  <system.webServer>                              ◁——  IIS 7.0+
    <modules runAllManagedModulesForAllRequests="true">    configuration
      <remove name="UrlRewriteModule"/>
      <add name="UrlRewriteModule"
       type="UrlRewritingNet.Web.UrlRewriteModule,
      UrlRewritingNet.UrlRewriter" />
```

```
    </modules>
  </system.webServer>

  <urlrewritingnet
    xmlns="http://www.urlrewriting.net/schemas/config/2006/07">
    <add name="Images"
         virtualUrl="^~/images/(.*)/(.*).jpg"
         rewriteUrlParameter="ExcludeFromClientQueryString"
         destinationUrl="~/myimages/site/image$1_$2.jpg"
         ignoreCase="true" />
  </urlrewritingnet>

</configuration>
```

In this listing, we're rewriting requests to a path like this one:

```
/images/150/home.jpg
```

to a path like this one:

```
/myimages/site/image150_home.jpg
```

Rewriting paths in this way can be especially useful if you need to provide a better-looking URL for automatically generated images.

If you prefer, you can define the rules in an external file, using the web.config delegation feature:

```
<urlrewritingnet configSource="Rewrite.config" />
```

Note that to use this module, you have to map the extension you want to ASP.NET if you're using IIS 6.0+ or IIS 7.0+ in Classic mode, or move the module declaration under system.WebServer section if you're using IIS 7.0+ in Integrated mode.

You can use UrlRewriting.NET with ASP.NET pages, and you'll get the same URL routing behavior; PostBacks are fully supported, too.

You can also use UrlRewriting.NET to perform redirects. When you're adding a rule, you have to specify the redirectMode attributes, as in this snippet:

```
<add name="FromHTMLToASPX"
  virtualUrl="^~/(.+).htm(.*)"
  redirectMode="Permanent"
  rewriteUrlParameter="ExcludeFromClientQueryString"
  destinationUrl="~/$1.aspx"
  ignoreCase="true" />
```

This rule automatically redirects the request to HTML static pages to ASP.NET ones, maintaining the same base URL. When you're dealing with a massive site refresh, you'll want to use this technique because you can continue to maintain the old URLs. And, thanks to the Permanent value in the redirectMode attribute, an HTTP 301 Moved Permanently status code will be sent, so search engine spiders update the referenced page URL automatically.

PERMANENT REDIRECTION WITH ASP.NET 4.0 ASP.NET 4.0 introduces a new method on the `HttpResponse` class from the `System.Web` namespace called `RedirectPermanent`. You can use it to emit a 301 HTTP status code where you need to do it in code.

UrlRewriting.NET fully supports providers, so you can extend the rule engine. You can also add the rules programmatically (via code) if you need to take control of rules using a control panel and assign them at runtime. You can find more information about this topic in the corresponding documentation at http://www.urlrewriter.net/.

DISCUSSION

URL rewriting is similar to URL routing, but lets you take more control over the results. You can even perform redirections using this technique.

URL routing and rewriting can help you increase both usability and search engine optimization. You can produce a better application, so you should definitely use them. If you only need to provide clean URLs in ASP.NET pages, consider URL routing; it's fully integrated in the runtime and provides you with advanced features, like an Expression Builder and a specific class to help you build correct URLs programmatically.

4.4 *Summary*

ASP.NET 4.0 introduces new features in Web Forms that will bridge the gap between better control over markup and ease of use. This chapter contained a brief overview of master pages, whose support has been improved both in the runtime and the VS 2010 IDE. Using master pages, you can manage the site layout easily. By nesting them, you'll have more control over different sections. By setting them programmatically, you'll get even more control over the results.

Web Form fundamentals remain the same as in previous versions, but in ASP.NET 4.0, standards compliance is a driving factor. New features in this area give you greater control over generated markup by removing automatically added HTML tags. The new `ClientID` mode will simplify your JavaScript code because you can refer to server control in an easier way.

Last, but not least, URL routing is now fully integrated in ASP.NET. You don't need to register anything. You can start using these good-looking (and SEO-friendly) URLs with little effort.

In general, though it's not revolutionary, Web Forms 4.0 introduces a lot of goodies for you as a developer. These improvements will continue to simplify your day-to-day work and assist you in creating great ASP.NET applications.

Moving on, but in the same general direction, the next chapter will cover a key aspect of web applications (and Web Forms in particular): how to display data from your sources (such as a database) in a page.

Data binding in
ASP.NET Web Forms

This chapter covers

- How data binding in ASP.NET works
- Using ASP.NET controls to display data
- New data binding features in ASP.NET 4.0
- Dynamic Data controls

Data binding plays a central role in ASP.NET Web Forms model. As you've seen in previous chapters, ASP.NET Web Forms are based on the notion of server controls. Server controls are objects placed on the page and programmed to offer a result. You can write specific code to intercept events and develop your pages using an event-driven methodology.

Data binding is essential in the ASP.NET ecosystem because web pages are often a gateway to display data coming from different sources, like a database, web service, or object. Data binding offers a simple way to implement the action to bind the data to the form and display the visual results easily.

Data binding itself hasn't changed in the last few versions of ASP.NET, but server controls and data access strategies have. As you learned in chapters 2 and 3, the past few years have seen the adoption of strongly typed collections versus the initial DataSet approach. New trends, like service-oriented applications and cloud computing, have amplified the notion of data and changed the way we think about storage. Plus, AJAX techniques are considered standard today. The initial concept of data binding has evolved because the environment has also evolved.

This chapter contains all you need to know about data binding in ASP.NET, with a focus on real-world techniques.

5.1 Displaying data

If you're not familiar with data binding, this section is for you. To understand how data binding influences ASP.NET, take a look at figure 5.1.

Data binding is integrated in both pages and controls life cycles, and is specifically tied to some magic performed under the hood by ASP.NET Page Parser.

Data binding-capable controls, often referred to as data controls, are special controls that provide a fast way to display data coming from different sources. From the control perspective, the source must implement an interface from the `IList`, `IEnumerable`, or `ICollection` interface. This requirement is always true for custom collections, data coming from a database using ADO.NET, and generally for LINQ expressions, too.

By setting the `DataSource` property of these controls, you can programmatically specify the source to be displayed. To avoid errors and simplify your work, these controls generally perform many of the tasks related to displaying data for you. They check for data, cycle through the items, and provide output. These controls are usually based on different templates that render different parts. These templates provide a simple way to personalize the markup to be generated.

Now that you've got some background, let's see how data binding works by looking at our first example.

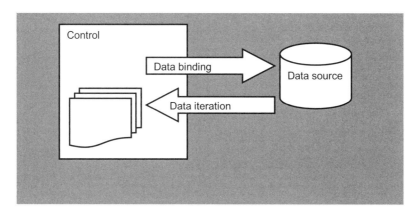

Figure 5.1 Data binding is tied into ASP.NET controls. When it's invoked, the data source is enumerated and its content is associated with the corresponding control.

How to display data using Repeater

`Repeater` is the simplest data control you'll find. As its name suggests, it can only repeat the templates specified in the markup. In this scenario, we'll display a set of customers coming from the Northwind database, mapped using Entity Framework.

PROBLEM

Displaying data from a database is probably the most common action that you'll perform while coding your applications. ASP.NET data binding can help you be more productive. Let's discover how this feature works.

SOLUTION

Before starting, let's take a step back to talk about how templates work. Templates are generally defined in markup, as shown in the following listing.

Listing 5.1   A simple Repeater with templates at work

```
<asp:Repeater id="MyView" runat="server">
  <HeaderTemplate>
    [Header markup goes here]
  </HeaderTemplate>
  <FooterTemplate>
    [Footers markup goes here]
  </FooterTemplate>
  <ItemTemplate>
    [Items markup goes here]
  </ItemTemplate>
</asp:Repeater>
```

When the ASP.NET Page Parser finds one of these templates, it automatically converts it at runtime to an instance of `System.Web.UI.CompiledTemplateBuilder`. (Note that templates are implemented by a generic `ITemplate` interface.) Later, every time the template is referenced to display the items inside the data source, the same template will be used. This setup has the advantage of letting you define the template via markup, instead of using code.

> **MORE ABOUT TEMPLATES IN ASP.NET**   We're going to address templates again in chapter 7, when we talk about custom controls. If you want to know even more about templates, you can take a look at the MSDN documentation at http://mng.bz/1g9v.

To simplify data binding, ASP.NET introduces a specific syntax, which is automatically converted to include an event handler for the `DataBinding` event:

```
<%# "Some text"%>
```

This sequence of characters is interpreted by the Page Parser so that the contained function is called only when the `DataBinding` event occurs. This event is called only when the `DataBind` method is explicitly called on the container control. In a simple form, you'll use the `Eval` method to extract the data. This method is exposed by the page itself, via the `TemplateControl` class:

```
<%#Eval("MyProperty")%>
```

`Eval` is a shortcut method that was introduced in ASP.NET 2.0. It maps to `Data-Binder.Eval`. In this case, the code will look similar to this:

```
<%#DataBinder.Eval(Container.DataItem, "MyProperty")%>
```

Both methods automatically retrieve the property `MyProperty` from the associated data source, via the `Container` property type `IDataItemContainer`.

> **EVAL, DATABINDER.EVAL, AND FORMATTING**   You can specify a format string to be applied to the property specified by `Eval/DataBinder.Eval` by simply passing the format as the last parameter:
>
> ```
> <%#Eval("Date", "{0:D}")%>
> ```
>
> This code will format the `Date` property, of `DateTime` type, using the `0:D` format (long date). You can find more information about string formatting on MSDN at http://mng.bz/t8xK.

Per convention, the `IDataItemContainer` interface is implemented by all the templates. The properties of this interface are listed in table 5.1.

Table 5.1   IDataItemContainer interface members

Member	Description
`DataItem`	An `Object` that contains the reference to the current element, which is taken from the data source.
`DataItemIndex`	The current element index in the data source.
`DisplayIndex`	The current element index in the rendering. Some controls can change the rendering and arrange items horizontally or vertically.

If you need to display a property from a specific class, you can also use this syntax:

C#:
```
<%#((MyClass)Container.DataItem).MyProperty%>
```

VB:
```
<%#DirectCast(Container.DataItem, MyClass).MyProperty%>
```

You should choose this syntax over the previous one (`Eval/DataBinder.Eval`) most of the time. It doesn't use reflection and it performs better. You don't need to perform casting because you're accessing the object directly. This syntax has a true compile-time syntax check, whereas the other will be controlled only at runtime. And runtime errors are a problem because you have less control over their testability.

You can adapt the code in listing 5.1 to show the customers as an unordered list, as shown in the following listing.

Listing 5.2   Adapting the Repeater to display a different layout

```
<asp:Repeater id="CustomerView" runat="server">
  <HeaderTemplate>
    <ul>
  </HeaderTemplate>
  <FooterTemplate>
    </ul>
  </FooterTemplate>
  <ItemTemplate>
    <li><%#((Customer)Container.DataItem).ContactName %></li>         ⟵── In C#
    <li><%#DirectCast(Container.DataItem, Customer).ContactName%></li>  ⟵
  </ItemTemplate>
</asp:Repeater>                                                              In VB
```

The code to retrieve the data using Entity Framework is easy to understand. The code in listing 5.3 is an example so it's simplified, but you can do the same thing we did in chapter 3: wrap the `ObjectContext` so it can be shared easily by different pieces of your page. The code that performs the data binding is shown in the following listing.

Listing 5.3   ObjectContext inside the page gets data and performs data binding

C#:
```
CustomerView.DataSource = ApplicationObjectContext.Current.Customers;
CustomerView.DataBind();
```

VB:
```
CustomerView.DataSource = ApplicationObjectContext.Current.Customers
CustomerView.DataBind()
```

If you run this code inside a browser, it produces a result similar to what's displayed in figure 5.2.

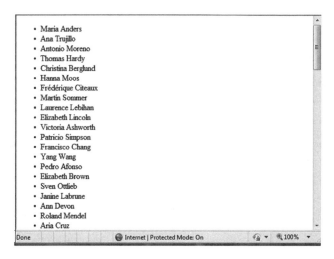

Figure 5.2
The `Repeater` produces a list after data binding. You can control the visual layout using the templates.

Because a `Repeater` has the ability to let you decide what your rendering strategy is and doesn't add any markup to what you specify, you can adapt the output to your needs.

DISCUSSION

Data binding in ASP.NET is so easy to understand. The power behind this simple syntax is that you can make it universally available without needing to provide different behavior when the data source types change. `Repeater` is the simplest control you can choose, but ASP.NET 4.0 also has new features for `ListView`. `ListView` is a control introduced by ASP.NET 3.5 and represents a complete solution to data binding in ASP.NET.

TECHNIQUE 27   ## ListView in ASP.NET 4.0

`ListView` was first introduced in ASP.NET 3.5 to simplify the problem of choosing a data control. Previously, if you needed to have maximum flexibility, you'd have to choose a `Repeater`. But this flexibility is limited. `Repeaters` don't support editing, inserting, paging, or sorting. If you needed any of those things, you'd need to choose a `GridView` instead, but that doesn't support a truly free template; you can use only its columns representation. `ListView` provides you with maximum flexibility, combining the advantages of the `Repeater` and `GridView`.

PROBLEM

Flexibility and control over markup is important. `ListView` in ASP.NET 4.0 has new features that make it even more useful when you require both. Let's take a look at them.

SOLUTION

`ListView` provides more flexibility in defining templates, and, at the same time, adds more support for advanced scenarios than `Repeater` gives you. This control supports paging, sorting, editing, inserting, and selecting. Generally speaking, it has templates for all the specific states. Support for template types is described in table 5.2.

Table 5.2 Templates supported by ListView

Template	Description
`ItemTemplate` and `AlternatingItemTemplate`	Represents the templates associated with the item and the alternating item. Generally, the alternating item is omitted because the difference between odd and even items is handled via CSS.
`EditItemTemplate`	Contains the templates to handle the editing process.
`EmptyDataTemplate`	Represents the template used when the data source has no data to display.
`EmptyItemTemplate`	Displays a specific template when the current item is empty.
`GroupTemplate` and `GroupSeparatorTemplate`	Used to display a specific template when the control is used with the `ListView` group feature.

Table 5.2   Templates supported by ListView *(continued)*

Template	Description
InsertItemTemplate	Includes a template to be used when inserting a new item.
LayoutTemplate	Represents the global template. This control has no specific templates for a footer and header, but uses a global template instead.
SelectedItemTemplate	Displays a specific template when an item is selected.

The simplest implementation that you could use in ASP.NET 3.5 is shown in the following listing.

Listing 5.4   The simplest implementation of ListView in ASP.NET 3.5

```
<asp:ListView ID="CustomerView" runat="server">
  <LayoutTemplate>
    <ul>
      <li ID="ItemPlaceHolder" runat="server" />
    </ul>
  </LayoutTemplate>
  <ItemTemplate>
    <li runat="server">
      <%#((Customer)Container.DataItem).ContactName%></li>
  </ItemTemplate>
</asp:ListView>
```

In ASP.NET 4.0, this implementation was simplified, and you don't need to specify a LayoutTemplate anymore. Omitting the LayoutTemplate can be useful when you're repeating different kinds of layout, as a series of divs or images. This solution is shown in the following listing.

Listing 5.5   Default implementation of ListView in ASP.NET 4.0

```
<asp:ListView ID="CustomerView" runat="server">
  <ItemTemplate>
    <div class="customer">
      <%#((Customer)Container.DataItem).CustomerName%>
    </div>
  </ItemTemplate>
</asp:ListView>
```

Figure 5.3 is the visual result of the markup in listing 5.5, enhanced using CSS.

You can use ListView in advanced scenarios, such as editing or paging. We'll discuss these features in section 5.2.

DISCUSSION

Even though ListView hasn't changed much in ASP.NET 4.0, this recap was useful to point out some of its features. If you're coming from ASP.NET 2.0, you can probably see why ListView is considered the premiere choice among ASP.NET developers when dealing with data binding.

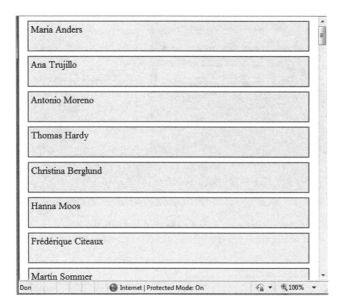

Figure 5.3   The minimum layout of `ListView` can produce interesting results. You can combine CSS styles to visually enhance the result.

5.2   Modifying data

Displaying data is important, but editing also plays a central role in modern web applications. In the last versions of ASP.NET, editing became easier to implement in Web Forms, thanks to a specific family of controls called data source controls. These controls offer the basic features of data binding, but they implement these features automatically. The idea behind these controls is to avoid writing code so you can concentrate on other aspects of your applications.

Let's look at how data source controls work so that you can better understand when this kind of control is valuable for your application.

TECHNIQUE 28   Using data source controls

Data source controls are web server controls, so you have to specify them in markup. To leverage this kind of feature, you don't have to write C# or VB code.

PROBLEM

We tend to write a lot of repetitive code. When the application is really data intensive, automation that speeds up development might increase your productivity. More productivity with less work? It is possible—read on!

SOLUTION

Data source controls were introduced to simplify two of the most common tasks in web applications: displaying and editing data.

Figure 5.4 shows a schematic overview of how data source controls work. ASP.NET 4.0 contains different data source controls, listed in table 5.3.

Of the controls in table 5.3, completely avoid using `SqlDataSource`. It will embed the queries directly in your markup. Although this will initially speed up your development,

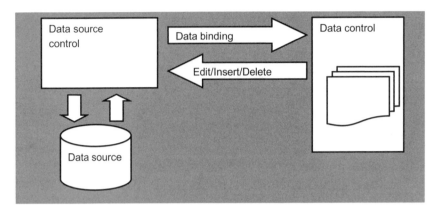

Figure 5.4   Data source controls automatically perform calls that instruct the data control. You don't need to write any code to implement the common scenarios.

Table 5.3   ASP.NET 4.0 data source controls

Template	Description
EntityDataSource	Simplifies the use of Entity Framework's object context.
LinqDataSource	Automatically uses LINQ to SQL DataContext or any LINQ-enabled provider.
ObjectDataSource	Used with custom entities and collections, against a specific business logic.
SiteMapDataSource	Wraps the access to SiteMap, a feature introduced in ASP.NET 2.0 to represent a site structure.
SqlDataSource	Can be used with any compatible database provider, such as SQL Server, Oracle, or MySQL. Some providers must be downloaded from the vendor websites.
XmlDataSource	Lets you associate an XML document to a data control.

you'll pay the price when maintaining this solution. Because the queries are embedded into the page, you don't have the business logic. No business logic is a problem from a design perspective because you're linking together the page and the database.

ObjectDataSource is useful when you have your own business logic, with your defined object model, and you want to use it. EntityDataSource and LinqData-Source, on the other hand, let you automatically leverage Entity Framework's Object-Context or LINQ to SQL's DataContext. You can add this control using the Visual Studio designer by simply accessing the smart task list, and then selecting the Configure Data Source option. Figure 5.5 shows the wizard associated with Entity Framework data sources.

All these controls are defined in markup, and you'll need to use the DataSourceID property of the data control to link them and get the data from the data source. Example markup is shown in the following listing.

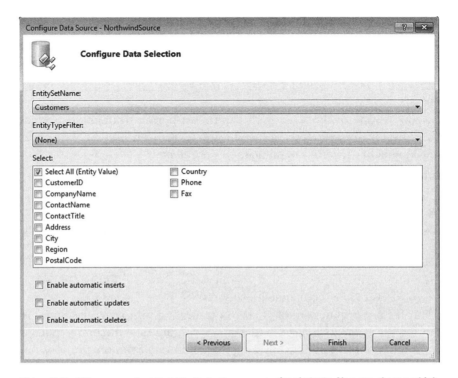

Figure 5.5 When you select `EntityDataSource`**, a wizard starts. You can choose which entity and properties you want to display, and enable insert, update, or delete.**

Listing 5.6   Using the DataSourceID property to link EntityDataSource to ListView

```
<asp:ListView ID="CustomerView" runat="server"
    DataSourceID="CustomerSource">          ← Data source
  <ItemTemplate>                               control ID
    <div class="customer">
       <%#((Customer)Container.DataItem).ContactName%>
    </div>
  </ItemTemplate>
</asp:ListView>

<asp:EntityDataSource ID="CustomerSource" runat="server"   ← Entity Framework
    ConnectionString="name=NorthwindEntities"                object context
    DefaultContainerName="NorthwindEntities"     ← EntitySet
    EntitySetName="Customers" />                    to be used
```

When you run this code, the results are similar to the example shown in figure 5.3. We changed only the code to retrieve the data, not the template to display it.

DISCUSSION

We personally believe that writing code in most situations is the best option: you'll have more control over what happens under the hood and spend less time hacking the data source controls to suit your needs. That said, the data source and `GridView` controls are useful when you're editing or inserting data, which we'll talk about next.

TECHNIQUE 29   **EntityDataSource and Entity Framework**

In situations where all you need is a simple CRUD (Create, Read, Update, and Delete) GUI over your data, data source controls come to the rescue. Next, we're going to look at the Entity Framework support offered by the ASP.NET 4.0 data-binding controls.

PROBLEM

Data entry is one of the most used—and most boring to implement—features you have to deal with in modern web applications. You can use `EntityDataSource` and Entity Framework together to mitigate this problem.

SOLUTION

Entity Framework is our preferred technology to implement data access logic. As an ORM, it has powerful features and the ability to treat the same kinds of operations (create, update, read, and delete) in the same way, with different mapped entities. This ability means that we can be sure that the same logical operational, say, inserting, is performed the same way for all the different entities that we've mapped. The magic, as we outlined in chapters 2 and 3, is performed by the Entity Framework engine itself, so we don't need to handle it manually.

This feature is quite handy when you're dealing with repetitive code. You're just repeating the same code again and again, changing only the entity that's used each time. You're not really adding anything that's different from the previous time.

`EntityDataSource` is specifically designed to work with the Entity Data Model (EDM) and with the newly introduced support for POCO entities.

You need to enable only the following properties to get the respective support from the data source:

- `EnableDelete` supports deleting
- `EnableInsert` creates new entities
- `EnableUpdate` updates existing entities

The following listing contains a simple example of using `EntityDataSource` (a `Grid-View` is used for brevity only).

Listing 5.7 Automatically enabling edit, insert, and delete with EntityDataSource

```
<asp:GridView ID="CustomerView" runat="server"
    AutoGenerateEditButton="true"
    AutoGenerateDeleteButton="true"
    AllowPaging="true"
    AllowSorting="true"
    DataKeyNames="CustomerID"
    DataSourceID="CustomerSource" />

<asp:EntityDataSource ID="CustomerSource" runat="server"
    ConnectionString="name=NorthwindEntities"
    DefaultContainerName="NorthwindEntities"
    EnableInsert="true" EnableDelete="true" EnableUpdate="true"
    EntitySetName="Customers" />
```

	CustomerID	CompanyName	ContactName	ContactTitle	Address	City	Region	PostalCode	Country	
Edit Delete	ALFKI	Alfreds Futterkiste	Maria Anders	Sales Representative	Obere Str. 57	Berlin		12209	Germany	03 00
Edit Delete	ANATR	Ana Trujillo Emparedados y helados	Ana Trujillo	Owner	Avda. de la Constitución 2222	México D.F.		05021	Mexico	(5) 47
Edit Delete	ANTON	Antonio Moreno Taqueria	Antonio Moreno	Owner	Mataderos 2312	México D.F.		05023	Mexico	(5) 39
Edit Delete	AROUT	Around the Horn	Thomas Hardy	Sales Representative	120 Hanover Sq.	London		WA1 1DP	UK	(1 77
Edit Delete	BERGS	Berglunds snabbköp	Christina Berglund	Order Administrator	Berguvsvägen 8	Luleå		S-958 22	Sweden	09 65
Edit Delete	BLAUS	Blauer See Delikatessen	Hanna Moos	Sales Representative	Forsterstr. 57	Mannheim		68306	Germany	06 08
Edit Delete	BLONP	Blondesddsl père et fils	Frédérique Citeaux	Marketing Manager	24, place Kléber	Strasbourg		67000	France	88
Edit Delete	BOLID	Bólido Comidas preparadas	Martin Sommer	Owner	C/ Araquil, 67	Madrid		28023	Spain	(9 82

| Done | | Internet \| Protected Mode: On | | 100% |

Figure 5.6 `EntityDataSource` **automatically handles editing, deleting, sorting, and paging. You have to enable the corresponding data control feature; in this scenario, we used** `GridView`**.**

At runtime, the code in this listing produces a grid in which you can edit, sort, page, and work with Entity Framework without writing any code. This grid is shown in figure 5.6.

This solution is extremely powerful. You don't need to write any code; all you have to do is change the `EntitySetName` property on the `EntityDataSource` instance to display (and manipulate) data coming from another table and map it to an entity. This solution also produces the best SQL code possible because it's converted before being executed. This behavior is contrary to that of `SqlDataSource`, which performs most of these operations in memory.

DISCUSSION

`EntityDataSource` supports all the typical features you need: paging, sorting, filtering, and CRUD. Even so, we understand that this solution isn't optimal in every situation. You gain a lot in terms of productivity, but you lose control over what's performed behind the scenes. You can use EDM extensibility (especially with POCO entities and n-layers architecture support) to further enforce your logic, but this solution will remain coupled with Entity Framework. If this outcome is acceptable to you, your mileage will be very good.

This feature is one of the most useful ones in ASP.NET when you have to deal with a simple interface to perform data entry operations. These benefits are expanded in Dynamic Data controls, which we'll address in section 5.4. Before we get to that though, we need to take a look at what's new in ASP.NET 4.0 for data controls.

TECHNIQUE 30   **What's new in GridView, FormView, and ListView**

Although not revolutionary, ASP.NET 4.0 contains some important tweaks and enhancements over previous versions. Specifically, `GridView`, `FormView`, and `ListView` now contain new features that produce better markup for implementing new scenarios.

PROBLEM

Let's suppose you're coming from ASP.NET 2.0/3.5, and you just want to understand what's new for these controls. If that's your situation, this scenario is for you.

SOLUTION

GridView, FormView, and ListView appear to be similar. They all display data coming from a data source, but each uses a different layout mechanism:

- GridView, as its name suggests, lets you arrange your data in a grid
- FormView gives you a free template, but supports only one item at time
- ListView is new to ASP.NET 3.5 and simplifies most of the annoyance of the other data controls

Each one has his own strategy; you can find a comprehensive guide to them on MSDN at http://mng.bz/7v8g.

To better understand the new features, let's look at them now.

FORMVIEW

FormView in ASP.NET 4.0 produces better markup than it used to by using the Render-OuterTable property, which is available on other controls, too. (We talked about the RenderOuterTable property in chapter 4.)

With this property set to false, you can remove the outer markup (usually a table) and render only your template code:

```
<asp:FormView ... RenderOuteTable="false">
...
</asp:FormView>
```

The default value for this property is true, which avoids compatibility issues.

GridView and ListView

When you select a row in the GridView and ListView controls, the item index is persisted on page change. So, if you selected the first item on the first page, the item remains selected when switching to another page.

To avoid this behavior, ASP.NET 4.0 introduces a new property for these controls, called EnablePersistedSelection. If you set it to true, it doesn't select the same row index on other pages, but maintains the correct selection across pages.

This behavior is off by default to maintain compatibility, so you have to explicitly set it.

GridView

GridView in ASP.NET 4.0 introduces new support for sorting styles. In previous versions, it was difficult to provide a specific style for the two statuses (ascending and descending). You can now specify a CSS class (or inline style) using two TableItem-Style properties, SortedAscendingHeaderStyle and SortedDescendingHeader-Style, to respectively indicate a style for ascending and descending sorting:

```
<asp:GridView ID="CustomerList" runat="server"
  AllowSorting="true"
  ...
```

```
  SortedAscendingHeaderStyle-CssClass="sortedAsc"
  SortedDescendingHeaderStyle-CssClass="sortedDesc">
  ...
</asp:GridView>
```

You can then provide an arrow, for example, by simply registering it in your CSS:

```
.sortedAsc a {
   background:url(asc.gif) right center no-repeat;
}

.sortedDesc a {
   background:url(desc.gif) right center no-repeat;
}
```

You can also specify the `SortedAscendingCellStyle` and `SortedDescendingCell-Style` properties to associate a specific style with a given sorted column:

```
<asp:GridView ID="CustomerList" runat="server"
  AllowSorting="true"
  ...
  SortedAscendingCellStyle-CssClass="sortdeCellAsc"
  SortedDescendingCellStyle-CssClass="sortedCellDesc">
...
</asp:GridView>
```

Take a look at the results in figure 5.7.

These enhancements to `GridView` are relatively minor over previous versions, but you can write less code to accomplish the same tasks.

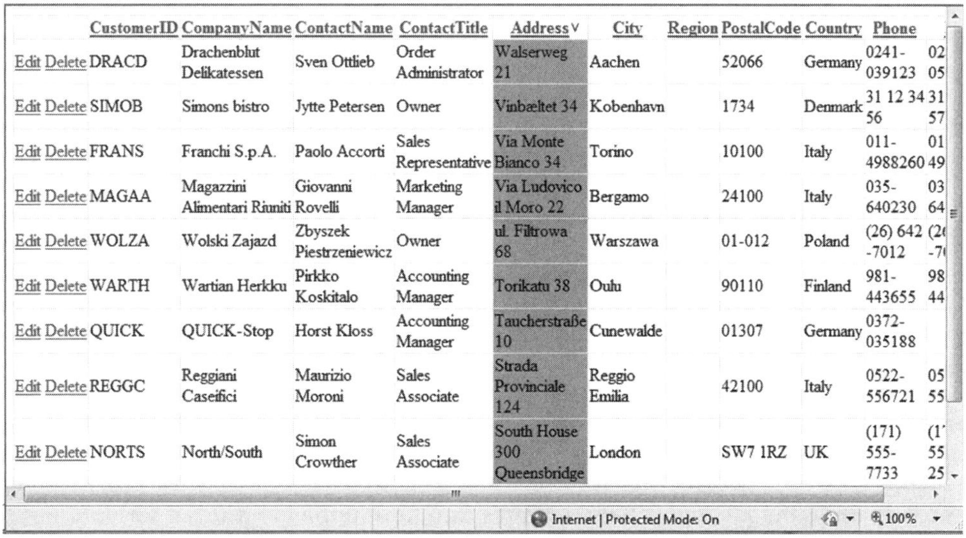

Figure 5.7 `GridView` **in ASP.NET 4.0 supports a new visual style for sorting. You can use CSS to highlight the column, as shown.**

DISCUSSION

These features are merely improvements of existing ones. They'll make your life easier though, because now you don't need to manually implement them or leverage some hacks to adapt them to your needs.

Now that you're ready to display and modify data, the next step is to filter data using some more new ASP.NET 4.0 features.

5.3   *Filtering and sorting data*

You can filter and sort data by simply modifying the selection routine. With emerging technologies like LINQ, the way we think about filtering and sorting has dramatically changed. Now that we're accustomed to manipulating data using query expressions in LINQ, the `EntityDataSource` and `LinqDataSource` controls can come to the rescue in many scenarios.

ASP.NET 4.0 introduces a new kind of control, called `QueryExtender`, which unifies and simplifies both data filtering and sorting.

TECHNIQUE 31   **The QueryExtender control**

The simplest way to understand how the `QueryExtender` control works is to use it. This control extends what you can do with filtering and sorting capabilities by using `EntityDataSource` and `LinqDataSource`. It also makes these controls similar to use.

PROBLEM

Filtering and sorting are tasks that get repeated in a lot of applications. Our aim in this example is to show you how to simplify them whenever possible.

SOLUTION

Data source controls aren't terribly flexible when you're dealing with runtime filtering. These controls are designed to be productive in the design-time world. You have to specify custom parameters using the specific filtering controls. If you want to specify custom filtering strategies, you can't use a declarative option because there isn't one.

The `QueryExtender` control, on the other hand, simplifies this kind of scenario. To use it, you declare it on your page with options, link it to a data source control, and that's it—you're done. This kind of control is called a control extender, because it extends another control's features. You specify the control to be extended using the `TargetControlID` property. Figure 5.8 contains a schema of this process.

This control works with the `IQueryableDataSource` interface. This interface is implemented by data source controls in the `System.Web.UI.WebControls` namespace, such as `EntityDataSource` and `LinqDataSource`. If you're writing custom controls and want to support these features, you must implement this interface.

Basic filtering

The simplest form of the `QueryExtender` control sorts an existing `EntityDataSource`. This kind of sorting is shown in the following listing.

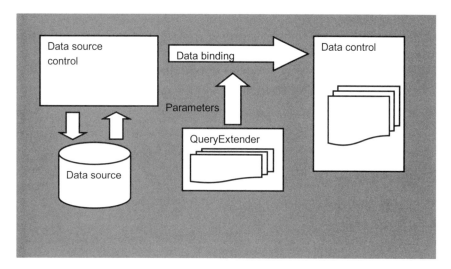

Figure 5.8 `QueryExtender` is a control extender. It extends the features of the specified control. In this case, the control to be extended is the data source control.

Listing 5.8 QueryExtender ties to a GridView to order the results

```
<asp:GridView ID="CustomerList" runat="server" AutoGenerateColumns="False"
  DataKeyNames="CustomerID"
  DataSourceID="CustomerDataSource">
</asp:GridView>

<asp:EntityDataSource ID="CustomerDataSource"
  runat="server"
  ConnectionString="name=NorthwindEntities"
  DefaultContainerName="NorthwindEntities"
  EntitySetName="Customers">
</asp:EntityDataSource>

<asp:QueryExtender ID="CustomerQueryExtender" runat="server"
  TargetControlID="CustomerDataSource">
  <asp:OrderByExpression DataField="Country" Direction="Ascending">
    <asp:ThenBy DataField="CompanyName" Direction="Ascending" />
  </asp:OrderByExpression>
</asp:QueryExtender>
```

Data source to be used

The markup used here is similar to the corresponding LINQ expression. Note that when you're dealing with multiple order by clauses, you have to use the `ThenBy` control, nested inside a main `OrderByExpression` control.

> **DESIGN-TIME SUPPORT FOR QUERYEXTENDER** At the time of this writing, `QueryExtender` doesn't have design-time support in VS 2010.

From a practical perspective, the controls used to represent the expressions are similar to the corresponding LINQ operators.

Filtering using properties

Filtering is a little more complicated than sorting. The simplest way to filter a data source is to specify a fixed value for a given property.

To filter the customer data source to retrieve only values where the Country property is Italy, you have to write this markup:

```
<asp:QueryExtender ID="CustomerQueryExtender" runat="server"
  TargetControlID="CustomerDataSource">
  <asp:PropertyExpression>
    <asp:Parameter Name="Country" Type="String" DefaultValue="Italy" />
  </asp:PropertyExpression>
</asp:QueryExtender>
```

Filtering by a single value couldn't be easier, could it?

Filtering using a range

With the RangeExpression control you can apply a range filter. You can use two ControlParameter controls in this kind of scenario to tie the high and low values to two controls. In the following listing, we'll retrieve all the products that have a UnitsIn-Stock property value that's between the specified values.

Listing 5.9   Specifying a range using the RangeExpression control to filter results

```
<asp:GridView runat="server" ID="ProductList"
  DataSourceID="ProductDataSource"
  AutoGenerateColumns="False" DataKeyNames="ProductID" >
...
</asp:GridView>

<asp:EntityDataSource ID="ProductDataSource" runat="server"
  ConnectionString="name=NorthwindEntities"
  DefaultContainerName="NorthwindEntities"
  EntitySetName="Products">
</asp:EntityDataSource>

<asp:QueryExtender ID=" ProductQueryExtender" runat="server"
  TargetControlID="ProductDataSource">
  <asp:RangeExpression DataField="UnitsInStock"          Operators
    MaxType="Inclusive"                                  <= and >=
    MinType="Inclusive">
    <asp:ControlParameter ControlID="LowerQuantity"                    Low value
      PropertyName="Text" Type="Int16" />                              control ID
    <asp:ControlParameter ControlID="HigherQuantity"
      PropertyName="Text" Type="Int16" />
  </asp:RangeExpression>                          High value
</asp:QueryExtender>                              control ID
```

You can see the resulting page in figure 5.9.

If you've used the declarative control filters offered by ObjectDataSource, you might've found this approach familiar.

In the next example, we'll take a look at how easy it can be to apply filters using custom methods.

Show only product with units in stock between 0 _____ and 5 _____ [Update]

ProductID	ProductName	SupplierID	CategoryID	QuantityPerUnit	UnitPrice	UnitsInStock	UnitsOnOrder	ReorderLevel	D
5	Chef Anton's Gumbo Mix	2	2	36 boxes	21,3500	0	0	0	☑
17	Alice Mutton	7	6	20 - 1 kg tins	39,0000	0	0	0	☑
21	Sir Rodney's Scones	8	3	24 pkgs. x 4 pieces	10,0000	3	40	5	☐
29	Thüringer Rostbratwurst	12	6	50 bags x 30 sausgs.	123,7900	0	0	0	☑
31	Gorgonzola Telino	14	4	12 - 100 g pkgs	12,5000	0	70	20	☐
45	Rogede sild	21	8	1k pkg.	9,5000	5	70	15	☐
53	Perth Pasties	24	6	48 pieces	32,8000	0	0	0	☑
66	Louisiana Hot Spiced Okra	2	2	24 - 8 oz jars	17,0000	4	100	20	☐
74	Longlife Tofu	4	7	5 kg pkg.	10,0000	4	20	5	☐

Figure 5.9   The RangeExpression data control displays only items whose property matches the range. This control makes this kind of scenario simple—you can use markup instead of code.

Filtering using custom methods

The truth is that you'll probably need filters that are more advanced than a simple range. When you do, you can use the MethodExpression controls that work against a classic LINQ query.

To filter using your own method, you have to provide markup similar to that shown in the following listing.

Listing 5.10   Using a custom method and the MethodExpression control to filter data

```
<asp:EntityDataSource ID="CustomerDataSource" runat="server"
  ConnectionString="name=NorthwindEntities"
  DefaultContainerName="NorthwindEntities" EntitySetName="Customers" />

<asp:QueryExtender ID="CustomerQueryExtender" runat="server"
    TargetControlID="CustomerDataSource">
  <asp:MethodExpression MethodName="GetFilter">        ◁─┐
    <asp:ControlParameter Name="CompanyName" ControlID="CompanyName"
    PropertyName="Text"
     Type="String" />                               Filter method │
  </asp:MethodExpression>
</asp:QueryExtender>
```

You have to define the method in your page code, or define it externally by setting the Type property on the MethodExpression declaration:

C#:
```
public static IQueryable<Customer> GetFilter(IQueryable<Customer>
                                    customers, string companyName)
{
  return customers.Where(c => c.CompanyName.Contains(companyName));
}
```

VB:

```
Public Shared Function GetFilter(ByVal customers As IQueryable(Of
    NorthwindModel.Customer), ByVal companyNameAs String) As IQueryable(Of
    NorthwindModel.Customer)
  Return customers.Where(
    Function(c)
      c.CompanyName.Contains(companyName)
    End Function)
End Function
```

As you can see, this is a standard LINQ query expression where you can apply all the filtering you need. The important things here are the parameter name and the return type, which must be identical to those defined in markup. You can see the results in figure 5.10.

This example works with strings, but you can also use it to implement complex filtering rules. If you just need to work with strings, you can use a specific control, which we'll talk about next.

Working with strings

If you need to search strings, you can use the SearchExpression control. The Search-Type property can assume a value that's between Contains, StartsWith, and End-sWith. This value will influence the operator to be used. The rest of the markup is similar to the previous example:

```
<asp:QueryExtender ID="CustomerQueryExtender" runat="server"
  TargetControlID="CustomerDataSource">
  <asp:SearchExpression
    ComparisonType="InvariantCultureIgnoreCase"
    DataFields="CompanyName"
    SearchType="Contains
    <asp:ControlParameter Name="customerName"
      ControlID="CustomerName" PropertyName="Text"
      Type="String" />
  </asp:SearchExpression>
</asp:QueryExtender>
```

Normally, empty values are ignored, unless you set the ConvertEmptyStringToNull property on the filter element to true. If you run this example, you'll notice that all the customers are shown the first time you run it.

The controls defined inside the SearchExpression are the same ones that you can specify in other filtering scenarios: you can filter by querystring, session, profile, route, controls, and so on. You can even write custom parameters if you need to accomplish specific tasks!

Search by company name: pi   [Update]

CustomerID	CompanyName	ContactName	ContactTitle	Address	City	Region	PostalCode	Country	Phone	Fax
GODOS	Godos Cocina Tipica	José Pedro Freyre	Sales Manager	C/ Romero, 33	Sevilla		41101	Spain	(95) 555 82 82	
LONEP	Lonesome Pine Restaurant	Fran Wilson	Sales Manager	89 Chiaroscuro Rd.	Portland OR		97219	USA	(503) 555-9573	(503) 555-9646
PICCO	Piccolo und mehr	Georg Pipps	Sales Manager	Geislweg 14	Salzburg		5020	Austria	6562-9722	6562-9723

Figure 5.10   You can add a simple search to your page using a MethodExpression control. Using this control, you can define your own filtering rule quickly.

DISCUSSION

You've got to be able to filter and sort your data. If you like to write declarative controls to query your objects, the query extender mechanism will fill a gap found in previous versions. If you prefer more control over what's happening under the covers, you can achieve the same results with code.

In the next part of this chapter, we'll cover Dynamic Data controls. This feature was introduced in ASP.NET 3.5 SP1. It simplifies common data-entry tasks by using Entity Framework or LINQ to SQL models to automatically generate all the masks used to display, alter, or insert data.

5.4 *Working with Dynamic Data controls*

Dynamic Data controls are a new wave of declarative controls that enable you to develop simpler data-based applications. Many applications are essentially data oriented; instead of relying on the typical n-layer architecture, they directly manipulate data. The idea behind Dynamic Data controls is to dynamically build the view and editing masks, using Entity Framework's `ObjectContext` or LINQ to SQL's `Data-Context`. ASP.NET 4.0 supports custom providers using the typical Provider Model design pattern.

If you need to quickly compose an editable area over your mapped objects, Dynamic Data controls are the best answer in terms of productivity. You can literally build an admin area for your sites in seconds.

TECHNIQUE 32 **The first application**

Visual Studio 2010 contains two templates specifically targeted to Dynamic Data controls. Choose the right one, depending on whether you'll use LINQ to SQL or Entity Framework. If you want to build your own provider, which is supported in version 4.0, the route you take might be different.

Dynamic Data controls are a group of controls (both custom and user controls) that leverage some of the most interesting new features of ASP.NET 4.0 (such as URL routing, or query extender).

PROBLEM

The problem that this scenario will solve is simple: provide a dynamic way to display, filter, sort, and manipulate data efficiently. Dynamic Data controls certainly fit the bill.

SOLUTION

To begin your first application based on this feature, you need to create a new project in Visual Studio 2010. The available options are shown in figure 5.11.

Our application will be based on Entity Framework (using the mapping you created in technique 26, based on Northwind, and that we analyzed in technique 31). Keep in mind that although the templates are similar, you can't switch from Entity Framework to LINQ to SQL (or vice versa) after you've created the project.

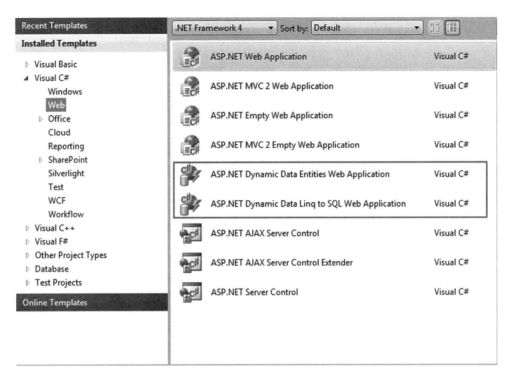

Figure 5.11   ASP.NET Dynamic Data controls have two templates in VS 2010. You must choose between a model based on Entity Framework or LINQ to SQL.

A typical Dynamic Data control application is based on the following concepts:

- `MetaModel`—Represents the logical model
- `MetaTable`—Contains the representation of the logical table, inside the `Meta-Model`
- `MetaColumn`—Represents the logical column, inside the `MetaTable`

Each `MetaTable` is inside a `MetaModel`, which holds all the information about the tables. Each `MetaTable` contains information about the columns, represented by an instance of `MetaColumn`. This information is registered at runtime, generally using the `RegisterContext` method of `MetaModel`. By default, all the tables and the columns are visible, but you can change that; we'll tell you how later.

It's not mandatory to register the model in global.asax, but that's the default behavior. You have to register the model at startup, and global.asax is the default option. You'll see code similar to that shown in the following listing.

Listing 5.11   Registering the model in global.asax

C#:

```
public class Global : System.Web.HttpApplication
{
```

```
  private static MetaModel s_defaultModel = new MetaModel();
  public static MetaModel DefaultModel
  {
    get
    {
      return s_defaultModel;
    }
  }

  public static void RegisterRoutes(RouteCollection routes)
  {
    ContextConfiguration config = new ContextConfiguration() {
                                      ScaffoldAllTables = true };
    DefaultModel.RegisterContext(typeof(NorthwindEntities), config);
  }
}
```

VB:

```
Public Class [Global]
    Inherits System.Web.HttpApplication
    Private Shared s_defaultModel As New MetaModel()
    Public Shared ReadOnly Property DefaultModel() As MetaModel
        Get
            Return s_defaultModel
        End Get
    End Property

    Public Shared Sub RegisterRoutes(ByVal routes As RouteCollection)
        Dim config As New ContextConfiguration()
        config.ScaffoldAllTables = True            ⟵ Shows all tables
        DefaultModel.RegisterContext(
                        GetType(NorthwindEntities),    ⟵ ObjectContext
                        config)
    End Sub
End Class
```

In this example, we're using Entity Framework, but with LINQ to SQL both the code and the concepts are identical. The ScaffoldAllTables property is important because by default its value is false. By setting it to true, you'll automatically show all the tables in the first page.

When you create a new application based on this project, you'll notice that all the code is already in place, and you don't need to write it! A new route is also registered:

C#:

```
routes.Add(new DynamicDataRoute ("{table}/{action}.aspx")
{
  Constraints = new RouteValueDictionary(new {
                                action = "List|Details|Edit|Insert" }),
  Model = DefaultModel
});
```

VB:

```
routes.Add(New DynamicDataRoute("{table}/{action}.aspx") With
{
  .Constraints = New RouteValueDictionary(New With {
```

```
                                                   .Action = "List|Details|Edit|Insert"}),
   .Model = DefaultModel
})
```

Dynamic Data controls work with a friendly URL, such as /Products/List.aspx. You can change the generated URL to reflect your needs. You can protect these URLs using standard authorization and authentication features from ASP.NET, such as `UrlAuthorization` and `FormsAuthentication`. When you're running the project, you'll receive a list of tables, shown in figure 5.12.

If you navigate to each table, you can see how the controls perform in different situations, such as filtering, paging, or inserting.

From a technical point of view, the page templates are defined under the Dynamic-Data/PageTemplates directory. The magic is performed by a special control, `DynamicControl`, which works with `GridView` and `DetailsView` to display fields dynamically. Traditionally, you had to use these controls with hard-coded fields, which limits the possibility of providing flexible masks. These controls have been adapted to work easily with these new features provided by Dynamic Data. You can also use other controls, like `ListView` or `FormView`, using the same approach.

> **INTEGRATING DYNAMIC DATA CONTROLS IN EXISTING SITES**   If you need to integrate this feature in existing applications, you need to copy the DynamicData directory and global.asax. You can set a different directory for the template using the `DynamicDataFolderVirtualPath` property on `ContextConfiguration`, as explained on MSDN at http://mng.bz/nNS4. You can read more about adding Dynamic Data to an existing website at http://mng.bz/uQn7.

The interesting part is that `DynamicControl` works with invisible, but useful, information called metadata. You can use the *data annotations* features from the `System.ComponentModel.DataAnnotations` namespace to decorate the classes and to provide additional information that Dynamic Data controls can read to understand how a column is composed, which type it holds, and so on. Data annotation is a transversal concept, and can be used outside Dynamic Data controls. For example, ASP.NET MVC uses it to automatically build the UI associated with a given model.

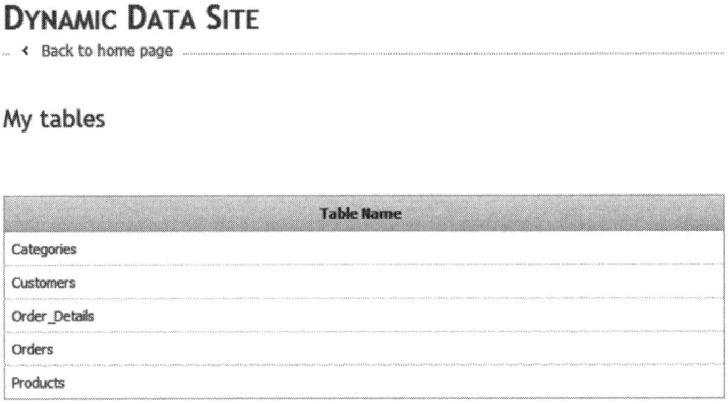

DYNAMIC DATA SITE

‹ Back to home page

My tables

Table Name
Categories
Customers
Order_Details
Orders
Products

Figure 5.12   The default page in Dynamic Data will display the list of mapped entities. In Dynamic Data, mapped entities are called tables.

DISCUSSION

Dynamic Data controls present a powerful technology that simplifies data entry, where your data strategy coincides with your mapped model. Thanks to data annotations, Dynamic Data controls automatically provide form validation, based on the metadata available. The rendering is associated with specific controls, depending on the data type.

Believe it or not, you can extend this behavior even further. You're going to see that in the next scenario.

TECHNIQUE 33   ## Working with metadata and templates

Dynamic Data controls work with templates, for both views and data types. Each column is rendered according to its type, using a simple mechanism. You can alter this behavior to achieve different results.

PROBLEM

When you're dealing with mapped entities coming from a database, the database schema infers some metadata information, such as data type, maximum length, and so on. When data is being displayed, the column name, the validation, or the UI data type might differ from the underlying database schema. Sometimes, you might need different templates.

SOLUTION

Dynamic Data templates are grouped by type. Page templates are in the Dynamic-Data/PageTemplates folder, where each page represents a different action:

- *List.aspx*—Contains a `GridView`, used to display data. You can specify foreign keys, boolean values, and custom filters using a special control, called `DynamicFilter`.
- *Edit.aspx*—Contains a `DetailsView`, used to display the data while in editing.
- *Insert.aspx*—Used to insert a new item, using a `DetailsView`.
- *ListDetails.aspx*—Can be used to override List.aspx behavior. Provides, on the same page, both a list and edit panel, using a master/detail approach.

All the templates share a common base, using a `DynamicDataManager` to instruct the data controls, a `ValidationSummary` to display validation errors, and an `UpdatePanel` to provide AJAX capabilities, using ASP.NET AJAX (see chapter 12).

Changing the display behavior

Each column is rendered according to its data type, using the appropriate template in the DynamicData/FieldTemplates directory. Table 5.4 describes the types that are supported.

Table 5.4 Default field templates in Dynamic Data

Template	Description
Boolean	Represents a boolean value using a `CheckBox`.
Children	Gets a link that navigates to the child entities, in a relation.
DateTime	Displays a `DateTime` value.

Table 5.4   Default field templates in Dynamic Data *(continued)*

Template	Description
Decimal	Displays a `Decimal` value.
EmailAddress	Represents an email address. The address is clickable.
Enumeration	Supports enumeration. New in verson 4.0.
ForeignKey	Displays a link to the foreign key column.
Integer	Displays an `Integer` value.
ManyToMany	Represents a many to many relationship, if that's supported by the provider.
MultilineText	Displays multiline text.
Text	Displays simple text.
Url	Displays a hyperlink to the given URL.

When the type of a column is a non-primitive data type, data annotations come to the rescue. Using the `DataTypeAttribute` attribute from `System.ComponentModel.DataAnnotations`, you can specify a type that's more specific than the CLR type. Using the templates listed in table 5.4, you could map a string property to be represented by the `Url` template, or by `MultilineText`. The CLR type, in this kind of situation, remains `System.String`, but for display purposes you would use a more specific one.

Because we're working with autogenerated entities, we need to use an attribute called `MetadataType` to tell Dynamic Data which class contains metadata information. If you're using Entity Framework's POCO support (see chapters 2 and 3), you can use the attribute directly. An example of using `MetadataType` is shown in the following listing.

Listing 5.12   Extending the Customer entity with custom attributes

C#:
```
[MetadataType(typeof(CustomerMetaData))]          ◁── Specify class containing
public partial class Customer                          annotations
{}
public class CustomerMetaData
{
  [DataTypeAttribute(DataType.MultilineText)]     ◁──
  public string Address { get; set; }
}
```

VB:
```
<MetadataType(GetType(CustomerMetaData))>         ◁──  Specify different
Partial Public Class Customer                          data type
End Class

Public Class CustomerMetaData
  <DataTypeAttribute(DataType.MultilineText)>     ◁──
  Public Address As String
End Class
```

Generally, the `DataTypeAttribute` holds one of the values from the `DataType` enum. (You can fine more information about this enum on MSDN at http://mng.bz/7d3n.) You can specify a string, which forces Dynamic Data to use the corresponding custom template. We'll talk about custom templates in technique 34.

To just control the selected control, without altering the data type, you can use `UIHintAttribute`, which is specifically targeted at visual rendering. When you specify this attribute, Dynamic Data bypasses the `DataTypeAttribute` value, which can be accessed in the corresponding custom field template.

Changing the display format

If you need to change how the value is handled at display time, you need to use `DisplayFormatAttribute`. This attribute has interesting properties that handle the format string, null display text, and whether the display should be applied in editing:

C#:
```
public class ProductMetadata
{
  [DisplayFormat(ApplyFormatInEditMode = false,
                 DataFormatString = "{0:C}",
                 NullDisplayText = "not set")]
  public decimal UnitPrice {get; set;}
}
```

VB:
```
Public Class ProductMetadata
    <DisplayFormat(ApplyFormatInEditMode := False,
                 DataFormatString := "{0:C}",
                 NullDisplayText := "not set")>
    Public Property UnitPrice As Decimal
End Class
```

You can see an example in figure 5.13.

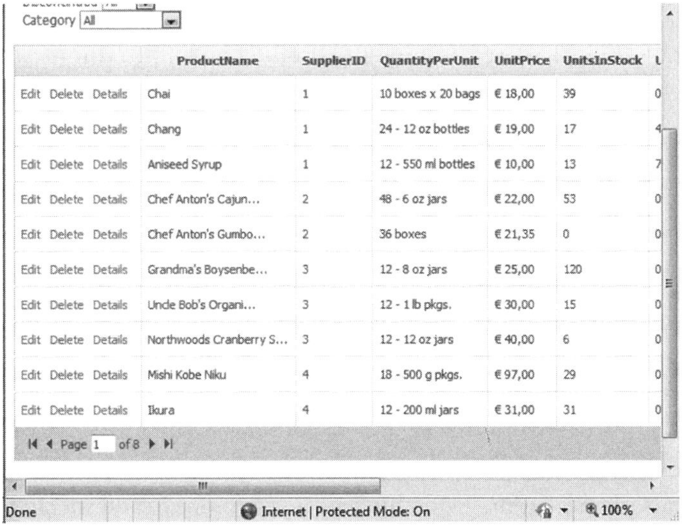

Figure 5.13 A custom display format is applied to the `UnitPrice` property. The results will influence how the data is rendered.

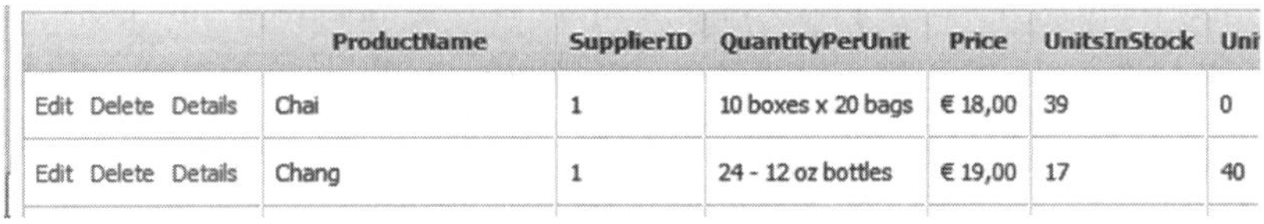

	ProductName	SupplierID	QuantityPerUnit	Price	UnitsInStock	Uni
Edit Delete Details	Chai	1	10 boxes x 20 bags	€ 18,00	39	0
Edit Delete Details	Chang	1	24 - 12 oz bottles	€ 19,00	17	40

Figure 5.14   You can specify a custom display name (in this example, Price instead of UnitPrice). Using custom names makes your page more user-friendly.

This attribute is useful because it provides an advanced format specific to the corresponding attribute and column combination.

Changing the display name

The model is used to represent the entities, which aren't directly exposed to your users. For this reason, you can specify a display name that's used to provide a better display name, using `DisplayNameAttribute`. You can find the results in figure 5.14.

The corresponding code is simple:

C#:

```
public class ProductMetadata
{
  [DisplayName("Price")]
  public decimal UnitPrice {get; set;}
}
```

VB:

```
Public Class ProductMetadata
    <DisplayName("Price")>
    Public Property UnitPrice As Decimal
End Class
```

If you need to specify a description, you can use `DescriptionAttribute`.

Hiding tables and columns

You can hide tables and columns from the layout completely by setting the `Scaffold-Table` or `ScaffoldColumn` property. To hide the Product table, you can use this code:

C#:

```
[ScaffoldTable(false)]
public class ProductMetadata
{
}
```

VB:

```
<ScaffoldTable(false)
Public Class ProductMetadata
End Class
```

If you need to hide a column, the code is similar.

DISCUSSION

Dynamic Data controls are designed to be extensible. You can control every aspect of page layout and data manipulation, using the data annotations to add specific meaning to tables and columns. If you need to extend its capabilities even more, read on. We're going to talk about address validation, custom templates, and searching.

TECHNIQUE 34   Extending Dynamic Data

It's easy to extend Dynamic Data and use advanced features, such as validation or searching. You can achieve interesting results by leveraging specific attributes.

PROBLEM

In a typical application, you need to validate user input, use a custom template, and integrate your own search criteria. Let's see how you can integrate these features into Dynamic Data.

SOLUTION

Validation is probably the most requested feature in data entry. You can't simply trust the user input; you need to provide a validation mechanism. We'll start our solution with this problem.

Validation

Dynamic Data uses the attributes of data annotations to perform validation. You can find more information about all the attributes at http://mng.bz/nqz1.

The most interesting attributes for validation are presented in table 5.5.

Table 5.5   Data annotation attributes used in validation

Template	Description
CustomValidationAttribute	New in ASP.NET 4.0. Using this attribute, you can define rules attached to the entity.
RangeAttribute	Can be used to specify the valid value range.
RegularExpressionAttribute	Contains a regular expression to validate the property value.
RequiredAttribute	Marks the property as required.
StringLengthAttribute	Defines the string length.
ValidationResult	Used in custom validation attributes to represent the validation result.

If you want to specify that the `UnitPrice` property on `Product` is mandatory and that its value must be between 0 and 100, you'll write the following code:

C#:
```
public class ProductMetadata
{
  [Required]
  [Range(0, 100, ErrorMessage="Valid only between 0 and 100")]
  public decimal UnitPrice;
}
```

VB:

```
Public Class ProductMetadata
  <Required>
  <Range(0, 100, ErrorMessage := "Valid only between 0 and 100")]
  Public UnitPrice As Decimal
End Class
```

If you run the Dynamic Data site using this modified property, you'll get the result shown in figure 5.15.

    You can also provide validation using LINQ to
SQL or Entity Framework extensibility. Data annotations use attributes and are easier to use in simple scenarios like this one.

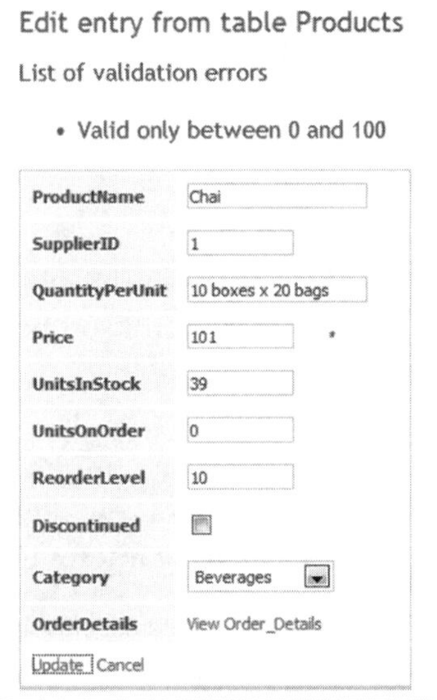

Building a custom template

To build a custom template, you need to create a
new user control under the DynamicData\Field-
Templates directory. The control must derive
from `System.Web.DynamicData.FieldTemplate-`
`UserControl`, which is the base class used by
Dynamic Data to define custom templates.

    You can define two custom templates: one for
the display status and the other for the editing. The
edit template must include _edit after the template
name and before the .ascx extension. If you omit
the edit template, the default one for the type will
be used.

Edit entry from table Products

List of validation errors

- Valid only between 0 and 100

ProductName	Chai
SupplierID	1
QuantityPerUnit	10 boxes x 20 bags
Price	101 *
UnitsInStock	39
UnitsOnOrder	0
ReorderLevel	10
Discontinued	☐
Category	Beverages ▾
OrderDetails	View Order_Details

Update Cancel

**Figure 5.15   Dynamic Data validation
is based on data annotations. You can
use attributes to specify custom rules
that maintain data consistency.**

    To specify a custom template, you must use the `UIHintAttribute` attribute:

C#:

```
[UIHintAttribute("Phone")]
public string Phone { get; set; }
```

VB:

```
<UIHintAttribute("Phone")
Public Property Address As String
```

Save the `Phone` template inside Dynamic Data's template directory. To create a simple
template, you can use one of the existing ones as a starting point. In our case, the
most similar is the `Url` template, so our new template code will be similar to that
shown in the following listing.

Listing 5.13   Defining a custom field template to display phone number

C#:

```
public partial class PhoneField :
                       System.Web.DynamicData.FieldTemplateUserControl
{
```

```
  protected override void OnDataBinding(EventArgs e)
  {
    HyperLinkUrl.NavigateUrl = GetUrl(FieldValueString);    ⟵── Display value
  }

  private string GetUrl(string phone)
  {                                                                    Format
    return string.IsNullOrEmpty(phone) ? "#"                          callto link
                      : string.Concat("callto:", phone);    ⟵┘

  }

  public override Control DataControl           ⟵┐ Control used
  {                                               │ by template
    get
    {
      return HyperLinkUrl;
    }
  }
}
```

VB: Display value
```
Public Partial Class PhoneField
    Inherits System.Web.DynamicData.FieldTemplateUserControl
    Protected Overloads Overrides Sub OnDataBinding(ByVal e As EventArgs)
        HyperLinkUrl.NavigateUrl = GetUrl(FieldValueString)    ⟵┘
    End Sub                                                        Format
                                                                   callto link
    Private Function GetUrl(ByVal phone As String) As String   ⟵┘
        Return If(String.IsNullOrEmpty(phone), "#",
                                  String.Concat("callto:", phone))
    End Function

    Public Overloads Overrides ReadOnly Property DataControl() As
⟹  Control                                          ⟵┐ Control used
        Get                                           │ by template
            Return HyperLinkUrl
        End Get
    End Property
End Class
```

In our example, the Phone property will be rendered as a hyperlink, using the callto protocol to automatically initiate a Voice over Internet Protocol (VoIP) conversation by clicking on the phone number. The resulting page is shown in figure 5.16.

You can extend this approach even further to use it on a complex type. You can use it to attach a WYSIWYG (What You See Is What You Get) editor to specific properties or to provide custom behavior for your application. By inspecting the existing template, you can learn a lot and create your own implementations.

Custom filter templates

You can customize the search mechanism by writing filter templates. Similar to display templates, you save a filter template under DynamicData\Filters, and the user control must inherit from System.Web.DynamicData.QueryableFilterUserControl.

To implement this behavior, you must understand how IQueryable works and know something about LINQ, lambda, and Func<T>. You can read more about this topic on MSDN at http://mng.bz/YKP4.

ctName	ContactTitle	Address	City	Region	PostalCode	Country	Phone	Fax	Orders
ders	Sales Representative	Obere Str. 57	Berlin		12209	Germany	<u>030-0074321</u>	030-0076545	View Orders
llo	Owner	Avda. de la Constituci...	México D.F.		05021	Mexico	(5) 555-4729	(5) 555-3745	View Orders
Moreno	Owner	Mataderos 2312	México D.F.		05023	Mexico	(5) 555-3932		View Orders
Hardy	Sales Representative	120 Hanover Sq.	London		WA1 1DP	UK	(171) 555-7788	(171) 555-6750	View Orders
Berglund	Order Administrator	Berguvsvägen 8	Luleå		S-958 22	Sweden	0921-12 34 65	0921-12 34 67	View Orders
oos	Sales Representative	Forsterstr. 57	Mannheim		68306	Germany	0621-08460	0621-08924	View Orders
e C...	Marketing Manager	24, place Kléber	Strasbourg		67000	France	88.60.15.31	88.60.15.32	View Orders
mmer	Owner	C/ Araquil, 67	Madrid		28023	Spain	(91) 555 22 82	(91) 555 91 99	View Orders

callto:030-0074321   Internet | Protected Mode: On   100%

Figure 5.16   The custom template for the phone number in action. You can specify custom behaviors and provide better usability for your users.

DISCUSSION

You can enhance and customize Dynamic Data controls to suit your needs. The new version available with ASP.NET 4.0 introduces some new, long-awaited features, like custom filters, custom page templates, new templates, and better integration with existing and custom providers.

If you need to provide a dynamic data entry interface, you can do it easily with Dynamic Data controls.

5.5   *Summary*

Data binding is a central topic in every ASP.NET application. Data binding isn't necessarily tied to a database as a data source. You can, in fact, get data from different kinds of sources, and perform the same step to display the data. This is the first advantage of using data binding: you can use the same techniques to display data coming from different sources.

ASP.NET supports data binding in different ways, by providing specific controls to display data (called data controls) and other controls to get data without writing code (called data source controls). You'll find that using controls to get data is useful in some situations, and you can always write code if you prefer more control over the results. The important thing to remember is that the data controls can display data, and provide sorting, paging, and editing capabilities. You choose whether you want to automate ASP.NET data source controls, or if you just want to write code.

Dynamic Data controls have a new, exciting platform that you can use to build powerful, visually rich data entry forms without writing code. Instead, you use the power behind Entity Framework and LINQ to SQL, which you can extend in ASP.NET 4.0 to custom providers. You can enhance the platform by writing specific code and achieve interesting and useful results.

We'll continue our examination of ASP.NET Web Forms by looking at how you can use custom controls to enhance componentization. Let's get to it.

Custom controls

6

This chapter covers

- An introduction to how to build custom controls
- Composite controls
- Handling PostBack in custom controls
- Complex controls
- Data binding and templates in custom controls

You can use custom controls in ASP.NET Web Forms to benefit from componentization. As you learned in previous chapters, ASP.NET Web Forms are based on the concept of controls, which are used as placeholders for their given features. Controls are useful when you're developing complex applications because you can avoid code duplication. Because custom controls are objects, you can use the typical features offered by OOP.

You can start from scratch with your own control, or use an existing control and enrich it. Depending on your needs, you can interact with the Web Form during PostBacks, or support data binding (introduced in chapter 5).

One of the most interesting aspects of custom controls is that you can encapsulate your logic and reuse it many times in your application, without rewriting it.

This feature will be a great help when you need to enhance the control even more because the modifications will reflect automatically.

When you're dealing with custom controls, you need to have a solid understanding of how ASP.NET Web Forms work because you're more exposed to some internals than you are in other situations. If you need to brush up on ASP.NET Web Forms, be sure that you've read chapters 4 and 5.

In this chapter, we'll take a look at how to build custom controls, starting with the simple ones. After that, we'll move on to analyzing more complex scenarios, such as data binding and templating. Most of the topics presented here aren't entirely new to ASP.NET 4.0, but they're definitely important if you're working with ASP.NET.

6.1 *The basics of custom controls*

A custom control is a class that handles a scenario and offers a solution. Typically, it generates a markup (HTML or XHTML), but some scenarios don't do that. For example, in chapter 5 we talked about data source controls, which don't generate markup.

When you write a custom control, you're trying to solve a recurring problem in order to avoid writing the same logic—and code—multiple times. Because the control will be available in the page's control tree, you need to code it accordingly.

Generally, custom controls are divided into the following groups, based on their features:

- *Basic controls* are the simplest ones
- *Composite controls* are created by composing existing controls to create new ones
- *Templated controls* use a template to give you advanced control over the generated markup
- *Data binding controls* help you display data coming from a data source
- *Control designers* are used to leverage Visual Studio's 2010 design surface
- *Control builders* let you use your own markup format in the control

In this chapter, we'll talk about most of these controls, but we won't peer too deeply. These scenarios can become quite complicated, depending on your needs; the space in this chapter is sufficient to cover only the most common—and interesting—approaches.

Simple controls and custom controls have some commonalities. Before you start writing custom controls, you should take a look at how to build a simple control. That's what we're going to do in our first scenario.

TECHNIQUE 35   **Simple controls**

Custom controls are built by inheritance. You can enhance complex controls and add your modifications, or start with the simplest one. If you want to build a simple control, or if you don't want additional features, you can start with `System.Web.UI.Control`.

The most interesting aspect of custom controls is that you'll generate the markup with code—you don't have to write it directly. If you want to build simple reusable objects, ASP.NET Web Forms embrace the concept of *user control* (which is similar to a partial view in ASP.NET MVC). A user control is a small piece of a page, with all the same peculiarities. It has markup and code that are well separated from each other, and you can freely define your markup using a designer. Keep in mind, though, that you can't use the approach you use to build custom controls to build user controls because the markup is generated fully in code.

PROBLEM

You need to start to reuse code to solve recurring problems. Our objective with this scenario is to save you time when you're adding more features. You want to write the code once and use it in different situations.

SOLUTION

When you're writing a custom control, you have to create a new class that inherits from the `Control` class. This base class has few members, the most important of which is the `Render` method. This class is responsible for generating the markup and holds a single instance of `HtmlTextWriter`. It's used to write the resulting markup to the buffer, and it inserts the generated output from the control in the final output stream. This approach is used by each control in the control tree, and, as you learned in chapter 5, the ASP.NET Web Form itself (the page) is a control; the rendering is performed in the same way as it is for the page.

When you need to provide output, the easiest way is to just generate it in the `Render` method. Even though the custom control we'll build in a moment is simple (it displays only the value of its `Text` property) you can appreciate some of the most common issues you'll need to deal with when building custom controls. The code for our custom control is shown in the following listing.

Listing 6.1 A simple custom control with a string property

```
C#:
[DefaultProperty("Text")]                        Default property in
                                                 Visual Studio's designer
[ToolboxData("<{0}:FreeText runat=server
[CA]text=\"Your text \"></{0}:FreeText>")]       Markup
public class FreeText : Control                   inserted by
{                                                 designer
  [Bindable(true)]                    Attributes
  [Category("Appearance")]            used to
  [DefaultValue("")]                  control
  [Localizable(true)]                 behavior
  public string Text
  {
    get
    {
      Return ViewState["Text"] as String;
    }
    set
    {
      ViewState["Text"] = value;
    }
  }
}
```

```
protected override void Render(HtmlTextWriter output)
{
  output.Write(Text);                    ◁─── Output is
}                                              generated
}
```

VB:

```
                                               ◁─ Default property in
                                                  Visual Studio's designer
<DefaultProperty("Text")>
<ToolboxData("<{0}:FreeText runat=server
➡  text=""Insert your text here""></{0}:FreeText>")>    ◁─ Markup inserted
Public Class FreeText                                        by designer
  Inherits Control
  <Bindable(True)>                       ◁─ Attributes used to
  <Category("Appearance")>                  control behavior
  <DefaultValue("")>  <Localizable(True)>
  Public Property Text() As String
    Get
      Return DirectCast(ViewState("Text"), String)
    End Get
    Set
      ViewState("Text") = value
    End Set
  End Property

  Protected Overrides Sub Render(output As HtmlTextWriter)
    output.Write(Text)                   ◁─ Output is
  End Sub                                   generated
End Class
```

As you can see from this code, attributes are widely used in custom controls to work with both the ASP.NET Page Parser and Visual Studio's designer. Most of these attributes aren't necessary to make the control work, but will be useful to other members on your team.

In figure 6.1, you can see how Visual Studio 2010 will host this control in its designer.

Now you've got the control on your page. But before you can use it, you have to register it.

Registering a control

You can register a control in two ways:

- *Locally on the page*—The control will be available only on this page
- *Globally*—The control will be available to the whole application

The syntaxes you use in each of these two cases are similar, and there isn't a preferred choice. If you need a set of controls in many pages and you don't want to repeat the registration every

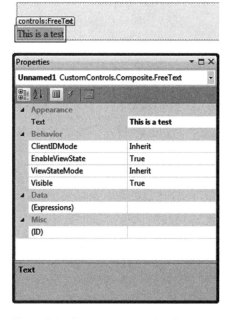

Figure 6.1   Our custom control as it appears when hosted in the designer. At the bottom are the properties related to our control.

time, the global approach is the best way to go. On the other hand, if you need them only on one page, it's better to register them on the page where you use them.

If you want to globally register a control, you need to open your web.config and place the registration under configuration\system.web\pages, as in the following snippet:

```
<controls>
  <add tagPrefix="controls"
      namespace="CustomControls.Composite"
      assembly="CustomControls.Composite" />
</controls>
```

You can locally register a control in a page (or user control) using the @Register directive:

```
<%@ Register TagPrefix="controls"
            Namespace="CustomControls.Composite"
            Assembly="CustomControls.Composite" %>
```

The TagPrefix attribute is used to represent the first part of the typical control declaration. The second part, the one after the :, is the class name itself. For our example, the definition in the markup will be:

```
<controls:FreeText runat="server" Text="This is a test" />
```

Because it will influence the way you declare the control in markup, the class name is important and must be chosen accordingly.

> **TIPS FOR CONTROL REGISTRATION**   If you can, avoid using a long name for your control and don't add the control suffix (it's not necessary).
>
> Don't use the default asp tag prefix either because it will slow down the control's lookup performance. Using this prefix will add more namespaces to consider when the Page Parser tries to understand where the control is defined; it's a system namespace, which is often used to clearly identify the fact that a control is coming from the Base Class Library (BCL) BCL.

Everything we've introduced with this scenario can be applied to user controls, too. For user controls, you specify the src property to specify the path.

DISCUSSION

Congratulations! Your first control is complete. This control is quite simple, but shows some of the fundamental aspects you'll have to deal with when you write custom controls. In the real world, it's more common to write custom controls that are based on existing controls. They will enhance and combine other controls' features in a single point and will provide an easier way of coding a feature. In the next scenario, we'll take a look at how these composite controls work in ASP.NET.

TECHNIQUE 36   Composite controls

Custom controls are often created by combining existing ones, enhancing their features. In most situations, this process consists of picking two or more controls and combining them to produce a single result. Knowing how to do this is important because you can reuse existing controls and add more features to simplify the use of common, recurring situations.

We're talking about composite controls separately because combining controls is more challenging than creating a new one from scratch. When you create composite controls, you'll encounter special problems. For example, the controls need to be wrapped, and their members need to be exposed in the corresponding control. This task is simple to perform but it's also time consuming. The reality is that you'll map only the most used and useful members, and add the others as you need them.

The problem with this class of controls is that you're hiding them from the outside, deciding what the external world may and may not use. For this reason, events handled internally by these controls can become a nightmare. You need to implement an *event bubbling* technique (to let events propagate through the control tree), or opt to define new events to expose just the existing ones outside the wrapped controls. To fully understand how all this will affect how you create a composite control, our next scenario will cover how to build composite controls using ASP.NET.

PROBLEM

Let's suppose you need to create a special `DropDownList` that, in a single declaration, can be used to both insert the description and the options to be selected by the user. By using this control, you can save a lot of time in terms of markup to be written, and you can reuse the same feature over and over in your projects.

SOLUTION

Composite controls are generally created by deriving from `CompositeControl` in `System.Web.UI.WebControls`. This class implements a lot of the logic necessary to implement custom controls that are web controls, too—composite controls support styling, for example. If you don't need these features, you can opt for the simple `Control` class from `System.Web.UI`. Using the `Control` class will ensure that the generated markup remains simple, but you'll need to manually add the missing features that `CompositeControl` already provides.

Figure 6.2 illustrates the concept of composite controls.

Whether you use the `CompositeControl` class or the `Control` class, you need to manipulate the page's control tree and dynamically instantiate controls at runtime.

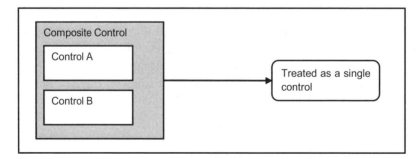

Figure 6.2   A composite control combines other controls. Externally, they're treated as a single control that encapsulates the entire logic.

Contrary to the previous example, where the `Render` method was used to compose the markup, composite controls work by combining controls together, so the controls are added using the `CreateChildControls` method.

The `CreateChildControls` method is called via a call to the `EnsureChildControls` method whenever a child control is needed. When you're manipulating the control tree, you need to be careful and remember that these are controls that will be nested into the control itself and then into the page. To add a control inside another, you have to access its `Controls` properties and add it via the `Add` method, as shown in the following listing.

Listing 6.2   CreateChildControl contains the nested controls declaration

C#:
```csharp
public class SuperDropDownList: CompositeControl, INamingContainer
{
  protected override void CreateChildControls()
  {                                                    ① Avoids control
    if (ChildControlsCreated)                             creation
      return;

    Controls.Clear();                        Removes existing
                                             controls
    Controls.Add(new LiteralControl("<p>"));

    Label labelText = new Label();
    labelText.Text = Description;
    Controls.Add(labelText);

    Controls.Add(new LiteralControl(
                  string.IsNullOrEmpty(Description)?

                          string.Empty:": "));
    DropDownList listControl = new DropDownList();

    Controls.Add(listControl);

    Controls.Add(new LiteralControl("</p>"));    ① Avoids control
                                                    creation
    ChildControlsCreated = true;
  }
...                              Continues
}                                code
```

VB:
```vb
Public Class SuperDropDownList
  Inherits CompositeControl
  Implements INamingContainer
  Protected Overrides Sub CreateChildControls()    ① Avoids control
    If ChildControlsCreated Then                      creation
      Return
    End If

    Controls.Clear()                       Removes existing
                                           controls
    Controls.Add(New LiteralControl("<p>"))
```

```
    Dim labelText As New Label()
    labelText.Text = Description
    Controls.Add(labelText)

    Controls.Add(New LiteralControl(If(String.IsNullOrEmpty(Description),
                                       String.Empty, ": ")))

    Dim listControl As New DropDownList()
    Controls.Add(listControl)

    Controls.Add(New LiteralControl("</p>"))                ❶ Avoids control
                                                               creation
    ChildControlsCreated = True
  End Sub                          Continues
...                                code
End Class
```

As you can see in this listing, we're basically adding some controls in order to display a DropDownList and a description. To remove unwanted controls from the control tree (which could be Literal controls that can be added in markup), we're performing a call to Controls.Clear to reset the control tree. The code in ❶ isn't actually necessary because it's already included by Composite-

Control. Listing 6.2 shows how to deal with this problem when another simpler base control (as Control) is used. Look at figure 6.3 to see the results.

We've omitted the declaration of the properties from listing 6.2 for brevity. When you need to set the properties for the inner controls, you have to use a special approach: you need to access an inner object's property from outside the control. In these situations, the preferred way to go is shown in the following snippet:

Figure 6.3   The new SuperDrop-
DownList **control is in action. This
control combines different controls
to provide a simple implementation.**

C#:
```csharp
public IList DataSource
{
  get
  {                                          Will call
                                             CreateChildControls
    EnsureChildControls();
    return ((DropDownList)Controls[3]).DataSource as IList;
  }
  set
  {
    EnsureChildControls();
    ((DropDownList)Controls[3]).DataSource = value;
  }
}
```

VB:
```vbnet
Public Property DataSource() As IList
  Get
```

```
   EnsureChildControls()
   Return TryCast(DirectCast(Controls(3), DropDownList).DataSource, IList)
 End Get

 Set
   EnsureChildControls()
   DirectCast(Controls(3), DropDownList).DataSource = value
 End Set
End Property
```

**Will call
CreateChildControls**

As you can see, we're referring to the control we created in listing 6.2 (in this case, the `DropDownList`), finding it by position, and directly exposing its inner property. Because you don't have to keep the inner property in sync (it's automatically performed using this pattern), this example shows you the best way to handle this situation.

> **HOW TO AVOID REFERENCING A CONTROL BY POSITION** To produce cleaner code, you can also save a reference to the controls in `CreateChildControls` and then refer to the controls using this syntax (instead of finding them by position).

The calls to `EnsureChildControls` are not only important—they're mandatory. These calls ensure that the controls are created before we access them.

Now that the infrastructure of our control is in place, let's take a look at how to use events in composite controls.

Events in composite controls

Events are used in custom controls to simplify the code necessary to handle a state. A composite control hides the child controls, so you need to propagate their events outside the container by implementing an event wrapper.

Redirecting an event is a simple technique. The event is sent outside by first intercepting it locally and then propagating it outside. Take a look at the following snippet to understand how it works. In this case, the code is worth 1,000 words.

C#:
```
public event EventHandler SelectedValueChanged;

protected void OnSelectedValueChanged(EventArgs e)
{
  if (SelectedValueChanged != null)
    SelectedValueChanged(this, e);
}
```

VB:
```
Public Event SelectedValueChanged As EventHandler

Protected Sub OnSelectedValueChanged(e As EventArgs)
  RaiseEvent SelectedValueChanged(Me, e)
End Sub
```

This snippet will expose a new event, called `SelectedValueChanged`, and a new `OnSelectedValueChanged` method, which is used to define the event handler in the markup. The last addition we need to make, in order to attach the event to the inner control, is to add this simple code in the `CreateChildControls` method, right after the `DropDownList` instance:

C#:

```
DropDownList listControl = new DropDownList();
listControl.SelectedIndexChanged += (object sender, EventArgs e) => {
  OnSelectedValueChanged(e);
};
```

VB:

```
Dim listControl as New DropDownList()
listControl.SelectedIndexChanged += Function(sender As Object,
                                        e As EventArgs) Do
    OnSelectedValueChanged(e)
End Function
```

This snippet ensures that when the `DropDownList`'s `SelectedIndexChanged` event is fired, our event will be fired, too. The result is that the event handler created inside the page will also be called, and our event will propagate outside the contained control.

DISCUSSION

When you're building composite controls, you need to pay attention to the fact that you're not generating markup, but composing your controls, mixing them together, and manipulating the page's control tree. This task is certainly easy to implement in a simple scenario like the one we covered here because you're leveraging existing controls, but it can also be prone to error. As you learned in this scenario, you need to understand how `CreateChildControls` and `EnsureChildControls` work.

Now that you've created the basic controls, we'll explore how you can add Post-Back to custom controls. This feature can be useful when you're building custom controls, and you can use it in composite controls to enhance the result by adding new behaviors.

TECHNIQUE 37   **Handling PostBack**

In the ASP.NET Web Form model, PostBack is important and is used to provide support for events. (We introduced this topic in chapter 1, so go back to that chapter if you need a refresh.) When you build custom controls, you'll need to provide PostBack when the control needs to be refreshed or its state is altered.

PROBLEM

ASP.NET pages are based on the concept of programmable controls. To intercept events fired by the controls present on a page, ASP.NET Web Forms use PostBacks. We want to write a control that can change its state and execute specific code attached to a defined event.

SOLUTION

A custom control that can perform a PostBack, fire an event, and alter the control state in response to the action performed by the user is what we need to create.

If you need to perform PostBacks, your control must implement the `IPostBack-EventHandler` interface from `System.Web.UI`. This interface provides a simple

RaisePostBackEvent method that must be implemented to capture the PostBack and handle it correctly. This method is the entry point for every PostBack generated by the control. It must contain the related logic to handle the multiple states that your control might have.

> **CONTROL VERSUS WEBCONTROL** You might have already noticed that we've mixed the use of Control and WebControl in this chapter. WebControl derives from Control and offers more properties, primarily related to styles, and wraps its content inside a tag.

Let's suppose you've created a new event called ValueChanged. (If you need to, take a look back at the previous scenario to discover how to add an event to a control.) Your control will look like the one shown in the following listing.

Listing 6.3   A simple control that supports PostBack

C#:
```csharp
public class PostControl : WebControl, IPostBackEventHandler
{
  public void RaisePostBackEvent(string eventArgument)
  {
    Value = DateTime.Parse(eventArgument);      // Get value from PostBack
    OnValueChanged(EventArgs.Empty);            // Fire event
  }

  public event EventHandler ValueChanged;       // Define event
  protected void OnValueChanged(EventArgs e)
  {
    if (ValueChanged != null)
      ValueChanged(this, e);
  }
}
```

VB:
```vb
Public Class PostControl
  Inherits WebControl
  Implements IPostBackEventHandler

  Public Sub RaisePostBackEvent(eventArgument As String)
    Value = DateTime.Parse(eventArgument)       ' Get value from PostBack
    OnValueChanged(EventArgs.Empty)             ' Fire event
  End Sub

  Public Event ValueChanged As EventHandler     ' Define event
  Protected Sub OnValueChanged(e As EventArgs)
    RaiseEvent ValueChanged(Me, e)
  End Sub
End Class
```

When the PostBack is fired, the control simply takes the parameter, assigns it to a property, and fires the associated event.

To fire the PostBack, we need to create an action that will perform a POST request to the page. You usually do this by adding a hyperlink to the page that calls the

JavaScript doPostBack function, which is dynamically added to every ASP.NET page. Although you can embed this call directly, it's better to have it generated by using the GetPostBackClientHyperlink method offered by ClientScript, which is accessible through the current Page instance. The code is shown in the following listing.

Listing 6.4   A simple control that generates a link for a PostBack

C#:

```
protected override void RenderContents(HtmlTextWriter writer)
{
  string postBackLink =
    Page.ClientScript.GetPostBackClientHyperlink(this,
                                     Value.ToString(), true);
  HyperLink link = new HyperLink();
  link.NavigateUrl = postBackLink;
  link.Text = "Test PostBack";
  link.RenderControl(writer);
}
```

VB:

```
Protected Overrides Sub RenderContents(writer As HtmlTextWriter)
  Dim postBackLink As String =
      Page.ClientScript.GetPostBackClientHyperlink(Me,
                                     Value.ToString(), True)
  Dim link As New HyperLink()
  link.NavigateUrl = postBackLink
  link.Text = "Test PostBack"
  link.RenderControl(writer)
End Sub
```

This code will generate a new link that will post the control back to the page. The RaisePostBackEvent from listing 6.3 will be raised, and the event will be fired. You can take a look at the results in figure 6.4.

The control you created in this scenario is simple, but it does show you how to add PostBack support in an easy way. Another important topic related to handling state that you should consider when you're writing a custom control that performs PostBack is ViewState. We're not going to cover that here though; we'll save that for chapter 13.

Figure 6.4   When the link is clicked, it causes a PostBack. Given the code that's associated with our control, our page will intercept the event and write the current date and time.

DISCUSSION

After working through this scenario, you've got a basic understanding of how to create custom controls in ASP.NET applications. You can generate custom markup, combining existing controls to provide a new way of using them together. Last, but not least, you know how to fire PostBacks and handle them in custom controls.

Now that you're comfortable with the basics, the next part of this chapter will cover how to write complex controls. In particular, we'll take a look at how to use templating and data binding, which will open a new set of more complex scenarios for you.

6.2   Complex controls

In most common situations, you'll need to build controls that are more complex than the ones we've previously introduced. In real-world scenarios, it's common to provide advanced features like templating or data binding to enhance control reusability.

You can personalize the visual appearance of the control depending on your need, without duplicating the inner code, by implementing templates. You can also do this with data binding to display data coming from external sources, like a database.

ASP.NET has special features related to data binding and templating, but before we can move on, we need to address what a container control is and how it works. This concept is important in this model, where controls are nested.

TECHNIQUE 38   **Container controls**

Container controls are a special kind of control that contain other controls. This is an important concept if you consider ASP.NET's page structure, where a control must have a unique ID. Container controls ensure that the contained controls have a unique ID across the container. As per the ASP.NET control tree, the generated ID (often referred to as `ClientID`) is composed by concatenating the parent and child IDs, to avoid conflicts across the page.

PROBLEM

You usually build complex controls by creating the controls programmatically and nesting them inside the parent. You need to know how to put the right pieces in the right positions to fully leverage ASP.NET's page framework and get the behavior you expect.

SOLUTION

The most important thing to remember about container controls is that most of the time, you'll need to implement a marker interface for your class or decorate it with some attributes. You have to do this because you need to tell the server how to deal with the control. Figure 6.5 shows how a container control works.

To instruct the Page Parser that the control is a container, you need to implement the `INamingContainer` interface. As previously noted, this interface is only a marker interface, so you don't have to write any code. The Page Parser will find the interface

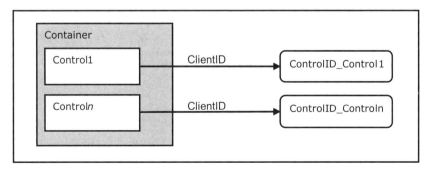

Figure 6.5   A container control influences the inner control's ID. To learn about how the ClientID is generated, see chapter 4.

and generate unique IDs for the child controls. You need unique IDs when you need different instances of your control in a single page, to avoid conflicts. To implement this behavior, you'll need to write some code like the following:

C#:
```
public class Message : Control, INamingContainer {}
```

VB:
```
Public Class Message
    Inherits Control
    Implements INamingContainer
End Class
```

You don't need to do anything else to support this feature.

Another interesting aspect of custom controls is how child controls are created. Let's suppose we want to declare our control using this form:

```
<controls:Message runat="server">
  <ItemTemplate>...</ItemTemplate>
</controls:Message>
```

The ItemTemplate tag used in this case is in fact a property, which is declared in this form because it can't be expressed by a simple literal property. You need to use a special attribute, called ParseChildrenAttribute, to instruct the Page Parser accordingly; otherwise, the Page Parser (by default) will treat the inner tag as a literal content and add a new LiteralControl under the control's tree. You declare this attribute on the class, as in the following snippet:

C#:
```
[ParseChildren(true)]
public class Message : Control, INamingContainer {}
```

VB:
```
<ParseChildren(true)>
Public Class Message
    Inherits Control
    Implements INamingContainer
End Class
```

This attribute can assume different meanings, depending on how you declare it. When it's present and set to true, child elements must correspond to the properties of the control; if they don't, a parser error is generated (like it would be for non-mapped properties or literal text). This behavior is especially useful in templating and data binding controls.

When you omit ParseChildrenAttribute or explicitly set it to false, the inner elements must be server controls. The Page Parser will create them by calling the AddParsedSubObject method, coming from the IParserAccessor interface. By default, IParserAccessor adds the child controls to the tree. All the remaining literal controls (like spaces or tabs between controls) are added to the tree as instances of LiteralControl. This outcome is the preferred behavior when you're building panels, where inner controls are placed directly inside the control definition.

Properties as inner tags

To define a property as an inner tag, as we did in the previous example, `ParseChildrenAttribute` isn't enough. You also need to define `PersistenceModeAttribute`, this time on the property itself:

C#:
```
[PersistenceMode(PersistenceMode.InnerProperty)]
public ITemplate ItemTemplate { get; set; }
```

VB:
```
<PersistenceMode(PersistenceMode.InnerProperty)>
Public Property ItemTemplate() As ITemplate
```

In this scenario, you define the property as an inner tag, but the options listed in table 6.1 are also available.

Table 6.1 PersistenceMode enum values to use with PersistenceModeAttribute

Value	Description
`Attribute`	The property or event is defined as an attribute. This is the default behavior.
`EncodedInnerDefaultProperty`	Similar to `InnerDefaultProperty`, but the property value is HTML encoded.
`InnerDefaultProperty`	The property is defined as the inner text and is the default property. Only one property can be marked this way.
`InnerProperty`	The property is defined as a nested tag.

Mixing the different values provided by `PersistenceMode` enum will give you different results. Experimentation will guide you in building a control that best suits your needs.

DISCUSSION

The topics covered in this scenario are extremely useful when you're dealing with templated controls, where data binding must be supported. In these situations, you've got to specifically instruct the Page Parser to achieve the behavior you're after.

The next scenario will cover the basics of templated controls and guide you in effectively supporting data binding.

TECHNIQUE 39 **Templated controls**

We've already explored how server controls maintain their values across PostBacks, how to combine them to build richer controls, and how to control the Page Parser. The next, natural evolution is to take a look at templating, which is the ability to reuse the control's inner behavior, but with the specific purpose of improving layout. Using templated controls gives you benefits in terms of code reusability; you can reuse more code and simply provide a new layout when you need one. Templated controls are especially useful when you're implementing data binding. We'll cover that here, too.

PROBLEM

Quite often, we tend to duplicate code only to provide different outputs, suited to different situations. In this scenario, all we need to do is provide a template that differs from case to case.

SOLUTION

Templated controls offer a template that you use to customize the visual appearance of your page. We discussed templates in chapter 5 when we talked about data binding because they're used specifically in a data-binding situation to provide flexibility when showing data coming from external sources, like a database. In this scenario, we're going to cover how to use them in custom controls. Figure 6.6 shows how templated controls work.

Remember that a template is represented by a special marker type, called ITem-plate. We'll declare our template properties this way:

C#:
```
[TemplateContainer(typeof(MessageItem))]
[PersistenceMode(PersistenceMode.InnerProperty)]
public ITemplate ItemTemplate { get; set; }
```

VB:
```
<TemplateContainer(GetType(MessageItem))>
<PersistenceMode(PersistenceMode.InnerProperty)>
Public Property ItemTemplate() As ITemplate
```

As you can see in this snippet, we've added a new TemplateContainerAttribute to the property definition, which indicates the template container type. This attribute is useful to enable correct IntelliSense in Visual Studio, too.

We'll get back to TemplateContainer soon. Right now, you need to understand how to instantiate the template. The preferred way is to override the CreateChild-Controls method and provide the correct initialization. Because ParseChildren-Attribute is added to the class, no LiteralControls will be created. Listing 6.5 shows the corresponding code.

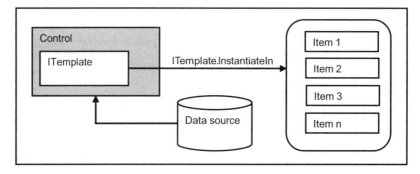

Figure 6.6 You usually use templated controls to repeat a given template when performing data binding. A templated control renders each item loaded from the data source using the same template.

Listing 6.5   A simple templated control

C#:
```csharp
[ParseChildren(true)]
public class Message : Control, INamingContainer
{
  [TemplateContainer(typeof(MessageItem))]
  [PersistenceMode(PersistenceMode.InnerProperty)]
  public ITemplate ItemTemplate { get; set; }

  public string Text
  {
    get { return ViewState["Text"] as string; }
    set { ViewState["Text"] = value; }
  }

  protected override void CreateChildControls()
  {
    if (ItemTemplate != null)
    {
      MessageItem template = new MessageItem(this);       ❶ Instantiates
      ItemTemplate.InstantiateIn(template);                  template...
      this.Controls.Clear();                              ❷ ...and adds
      this.Controls.Add(template);                           to tree
    }
    else
    {                                                      Used if template's
      Controls.Add(new LiteralControl(Text));              omitted
    }
  }

  protected override void OnDataBinding(EventArgs e)
  {                                                        ❸ Calls
    EnsureChildControls();                                   EnsureChildControls
    base.OnDataBinding(e);
  }
}
```

VB:
```vbnet
<ParseChildren(True)>
Public Class Message
  Inherits Control
  Implements INamingContainer
  <TemplateContainer(GetType(MessageItem)),
      PersistenceMode(PersistenceMode.InnerProperty)>
      Public Property ItemTemplate() As ITemplate

  Public Property Text() As String
    Get
      Return TryCast(ViewState("Text"), String)
    End Get
    Set
      ViewState("Text") = value
    End Set
  End Property

  Protected Overrides Sub CreateChildControls()
```

```
    If ItemTemplate IsNot Nothing Then                ❶ Instantiates
      Dim template As New MessageItem(Me)                  template...
      ItemTemplate.InstantiateIn(template)
      Me.Controls.Clear()                             ❷ ...and adds
      Me.Controls.Add(template)                          to tree
    Else
      Controls.Add(New LiteralControl(Text))          Used if template's
    End If                                             omitted
  End Sub

  Protected Overrides Sub OnDataBinding(e As EventArgs)  ❸ Calls
    EnsureChildControls()                                   EnsureChildControls
    MyBase.OnDataBinding(e)
  End Sub
End Class
```

In this example, a strongly typed template is defined. First, the code instantiates the container ❶ and then performs the rendering inside the container itself, which is then added to the control tree ❷. The template container is a simple class, which is used to simplify the data binding.

The OnDataBinding method inherited from Control is overridden to invoke the EnsureChildControls method ❸; this guarantees that child controls in the template are created before the data binding takes place.

Because our template will just show some text, the corresponding template container has only one property, which makes things simple. All the code is contained in the following listing.

Listing 6.6   A custom implementation for a template container

C#:
```
public class MessageItem : Control, INamingContainer
{
  private Message parentControl;
  public MessageItem(Message parent)
  {                                           Parent control
    parentControl = parent;                   is passed...
  }

  public string Text
  {
    get
    {                                         ... so its Text property
      return parentControl.Text;              can be used
    }
  }
}
```

VB:
```
Public Class MessageItem
  Inherits Control
  Implements INamingContainer
  Private parentControl As Message
  Public Sub New(parent As Message)
```

```
    parentControl = parent                        ◁──┐ Parent control
  End Sub                                            │ is passed...

  Public ReadOnly Property Text() As String
    Get
      Return parentControl.Text                   ◁──┐ ... so its Text property
    End Get                                          │ can be used
  End Property
End Class
```

Now you can use this template with the following markup:

```
<controls:Message runat="server" ID="MyMessage"
                  Text="This is test">
<ItemTemplate>
    <p>Here's a formatted template: <%#Container.Text %></p>
</ItemTemplate>
</controls:Message>
```

When you define a template, the control will render it. Thanks to our custom template container, we can reference the Text property via the Container property that's defined on the template. In real-world situations, you can define the container even more to better represent your needs. Figure 6.7 show the result of our work in this section.

> Here's a formatted template: This is a test

Figure 6.7 You can use a template container to enhance the look of your control. In this example, we're taking a value from the control and formatting it.

Although this exercise was useful so that you could understand how templated controls work, this example is limited in use because data binding isn't performed in the strict sense of its meaning.

DISCUSSION

Templating is an important thing to keep in mind when you're building custom controls. It lets you freely define a visual appearance for your page that can be changed without you rewriting the code.

This scenario leads us directly into the next one, where we're going to address how to use data binding in custom controls.

TECHNIQUE 40   Data binding in custom controls

To show how data binding works, we need to define a scenario that's more complex than the previous one. The basics are similar; what changes is the base class that you use. ASP.NET, via the .NET Framework's BCL, provides a lot of base classes to use as a starting point, without the need to manually implement every single feature. In this scenario, we'll cover how to build simple custom controls that support data binding and implement all the techniques we've covered so far.

PROBLEM

ASP.NET already provides support for the most common situations related to data binding. We want to write a lightweight custom control that can display a single item (using a template) and directly handle the empty state.

SOLUTION

Data binding is so powerful that it's often used with custom layouts because of its flexibility. Although it's perfectly legitimate to use a Repeater to display one item from a collection, that's not the best way to go.

Data-binding controls accept only collections as a data source, so you need to add your item to a fictitious collection in order to display it. In other words, you're wasting a lot of power to perform a simple operation that involves two templates and a couple of lines of code. In this kind of situation, a custom control might be just what you need.

We'll start with CompositeDataBoundControls in System.Web.UI.WebControls, which is the preferred starting point when you need to build a custom composite control. Because this control is a container control, the INamingContainer interface is implemented, too. By default, the DataSource property supports only IEnumerable as the source, so the property itself is overridden.

To support data binding, you need to override the CreateChildControls method with parameters. This method is called several times in different stages:

C#:
```csharp
protected override int CreateChildControls(IEnumerable dataSource, bool
      dataBinding)
{
  if (ItemTemplate == null)
    throw new ArgumentNullException("ItemTemplate");

  RepeaterItem container = new RepeaterItem(0, ListItemType.Item);
  Controls.Add(container);                                          ◁──┐ Add the template
  ItemTemplate.InstantiateIn(container);                              │ container
```

VB:
```vb
Protected Overrides Function CreateChildControls(ds As IEnumerable,
      dataBinding As Boolean) As Integer
  If ItemTemplate Is Nothing Then
    Throw New ArgumentNullException("ItemTemplate")
  End If

  Dim container As New RepeaterItem(0, ListItemType.Item)        ┌ Add the template
    Controls.Add(container)                                    ◁─┘ container

  ItemTemplate.InstantiateIn(container)
```

We don't need a special template container, so we reused the one provided by Repeater. If you prefer to provide your own implementation, take a look at how it's implemented. This control has an EmptyTemplate property that defines a template to be used when the DataSource property is null. The following code checks the Data-Source property and adds EmptyTemplate if it's needed:

C#:
```csharp
  if (dataBinding)
  {
    if (DataSource == null)
    {
      if (EmptyTemplate != null)
```

```
      {
        this.Controls.Clear();
        EmptyTemplate.InstantiateIn(this);
      }
    }
    else
...
  }
```

VB:

```
  If dataBinding Then
    If DataSource Is Nothing Then
      If EmptyTemplate IsNot Nothing Then
        Me.Controls.Clear()
        EmptyTemplate.InstantiateIn(Me)
      End If
    Else
...
  End if
```

The remaining part of the code, after the `else` block, picks the `DataSource` property and assigns it to the template container, via the `DataItem` property:

C#:

```
container.DataItem = DataSource;
if (!Page.IsPostBack)
  container.DataBind();
container.DataItem = null;
```

To support data binding ←

VB:

```
container.DataItem = DataSource
If Not Page.IsPostBack Then
  container.DataBind()
End If
container.DataItem = Nothing
```

To support data binding ←

As you can see from the following code snippet, the controls can be used as a normal data binding control:

```
<controls:SingleView runat="server" ID="AuthorView">
  <ItemTemplate>
    <p><%#Eval("FirstName") %>
       <%#Eval("LastName") %></p>
  </ItemTemplate>
  <EmptyTemplate>
    <p>No author specified.</p>
  </EmptyTemplate>
</controls:SingleView>
```

Because the `ItemTemplate` property is marked for two-way data binding, this template can also be used to alter existing data. Figure 6.8 contains different examples of the control at work.

This example shows how to combine all the different techniques that you've learned in this chapter. By combining attributes, templates, `INamingContainer`, and

Figure 6.8
Two outcomes for our data-binding control. On the left, the `ItemTemplate` property is displaying the source. On the right, the `EmptyTemplate` was instantiated.

data binding, you can build a powerful control in few lines, and you get great performance with maximum flexibility.

DISCUSSION

Data binding is a powerful feature in ASP.NET Web Forms. You can build rich layouts without duplicating any code. If you need special behavior in data binding, you can create a custom control to suit your needs with little effort, thanks to ASP.NET's page framework.

To complete our examination of custom controls, we'll turn now to advanced controls that you can use to control the way you declare your controls.

6.3   *Advanced controls*

You're going to either love or hate the level of customization that ASP.NET lets you achieve with custom controls. Using custom controls puts you in charge of how to write the markup inside the control. You can also achieve extreme customization by implementing design-time support. We're not going to address this topic directly here because it's not mandatory for using custom controls. Implementing design-time support is a matter of deciding whether to support a rich design-time experience. You can find more information about this topic on MSDN at http://www.mng.bz/URn5.

The next topic addresses a special scenario, showing you how to control the declaration of nested controls. You'll be using a special kind of control, called control builders.

TECHNIQUE 41   **Control builders**

These controls are called control builders because they're responsible for regulating how nested controls are built. In this scenario, you'll learn how to simplify the markup you use when you're declaring a control.

PROBLEM

We want to control how the markup inside the control is defined by building our own semantic. Having your own semantic will help you simplify the control's declaration.

SOLUTION

In most situations, you don't want the verbosity of ASP.NET's control declaration that the *prefix:controlname* pattern uses. For example, when you're building a CMS, it's important to have a simplified markup if you plan to let non-technical users rearrange some parts of it. In this scenario, you'll learn how to build our own semantic to simplify the control declaration.

You can use control builders in a lot of situations. They're frequently used in ASP.NET to simplify control markup. For example, let's compare this pseudo-markup:

```
<controls:Tabs runat="server">
  <Tab Title="Tab A">Content</Tab>
  <Tab Title="Tab B">Content</Tab>
  <Tab Title="Tab C">Content</Tab>
</controls:Tabs>
```

To this:

```
<controls:Tabs runat="server">
  <controls:Tab Title="Tab A">Content</controls:Tab>
  <controls:Tab Title="Tab B">Content</controls:Tab>
  <controls:Tab Title="Tab C">Content</controls:Tab>
</controls:Tabs>
```

Even though the difference isn't huge, the first version is simpler to declare, less error prone, and easier to understand for a user who knows basic HTML. You can use control builders to transform the second version into the first one.

A control builder is a special class that inherits from the `System.Web.UI.Control-Builder` class. This class offers basic infrastructure and has a method called `GetChildControlType`, which will be overwritten to include the logic. Before we create our control builder, we need to focus on our scenario. First, we'll implement a markup dialect to be used in a mini-CMS solution. In a situation like this, the page is typically divided into blocks, also called *zones*. A zone can both contain controls and be contained by controls. Its role is only to be a placeholder for other controls. Let's step back to the example pseudo-markup and try to provide our final markup. It will look like this:

```
<controls:Zone runat="server">
  <box title="First box">
    <articles PageSize="10" Category="ASP.NET" />
  </box>
  <box title="Second box">
    <articles PageSize="5" Category="Silverlight" />
  </box>
</controls:Zone>
```

This code is self-explanatory. It's composed of only ASP.NET custom controls, where `box` represents a box (a container for something), and `articles` is special syntax that will instantiate a control with a list of articles, organized by category. Figure 6.9 contains a schema of this concept.

If you take a deeper look at the code, you'll see how simple this markup is for a user who knows HTML. It uses no special ASP.NET-only tags! (In chapter 15, when we analyze how to dynamically load and compile markup from other sources, like a database, you'll learn how you can use the virtual path provider to close this circle. You'll

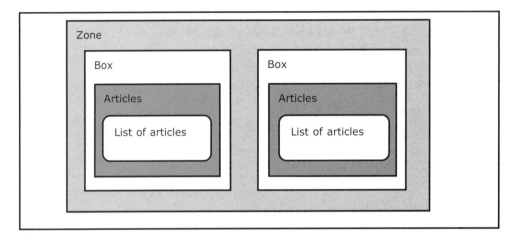

Figure 6.9   A zone contains one or more boxes. Each box can contain one or more lists of articles (or other views). This schema can be expanded easily to represent different needs.

be able to load this content from a database where the user has stored it). The markup is stored in a pared-down format that's transformed in control instances at runtime. You don't need to transform them by hand because the Page Parser will do the trick for you.

Before moving on, let's take a look at the Zone class, which holds most of the logic. The code is in the following listing.

Listing 6.7   The Zone control contains other controls

C#:

```
[ControlBuilder(typeof(ZoneBuilder))]          Indicates
                                               control builder
[ParseChildren(false)]
public class Zone : CMSPartBase                 Controls how
                                                children are parsed
{
    protected override void RenderContents(HtmlTextWriter writer)
    {
        for (int i = 0; i < this.Controls.Count; i++)
        {
            Controls[i].RenderControl(writer);
        }
    }
}
```

VB:

```
                                               Indicates
                                               control builder
<ControlBuilder(GetType(ZoneBuilder))>
<ParseChildren(False)>                          Controls how
Public Class Zone                               children are parsed
    Inherits CMSPartBase
    Protected Overrides Sub RenderContents(writer As HtmlTextWriter)
        For i As Integer = 0 To Me.Controls.Count - 1
            Controls(i).RenderControl(writer)
```

```
            Next
        End Sub
End Class
```

The `Zone` class is simple but holds two special attributes:

- `ParseChildrenAttribute`—Regulates how the child controls are parsed
- `ControlBuilderAttribute`—Points to the class that specifies how the markup is declared

The `CMSPartBase` class is a simple base class, one that's shared by all the controls involved in this scenario and that gives them a common set of properties. Using this class will help you to have a set of tags that share some common properties and will simplify the general effort to write a consistent markup.

Now let's get back to the control builder. The code for it is in the following listing.

Listing 6.8   The ZoneBuilder class takes care of markup

C#:
```
public class ZoneBuilder : ControlBuilder
{
  public override Type GetChildControlType(string tagName,       Add more
                                     IDictionary attribs)         options
  {                                                               here
...
    if (tagName.Equals("articles",
                  StringComparison.InvariantCultureIgnoreCase))
      return typeof(ArticleView);
    else if (tagName.Equals("box",
                  StringComparison.InvariantCultureIgnoreCase))
      return typeof(Box);                                         Convert from
                                                                  markup to
    return null;                                                  control
  }
}
```

VB:
```
Public Class ZoneBuilder
  Inherits ControlBuilder
  Public Overrides Function GetChildControlType(
                            tagName As String,         Add more
                            attribs As IDictionary) As Type   options
...                                                           here
    If tagName.Equals("articles",
            StringComparison.InvariantCultureIgnoreCase) Then
      Return GetType(ArticleView)
    ElseIf tagName.Equals("box",
            StringComparison.InvariantCultureIgnoreCase) Then
      Return GetType(Box)                              Convert from
    End If                                             markup to
                                                       control
    Return Nothing
  End Function
End Class
```

The code is self-explanatory. We're converting the tag name coming from our control to the effective instance of the corresponding controls. Controls that aren't mapped inside this method (as plain HTML markup) will be ignored and output as written. This is another advantage of this technique, which you can use to easily mix server-generated parts with plain HTML.

To make nesting easy, the `Box` class inherits from `Zone`. We can nest more boxes into a zone to compose complex markups. In contrast, the `ArticleView` class corresponds to the `article` tag and has a simple structure:

C#:
```
public class ArticleView : CMSPartBase
{
  public string Category { get; set; }

  protected override void Render(HtmlTextWriter writer)
  {
    writer.Write("<h1>" + Title + "</h1>");
    writer.Write("<p>This is a list of " + PageSize.ToString() +
                " articles in " + Category + ".</p>");
  }
}
```

VB:
```
Public Class ArticleView
  Inherits CMSPartBase

  Public Property Category() As String

  Protected Overrides Sub Render(writer As HtmlTextWriter)
    writer.Write("<h1>" & Title & "</h1>")
    writer.Write("<p>This is a list of " + PageSize.ToString() &
                " articles in " & Category & ".</p>")
  End Sub
End Class
```

This scenario provides a simple explanation of how you can build controls that live inside this ecosystem. In a real-world situation, the control you've built would pick the list of articles from the data source and display them in the page. Figure 6.10 shows the results of this page when browsed.

First box

This is a list of 10 articles in ASP.NET.

Second box

This is a list of 5 articles in Silverlight.

Test: I'm a plain HTML markup

Figure 6.10   Our control instantiates the contained controls, using our control builder. A control builder will let you use a personalized markup.

Control builders are a powerful tool to have because you can decide how your markup will be declared. We've explored only a fraction of what you can do with control builders, but you can find more information on MSDN at http://www.mng.bz/Cpk.

DISCUSSION

With this last scenario, our journey of exploration into the features provided by custom controls in ASP.NET Web Forms is complete. This last scenario will come in handy when you need to take your controls to the next level. Now you can control how the markup is written or how the control reacts when other controls are nested.

By combining all the techniques you've learned in this chapter, you can build powerful custom controls to take your ASP.NET Web Form-based application to the limit!!

6.4 *Summary*

Building custom controls is often treated as an art. In fact, it's one of the most challenging aspects of ASP.NET.

Getting starting with custom controls isn't difficult, but advanced scenarios, like the last one we presented in this chapter, involve a deep understanding of ASP.NET. In more simple situations, custom controls can help you avoid code duplication by implementing and supporting repetitive tasks. You can easily add PostBack and templates to every control, and implementing support for data binding isn't all that difficult.

For brevity, we omitted some specialized scenarios, like control designer and support in Visual Studio. The idea behind this chapter was to offer you a glimpse of what ASP.NET has to offer in this area. It's up to you to find out more on your own.

The next chapter is going to show you how to control the way markup is generated by controls. Most of what we'll reveal will also come in handy when you're building custom controls.

Taking control of markup

This chapter covers

- Adaptive rendering
- How to build control adapters
- Browser capabilities providers in ASP.NET 4.0

Although ASP.NET MVC is the ideal choice when you want to precisely control the markup generated by your pages, you can use an ASP.NET Web Form to achieve similar results. Plus, the truth is that you probably have investments in Web Form-based applications. You can't rewrite them because that will cost you money—and time.

As you learned in chapter 4, ASP.NET 4.0 is committed to generating better markup and providing better adherence to web standards, so in most situations you won't need to modify the standard output. At the risk of repeating ourselves, remember that ASP.NET is built with extensibility in mind, so if you need to adapt a control rendering to a specific need, you can leverage one of the most underestimated features—and the hidden gem—of ASP.NET: *adaptive rendering*.

Adaptive rendering isn't entirely new to ASP.NET 4.0, but its features are enhanced in this version, with a new pluggable provider model added to the browser capabilities engine. By writing a new provider, you can alter the rendering process without changing your code.

Adaptive controls, on the same hand, can be used to modify the output generated by a single control, to adapt it to different browsers, or simply to provide a different output without needing to change the markup already in place.

Both adaptive rendering and browser capabilities work together, so this chapter will address their respective features and highlight how they interact.

7.1   *ASP.NET adaptive rendering*

Adaptive rendering was introduced in the first version of ASP.NET to provide different rendering for different devices. The first incarnation was used to differentiate between browsers and platforms: Internet Explorer, Netscape, Palm, and so on. It might seem that we're talking about something that happened ages ago. In fact, the first version of ASP.NET was shipped in 2002, and the web was very different than it is now. Things like XHTML and HTML 4.01 support, cookies, and tables are established features in today's browsers, but they weren't then. The idea behind this adaptive rendering engine was to adapt the output to different devices to provide better results with different features. To accomplish this task, a database with different browser profiles (called browser capabilities) was created.

You can access the current browser capabilities by querying the `Browser` property on the `HttpRequest` class, which contains an instance of the `HttpBrowserCapabilities` class. For example, if you want to know whether the current browser supports a specific feature, such as XMLHTTP (used in Ajax applications), you can simply write something like this:

```
<%=Request.Browser.SupportsXmlHttp%>
```

You can find more information on this class on MSDN at http://mng.bz/N94X.

Where ASP.NET browser capabilities failed in the past was in the lack of updates for new browsers and devices. To name a few, FireFox wasn't supported by ASP.NET 1.1, and iPhone wasn't recognized by ASP.NET 3.5. What that means is that specific features (like Ajax, validator controls, or mobile controls) couldn't be activated, and the rendered markup probably didn't reflect the true power of the device requesting the resource. Unfortunately, the definitions weren't updated after the initial version, so they didn't reflect the current market.

> **NEW BROWSER CAPABILITIES DEFINITION FILE IN ASP.NET 4.0** The browser capabilities definition format was updated for ASP.NET 4.0 with a new format that isn't compatible with the previous one. If you need to migrate your definitions, you have to copy the old files under the global configuration directory.

Version 4.0 introduces a new set of devices previously not supported, such as Google's Chrome, RIM's BlackBerry, and Apple's iPhone. Major browsers like Internet Explorer, FireFox, Opera, and Safari (for different platforms, where available) are already supported.

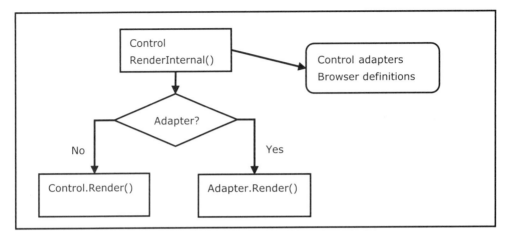

Figure 7.1   ASP.NET adaptive rendering works at both the page and control level. You can modify the output of any controls before rendering. If an adapter is associated with the control, rendering is performed by calling its Render method; otherwise, normal control rendering occurs.

You can specify browser definitions globally (under %SystemRoot%\Microsoft.NET\ Framework\v4.0.30319\Config\Browsers\), or locally for a single application using a .Browser file under the special directory \App_Browsers\.

Figure 7.1 gives you a look at how adaptive rendering works.

When a specific control is ready to generate its markup, the ASP.NET infrastructure looks for a special class, called the control adapter. A control adapter indicates the rendering strategy associated with a particular control. By changing the control adapter (via browser capabilities), you can change the rendering strategy implemented by a control. You can change the strategy for a built-in control, for a given set of browsers, or globally. Implementing a control adapter can be an easy and fun task, and you can adapt your controls to your specific needs. You can find more information about control adapter architecture on MSDN at http://mng.bz/gz37.

TECHNIQUE 42   Add OptionGroups to DropDownList

When you need to change the markup of a simple control, you have the choice of completely replacing it with another one. Doing this is easy, except when you're substituting complex controls, and reproducing all the features by hand costs you time. There are cases where you need to modify the output globally, and though you can do that by writing a custom control and replacing the previous one, that will also cost you some time.

To simplify these scenarios, you can modify the output generated by a given control globally by simply implementing a control adapter. And you can reuse it in other projects if you need to.

PROBLEM

The problem with this scenario involves markup generation and how you can adapt the output to your specific needs. In this first dive into ASP.NET adaptive rendering, we'll take a look at how you can increase the benefits of using the classic `DropDown-List` by adding support for option groups.

SOLUTION

To build a control adapter, you have to implement a class that overrides `System. Web.UI.Adapters.ControlAdapter` or `System.Web.UI.WebControls.Adapters.WebControl-Adapter`. You'll have to override `System.Web.UI.WebControls.Adapters.WebControlAdapter` for web controls, and it includes some basic features. If you want more control, the first option is the preferred choice. You can also specify a page adapter to alter page rendering, but this technique isn't widely used; it's more common to alter a single control markup than the `Page` markup.

A control adapter typically overrides the rendering logic. As we talked about in chapter 6, server controls usually generate their markup in a series of Render*Something* methods, such as `RenderBeginTag`, `RenderInput`, and so on. These methods, per convention, are invoked from the `Render` method, which is associated with the rendering of the control in the page.

Note that a control adapter is not the way to go if you need to alter the behavior of a control. If you use a control adapter, you can't add new properties or methods to the original control; you can only overwrite its rendering.

Figure 7.2 Option groups are used in a drop-down list to visually group elements. By organizing elements with groups, you can increase the usability of your page.

To understand what we're going to do, look at the option groups in figure 7.2.

From a markup point of view, option groups are based on the following tags:

```
<select name="ProductsList" id="ProductsList">
  <optgroup label="Milk and dairy product">
    <option value="Yogurt">Yogurt</option>
    <option value="Butter">Butter</option>
  </optgroup>
  <optgroup label="Eggs">
    <option value="Eggs">Eggs</option>
  </optgroup>
  ...
</select>
```

Unfortunately, the classic `DropDownList` doesn't support option groups. You can only add `ListItem` inside the controls, so you have to change the control rendering.

To implement this feature, you have to write a new control adapter that will generate the child controls, honoring a new `OptionGroup` attribute. This attribute on the list item will be passed to the container, thanks to the `IAttributeAccessor` interface that `List-Item` implements. This interface lets you specify custom attributes inside a control. By default, these attributes are rendered as they're written. In our scenario, we'll take advantage of this behavior to intercept the value and generate the markup accordingly.

To modify the output, we have to override the RenderContents method. In this method, the control generates its output. (To understand how the control works, we suggest that you get Red Gate's .NET Reflector at http://reflector.red-gate.com/.) The rendering is performed by the ListControl class, which DropDownList inherits from. The following listing contains the code to reproduce the original behavior.

Listing 7.1   The control adapter code

C#:
```csharp
public class DropDownListAdapter : WebControlAdapter
{
  protected override void RenderContents(HtmlTextWriter writer)
  {
    DropDownList list = this.Control as DropDownList;        // Adapt control

    uniqueID = list.UniqueID;

    string lastOptionGroup = null;                           // Cycle through items
    string currentOptionGroup = null;
    foreach (ListItem item in list.Items)
    {
      currentOptionGroup = item.Attributes["OptionGroup"] as string;

      if (currentOptionGroup != null)
      {
        if (lastOptionGroup == null ||
            !lastOptionGroup.Equals(currentOptionGroup,
                  StringComparison.InvariantCultureIgnoreCase))
        {
          if (lastOptionGroup != null)                       // Render closing tag
            RenderOptionGroupEndTag(writer);

          RenderOptionGroupBeginTag(currentOptionGroup, writer);   // Render by item
        }

        lastOptionGroup = currentOptionGroup;
      }

      RenderListItem(item, writer);
    }

    if (lastOptionGroup != null)
      RenderOptionGroupEndTag(writer);
  }
}
```

VB:
```vb
Public Class DropDownListAdapter
  Inherits WebControlAdapter
  Protected Overloads Overrides Sub RenderContents(
                    ByVal writer As HtmlTextWriter)          ' Adapt control
    Dim list As DropDownList = TryCast(Me.Control, DropDownList)

    uniqueID = list.UniqueID
```

```
    Dim lastOptionGroup As String = Nothing                           Cycle through
    Dim currentOptionGroup As String = Nothing                        items
    For Each item As ListItem In list.Items
      currentOptionGroup = TryCast(item.Attributes("OptionGroup"), String)

      If Not currentOptionGroup Nothing Then
        If lastOptionGroup Is Nothing OrElse
          Not lastOptionGroup.Equals(currentOptionGroup,
            StringComparison.InvariantCultureIgnoreCase) Then
          If Not lastOptionGroup Is Nothing Then          Render
            RenderOptionGroupEndTag(writer)               closing tag
          End If

          RenderOptionGroupBeginTag(currentOptionGroup, writer)
        End If

        lastOptionGroup = currentOptionGroup
      End If
                                                          Render by
      RenderListItem(item, writer)                        item
    Next

    If lastOptionGroup IsNot Nothing Then
      RenderOptionGroupEndTag(writer)
    End If
  End Sub
End Class
```

The markup to include the control remains the same, but a new attribute is added to every `ListItem` (unfortunately, this attribute isn't supported by IntelliSense):

```
<asp:DropDownList runat="server" ID="ProductsList" AutoPostBack="true">
  <asp:ListItem OptionGroup="Milk and dairy product">Yogurt</asp:ListItem>
  <asp:ListItem OptionGroup="Milk and dairy product">Butter</asp:ListItem>
  <asp:ListItem OptionGroup="Nuts">Tree nuts (walnuts)</asp:ListItem>
  <asp:ListItem OptionGroup="Soy">Soy</asp:ListItem>
  <asp:ListItem OptionGroup="Other">Other</asp:ListItem>
</asp:DropDownList>
```

Thanks to the `IAttributeAccessor` interface implemented by `ListItem`, you can add the attribute without any problem. In the following listing, you'll find the code that generates the single option in the list.

Listing 7.2   Code necessary to generate a single item

C#:
```
private void RenderListItem(ListItem item, HtmlTextWriter writer)
{
  writer.Indent++;
  writer.WriteBeginTag("option");
  writer.WriteAttribute("value", item.Value, true);

  if (item.Selected)
    writer.WriteAttribute("selected", "selected", false);

  foreach (string key in item.Attributes.Keys)
  {
```

```
    if (!key.Equals("optiongroup",
                 StringComparison.CurrentCultureIgnoreCase))

      writer.WriteAttribute(key, item.Attributes[key]);
  }

  writer.Write(HtmlTextWriter.TagRightChar);

  if (Page != null)
  {
    Page.ClientScript.RegisterForEventValidation(uniqueID,
                                      item.Value);

  }

  HttpUtility.HtmlEncode(item.Text, writer);
  writer.WriteEndTag("option");
  writer.WriteLine();
  writer.Indent--;
}
```

Every attribute will be rendered

Necessary for PostBack

VB:

```
Private Sub RenderListItem(ByVal item As ListItem,
                         ByVal writer As HtmlTextWriter)
  writer.Indent += 1
  writer.WriteBeginTag("option")
  writer.WriteAttribute("value", item.Value, True)

  If item.Selected Then
    writer.WriteAttribute("selected", "selected", False)
  End If

  For Each key As String In item.Attributes.Keys
    If Not key.Equals("optiongroup",
      StringComparison.CurrentCultureIgnoreCase) Then
      writer.WriteAttribute(key, item.Attributes(key))
    End If
  Next

  writer.Write(HtmlTextWriter.TagRightChar)

  If Page IsNot Nothing Then
    Page.ClientScript.RegisterForEventValidation(uniqueID,
                                        item.Value)
  End If

  HttpUtility.HtmlEncode(item.Text, writer)
  writer.WriteEndTag("option")
  writer.WriteLine()
  writer.Indent -= 1
End Sub
```

Every attribute will be rendered

Necessary for PostBack

Much of the code in listing 7.2 reflects the code implemented by the original Drop-DownList control. The changes to the behavior are, in fact, included in listing 7.1 to support the <optgroup/> tag. The code to generate the optgroup tag is simple and is shown in the following listing.

Listing 7.3   Each option group is generated when needed

C#:

```
private void RenderOptionGroupBeginTag(string name, HtmlTextWriter writer)
{
  writer.Indent++;
  writer.WriteBeginTag("optgroup");
  writer.WriteAttribute("label", name);
  writer.Write(HtmlTextWriter.TagRightChar);
  writer.WriteLine();
}
```

VB:

```
Private Sub RenderOptionGroupBeginTag(ByVal name As String,
                                      ByVal writer As HtmlTextWriter)
  writer.Indent += 1
  writer.WriteBeginTag("optgroup")
  writer.WriteAttribute("label", name)
  writer.Write(HtmlTextWriter.TagRightChar)
  writer.WriteLine()
End Sub
```

To apply the adapter to the control, you need to create a new file with the extension .browser under the \App_Browsers\ directory. This file will register the adapter locally to the application:

```
<browsers>
  <browser refID="Default">
    <controlAdapters>
      <adapter
        controlType="System.Web.UI.WebControls.DropDownList"
        adapterType=" ASPNET4InPractice.DropDownListAdapter,App_Code" />
    </controlAdapters>
  </browser>
</browsers>
```

The refID attribute is used to specify the kind of browser the adapter should be applied to. If you use Default, the adapter will be applied globally.

> **DISABLING AND FORCING ADAPTIVE RENDERING**   If you don't want to let ASP.NET decide on the adapter for a particular control, you can set the Adapter-Enabled property to false. The original markup is generated with that value. If you want to specify an attribute for only a particular set of browsers, you can use this syntax:
>
> ```
> <asp:label IE:Text="IE only text" Text="Other browsers text" runat="server" />
> ```
>
> The IE: filter sets the Text property only when the page is accessed via Internet Explorer.

If you omit the OptionGroup property, the DropDownList will work like it usually does; using the control adapter isn't intrusive and will preserve your existing forms. When you need to, you can leverage this new feature by simply writing the correct markup.

DISCUSSION

The scenario we've covered here is simple and pretty self-explanatory. By registering the control adapter, you can alter the control behavior without changing the markup already present in your application. Being able to do this is a big advantage because you can enhance the markup produced without compromising the functionalities. A custom control will achieve the same goals, but a control adapter has the advantage of letting you decide when to implement the markup, from project to project, at a central point and without changing anything in the application.

To better understand how deeply you can influence the inner workings of a custom control, the next scenario will cover an advanced solution: how to modify the `DataList` control to produce a table-less layout, using `<div />` tags instead of a table.

TECHNIQUE 43   **Build a table-less control adapter for the DataList**

`DataList` is probably considered obsolete in ASP.NET applications. You might be asking, why are they even mentioning `DataList` in this book? We already have `ListView`, `GridView`, and all their friends. The answer is simple: `DataList` is the only control capable of displaying more than one item per row (natively, without having to do any CSS hacking).

To implement this formatting, `DataList` generates a table. Tables are good for displaying numerical data or reports, but they're not intended to be used as the basis for the layout. For layout problems, the solution is to use CSS.

PROBLEM

Tables aren't intended to be used to compose layout, but rather to display tabled data, such as financial lists and similar information. If you need to work with accessibility constraints, using a table for layout purposes could represent a problem. You can achieve the same results by using a table-less, CSS-based layout. By implementing a control adapter for the `DataList` control, you can continue to use a built-in control and change its behavior globally, like we did in the previous scenario.

SOLUTION

The solution proposed to handle this scenario is to use a new control adapter to modify the markup generated by `DataList`, without replacing the control in the markup. `DataList` can show multiple items per row by setting the `RepeatColumns` and `Repeat-Direction` properties. You can specify a vertical or horizontal alignment, and the items will be organized automatically in rows. This effect might be useful in a lot of situations. From product catalogs to image galleries, it can help you organize the layout visually in a better way.

As in the previous example, the central task is to write a new class that inherits from `WebControlAdapter` and change the rendering process by overriding the `Render-Contents` method. This example differs from the previous one in that `DataList` is a *templated control*, but this isn't a critical problem; we can create the inner controls manually as the control does originally. This new adapter ignores `SeparatorItemTemplate`, but if you think that template might be useful to you, you can always implement the corresponding code. As a good starting point, we suggest that you take a look at the code that's generated with Red Gate's .NET Reflector disassembler. The following listing shows the code that generates the structure.

Listing 7.4   Code that generates the markup structure

C#:

```csharp
protected override void RenderContents(HtmlTextWriter writer)
{
  DataList dataList = Control as DataList;
  if (dataList != null)
  {
    if (dataList.HeaderTemplate != null)          ←── Render HeaderTemplate
      RenderHeader(writer, dataList);

    if (dataList.ItemTemplate != null ||
        dataList.AlternatingItemTemplate != null)
    {                                              ←── Add items
      RenderItem(writer, dataList);

      if (dataList.RepeatDirection == RepeatDirection.Horizontal)
        return;
    }                                              ←── Add final div
    if ((dataList.Items.Count % RepeatColumns) != 0)
    {
      writer.Indent--;
      writer.WriteLine();
      writer.WriteEndTag("div");
    }

  }

  writer.Indent--;
  writer.WriteLine();

  if (dataList.FooterTemplate != null)            ←── Render FooterTemplate
    RenderFooter(writer, dataList);
}
```

VB:

```vb
Protected Overloads Overrides Sub RenderContents(
                   ByVal writer As HtmlTextWriter)
  Dim dataList As DataList = TryCast(Control, DataList)
  If dataList IsNot Nothing Then
    If Not dataList.HeaderTemplate Is Nothing Then   ←── Render HeaderTemplate
      RenderHeader(writer, dataList)
    End If

    If Not dataList.ItemTemplate Is Nothing OrElse
      Not dataList.AlternatingItemTemplate Is Nothing Then   ←── Add items
      RenderItem(writer, dataList)

      If dataList.RepeatDirection = RepeatDirection.Horizontal Then
        Exit Sub
      End If
    End If
```

```
    If (dataList.Items.Count Mod RepeatColumns) <> 0 Then
      writer.Indent -= 1
      writer.WriteLine()
      writer.WriteEndTag("div")

    End If
  End If

  writer.Indent -= 1
  writer.WriteLine()

  If dataList.FooterTemplate IsNot Nothing Then
    RenderFooter(writer, dataList)
  End If
End Sub
```

◁─┐ **Add**
   final div

◁── **Render FooterTemplate**

The complex part is encapsulated in the RenderItem method. You have to address the fact that, depending on the RepeatDirection value, you need to display a specific index. Take a look at the next listing.

Listing 7.5 The DataList adapter renders templates and content

C#:
```
private void RenderItem(HtmlTextWriter writer, DataList dataList)
{
  DataListItemCollection items = dataList.Items;

  writer.WriteLine();
  DataListItem currentItem;

  int itemsPerColumn = (int)Math.Ceiling(
          ((Double)dataList.Items.Count) / ((Double)RepeatColumns));

  int rowIndex, columnIndex, currentIndex = 0;

  for (int index = 0; index < dataList.Items.Count; index++)
  {
    rowIndex = index / RepeatColumns;
    columnIndex = index % RepeatColumns;
    currentIndex = index;

    if (dataList.RepeatDirection == RepeatDirection.Vertical)

      currentIndex = (columnIndex * itemsPerColumn) + rowIndex;
    currentItem = items[currentIndex];
```

❶ Calculate page size

❷ Get row and column index

❸ Calculate index

❹ Get item

VB:
```
Private Sub RenderItem(ByVal writer As HtmlTextWriter,
                       ByVal dataList As DataList)
  Dim items As DataListItemCollection = dataList.Items

  writer.WriteLine()
  Dim currentItem As DataListItem

  Dim itemsPerColumn As Integer =
    Convert.ToInt32(Math.Ceiling(
        Convert.ToDouble(dataList.Items.Count) /
        Convert.ToDouble(RepeatColumns)))

  Dim rowIndex As Integer, columnIndex As Integer,
      currentIndex As Integer = 0
```

❶ Calculate page size

```
For index As Integer = 0 To dataList.Items.Count - 1
  rowIndex = Convert.ToInt32(Math.Floor(
       Convert.ToDouble(index) /
       Convert.ToDouble(RepeatColumns)))              ❷ Get row and
  columnIndex = index Mod RepeatColumns                  column index
  currentIndex = index

  If dataList.RepeatDirection = RepeatDirection.Vertical Then   ❸ Calculate
    currentIndex = (columnIndex * itemsPerColumn) + rowIndex       index

  currentItem = items(currentIndex)                    ◄── ❹ Get item
```

In the first part of this listing, you'll see the formula that calculates the index to display ❶ before getting the row and column index ❷. Next, based on the items to be displayed per row, a new width property is added (via CSS) to every element, wrapped inside a div. Finally, `ItemTemplate` (or `AlternatingItemTemplate`) is instantiated in the container to display the template specified in the page, using the markup. After we have the current item index ❸, we need to get the item ❹.

At this point, we're ready to produce the output for the first row:

C#:

```csharp
if ((index % RepeatColumns) == 0)
{
  writer.WriteLine();
  writer.WriteBeginTag("div");

  writer.WriteAttribute("style", "clear:both");

  writer.Write(HtmlTextWriter.TagRightChar);
  writer.Indent++;
}
```

VB:

```vb
If (index Mod RepeatColumns) = 0 Then
  writer.WriteLine()
  writer.WriteBeginTag("div")

  writer.WriteAttribute("style", "clear:both")

  writer.Write(HtmlTextWriter.TagRightChar)
  writer.Indent += 1
End If
```

The next step is to write the current element in the markup:

C#:

```csharp
writer.WriteBeginTag("div");

TableItemStyle style = (currentItem.ItemType == ListItemType.Item) ?
            dataList.ItemStyle :
            (dataList.AlternatingItemStyle == null ?
                dataList.ItemStyle :
                 dataList.AlternatingItemStyle);

style.Width = new Unit((int)Math.Abs((double)100 / RepeatColumns),
                    UnitType.Percentage);

CssStyleCollection finalStyle = GetStyleFromTemplate(dataList, style);
```

```
    if (dataList.RepeatColumns > 1)
      finalStyle.Add("float", "left");

    writer.WriteAttribute("style", finalStyle.Value);

    writer.Write(HtmlTextWriter.TagRightChar);
    writer.Indent++;

    foreach (Control itemCtrl in currentItem.Controls)
    {
      itemCtrl.RenderControl(writer);                         ◁────┐ Render inner
    }                                                              │ controls

    writer.Indent--;
    writer.WriteLine();
    writer.WriteEndTag("div");
```

VB:

```
    writer.WriteBeginTag("div")

    Dim style As TableItemStyle = If(
        (currentItem.ItemType = ListItemType.Item),
          dataList.ItemStyle,
          (If(dataList.AlternatingItemStyle Is Nothing,
              dataList.ItemStyle,
              dataList.AlternatingItemStyle)
          )
        )

    style.Width = New Unit(CInt(Math.Abs(CDbl(100) / RepeatColumns)),
                          UnitType.Percentage)

    Dim finalStyle As CssStyleCollection =
                    GetStyleFromTemplate(dataList, style)
    If dataList.RepeatColumns > 1 Then
      finalStyle.Add("float", "left")
    End If

    writer.WriteAttribute("style", finalStyle.Value)

    writer.Write(HtmlTextWriter.TagRightChar)
    writer.Indent += 1

    For Each itemCtrl As Control In currentItem.Controls
      itemCtrl.RenderControl(writer)                          ◁────┐ Render inner
    Next                                                           │ controls

    writer.Indent -= 1
    writer.WriteLine()
    writer.WriteEndTag("div")
```

Finally, we need to close the div element we opened in the first part of this code (listing 7.5) when a new row is needed:

C#:

```
if (((index + 1) % RepeatColumns) == 0)
{
  writer.Indent--;
  writer.WriteLine();
  writer.WriteEndTag("div");
}
```

VB:
```
If ((index + 1) Mod RepeatColumns) = 0 Then
  writer.Indent -= 1
  writer.WriteLine()
  writer.WriteEndTag("div")
  End If
Next
```

As you can see, the code isn't complex, but it requires that you understand how the DataList (and template controls) works. To complete the scenario, we need to show you how to render the header (and footer). The following listing contains the code.

Listing 7.6   Rendering the header with a special function

C#:
```
private void RenderHeader(HtmlTextWriter writer, DataList dataList)
{
  writer.WriteBeginTag("div");

  CssStyleCollection style = GetStyleFromTemplate(dataList,
                                    dataList.HeaderStyle);

  if (!String.IsNullOrEmpty(style.Value))             ◁─────┐  Preserve style,
    writer.WriteAttribute("style", style.Value);         ❶  if specified

  writer.Write(HtmlTextWriter.TagRightChar);

  PlaceHolder container = new PlaceHolder();
  dataList.HeaderTemplate.InstantiateIn(container);   ◁─────┐  Instantiate and
  container.DataBind();                                  ❷  bind template

  if ((container.Controls.Count == 1) &&
      typeof(LiteralControl)
        .IsInstanceOfType(container.Controls[0]))                    {
    writer.WriteLine();                               ◁─────┐  Specific to text-
                                                         ❸  only controls
    LiteralControl literalControl =
                          container.Controls[0] as LiteralControl;
    writer.Write(literalControl.Text.Trim());
  }
  else
  {
    container.RenderControl(writer);
  }

  writer.WriteEndTag("div");
}
```

VB:
```
Private Sub RenderHeader(ByVal writer As HtmlTextWriter,
                  ByVal dataList As DataList)
  writer.WriteBeginTag("div")

  Dim style As CssStyleCollection = GetStyleFromTemplate(dataList,
                                    dataList.HeaderStyle)

  If Not String.IsNullOrEmpty(style.Value) Then      ◁─────┐  Preserve style,
    writer.WriteAttribute("style", style.Value)         ❶  if specified
```

```
   End If

   writer.Write(HtmlTextWriter.TagRightChar)

   Dim container As New PlaceHolder()
   dataList.HeaderTemplate.InstantiateIn(container)
   container.DataBind()
   If (container.Controls.Count = 1) AndAlso
         GetType(LiteralControl)
               .IsInstanceOfType(container.Controls(0)) Then
      writer.WriteLine()

      Dim literalControl As LiteralControl =
               TryCast(container.Controls(0), LiteralControl)
      writer.Write(literalControl.Text.Trim())
   Else
      container.RenderControl(writer)
   End If

   writer.WriteEndTag("div")
End Sub
```

❷ Instantiate and bind template

❸ Specific to text-only controls

The interesting part in this code listing is how the styles are restored (which is performed for the ItemTemplate, too). This code lets you specify a CSS style using the ItemStyle ❶ or HeaderStyle properties, so you won't lose any features from the standard DataList. Data binding ❷ is also supported, as well as Literal-only controls ❸.

The RenderFooter method is similar to RenderHeader, so we've omitted it from the code (you can find it in the downloadable samples). Just as with the header, the footer is rendered if a template is specified.

If you register this control adapter (as we did in the previous scenario), you can adapt the DataList rendering to be more standard-friendly. Figure 7.3 shows you the result. This layout is identical to what you would get if you didn't use the adapter.

To produce this result, both the RenderBeginTag and RenderEndTab methods are overridden to generate a container <div /> tag, instead of the original <table /> tag. In this way, you can replace all the tags with your own. 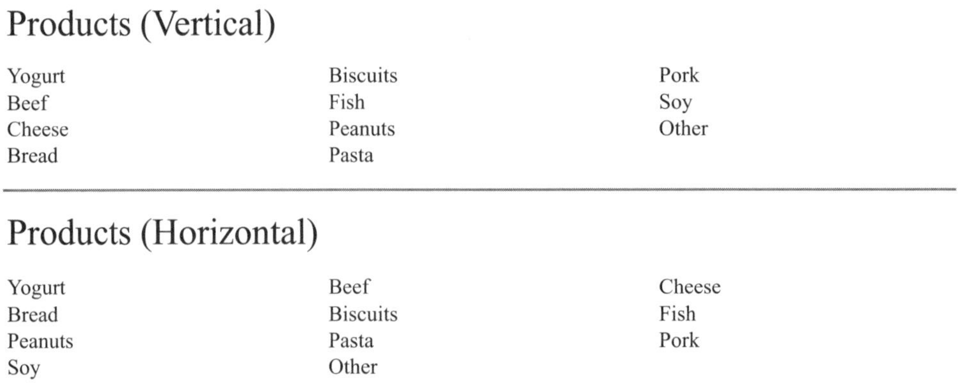

Products (Vertical)

Yogurt	Biscuits	Pork
Beef	Fish	Soy
Cheese	Peanuts	Other
Bread	Pasta	

Products (Horizontal)

Yogurt	Beef	Cheese
Bread	Biscuits	Fish
Peanuts	Pasta	Pork
Soy	Other	

Figure 7.3   The layout generated for the DataList control remains the same as the original. You can use control adapters to enhance the visual results without changing the control declaration.

DISCUSSION

Control adapters are incredibly powerful, as you might have noticed by examining the two scenarios we covered in this chapter. Because you can also write page adapters—after all, a page is a control, so this makes sense—the sky's the limit when it comes to what control adapters can do for you.

You can use adaptive rendering to selectively adapt the control rendering to different devices or to globally change its behavior if you need to. Even though the focus of ASP.NET 4.0 is to be friendlier to web standards, old controls like `DataList` might benefit from a little makeup.

7.1.1   *Mobile controls and the Control Adapter Toolkit*

Mobile controls were the first example of adaptive rendering. Introduced in ASP.NET 1.0, they were intended to provide the right markup for different kinds of mobile devices automatically. At the time, mobile devices were quite different from each other: there was cHTML, XHTML, WML, and so on.

Right now, it's clear that the mobile web is composed of smart devices capable of rendering complex layouts, and these original control adapters (and their respective controls) aren't needed any more. For that reason, mobile controls are deprecated in ASP.NET 4.0.

If you need to maintain a solution based on this technology, you can update the browser definitions on this page: http://mdbf.codeplex.com/. (Note that the information on this website is no longer updated or supported.) From http://www.asp.net/mobile/, you can browse for more content and access the original controls source code.

CSS Friendly Control Adapters, also known as the CSS Control Adapter Toolkit, is a pack of control adapters shipped after ASP.NET 2.0 that increases adherence to web standards for controls like `Login`, `Menu`, and so on. They were intended to provide more CSS-friendly controls, with a cleaner markup structure.

At the time of this writing, a Control Adapter Toolkit equivalent doesn't exist for ASP.NET 4.0, which actually makes sense if you think about it. In chapter 6, we explained the new features of ASP.NET web controls, and the short story is that they now embed a set of adapters to produce better markup without adding external classes.

At http://www.asp.net/cssadapters/ you can download the original implementation. We're recommending that you download this implementation because you can look at it to understand how to implement control adapters. The download contains great examples of how to deal with adaptive rendering.

Now that we're done with adaptive rendering, the next part of the chapter is dedicated to how you can influence this feature by specifying the browser capabilities. Some new features in ASP.NET 4.0 make this area more interesting than ever.

7.2   *ASP.NET 4.0 browser capabilities*

We've talked about ASP.NET browser capabilities before. They work in conjunction with adaptive rendering. To be more precise, browser capabilities influence the way control adapters are used by ASP.NET for rendering infrastructure, for both pages and controls.

This feature is innate in ASP.NET and is based on a set of file definitions that include the most common user agents, from both stand-alone and mobile device browsers.

Time has proven that it's practically impossible for Microsoft to maintain this list and keep it updated, so new alternatives have emerged. To maintain updated definitions before ASP.NET 4.0, you had to do it manually. Now several different sources provide the definitions, and one of the most authoritative is the definition distributed at http://mdbf.codeplex.com/.

In the current version of ASP.NET, the following browsers and platforms are directly supported:

- RIM's Blackberry
- Google Chrome
- Mozilla FireFox
- Internet Explorer
- Internet Explorer Mobile
- Apple's iPhone
- Opera
- Apple's Safari

Plus, there's a generic profile, a profile for search engine crawlers/spiders, and a default profile to cover the other platforms and browsers.

Even though the file definitions represent a useful way to instruct browser capabilities and adaptive rendering, it's sometimes better to control the way the capabilities are provided via code. Even if .browser files (and everything else in ASP.NET) are converted in objects, having complete control over the process can produce simpler results than editing or updating those XML files. That's why ASP.NET 4.0 introduces the concept of *browser capabilities providers*.

TECHNIQUE 44   Building a custom browser capabilities provider

You can use ASP.NET browser capabilities providers to totally replace the standard capabilities definition mechanism or to expand it by adding new functionalities. By replacing the standard definition, you can alter the way ASP.NET produces output.

PROBLEM

One of the problems of the default file definitions is that they're not updated regularly. We want to bypass the standard mechanism and provide a new one that will produce, for every request, the best markup possible.

SOLUTION

ASP.NET 4.0 introduces a new class, named `HttpCapabilitiesProvider`. This feature implements the Provider Model pattern, which we'll explain in chapter 11. Basically, it works the same way as the Membership Provider pattern: you can define a provider to implement a specific behavior, using a base class as the interface to implement. The providers are guaranteed to have the same identical structure, so they can be defined in the configuration. The advantage is that you don't need to write specific adapters or define file configurations, but you can express your own rules in code.

To implement a custom engine, you have to overwrite the `GetBrowserCapabilities` method and provide a new instance of `HttpBrowserCapabilities`. Because this method will be called several times during the page lifecycle, you need to specify a caching pattern. (If you don't know how cache works, you can find more information in chapter 14.)

The following listing shows a basic implementation of a provider.

Listing 7.7 The custom browser capabilities provider

C#:
```
public class MyBrowserProvider : HttpCapabilitiesProvider
{
  public override HttpBrowserCapabilities GetBrowserCapabilities(HttpRequest
    request)
  {
    string cacheKey = "MyBrowserProvider_"+              Unique key for
                    request.UserAgent??"empty";          user agent
    int cacheTimeout = 360;

    HttpBrowserCapabilities browserCaps = HttpContext.Current.Cache[cacheKey]
     as HttpBrowserCapabilities;
    if (browserCaps == null)
    {
      browserCaps = new HttpBrowserCapabilities();
      Hashtable values = new Hashtable(20, StringComparer.OrdinalIgnoreCase);
      values["browser"] = request.UserAgent;              Standard
      values["tables"] = "true";                          capabilities
      values["supportsRedirectWithCookie"] = "true";
      values["cookies"] = "true";
      values["ecmascriptversion"] = "3.0";
      values["w3cdomversion"] = "1.0";
      values["jscriptversion"] = "6.0";
      values["tagwriter"] = "System.Web.UI.HtmlTextWriter";

      values["IsIPhone"] = ((request.UserAgent ??          Custom
        string.Empty).IndexOf("iphone") > -1).ToString();  capabilities

      browserCaps.Capabilities = values;
      HttpRuntime.Cache.Add(cacheKey,
                  browserCaps,
                  null,
                  DateTime.Now.AddSeconds(cacheTimeout),
                  TimeSpan.Zero,
                  CacheItemPriority.Low,
                  null);
    }

    return browserCaps;
  }
}
```

VB:
```
Public Class MyBrowserProvider
  Inherits HttpCapabilitiesProvider
  Public Overloads Overrides Function GetBrowserCapabilities(
          ByVal request As HttpRequest) As HttpBrowserCapabilities
    Dim cacheKey As String = If("MyBrowserProvider_" &
```

```
                              request.UserAgent, "empty")         ◁──┐ Unique
                                                                      │ key for
      Dim cacheTimeout As Integer = 360                              │ user
                                                                      │ agent
      Dim browserCaps As HttpBrowserCapabilities =
                TryCast(HttpContext.Current.Cache(cacheKey),
                        HttpBrowserCapabilities)
      If browserCaps Is Nothing Then
        browserCaps = New HttpBrowserCapabilities()
        Dim values As New Hashtable(20, StringComparer.OrdinalIgnoreCase)
        values("browser") = request.UserAgent                 ◁──┐ Standard
        values("tables") = "true"                                 │ capabilities
        values("supportsRedirectWithCookie") = "true"
        values("cookies") = "true"
        values("ecmascriptversion") = "3.0"
        values("w3cdomversion") = "1.0"
        values("jscriptversion") = "6.0"
        values("tagwriter") = "System.Web.UI.HtmlTextWriter"

        values("IsIPhone") = (
                        ( If(request.UserAgent,
                          String.Empty)).IndexOf("iphone") > -1)
                        .ToString()                           ◁──┐ Custom
        browserCaps.Capabilities = values                         │ capabilities
        HttpRuntime.Cache.Add(cacheKey,
                          browserCaps,
                          Nothing,
                          DateTime.Now.AddSeconds(cacheTimeout),
                          TimeSpan.Zero,
                          CacheItemPriority.Low,
                          Nothing)

      End If

      Return browserCaps
    End Function
End Class
```

As you see in this listing, we're defining a set of capabilities. The ones we've defined
are the minimum you need to make the page work. They'll instruct the server controls
to use the most advanced markup and JavaScript code. Figure 7.4 contains the results
of the default provider and of our custom provider.

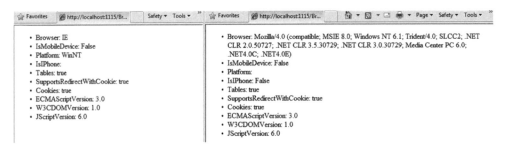

**Figure 7.4   The new provider populates the properties according to its code. You can see the default
provider using IE 8.0 on the left and the custom provider on the right.**

You can specify the provider you want to use in web.config, using this code:

```
<configuration>
  <system.web>
    <browserCaps
          provider="ASPNET4InPractice.MyBrowserProvider, App_Code" />
  </system.web>
</configuration>
```

Or, if you prefer, you can define the provider programmatically in global.asax, using the Application_Start event (or using an equivalent HttpModule):

C#:
```
void Application_Start(object sender, EventArgs e)
{
  HttpCapabilitiesBase.BrowserCapabilitiesProvider =
                                              new MyBrowserProvider();
}
```

VB:
```
Private Sub Application_Start(ByVal sender As Object, ByVal e As EventArgs)
  HttpCapabilitiesBase.BrowserCapabilitiesProvider =
                                              New MyBrowserProvider()
End Sub
```

You can define both standard and non-standard capabilities in your definition, and you can query them using a similar syntax:

```
<ul>
  <li>IsMobile device: <%=Request.Browser.IsMobileDevice %></li>
  <li>Platform: <%=Request.Browser.Platform %></li>
  <li>IsIPhone: <%=(Request.Browser["IsIPhone"] as string)%></li>
</ul>
```

As we already noted, you can see the result of all this code in figure 7.4. Note that you should express the values as strings, even if the capabilities are then exposed as a boolean. This behavior is probably caused by the first implementation in ASP.NET 1.0, where text is mandatory (because it was based on XML tags), and you need to address this problem if you want to make the code work.

DISCUSSION

Browser capabilities providers are super useful when you want to add new properties or provide a new way to define the default capabilities. In its simplest form, a provider is composed of few lines of code, but, as you might have noticed in the case of the new IsIPhone property, you can also define new properties based on code evaluation.

This solution has no drawbacks, because even the XML definition files are compiled. You don't need to worry about performance impacts—there aren't any!

Speaking of browser capabilities, the last scenario of this chapter addresses a common problem: how to validate your markup against the World Wide Web Consortium (W3C) Markup Validation Service.

TECHNIQUE 45   **Validating ASP.NET pages with the W3C validator**

Adaptive rendering can be both a joy and a pain. An example of the latter is certainly the absence of the W3C validator user agent from the default, recognized browsers. The W3C validator is a service from W3C (an international community that develops web standards) that aims to help web developers verify that their pages are using the right markup.

The fact that this validator isn't included can be a problem if you want to validate your page's markup, mainly because the output generated for an unknown browser is a conservative HTML 3.2.

PROBLEM

If you try to validate the markup generated by an ASP.NET page with the W3C validator, you'll probably have trouble. ASP.NET doesn't recognize the user agent and serves the least advanced markup that it can handle—HTML 3.2. This outcome isn't a problem per se, but it can become annoying if you want to validate the markup that's likely to be served to most of the browsers.

SOLUTION

As we've mentioned before, ASP.NET uses the browser capabilities to produce specific output for specific browsers. If you need to produce better markup by default, you can use the example in technique 44, where a unique behavior is applied to all the requests.

If you don't want to override the default provider, you can define a custom file definition. The W3C validator user agent contains W3C_Validator in the sent string. To identify it, all you need is to produce a rule, which is shown in the following listing.

Listing 7.8   The .browser file to support WC3 validator user agent

```
<browsers>
  <browser id="W3C_Validator" parentID="default">
    <identification>                                        RegEx intercepts
      <userAgent match="^W3C_Validator" />        ◁────┤ browser
    </identification>
    <capabilities>
      <capability name="browser" value="W3C Validator" />
      <capability name="ecmaScriptVersion" value="1.2" />
      <capability name="javascript" value="true" />
      <capability name="supportsCss" value="true" />
      <capability name="tables" value="true" />
      <capability name="w3cdomversion" value="1.0" />
      <capability name="tagWriter"                           Tag
              value="System.Web.UI.HtmlTextWriter" />  ◁────┤ writer
    </capabilities>
  </browser>
</browsers>
```

As you can see in this listing, by specifying HtmlTextWriter instead of Html32TextWriter, you can produce XHTML/HTML 4.01 markup, instead of HTML 3.2. The other properties will do the rest to enable DOM, JavaScript, and CSS support.

You can register the adapter globally or locally by saving this file as w3c.browser in your \App_Browsers\ folder.

DISCUSSION

ASP.NET 4.0 provides great flexibility in terms of markup generation and browser capabilities. You can leverage the new features to enrich your applications with less effort than in the past.

This last scenario is a great example of how you can add more features by simply understanding how the infrastructure works. Even if these scenarios don't fit in every application you'll build, they can help you when you need a bit more control.

7.3   *Summary*

Adaptive rendering and control adapters aren't entirely new to ASP.NET 4.0, but they're great examples of flexibility. You can control virtually any server control and alter the markup.

As you learned in this chapter, generating a new markup and substituting the original one is pain-free. All you need to do is write a control adapter, register it, and then ASP.NET automatically performs the choice. Sometimes this isn't easy (it depends on how complex the original control is), but the results are always interesting and worth the effort.

On the other hand, browser capabilities do have new features in version 4.0. Now you can completely substitute the entire engine to define your own set of definitions. When you want to force a particular feature in your output, this capability is priceless. ASP.NET uses the browser capabilities to drive adaptive rendering, and to provide better output when the user agent is recognized and a specific markup profile is loaded.

By controlling both adaptive rendering and browser capabilities, you can't only produce better markup. You can also help put into practice a better web by implementing correct support for web standards and at the same time promoting accessibility. You can even boost your old, existing applications by moving them to ASP.NET 4.0

Now that the story behind ASP.NET Web Forms is almost complete, we can take a look at how ASP.NET MVC lets you build the user interface in a way that's quite different. The next chapter will focus on how you can use ASP.NET MVC even if you're a novice developer, by leveraging your ASP.NET Web Forms skills.

Part 3

ASP.NET MVC

In part 2, we took a look at ASP.NET Web Forms. You might not know it, but using ASP.NET Web Forms isn't the only way to produce the UI; in part 3, we're going to investigate the option of building your UI with ASP.NET MVC.

ASP.NET MVC is a new option added in ASP.NET 3.5 SP1 and directly integrated into ASP.NET 4.0 as ASP.NET MVC 2.0. It's not the new Web Forms, but a completely different approach to solving the same problems. ASP.NET MVC lets you use the Model-View-Controller (MVC) pattern and is built with testability and great markup control in mind.

Chapter 8 gives you an introduction to ASP.NET MVC and shows the potential that this new toolkit offers when you're building the UI. You'll learn how to perform the basic actions that you're already acquainted with in ASP.NET Web Forms.

Chapter 9 covers customizing and extending ASP.NET MVC to unlock its full potential.

Introducing
ASP.NET MVC

8

This chapter covers
- Anatomy of the Model-View-Controller pattern
- Building your first page with ASP.NET MVC
- The routing infrastructure
- How to receive user input and validate it

ASP.NET, and specifically Web Forms, is an awesome technology for building software for the World Wide Web. When Microsoft introduced it back in 2002, it represented an absolute break from the past. It became possible to program for the web platform with a high-level infrastructure that provided abstractions typical of a smart client environment, like holding state across multiple requests or adopting an event-driven approach to handle what was going on with the UI.

ASP.NET grew in popularity in the developer community until some people began asking for more control over markup and the possibility of effectively testing web apps. These demands are the reason Microsoft began thinking about a new incarnation of ASP.NET technology, based on a simpler model that leverages a widely known pattern for the UI layer, called Model-View-Controller (MVC). This vision led to the birth of ASP.NET MVC.

Although ASP.NET MVC is still ASP.NET, its programming model is different than that of Web Forms, so it deserves its own chapter to introduce its basic concepts. We'll start with a simple project and then move toward more complex requirements and features.

This chapter will get you comfortable with ASP.NET MVC. You'll learn how to design your first pages and how the code you write fits into the overall MVC architecture. The last part of the chapter will look at handling user input, which involves building forms that get posted to the server and applying validation logic to the data coming from the browser. To better understand how all these concepts relate to a real-world scenario, we're going to use a real application, specifically a blog engine, as our practice field.

8.1   *A new way to build web applications*

ASP.NET uses a revolutionary, event-based model to program web applications. Building a page based on Web Forms is similar to building forms for desktop and client-server scenarios. These processes are similar because the framework tends to hide a lot of details that are intrinsic to the web platform from the developer, who can concentrate on the business problem his software is supposed to solve. Unfortunately, all these comforts have their drawbacks.

When you build enterprise applications, the only way to deal with a high level of complexity is to adopt a layered architecture, similar to the schema shown in figure 8.1. The complexity is spread across multiple, simpler components, separating UI concerns from business logic or data access strategies.

Even if you rigorously follow this path, what often happens is that handling user interactions quickly becomes tricky, and the UI code becomes cumbersome and difficult to maintain. ASP.NET Web Forms are no exception: despite the awesome stateful and event-driven programming model it provides, the risk of ending up having monolithic pages with methods running for hundreds lines of code is quite high.

During the last few years, the need for writing automated tests has gained popularity in the software industry. Developers want a test suite that ensures their code is correct and will do its job. Writing unit tests for the UI layer is unfortunately a tricky task if you have a Web Forms application because, as figure 8.2 shows, its logic is (usually) tightly coupled with the overall infrastructure and is sometimes embedded in the server controls.

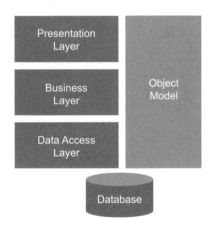

Figure 8.1   A typical 3-layer partitioning schema. The Presentation, Business Logic, and Data Access Layers have their own responsibilities and communicate with each other using a shared object model.

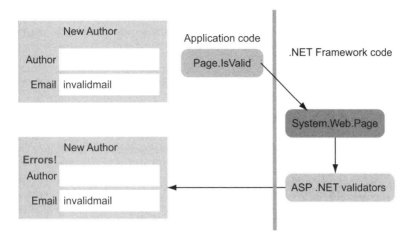

Figure 8.2 How form validation works in Web Forms. The user code checks only whether the page is valid; everything else is handled by .NET Framework code, based on validators on the page. Entry points for plugging in unit test code don't exist.

ASP.NET Web Forms deliberately hide the details of markup generation from the developer, who's just supposed to add a `GridView` control to obtain a tabular representation of the data without worrying about how the markup is rendered. It's a valuable feature, although interactions with graphic designers, who speak in terms of HTML nodes and CSS styles, tend to become more difficult.

This state of affairs recently pushed Microsoft in the direction of creating another platform, parallel to Web Forms. This platform proposes a different model to develop web applications, but still shares the same ASP.NET infrastructure. The platform is ASP.NET MVC.

8.1.1 The Model-View-Controller pattern

Model-View-Controller—we'll refer to it using its acronym MVC from now on—is a common and widely known pattern for designing the UI layer. It was first introduced in Smalltalk during the late 70s. Since then, it's gained a lot of popularity, becoming the pillar upon which web development platforms such as Ruby on Rails (and MonoRail, its unofficial porting for the .NET world), JavaServer Pages and, of course, ASP.NET MVC, are based. Figure 8.3 shows its conceptual schema.

The MVC pattern aims to reduce UI code complexity by splitting it into three

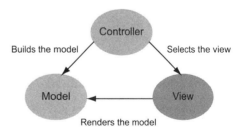

Figure 8.3 The Model-View-Controller pattern's conceptual schema. The controller handles a user request: first, it builds the model, which represents the data being shown on the UI, and then it forwards it to a view, which knows how to represent it.

components, in the same way a layered architecture does for the whole application logic. Each component has its own goals and responsibilities, which are described in table 8.1.

Table 8.1   Components of the MVC pattern

Name	Description
Model	This component acts as a data container and represents all the information you want to send back to the user. This information often comes in the form of plain .NET classes, exposing only properties and containing almost no logic at all. This form doesn't have to be strictly enforced, although it's a best practice when applications already have a business layer that encompasses the business logic.
View	The view is responsible for rendering the model and translating it into HTML. It contains only the specific logic needed to accomplish this task. For example, if the model contains a list of items, the associated view will probably have the logic to loop over them and repeat a particular HTML template for each one.
Controller	The controller acts as a bridge between the other two components. It inspects and validates the request coming from the browser, builds the model (perhaps leveraging BLL services), and forwards it to the appropriate view to generate the response.

For the rest of this chapter, we're going to deeply explore all these concepts and try to help you understand how you can take advantage of ASP.NET MVC to build a simple application. You'll learn how to simplify and rationalize the UI logic in a more structured design to keep code simple, maintainable, and testable.

8.2   *Your first experience with ASP.NET MVC*

The first release of ASP.NET MVC was available only as a separate download. Today, ASP.NET MVC 2 is officially part of ASP.NET 4.0. The corresponding project template is natively available in Visual Studio 2010, as figure 8.4 shows.

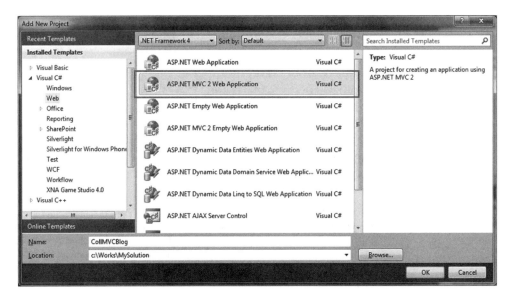

Figure 8.4   Creating a new ASP.NET MVC 2 application project from Visual Studio 2010

Figure 8.5 CoolMVCBlog's homepage mockup. You're going to achieve this result when you build your first ASP.NET MVC page.

To give you a better understanding of how ASP.NET MVC works, we're going to show you how to build a simple blog engine called CoolMVCBlog. The first feature you're going to deal with is its homepage, whose mockup is shown in figure 8.5. To simplify all the explanations, let's suppose that you already have an object model available, along with its ADO.NET Entity Framework data context.

Let's start examining the page components from the MVC pattern point of view.

TECHNIQUE 46   **The model**

Generally speaking, a model in ASP.NET MVC is a series of classes, preferably simple and possibly, without any logic, whose purpose is to hold all the data that's going to be on the page. It's probably the simplest part of the MVC pattern. Although ASP.NET MVC doesn't impose any specific rules on how to design it, neither does Visual Studio 2010 provide facilities to guide you while building it. Let's take a look at how to build a model for CoolMVCBlog's homepage.

PROBLEM

We need to build a proper model for CoolMVCBlog's homepage, reusing our application's object model whenever possible.

SOLUTION

When developers build layered applications, they often use an object model to represent the various business entities. This model might be generated using ADO.NET Entity Framework's designer, as you learned in chapter 3.

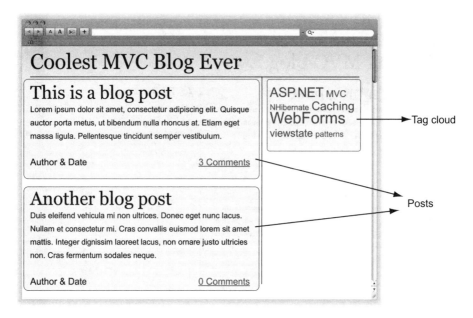

Figure 8.6   CoolMVCBlog homepage revisited. Notice how every dynamic homepage component maps to a distinct model object.

The model in the MVC pattern has a slightly different meaning. An application object model is made of entities that have a business purpose, like customers, bills, or orders. On the other hand, an MVC's model strictly relates to what you're going to show to the UI, which often results in a composition of both business entities and interface-specific objects. In figure 8.6, we'll consider once again the homepage mockup that you saw in figure 8.5.

This time we've highlighted the components that contribute to our page. Putting it all together, we can represent them with a `HomepageModel` class like the one shown in the following listing and store it in the Models subfolder.

Listing 8.1   Homepage model

C#:
```
public class HomepageModel
{
  public List<Post> Posts { get; set; }          ❶ Model class
  public List<TagCloudItem> TagCloudItems { get; set; }    for homepage
}

public class TagCloudItem                         ❷ Item belonging
{                                                    to TagCloud
  public int CategoryId { get; set; }
  public string Description { get; set; }
  public string Size { get; set; }
}
```

```
public class TagCloudService
{
  public List<TagCloudItem> GetTagCloudItems()
  {
    List<TagCloudItem> res =
      from p in context.PostSet // more Linq code here...

    return res;
  }
}
```

❸ Service to calculate TagCloud

VB:

```
Public Class HomepageModel
  Public Property Posts As List(Of Post)
  Public Property TagCloudItems As List(Of TagCloudItem)
End Class

Public Class TagCloudItem
  Public Property CategoryId As Integer
  Public Property Description As String
  Public Property Size As String
End Class

Public Class TagCloudService
  Public Function GetTagCloudItems() As List(Of TagCloudItem)

    Dim res as List(Of TagCloudItem) =
      From p In context.PostSets ' more Linq code here...

    Return res
  End Function

End Class
```

❶ Model class for homepage

❷ Item belonging to TagCloud

❸ Service to calculate TagCloud

As you can see, we used our domain model's `Post` entity ❶. We did that because it exactly matches what we're going to show on the page. Our model also contains a new class, named `TagCloudItem` ❷, which is a concept that belongs strictly to our Presentation Layer. This class isn't part of our domain model, and it doesn't have a corresponding table on the database, but it's created using an ad-hoc LINQ To Entities query in `TagCloudService` ❸, which is also part of our MVC model.

> ### Wasn't our model supposed to just hold data?
> The model we just introduced isn't as anemic as we previously indicated it would be. It exposes a service and executes a query to retrieve the `TagCloudItems`. You need to do this every time you have to deal with classes that belong only to the Presentation Layer or when the application is simple and doesn't have a BLL on its own. In these scenarios, exposing services at the model level results in code that's centralized in a single place and that's easily reusable.

DISCUSSION

In the last example, you built a model for CoolMVCBlog's homepage, which holds a list of posts and a tag cloud. Your model also contains a service that queries the database to retrieve and calculate the tag cloud composition, with the purpose of having this UI logic centralized in a single specific location.

When you're building a page in ASP.NET MVC, the first thing you should take care of is creating a model for it, which is a bunch of classes that represent the information you're going to show the user. This process is significantly different from what you do with ASP.NET Web Forms. When you're using Web Forms, you're pushed to think in terms of controls (grids, buttons, textboxes), but ASP.NET MVC takes into greater account the nature of the data that will populate the page.

The model is also the preferred entry point for storing high-level services that respond to UI-specific needs. As you just saw in this example of building the tag cloud, when you need to introduce additional logic to what is already provided by the BLL (or if there isn't a BLL at all) the best way to proceed is to create a service class at the model level.

In the next section, you'll see how these classes and services are involved in the process of handling a browser request. This process introduces the next component of the MVC pattern: the controller.

TECHNIQUE 47   **The controller**

When an ASP.NET MVC application receives an HTTP request, the framework must execute some code to generate the response. This concept is better expressed in the MVC idiom by saying that the framework handles the request by selecting the proper controller. The logic that does this is contained within an action method, which the runtime automatically invokes based on the particular URL the user requested.

To be able to show our blog's homepage to the user, we have to build a controller class. The controller class will take care of generating a valid instance for the model we designed in the previous section and forwarding it to a view.

PROBLEM

We want to build a controller to handle all the requests that come to our application's homepage.

SOLUTION

Our blog engine still lacks a controller that can handle homepage visualization. To fill this gap, you can create a new one. Right-click the Controllers folder (the location where all the application controllers conventionally reside) and select the Add Controller option; the dialog box shown in figure 8.7 opens. When you choose the controller name, you should follow the ASP.NET MVC naming convention and always terminate it with the -Controller suffix.

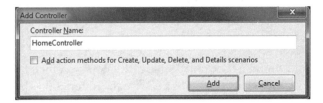

Figure 8.7   The Add Controller dialog box in Visual Studio 2010. Notice how the proposed name follows the controller naming convention. This dialog box can optionally generate methods for typical controller actions.

When you click the Add button, Visual Studio creates a class that inherits from the `Controller` base class and contains an empty method named `Index`. This method is called an action method and represents the actual handler of a request. In fact, as you'll see shortly, ASP.NET MVC associates a URL to a controller/action pair that then executes to generate the response; this process happens via the routing infrastructure. The code you need to show the homepage is in the following listing.

Listing 8.2 HomeController and its Index action

C#:

```csharp
public class HomeController : Controller
{
  public ActionResult Index()
  {
    using (var ctx = new BlogModelContainer())
    {
      var model = new HomepageModel();
      model.Posts = ctx.PostSet
        .OrderByDescending(p => p.DatePublished)
        .Take(3)
        .ToList();

      var service = new TagCloudService(ctx);
      model.TagCloudItems = service.GetTagCloudItems();

      return View(model);
    }
  }
}
```

❶ Fetch latest posts

❷ TagCloud composition via **TagCloudService**

VB:

```vb
Public Class HomeController
  Inherits Controller

  Public Function Index() As ActionResult
    Using ctx As New BlogModelContainer

      Dim model As New HomepageModel()
      model.Posts = ctx.PostSets.
        OrderBy(Function(p) p.DatePublished).
        Take(3).
        ToList()

      Dim service = New TagCloudService(ctx)
      model.TagCloudItems = service.GetTagCloudItems()

      Return View(model)
    End Using
  End Function
End Class
```

❶ Fetch latest posts

❷ TagCloud composition via **TagCloudService**

This method is pretty straightforward. It does nothing more than build a new `HomepageModel` instance and populate its two properties, `Posts` and `TagCloudItems`. The method populates the first property by executing a LINQ to Entities query ❶ (which retrieves the last three posts) and the second one by using `TagCloudService` ❷.

Web application code made simple

Although the controller we just made is part of a simple example, it highlights a fundamental peculiarity of ASP.NET MVC: the application code is intrinsically simpler than in Web Forms and is absolutely decoupled from any infrastructure. Our controller is a plain .NET class that exposes a method; the controller base class just provides some helpers. For this reason, we can create a console application and manually invoke an action to check whether it works as expected (or, better yet, we can easily create unit tests to validate our UI features).

The `Index` action ends by invoking the `View` method, passing the model as a parameter. In turn, the `View` method generates a `ViewResult` return value.

DISCUSSION

In this example, we built a controller, along with its action, to create a new instance of a `Homepage` class and then send it to a view, using the `View` method. An action doesn't always end with this kind of result. ASP.NET MVC doesn't impose any restriction on actions signatures, and the controller base class itself provides several helper methods to generate different response types. The possible results are listed in table 8.2.

Table 8.2   Results that an action can return

Name	Description
`ContentResult`	Represents a user-defined content result. This class allows you to manually specify the content encoding and type.
`FileResult`	The base class for sending a binary file to the browser. Its three inherited classes identify this file starting from a path (`FilePathResult`), a stream (`FileStreamResult`), or a byte array (`FileContentResult`).
`JavaScriptResult`	Represents JavaScript code sent back to the browser.
`JsonResult`	Uses a JavaScript Object Notation (JSON) serializer to serialize an object and send its representation as a response.
`RedirectResult`	Redirects the browser to the given URL.
`RedirectToRouteResult`	Builds a URL using the route settings and redirects the browser to it.
`ViewResult`	Uses a view to render a model and sends the HTML to the browser.

We've managed to build an object model for the data that we want to show in the homepage. We've also added some logic to load it from a database in response to a request coming from a browser. If we stopped here, you wouldn't be able to see anything in the browser because there's still one component missing for our application to actually produce HTML. That component is the view, which is the topic of the next section.

TECHNIQUE 48   The view

The view is the MVC component that's responsible for building the actual HTML and sending it to the browser. In the default ASP.NET MVC implementation, view data is stored in .aspx or .ascx files similar to the Web Form's files. They're contained inside a particular folder structure, which has a Views folder as the root and a list of subfolders, similar to the one shown in figure 8.8.

Each subfolder has a name that matches the name of a controller and contains all the views owned by that controller. Besides that, there's a Shared folder to which all the views shared by two or more controllers and the application master pages belong.

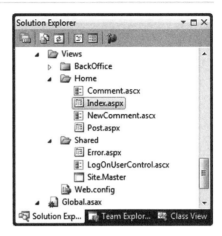

Figure 8.8   Views folder structure. The Views folder has a subfolder for each controller that stores its views, plus a Shared subfolder to contain all the shared views.

PROBLEM

We must build a view to render CoolMVCBlog's homepage that will accept an instance of HomepageModel and render the HTML. It must be the default view for the HomepageController's Index action.

SOLUTION

As we stated in technique 47, a ViewResult isn't the sole kind of response an action can return, but it's the most common one. Visual Studio provides a facility to automatically create a view from within an action code. All you have to do is right-click its code and select the Add View option from the contextual menu (see figure 8.9).

Figure 8.9   Adding a new view to the project is made easy by this dialog box provided by Visual Studio 2010.

The dialog box in figure 8.9 provides the following options to customize how the view is created:

- The master page you might want to use
- Whether the new view must be a partial view (more on this shortly)
- The model class the new view must be based on, if you want to create a strongly typed view

The following listing contains the code needed to properly render an instance of HomepageModel.

Listing 8.3   Homepage view code

C#:

```
<asp:Content ContentPlaceHolderID="MainContent"
            runat="server">
  <div class="content">
    <% foreach (var i in this.Model.Posts) { %>
      <h2>
        <%: Html.ActionLink(i.Title, "Post",         ❶ Link to post's
new { Id = i.Id }) %>                                    page
      </h2>
      <div><%: i.Text %></div>                       ❷ Show post
    <% } %>                                             content
  </div>
  <% Html.RenderPartial("TagCloud", this.Model.TagCloudItems); %>
</asp:Content>
```

VB:

```
<asp:Content ContentPlaceHolderID="MainContent"
            runat="server">
  <div class="content">
    <% For Each i in me.Model.Posts %>
      <h2>
        <%: Html.ActionLink(i.Title, "Post",         ❶ Link to post's
New With {.id = i.Id})%>                                 page
      </h2>
      <div>
        <%: i.Text %>                                ❷ Show post
      </div>                                            content
    <% Next%>
  </div>
  <% Html.RenderPartial("TagCloud", this.Model.TagCloudItems) %>
</asp:Content>
```

For those of you with experience building ASP or PHP applications, this code might seem familiar because it's mostly HTML markup mixed with C# or VB.NET. This similarity is apparent only because the view code contains just the logic needed to render the model. For example, the code repeats a specific template using a foreach block, which accesses the model using the Model property and iterates on every post it contains. You have absolute control over the generated markup (as opposed to what you have with Web Forms), without hiding it behind the server controls abstraction.

In our design, every post title must be a link to open the specific post page point-ing to a URL that follows the */Home/Post/postId* pattern. Although it's obviously possi-ble to manually construct that link, the code in ➊ uses the ActionLink HTML helper and dynamically composes the link based on routing settings (we'll cover this topic in section 8.3).

Last of all, the <%: ... %> syntax used in ➋ allows us to show that any special char-acters that the post body contains are automatically encoded, thus avoiding cross-site scripting (XSS) attacks. The view engine leverages the provider-based encoding archi-tecture of ASP.NET that you saw in chapter 4.

Am I allowed to add Web Forms server controls?

As you've already seen, ASP.NET MVC and Web Forms share the same ASP.NET in-frastructure as their basis; in fact, we've been able to reuse a lot of ASP.NET con-cepts, like pages to build the views, master pages, and ContentPlaceHolders. When you're creating a view, you can also use Web Forms server controls, as you'll see in the next chapter, although generally speaking this isn't an advisable approach. You lose absolute control over the generated markup, which is one key point in favor of ASP.NET MVC.

The tag cloud is part of the UI that will likely be part of many pages of our blog appli-cation, so it's worth building as a reusable component. In this case, we can render it via the RenderPartial method, which invokes a TagCloud view and passes the list of TagCloudItems.

TagCloud is a *partial view*, which is a componentized version of a particular markup. You can create a partial view by selecting Create A Partial View in the Add View dialog box shown in figure 8.9. The TagCloud code is in the following listing.

Listing 8.4   Content of TagCloud.ascx partial view

C#:
```
<%@ Control Language="C#"
    Inherits="ViewUserControl<IEnumerable<TagCloudItem>>" %>

<div class="cloud">
  <div class="cloud_title">
    Tag cloud
  </div>
  <% foreach (var i in this.Model) { %>
    <%= Html.ActionLink(i.Description, "Tag",
          new { Id = i.CategoryId },
          new { style = "font-size: " + i.Size,
                @class = "cloud_item" }) %>
  <% } %>
</div>
```

VB:
```
<%@ Control Language="VB"
    Inherits="ViewUserControl(Of IEnumerable (Of TagCloudItem))" %>
```

```
<div class="cloud">
  <div class="cloud_title">
    Tag cloud
  </div>
  <%For Each i In Me.Model%>
    <%= Html.ActionLink(i.Description, "Tag",
                  New With {.Id = i.CategoryId},
                  New With {.style = "font-size: " + i.Size,
                            .class = "cloud_item"})%>
  <%Next%>
</div>
```

The tag cloud template is just a bunch of links, again built using the `ActionLink` method. The size of this template is dynamically modified on the basis of the `Tag-CloudItem.Size` property.

DISCUSSION

Designing views in ASP.NET MVC is just a matter of combining markup and code to build intelligent templates able to render instances of model objects. You can leverage special methods, called HTML helpers, which encapsulate some useful logic. For example, the `ActionLink` method calculates a link based on the application routing settings. Partial views, on the other hand, provide the ability to build reusable components, which are the best way to ensure that the same markup is rendered consistently across the different pages of the application.

Successfully building the view concludes our first overview of the main components of the MVC pattern, but this isn't enough for our application to work properly. We still have to link URLs and actions together. Creating these links is called URL routing. In the next section, we'll delve into how it works in an ASP.NET MVC application.

8.3   Routing in ASP.NET MVC

So far, we've managed to build a controller class that incorporates the logic needed to display the homepage. In fact, its `Index` action is able to create a model instance and use some services to populate it; then it selects a view that translates all those bits into HTML.

We're still missing the trigger that executes that action. A user starts a request by typing our blog's URL into their browser, but there must be some additional logic that links that URL to the actual C# code you just finished writing. Enter URL routing.

8.3.1   Basic routing concepts in ASP.NET MVC

We introduced the concept of routing in chapter 4, when you saw how easy it is to plug it into a Web Forms application to map human-readable URLs to the pages. Thanks to the pluggable architecture of its infrastructure, routing is so flexible that it can be easily expanded to support different situations, such as a Dynamic Data controls-based website or ASP.NET MVC applications.

In ASP.NET MVC, routing plays a central role during the handling of an HTTP request. It connects the URL coming from the browser to the specific controller and

---

Routing was originally only an ASP.NET MVC peculiarity

Routing in ASP.NET was originally part of the first release of ASP.NET MVC. It signaled a break from the past, giving the URLs a functional meaning instead of just being a physical path. Routing gained a lot of popularity among developers and was easily portable to Web Forms, too, thanks to its open architecture. The ASP.NET team decided to promote it as one of the core features in ASP.NET 3.5 SP1. Today, it remains one of ASP.NET MVC's pillars, as you'll see.

---

the action, which are going to be executed to fulfill the request. A valid URL for an ASP.NET MVC application, by default, follows the RESTful (Representational State Transfer-compliant) schema:

```
http://myDomain/{Controller}/{Action}/{id}
```

This structure allows the runtime to easily locate the resources needed to handle the request, while at the same time giving your URLs a meaning that's easy to understand. For example, a URL like http://myDomain/Posts/Show/4 maps to the Posts-Controller controller (specifically to its Show action); the value 4 will be given to its id parameter.

Routes are usually registered in the global.asax file during the Application.Start event. The typical routes configuration is shown in the following listing.

Listing 8.5   Registering URL routes in global.asax

C#:
```
public static void RegisterRoutes(RouteCollection routes)
{                                                                    ❶ Ignored by
  routes.IgnoreRoute("{resource}.axd/{*pathInfo}");          ◁──┘      routing

  routes.MapRoute(
    "Default",
    "{controller}/{action}/{id}",
    new
    {
      controller = "Home",
      action = "Index",
      id = UrlParameter.Optional
    }
  );
}
```

VB:
```
Shared Sub RegisterRoutes(ByVal routes As RouteCollection)
  routes.IgnoreRoute("{resource}.axd/{*pathInfo}")
                                                                     ❶ Ignored by
  routes.MapRoute( _                                         ◁──┘      routing
    "Default", _
    "{controller}/{action}/{id}", _
    New With {
      .controller = "Home",
```

```
        .action = "Index",
        .id = UrlParameter.Optional} _
  )
End Sub
```

We can define a route configuration using the `routes.MapRoute` method ❶, providing a name (`Default` in our example) and a schema. The schema uses the reserved `{controller}` and `{action}` tags to identify which portion of the URL maps to the controller and action name, respectively. This method also accepts an anonymous type as a third parameter, which provides default values for the variables in the schema in case they're not present in the requested URL.

Routing doesn't necessarily affect every request. For example, the ASP.NET runtime uses the .axd extension to retrieve resources from assemblies. Requests to this kind of URL must not be redirected to an ASP.NET MVC controller, which is why we're using the `routing.IgnoreRoute` method at the top of the routes mapping section, before defining any actual route.

We can obviously alter routing settings to inject our customized rules. For example, if we wanted the URL of a search page to be something like http://myDomain/Posts/August/2008, we could add the new mapping to global.asax, as shown in the following listing.

Listing 8.6   Custom URL route for post search

C#:
```csharp
public static void RegisterRoutes(RouteCollection routes)
{
  routes.IgnoreRoute("{resource}.axd/{*pathInfo}");

  routes.MapRoute(
    "PostsByMonth",
    "Posts/{month}/{year}",
    new { controller = "Posts", action = "Search" });

  routes.MapRoute(
    "Default",
    "{controller}/{action}/{id}",
    new
    {
      controller = "Home",
      action = "Index",
      id = UrlParameter.Optional
    }
  );
}
```
❶ Additional route rule

VB:
```vb
Shared Sub RegisterRoutes(ByVal routes As RouteCollection)
  routes.IgnoreRoute("{resource}.axd/{*pathInfo}")

  routes.MapRoute( _
    "PostsByMonth", _
    "Posts/{month}/{year}", _
    New With { controller = "Posts", action = "Search" })
```
❶ Additional route rule

```
    routes.MapRoute( _
        "Default", _
        "{controller}/{action}/{id}", _
        New With {
            .controller = "Home",
            .action = "Index",
            .id = UrlParameter.Optional} _
        )
End Sub
```

In this code, all we did was add a new mapping ❶ called `PostsByMonth`, using the same `routes.MapRoute` method you've seen before. The URL schema has just two placeholders, month and year; controller and action names (`Posts` and `Search`) are provided by the routing defaults.

> ### Be careful with routing definitions order
> A real-world application typically defines multiple routing schemas. The order you use when declaring them plays a key role in how requests are handled. When the routing engine looks for the schema that's compliant with the request's URL, these schemas are evaluated by the definition order. That's the reason was in first position in listing 8.5; otherwise, if a URL was valid for, it would be handled by ASP.NET MVC, whether or not it contained the .axd extension.

When you're building a view, if you want to create a link that points to another page, you can use the `ActionLink` or `RouteLink` HTML helpers, shown in the following listing.

Listing 8.7 HTML helpers for creating links to other controllers

C#:
```
<%: this.Html.ActionLink(
        "Go back to Homepage",                    <--- Link text
        "Index",
        "Home") %>

<%: this.Html.RouteLink(
        "Search July 2010",
        "PostsByMonth",
        new { month = "July", year = 2010})%>
```

VB:
```
<%: this.Html.ActionLink( _
        "Go back to Homepage", _              <--- Link text
        "Index",
        "Home") %>

<%: this.Html.RouteLink( _
        "Search July 2010", _
        "PostsByMonth", _
        New With { .month = "July", .year = 2010})%>
```

You can use either `ActionLink` or `RouteLink`, depending on how you want to reference the linked page. `ActionLink` works with the action (`Index`) and controller (`Home`) names and exposes explicit parameters for them. `RouteLink` talks in terms of routes and routing variables.

Whichever one you choose, take a moment to realize how powerful this way of referencing pages is. You're not forced to hardcode URLs in your views because they're dynamically built using the routing settings and automatically recalculated if these settings change in the future.

Routes are a great and effective way to improve URL readability. ASP.NET MVC natively sets up a routing scheme that avoids query string parameters where possible, giving the application URLs a static look. Unfortunately, as applications grow in size, routing definitions quickly tend to become a maintenance nightmare. You can mitigate this problem by partitioning the projects in functional sections, called Areas.

TECHNIQUE 49   **Partitioning using Areas**

Enterprise applications are often made of different modules, each one providing its own pages and services. These modules cooperate together to implement complex business logic. Let's think about software that manages orders and deliveries for products. As figure 8.10 shows, you're most likely going to split it up into the following modules:

- A master module that stores data about products and clients
- An orders management module that keeps track of and records orders placed by customers
- A billing module
- A delivery tracking module

Integrating all these modules into a single, monolithic ASP.NET MVC application could be tricky. You could easily end up with dozens of controllers (and hundreds of related views), all mixed up in the same folder structure. The concept of project *Areas* can help you handle this scenario in a more structured way.

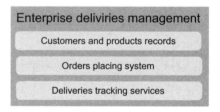

Figure 8.10   An enterprise application often consists of many modules interacting together to implement complex business logic.

PROBLEM

You have an application that is composed of different functional sections. You want to keep them separated from each other, so that your project structure reflects the logical partitioning of the application itself.

SOLUTION

When you have a set of functionalities that all together implement a single, distinct logical module of your application, encompassing them within a separated area can be a good way to rationalize how your ASP.NET MVC project is designed. The first step

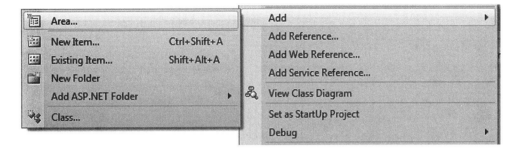

Figure 8.11   The project's contextual menu lets you add a new Area to the project.

toward this goal is to add a new Area to the project, using the contextual menu shown in figure 8.11.

After you give a name to the new Area, Visual Studio 2010 creates a corresponding folder in your project that internally replicates the subfolder structure typical of ASP.NET MVC. If you add an Area called Backoffice, the result that you'll get is similar to the one in figure 8.12.

Now you've got a new container available for the application's backoffice module. Controllers, modules, and views that implement the logic for inserting new posts to our blog application are kept separated from the front office ones, resulting in a more consistent and better-designed project

Figure 8.12   When Visual Studio 2010 creates the Backoffice Area, it replicates the folder structure typical of an ASP.NET MVC project.

structure. This separation doesn't happen just at the file level; Visual Studio 2010 automatically stores the classes in separate namespaces, so our application's object model reflects the logical partitioning we've just made.

Our new Backoffice Area also has its own routing rules, which are stored in the BackofficeAreaRegistration.cs file, which you can see in figure 8.12. The following listing shows its content.

Listing 8.8   BackofficeAreaRegistration content

C#:

```
public class BackofficeAreaRegistration : AreaRegistration
{
  public override string AreaName
  {
```

1 Area name registration

```
    get
    {
      return "Backoffice";
    }
  }

  public override void RegisterArea(AreaRegistrationContext context)
  {
    context.MapRoute(
      "Backoffice_default",
      "Backoffice/{controller}/{action}/{id}",
      new { action = "Index", id = UrlParameter.Optional }
    );
  }
}
```

① Area name registration

② Area-specific routing rules

VB:

```
Public Class BackofficeAreaRegistration
  Inherits AreaRegistration

  Public Overrides ReadOnly Property AreaName() As String
    Get
      Return "Backoffice"
    End Get
  End Property

  Public Overrides Sub RegisterArea( _
      ByVal context As AreaRegistrationContext)
    context.MapRoute( _
      "Backoffice_default", _
      "Backoffice/{controller}/{action}/{id}", _
      New With {.action = "Index", .id = UrlParameter.Optional} _
    )
  End Sub
End Class
```

① Area name registration

② Area-specific routing rules

BackofficeAreaRegistration inherits from the base AreaRegistration class and overrides its AreaName **①** and RegisterArea **②** members to provide the Area name and the routing rules. This code is automatically executed when the application starts, as shown in the following listing.

Listing 8.9   Global.asax registers all areas when the application starts

C#:

```
protected void Application_Start()
{
  AreaRegistration.RegisterAllAreas();

  RegisterRoutes(RouteTable.Routes);
}
```

VB:

```
Sub Application_Start()
  AreaRegistration.RegisterAllAreas()

  RegisterRoutes(RouteTable.Routes)
End Sub
```

The `Application_Start` event handler invokes a static `RegisterAllAreas` method, which dynamically explores the application assemblies, looking for classes that inherit from `AreaRegistration` to execute their `RegisterArea` method.

Can areas be componentized?

Areas are a great way to rationalize the application structure by splitting it into modules, but they belong strictly to the project where they were defined. Even so, sometimes applications can share some functional modules. Consider a security module that provides controller and logic to register users, lets them authenticate themselves, or lets an administrator manage roles.

Unfortunately, ASP.NET MVC areas can't be stored directly in a class library and referenced by many applications. Developers are forced to copy the same code over and over. A possible solution to that problem is called Portable Areas, which is part of the MvcContrib side project. You can download source and binaries and read the documentation at its Codeplex web site (http://mvccontrib.codeplex.com/).

DISCUSSION

When applications are composed of many functional modules, it might be worth organizing them into specific Areas so that you'll have a more maintainable and structured ASP.NET MVC project. When you're creating an Area, Visual Studio 2010 automatically sets up the folder structure and the code to register it at application startup.

Each application Area comes with its own controllers, models, and views, and has specific routing rules that you can customize to fit your needs.

8.4   Accepting user input

Congratulations! You've built your first page in ASP.NET MVC. Your application can respond to a browser that's requesting its homepage and show the last blog posts. These requests are called GET requests; they always originate from a user typing an address into the browser.

A real-world web application is also made of forms in which someone can insert data and that result in POST requests to your web server. The overall approach in ASP.NET MVC isn't different from what happens for GETs: an action receives some parameters from the request and executes the business logic. In this section, we're going to explore how this process occurs in ASP.NET MVC and which facilities you can leverage to build forms easily.

TECHNIQUE 50   **Handling user input at the controller level**

Let's imagine you want to let your CoolMVCBlog readers write comments on blog posts. When the user asks to view a single post, the corresponding view must provide a form to accept their input. Assume that you've already defined a Post.aspx view to specify how a post is rendered. Now, to better isolate the markup of the form from the

First post

Lorem ipsum dolor sit amet, consectetur adipiscing elit. Nunc ultrices accumsan pretium. Aliquam luctus odio leo, eget vehicula orci. Aenean dui nisl, rutrum in consectetur eget, interdum vitae sem. Donec condimentum porttitor nunc, sed tempus mi pellentesque ultrices. Etiam tortor nunc, consequat in porta ut, euismod id odio. Phasellus suscipit tellus nec leo auctor in laoreet felis mattis. Nunc eget nulla vitae neque vehicula dignissim. Suspendisse placerat mattis elit, sit amet mattis dui lobortis sit amet. Nullam ligula sapien, semper nec venenatis at, blandit malesuada felis. Nunc nec tortor mattis dolor sollicitudin vehicula sit amet at nisl. Fusce id tincidunt orci.

No comments posted yet...   **NewComment.ascx**

Author	
Email	
WebSite	
Text	

[Post comment]

Figure 8.13   A complete look at the Post.aspx view. This view leverages a NewComment.ascx partial view to render the comment input form.

rest of the page, we're going to build an additional partial view for it, like the one shown in figure 8.13.

As you can see in the next listing, Post.aspx internally uses a partial view, named NewComment.ascx, to encapsulate the form template within a discrete and reusable component.

Listing 8.10   Post.aspx referencing NewComment.ascx partial view

C#:

```
<asp:Content ContentPlaceHolderID="MainContent" runat="server">
  <div class="content">
    .. markup here ..
    <% Html.RenderPartial("NewComment",
       new CoolMVCBlog.Models.Comment()); %>
  </div>
</asp:Content>
```
❶ HTML helper renders the partial view

VB:

```
<asp:Content ContentPlaceHolderID="MainContent" runat="server">
  <div class="content">
    .. markup here ..
    <% Html.RenderPartial("NewComment",
       New CoolMVCBlog.Models.Comment()) %>
  </div>
</asp:Content>
```
❶ HTML helper renders the partial view

Because NewComment works on a model of Comment type, the Post.aspx view in this listing renders it by providing an empty instance ❶. Let's get started on the process that will retrieve the model, along with its values, when the form is posted to the server. Then we'll use it to actually attach a new comment to the original post.

PROBLEM

You want to give your readers the chance to send comments to blog posts by using a form. This data must be handled by a controller that adds it to the post's comments collection.

SOLUTION

As we've mentioned, we want to encapsulate the form to input the new comment within a reusable component. To do this, we created a strongly typed partial view that provides an editing template for a Comment instance. We won't provide the complete listing here (its code is very repetitive), but the next listing is worth a look because of a couple of interesting points that we'll discuss.

Listing 8.11 NewComment.ascx partial view

C#:

```
<%@ Control Language="C#" ... %>

<% using (Html.BeginForm()) {%>

  <div class="editor-label">
     <%: Html.LabelFor(model => model.Author) %>
  </div>
  <div class="editor-field">
     <%: Html.EditorFor(model => model.Author)%>
     <%: Html.ValidationMessageFor(model => model.Author, "*") %>
  </div>
  <div class="clear"></div>

  ... more fields here ...

  <div class="editor-label"> </div>
  <div class="editor-field">
     <input type="submit" value="Post comment" />
  </div>
  <div class="clear"></div>
<% } %>
```

VB:

```
<%@ Control Language="VB" ... %>

<% Using Html.BeginForm()%>

  <div class="editor-label">
    <%: Html.LabelFor(Function(model) model.Author)%>
  </div>
  <div class="editor-field">
    <%: Html.EditorFor(Function(model) model.Author)%>
    <%: Html.ValidationMessageFor(Function(model) model.Author, "*")%>
  </div>
  <div class="clear"></div>

  ... more fields here ...

  <div class="editor-label"> </div>
  <div class="editor-field">
    <input type="submit" value="Post comment" />
```

```
  </div>
  <div class="clear"></div>
<% End Using%>
```

Every input control in an HTML form must reside within a <FORM> tag, which posts to some URL. ASP.NET MVC provides you with an HTML helper called `BeginForm` to do this. You can use `BeginForm` with a `using` statement that will encompass the form's content. Then, every field we want to edit gets rendered with a `LabelFor`, an `EditorFor`, and a `ValidationMessageFor` HTML helper, which leverage a type-safe, lambda-expression-based syntax to identify the property they're referring to. ASP.NET MVC can automatically infer which kind of editor is optimal for particular data by looking at its type.

Why do editors for string properties render differently?

Listing 8.11 uses the same `EditorFor` syntax for every field; however, if you look back at the screenshot in figure 8.13, you might notice how the same syntax for two string properties (for example `Author` and `Text`) renders two different editors, a `TextBox` and a multiline `TextArea`, respectively. This magic happens thanks to the ASP.NET MVC templated editor infrastructure, which we're going to cover in detail in chapter 9.

Finally, a submit button gives the user the chance to post the form back to the server (in our case, back to the same URL), which triggers the action that's shown in the following listing.

Listing 8.12   HomeController action that handles the POST request

C#:

```
[HttpPost]
public ActionResult Post(int id, Comment newComment)        ●❶ Accepting Comment instance
{
  using (var ctx = new BlogModelContainer())
  {
    var post = ctx.PostSet
      .Include("Comments").Where(p => p.Id == id).Single();

    // .. more code here ..

    newComment.Date = DateTime.Now;
    post.Comments.Add(newComment);                           ❷ Saving new comment
    ctx.SaveChanges();

    return RedirectToAction(
      "Post",
      new { id = id });                                      ❸ Redirecting to GET action
  }
}
```

VB:

```
<HttpPost()>
Public Function Post(                                        ❶ Accepting Comment instance
```

```
  ByVal id As Integer, ByVal newComment As Comment) As ActionResult
  Using ctx = New BlogModelContainer()
    Dim thePost = ctx.PostSets.
      Include("Comments").
      Where(Function(p) p.Id = id).
      Single()

    ' .. more code here ..

    newComment.Date = DateTime.Now
    thePost.Comments.Add(newComment)
    ctx.SaveChanges()

    Return Me.RedirectToAction(
      "Post", New With {.id = id })
  End Using
End Function
```

❷ Saving new comment

❸ Redirecting to GET action

The `HttpPostAttribute` instructs the framework to use this action only in response to a POST type request. This method (among others) accepts a parameter of type `Comment` ❶, which holds all the data coming from the browser. The method's implementation is definitely trivial; it just needs to add that object to the post comments collection ❷ and then save all the changes. Everything ends with a redirection to the same page, which prevents a page refresh from triggering another insert ❸.

How does that Comment instance get populated?

Having a `Comment` instance among the `Post` arguments gives us the chance to completely ignore what's going on under the hood. Under there is an array of strings contained within the request's form. Thanks to the editors we used to create the input form and an infrastructural object called *Model Binder*, ASP.NET MVC is able to recreate the object this form represents.

This level of abstraction is exceptional and is also pluggable to inject customized binders to handle different kinds of data. In this way, you can work with strongly typed, high-level objects. We'll delve deeper into that topic in the next chapter.

DISCUSSION

ASP.NET MVC has the awesome peculiarity of letting you write controller methods without having to worry too much about the fact that you're actually handling web requests. Your methods interact with the web infrastructure in terms of strongly typed objects, and POST requests aren't an exception.

In this scenario, we managed to write an action that gets activated in response to a form posted to the server. This action can also reconstruct an instance of a `Comment` object and insert it into the database, as figure 8.14 summarizes.

As far as building the corresponding view goes, the effort required is trivial thanks to editor templates. These templates help you build forms by simply specifying the model properties you want to edit; the infrastructure then takes care of rendering the proper HTML element based on the data type.

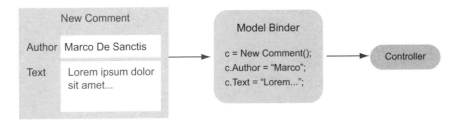

**Figure 8.14   When a form is posted to the server, a model binder uses its content to build a
new `Comment` instance. This object is then used as a parameter for the controller.**

To get back to our website—some functionality is still missing. We don't actually check
the user input for correctness. Some data is mandatory (think about the comment's
body) or requires a particular format to be considered valid (like the email field).
Let's see how we can take care of all this, too.

TECHNIQUE 51   **Validating posted data**

Whenever data comes from the outside world, you should never trust it. This rule is a
key to writing good applications. You need to validate incoming data not only because
of the security impact (we'll take care of those later on in the book), but because the
data might be invalid, based on how your application is supposed to work.

To deal with a new comment posted by the user, we need to follow some integrity
rules. We have a business requirement to trace the author's email address, so we
designed our database schema to have a not-nullable column in which to store it. In
addition, we definitely don't want to allow any comments that don't include one.

Every evolved web development framework provides an infrastructure that eases
the data validation process. ASP.NET Web Forms, for example, have some validator
server controls and their logic plugged into the page's `IsValid` property. ASP.NET
MVC has a model-centric validation architecture, based on a series of attributes called
data annotations. You can use data annotations to decorate the model properties to say
that the Email field is required or that the Author's name can be no more than 50
characters. If you think about it, this is pretty clever of the MVC pattern because it
shares the responsibilities among the components according to each one's responsibility. Figure 8.15 shows the highlights of this concept.

If any of these rules change in the future, you only have to modify the model, without touching the various controllers that use it.

In the next few pages, you'll learn how to leverage data annotations to check that
the input you receive is compliant with your rules.

PROBLEM

We want to be sure that a user can insert a comment into the database only if it's considered valid. Validation rules must be checked outside the controller code—you
don't want to pollute its logic with something that relates strictly to the model.

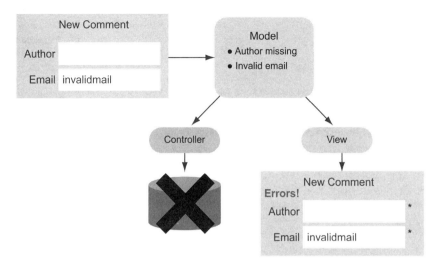

Figure 8.15   The validation process flows across the components of an ASP.NET MVC application. When a form is posted to the server, the associated model is validated using data annotations. Invalid data is handled at the controller level by avoiding saves and at the view level by showing error messages to the user.

SOLUTION

Data annotations are a series of attributes that were initially introduced to support ASP.NET Dynamic Data controls. These attributes are now supported by ASP.NET MVC to validate user inputs. You can use them to decorate a class definition to express the business constraints an instance has to fulfill to be considered valid, similar to the code shown in the following listing.

Listing 8.13   Sample use of data annotations on an ideal Comment class

C#:
```
public class Comment
{
  // .. more code here ..

  [Required(ErrorMessage="Author is mandatory")]
  public string Author { get; set; }

  [Required(ErrorMessage="Email is mandatory")]
  [RegularExpression(
    @"\b[A-Za-z0-9._%+-]+@[A-Za-z0-9.-]+\.[A-Za-z]{2,4}\b",
    ErrorMessage="Please provide a valid Email address")]
  public string Email { get; set; }

  [Required(ErrorMessage="You should post some text")]
  [StringLength(int.MaxValue, MinimumLength=5,
    ErrorMessage="Please provide a meaningful text")]
  public string Text { get; set; }
}
```

❶ Mandatory field

❷ Regular expression rule

❸ Minimum text length

VB:
```
Public Class Comment                                          ❶ Mandatory
                                                                 field
  <Required(ErrorMessage:="Author is mandatory")>       ◄─┘
  Public Property Author As String

  <Required(ErrorMessage:="Email is mandatory")>
  <RegularExpression(                                         ❷ Regular
    "\b[A-Za-z0-9._%+-]+@[A-Za-z0-9.-]+\.[A-Za-z]{2,4}\b",       expression
    ErrorMessage:="Please provide a valid Email address")>       rule
  Public Property Email As String                       ◄─┘

  <Required(ErrorMessage:="You should post some text")>
  <StringLength(int.MaxValue, MinimumLength:=5,               ❸ Minimum
    ErrorMessage:="Please provide a meaningful text")>           text length
  Public Property Text As String                        ◄─┘

End Class
```

In this example, a comment's Author field is considered mandatory ❶, as are the
Email field and the actual text. The Email property has a RegularExpression attribute to validate whether its content matches the given pattern ❷, and the Text isn't
correct if it's too short ❸. Other attributes are also out there, which, for example,
check whether a date or an integer value falls within a given range. A CustomValida-
tion attribute invokes a given method to provide custom validation logic.

Unfortunately in our case, we can't use data annotations on our model classes
directly because they're generated by Entity Framework's designer. Any manual
change will be lost as soon as the custom tool executes, forcing us to describe our
rules using a metadata type. To avoid this problem, we can create a metadata class like
the one in the following listing.

Listing 8.14   Using a metadata type for generated classes

C#:
```
public class CommentMetadata                                ❶ The metadata
{                                                       ◄─┘    type
  [Required(ErrorMessage="Author is mandatory")]
  public string Author { get; set; }

  // .. more properties here ..

}
[MetadataType(typeof(CommentMetadata))]                     ❷ Metadata reference
public partial class Comment                            ◄─┘    added to partial class
{ }
```

VB:
```
Public Class CommentMetadata                                ❶ The metadata
                                                        ◄─┘    type
  <Required(ErrorMessage:="Author is mandatory")>
  Public Property Author As String

  ' .. more properties here ..
End Class
```

```
<MetadataType(GetType(CommentMetadata))>
Partial Public Class Comment
```
❷ **Metadata reference added to partial class**

```
End Class
```

The new `CommentMetadata` ❶ class has the same properties of the actual `Comment` class, but it's not autogenerated. We can decorate them without worrying about losing our changes at every code generation. This class can be referenced from within `Comment` by the `MetadataType` attribute ❷.

Now let's turn our attention to the controller. Having all these attributes on the model class allows us to check for its correctness by simply evaluating the `Model-State.IsValid` property, as in the following listing.

Listing 8.15 Post action implementation taking model validation into account

C#:

```
[HttpPost]
public ActionResult Post(int id, Comment newComment)
{
  using (var ctx = new BlogModelContainer())
  {
    var post = ctx.PostSet.Include("Comments")
      .Where(p => p.Id == id).Single();

    if (!this.ModelState.IsValid)
    {
      return this.View(post);
    }

    // .. here we save the comment as seen before ..
  }
}
```
❶ **Invalid data not saved**

VB:

```
<HttpPost()>
Public Function Post(
  ByVal id As Integer, ByVal newComment As Comment) As ActionResult

  Using ctx = New BlogModelContainer()
    Dim thePost = ctx.PostSets.
      Include("Comments").
      Where(Function(p) p.Id = id).
      Single()

    If Not Me.ModelState.IsValid Then
      Return Me.View(thePost)
    End If

    '.. here we save the comment as seen before ..

  End Using
End Function
```
❶ **Invalid data not saved**

As you can see, plugging model validation into the controller is as easy as adding an `if` statement that might return the same view without saving the comment ❶. This view instance will be responsible for showing the error messages, which are directly

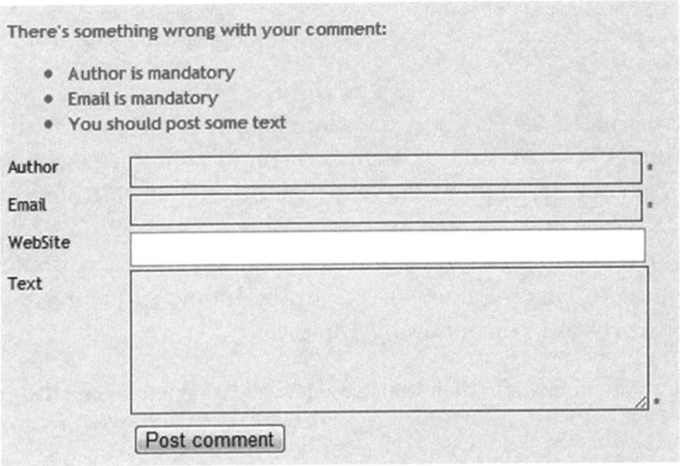

There's something wrong with your comment:

- Author is mandatory
- Email is mandatory
- You should post some text

Author

Email

WebSite

Text

Post comment

Figure 8.16
The comment form
displaying validation
errors. The errors
are automatically
activated when the
user input isn't
considered valid
according to the
data annotations.

inferred from the ErrorMessage properties we set up on the model. The result is
shown in figure 8.16.

The validation summary section can be included using the proper HTML helper in
the view definition, as in the following listing.

Listing 8.16   The view showing validation errors

C#:

```
<%@ Control Language="C#" ... %>

<% Html.EnableClientValidation (); %>
<% using (Html.BeginForm()) {%>
  <%: Html.ValidationSummary(
      "There's something wrong with your comment:") %>

  <div class="editor-label">
    <%: Html.LabelFor(model => model.Author) %>
  </div>
  <div class="editor-field">
    <%: Html.EditorFor(model => model.Author)%>
    <%: Html.ValidationMessageFor(
model => model.Author, "*") %>
  </div>

  .. more markup here ..
<% } %>
```

❶ Enable client-side
JavaScript validation

Inject validation
summary

Shows * on
invalid field

VB:

```
<%@ Control Language="VB" ... %>

<% Html.EnableClientValidation() %>
<% Using Html.BeginForm()%>
  <%: Html.ValidationSummary(
      "There's something wrong with your comment:") %>

  <div class="editor-label">
```

❶ Enable client-side
JavaScript validation

Inject validation
summary

```
    <%: Html.LabelFor(Function(model) model.Author)%>
  </div>
  <div class="editor-field">
     <%: Html.EditorFor(Function(model) model.Author)%>
     <%: Html.ValidationMessageFor(
Function(model) model.Author, "*") %>
  </div>

  .. more markup here ..
<% End Using%>
```

Shows * on
invalid field

The code in this listing is all we need to dynamically show validation messages on the form when the user enters invalid data. The helper method in ❶ automatically injects JavaScript code to validate the model on the client-side also. For this to work, we have to add to the page (or preferably to the site's master page) the script references shown in the following listing.

Listing 8.17 Script references needed for client-side validation

```
<script src="/Scripts/MicrosoftAjax.js"
  type="text/javascript"></script>
<script src="/Scripts/MicrosoftMvcAjax.js"
  type="text/javascript"></script>
<script src="/Scripts/MicrosoftMvcValidation.js"
  type="text/javascript"></script>
```

That's it! Now you've got a validation implementation that will ensure that your users' input is complete and valid.

DISCUSSION

Data validation in ASP.NET MVC has an excellent architecture that leverages attribute use to decorate model classes and encapsulate the business rules within this component of the MVC pattern. That said, we need our controllers to check the ModelState's property to find out whether it's valid or not.

Validation helpers the view close the circle. They automatically detect which rules are unsatisfied, and they show error messages. These helpers also easily support client-side validation, thanks to dynamically injected JavaScript code.

This powerful mechanism is also easily expandable. You can build custom validators to enforce particular business rules that aren't easily expressed by default attributes provided by the data annotations infrastructure. We'll continue our discussion of this topic in chapter 9.

8.5   *Summary*

This first chapter about ASP.NET MVC was an introduction to the new concepts this framework offers. Building an application without Web Forms is a completely different approach that lacks the immediacy of server controls, but at the same time it offers more control over markup. More importantly, this approach gives you a simpler and componentized model upon which to build modern web applications.

First we explored how the MVC pattern flows to handle a browser request. You learned how models, controllers, and views organically cooperate to return a response to the user.

Then we turned our attention to the routing infrastructure, especially to how it integrates with ASP.NET MVC. URL routing is an extremely powerful technique that replaces the old-looking query-string-based URLs with more meaningful ones.

The third part of the chapter was dedicated to handling user input. Instead of working with raw request form fields, ASP.NET MVC provides a great feature that places you at a higher abstraction level, automatically translating the posted data into custom model classes. Input validation is also easily defined on model-based logic using custom attributes. After you apply these attributes to your model's properties, they get translated into client- and server-side integrity checks.

Even with all these goodies, the greatest ASP.NET MVC power lies in its pluggability and expandability. In the next chapter, we'll focus on these advanced topics, and you'll learn how to bend the framework to fit your needs at the maximum level of customization.

Customizing and
extending ASP.NET MVC

Chapter 8 introduced you to the pillars of ASP.NET MVC: controllers, views, models, and routing. These concepts are the basic ones you have to master to start writing applications with this new web development platform. But when we move to real-world contexts, things tend to get a bit more complicated.

So far, you've learned a lot. You know how to handle a web request by using an appropriate combination of a controller, a model, and a view, but in more complex scenarios, these notions alone aren't usually enough. In fact, enterprise-level applications are often made of multifaceted pages, which are difficult to build and maintain unless you can split them into simpler and discrete components. Sometimes things get even harder, requiring you to plug your own custom logic into the framework itself to make it tie in to your specific needs.

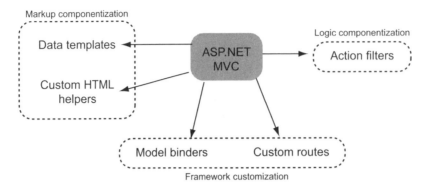

Figure 9.1   **The areas of ASP.NET MVC customization we're going to explore in this chapter. These features are the key ones you'll need in real-world application design. You can build discrete components, each one with its own responsibilities, and reuse them throughout the whole project.**

ASP.NET MVC has several entry points you can use to inject your own code to extend and customize it. In this chapter, we're going to explore some of these features, specifically the ones shown in figure 9.1.

As usual, we'll cover these topics starting with typical issues you'll face while building a real-world application. An improved version of CoolMVCBlog will once again be our guest on this journey. Markup and code componentization, transparent interaction with ADO.NET Entity Framework, and routes optimized for search engines are common needs. They're perfect for explaining how, in ASP.NET MVC, writing the right code in the right place can push your product's quality one step further. So, let's get started!

9.1   *Building reusable elements in ASP.NET MVC*

When you're building a big web application, you'll often come across situations in which pages share the same functionalities and UI elements. In these cases, it's important to have features that allow you to build reusable components, so that you can avoid code and markup duplication. Reusable components mean you don't waste time building the same functionalities again.

In ASP.NET Web Forms, we typically address these needs by building custom controls, but as you've learned, one key difference between Web Forms and ASP.NET MVC is that the latter lacks the notion of a server control; we need to find something else to build reusable components. It goes without saying that this isn't a weakness of ASP.NET MVC, but rather that the programming model is different. In the upcoming pages, you're going to discover the tools it provides to achieve similar results.

9.1.1   *Using templates to represent data*

In the previous chapter, and specifically in section 8.4, you saw how ASP.NET MVC provides an `EditorFor` HTML helper that you can leverage to build input forms easily. We barely touched on how this method is able to produce different HTML elements based on the data type of the property you're going to edit, as figure 9.2 schematizes.

Figure 9.2
The `Html.EditorFor` helper can render different editors for object properties, based on their type.

This feature is part of a bigger picture that helps you to componentize how a view renders data. When you build a view, you must write the HTML elements that will represent the data on the actual page. Because the same data types will hopefully be rendered similarly across many views, the idea behind data templates is to define these elements once for all and reference them by using just two distinct HTML helpers:

C#:

```
<%: Html.DisplayFor (model => model.myProperty)%>
<%: Html.EditorFor(model => model.myProperty)%>
```

VB:

```
<%: Html.DisplayFor(function(model) model.myProperty)%>
<%: Html.EditorFor(function(model) model.myProperty)%>
```

The engine itself then takes care of analyzing what `myProperty` is and selects the correct template for its representation.

ASP.NET MVC already provides some templates that render common data types such as booleans or strings, although there are actually just a few and they're quite basic. The good news is that you can easily customize them or provide new ones. You're going to learn how in the next section.

TECHNIQUE 52 **Building customized data templates**

A common requirement when you're building large web applications is to have the same kind of data rendered consistently in every page. If you want to address this issue with minimal effort, you should concentrate your efforts on building a data template to handle it.

A data template is no more than a partial view bound to a particular data type. When the ASP.NET MVC view engine encounters an `EditorFor` or a `DisplayFor` statement for a property of a certain type, if you've provided a data template for it, it's automatically instantiated. Let's see how all this works in a common scenario.

PROBLEM

You just downloaded the jQuery UI Datepicker, and you want to automatically plug it in throughout your whole website so that you can use it each time a date object must be edited.

SOLUTION

The jQuery UI Datepicker is a great piece of JavaScript code that leverages jQuery to display a fancy calendar to input a date, as shown in figure 9.3.

Figure 9.3   **The jQuery UI Datepicker applied to a text box shows a calendar when focused. Showing a calendar makes selecting a date easier.**

We're not going to deeply explore Datepicker features or how jQuery works; despite being dramatically interesting, these concepts are unfortunately beyond the scope of this book.

> **INTERESTED IN KNOWING MORE ABOUT JQUERY?**   If you want to expand your knowledge of jQuery, you'll find *jQuery in Action*, part of Manning's *In Action* book series, to be a great reference guide. This book provides in-depth coverage of this powerful JavaScript library.

All you need to know for our purposes is that you have to follow a couple of steps for a datepicker to be displayed automatically when a user clicks on an input box:

1 Reference jQuery and jQuery UI scripts.
2 Select all the date input boxes on the page and activate the datepicker functionality.

Because we're going to need this functionality in our whole web application, a good idea is to place this code in the master page file, like in the following listing.

Listing 9.1   Master page code that activates jQuery UI Datepicker

```
<%@ Master Language="C#" ... %>
<head>
  <script src="/Scripts/jquery-1.4.1.js"
       type="text/javascript" />
  <script src="/Scripts/jquery-ui-1.8.2.custom.min.js"       References to
    type="text/javascript"></script>                          scripts and CSS
  <link href="/Content/jquery-ui-1.8.2.custom.css"
    rel="stylesheet"          type="text/css" />
</head>
...
<script type="text/javascript">
    $(function () {                            ❶  Code that activates
        $('.dateInput').datepicker();              jQuery UI Datepicker
    });
</script>
```

Because this code applies to every page, we don't know how many input boxes there will be. A good way to proceed is to leverage the jQuery selector flexibility to pick elements by their CSS class (`dateInput` in our case) and then invoke the `datepicker` JavaScript method ❶ to activate the calendar on them. Note that `dateInput` isn't an actual style defined somewhere in a CSS file, but just a marker that lets us identify the elements for which all this has to happen.

Now that everything has been set up on the jQuery side, we can turn our attention to our application's views; we still have to make every date's input box reference that CSS class. We can obviously do this by manually specifying it each time we come across a date editor, or we can define a custom editor template for the `System.DateTime` type. To use a custom editor template, we must add an EditorTemplates subfolder under the Shared views folder and then create a new partial view with the same name of the type we want to edit (DateTime for our example). Figure 9.4 shows the final folder structure.

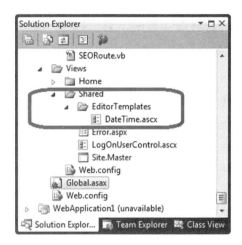

Figure 9.4   The location of DateTime.ascx in the folder structure of an ASP.NET MVC project

The following listing shows how the code we have to write in the view is trivial.

Listing 9.2   DateTime editor template

C#:
```
<%@ Control Language="C#" Inherits="System.Web.Mvc.ViewUserControl" %>
<script runat="server">
  private string dateString                        ◁──── ❶ String representation
  {                                                         of model
    get
    {
      if (this.Model == null)
        return null;

      return ((DateTime)this.Model).ToShortDateString();
    }
  }
</script>
<%= Html.TextBox("",                               ❷ TextBox
    dateString, new { @class = "dateInput" })%>       rendering
```

VB:
```
<%@ Control Language="VB" Inherits="System.Web.Mvc.ViewUserControl" %>
<script runat="server">
  Private ReadOnly Property DateString As String   ◁──── ❶ String representation
    Get                                                     of model
      If Me.Model Is Nothing Then
        Return Nothing
```

```
      End If

      Return DirectCast(Me.Model, DateTime).ToShortDateString
    End Get
  End Property
</script>
<%= Html.TextBox("", _
    DateString, New With {.Class = "dateInput"})%>
```

② TextBox rendering

Our DateTime.ascx view uses an internal property **①** to produce the string representation of the corresponding date. Then it leverages the `TextBox` HTML helper **②** to render an input box styled with the `dateInput` CSS class, which is what we originally wanted.

Now that all this is in place, we just have to use the `EditorFor` HTML helper to get ASP.NET MVC to resolve the newly created custom template and to use it to render the editor. So, for example, if we wanted to edit the date of publishing in the Edit Post view of CoolMVCBlog, we could write:

C#:
```
<%: Html.EditorFor(model => model.DatePublished)%>
```

VB:
```
<%: Html.EditorFor(Function(model) model.DatePublished)%>
```

> ### What if I just want to display data?
> Display templates let you design data-type-specific templates to define how this kind of data has to be visualized. They work exactly the same way as Editor templates, except that they must be stored in the DisplayTemplates subfolder and are triggered by using the `DisplayFor` HTML helper.

This example shows how easy is to create a custom template and bind it to a particular CLR type: it's just a matter of building a partial view with the same name and putting it in a carefully named folder.

Sometimes properties of the same CLR type require different templates because the data they represent is different. Think about a `Post` entity for our CoolMVCBlog; although its `Title` and `Text` properties are both of type `string`, we might want to have different templates to edit them, perhaps a plain text box for `Title` and a multi-line text editor for `Text` (if not a WYSIWYG editor such as CKEditor). In other words, we might need to handle types at a higher level of abstraction and use a more expressive way to tell the framework that they represent different kinds of data, as shown in figure 9.5

To define these custom data types, you can mark the corresponding properties with `DataTypeAttribute` or `UIHintAttribute` (their use is equivalent), like in listing 9.3.

Figure 9.5 Although `Title` and `Text` are both strings, we need `EditorFor` to produce different templates because each has a different business meaning.

Listing 9.3 Marking property type with UIHintAttribute

C#:

```
public class PostMetadata
{
  [DataType(DataType.MultilineText)]              ❶ Standard data
  public string Text { get; set; }                    type definition

  [UIHint("Author")]                              ❷ Custom data
  public int AuthorId { get; set; }                   type definition
}

[MetadataType(typeof(PostMetadata))]              Metadata type
public partial class Post                          reference
{ }
```

VB:

```
Public Class PostMetadata
  <DataType(DataType.MultilineText)>              ❶ Standard data
  Public Property Text As String                      type definition

  <UIHint("Author")>                             ❷ Custom data
  Public Property AuthorId As Integer                 type definition
End Class

<MetadataType(GetType(PostMetadata))>            Metadata type
Partial Public Class Post                         reference
End Class
```

When it comes across properties marked like those at ❶ and ❷, the ASP.NET MVC view engine looks in the Shared View folder for data templates that have the same names. If it finds any such templates, it renders them.

DISCUSSION

Modern development platforms provide features that help us build consistent and maintainable UIs. Web Forms, for example, uses the abstraction of custom server controls to let the developer build discrete and reusable interface portions. ASP.NET MVC provides a different model, called data templates, which is based on the data type you want to represent or edit in your page. Anytime you realize there's a particular object among your models that appears many times in many pages, and you want to componentize how it gets displayed or how its editor looks when it's placed in a form, reach for a custom data template.

Think about how many times you've built a drop-down list to let the user choose a customer. It doesn't matter whether that user is going to associate it with an order or an invoice, a property of type Customer is always going to be there to fill; building a single editor template for it is enough to automatically have it injected wherever it's needed.

Even though they're powerful, templates almost always require an association to a specific data type, but this isn't always the rule. Consider items like buttons, hyperlinks, or pop ups, just to name a few: although they aren't necessarily bound to a DateTime or Customer object, you might still want to build discrete components and avoid writing the same markup again and again in your pages. HTML helpers are much more helpful in these situations, as you're going to see in the next section.

TECHNIQUE 53   **Componentized markup through HTML helpers**

Data templates are an extremely smart solution when you must quickly build input forms, or when you need to display complex data. On the other hand, sometimes you need to include a bunch of markup code in something that must be as easily reusable as templates, but not necessarily bound to a particular model type.

Let's think about what happens every time we have to insert a link into a view. The link can come from data of different types, involve more than just one property of an object, or even originate from hardcoded values such as the Back To Index link on the post edit page of CoolMVCBlog. In all these cases, you'll find that using an HTML helper called ActionLink is a solution you'll be satisfied with. Besides generating markup, this solution also holds the logic to determine a target URL, given action, and controller names.

Similar situations are common in real-world applications, and having a library of customized HTML helpers can surely make the difference for how consistent and maintainable your product will be. For that reason, it's worth trying to learn to build some of your own.

PROBLEM

Our application allows registered users to perform login and logout operations using the corresponding actions of SecurityController. We want to build a custom component that we can re-use to easily build a form to insert login credentials or, if the user is already authenticated, to show a welcome message to the user.

SOLUTION

HTML helpers are methods you can call from within a view to generate HTML, encapsulating all the logic needed to render it. Every time we used the ActionLink extension method in chapter 8, we used it not only because we didn't want to manually write a hyperlink like <a href="someURL" ...>Link text</a>, but also because it allowed us to reason in terms of controller and actions, and, fortunately, it also translates it to actual URLs, as in figure 9.6.

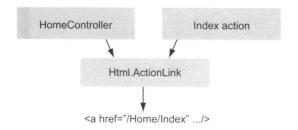

Figure 9.6 `ActionLink` **can generate URLs consistent with application routing settings.**

The idea we'll use to solve our problem is to create a new HTML helper that can evaluate the request authentication status and generate a login form or welcome message, whichever is appropriate. We could easily include the helper in a view, or perhaps in the master page with just this code:

C# and VB:

```
<%: Html.Login("Security", "Login", "Logout") %>
```

Building such an HTML helper is the same as writing a method like the one in the next listing. This method accepts actions and a controller name that we want to use when the user is logging in or out.

Listing 9.4   Main code of Login HTML helper

C#:

```
public static HtmlString Login(this HtmlHelper html,
  string controller, string loginAction, string logoutAction)
{
  if (HttpContext.Current.User.Identity.IsAuthenticated)
    return WelcomeMessage(html, logoutAction, controller);
  else
    return LoginInput(html, loginAction, controller);
}

private static HtmlString WelcomeMessage(HtmlHelper html,
  string logoutAction, string controller)
{
  return new HtmlString(string.Format("Welcome {0} :: {1}",
    HttpContext.Current.User.Identity.Name,
    html.ActionLink("Logout", logoutAction, controller)));
}
```

❶ **HtmlHelper's extension method**

❷ **Output selection logic**

❸ **Composition of welcome message**

VB:

```
<Extension()>
Public Function Login(ByVal html As HtmlHelper,
    ByVal controller As String, ByVal loginAction As String,
    ByVal logoutAction As String) As HtmlString

  If HttpContext.Current.User.Identity.IsAuthenticated Then
    Return WelcomeMessage(html, logoutAction, controller)
  Else
    Return LoginInput(html, loginAction, controller)
  End If
```

❶ **HtmlHelper's extension method**

❷ **Output selection logic**

```
End Function

Private Function WelcomeMessage(ByVal html As HtmlHelper,
    ByVal logoutAction As String, ByVal controller As String) As HtmlString

  Return New HtmlString(String.Format("Welcome {0} :: {1}",
    HttpContext.Current.User.Identity.Name,
    html.ActionLink("Logout", logoutAction, controller)))
End Function
```

❸ **Composition
of welcome
message**

Our `Login` HTML helper is an extension method for the `HtmlHelper` class ❶, whose main code checks whether the current user is authenticated. It also chooses whether it must render a welcome message or a login form ❷. The implementation of the first option is trivial, because `WelcomeMessage` just builds the output by concatenating some strings ❸.

Notice how we leverage another HTML helper, `ActionLink`, to build the hyperlink. Then we wrap the whole result using an `HtmlString` class. This class represents a string that contains already encoded HTML, which won't be affected when it's displayed in a `<%: %>` tag.

Conversely, when the user isn't authenticated, our helper invokes a `LoginInput` method. This method is slightly more complex, because it must use the code shown in the following listing to build an actual HTML form.

Listing 9.5 Building an HTML form via code

C#:
```
private static HtmlString LoginInput(HtmlHelper html,
  string loginAction, string controller)
{
  TagBuilder form = new TagBuilder("form");

  form.MergeAttribute("action",
    UrlHelper.GenerateUrl(null, loginAction,
      controller, new RouteValueDictionary(), html.RouteCollection,
      html.ViewContext.RequestContext, true));

  form.MergeAttribute("method", "post");

  form.InnerHtml = string.Format("User: {0} Pass: {1} {2}",
    html.TextBox("username"),
    html.Password("password"),
    "<input type=\"submit\" value=\"Login\" />");

  return new HtmlString(form.ToString());
}
```

**Composition of
Action attribute** ❶

**Form's HTML
content**

VB:
```
Private Function LoginInput(ByVal html As HtmlHelper,
    ByVal loginAction As String, ByVal controller As String)
    As HtmlString

  Dim form As New TagBuilder("form")

  form.MergeAttribute("action",
```

```
    UrlHelper.GenerateUrl(Nothing, loginAction,
      controller, New RouteValueDictionary,
      html.RouteCollection, html.ViewContext.RequestContext,
      True))

  form.MergeAttribute("method", "post")

  form.InnerHtml = String.Format("User: {0} Pass: {1} {2}",
    html.TextBox("username"), html.TextBox("password"),
    "<input type=""submit"" value=""Login"" />")

  Return New HtmlString(form.ToString())
End Function
```

❶ Composition of Action attribute

Form's HTML content

This code takes advantage of an object called `TagBuilder`, which eases the task of building HTML tags and decorating them with the attributes we need. For an HTML form, for example, we must indicate that we want to post it to a certain destination URL, which we can obtain from the `controller` and `loginInput` parameters through ASP.NET MVC's `UrlHelper` class ❶.

DISCUSSION

HTML helpers are a simple way to include in a method the logic required to generate HTML code, so that we can easily replicate it when we need it. Building them is only a matter of creating an extension method for the `HtmlHelper` type and returning an `HtmlString` instance (although the return type can be also a plain `string`).

Given its extremely versatile nature, these tools give you a great advantage when you're developing applications in ASP.NET MVC. Even though everything you make with an HTML helper can also be made using partial views, HTML helpers are usually more immediate and easy to use; after all, you just have to invoke a method, and you don't have to deal with models and types like you do with views and templates. Moreover, they're just code, so you can build class libraries and reuse them across many projects.

Of course, there's always a downside to every great solution. You want to be careful not to overuse HTML helpers; they're usually a bit verbose and tend to replace the actual markup. You don't want to bury the logic that generates the markup because that lessens your control over the HTML—one of the key advantages of using ASP.NET MVC in the first place.

In summary, HTML helpers and data templates are two key features of ASP.NET MVC that you can leverage to avoid duplicating the same markup over and over in your views. But these techniques cover only half the problem—code duplication often happens in controllers, too. The next section will show you a useful trick for avoiding it.

TECHNIQUE 54   Inject logic using action filters

The previous section was about componentizing markup, but sometimes markup requires code on the controller side to render correctly. If you were forced to replicate the code each time you wanted to use an HTML helper, a partial view, or a data template, you would lose almost all the advantages of building these reusable components.

Let's recall for a moment the homepage we built in chapter 8. It should look like the one in figure 9.7, which highlights a particular portion of it.

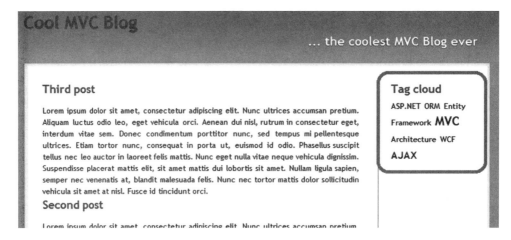

Figure 9.7 Our blog engine's homepage; it contains a tag cloud that will likely be shared among multiple pages.

When we built the corresponding view, we thought the tag cloud would be a shared UI element, which was supposed to be present in multiple pages; this was one of the reasons we decided to design it as a partial view. Unfortunately, although the template is actually reusable, we still need some code on the controller to populate the model with the data the cloud will represent. The `HomePageController` did it by invoking a `TagCloudService`, as shown in the following listing. If things remain as they are, we'll have to replicate this code for each action that ultimately shows a tag cloud.

Listing 9.6 HomeController fetching tag cloud items

C#:
```
public ActionResult Index()
{
  // more code here

  var service = new TagCloudService(ctx);
  model.TagCloudItems = service.GetTagCloudItems();

  return View(model);
}
```

VB:
```
Public Function Index() As ActionResult
  ' more code here

  Dim service = New TagCloudService(ctx)
  model.TagCloudItems = service.GetTagCloudItems()

  Return View(model)
End Function
```

It goes without saying that we definitely want to avoid replicating all this. We can do it by using a powerful ASP.NET MVC feature: action filters.

PROBLEM

We want to show our blog's tag cloud in multiple pages, but we don't want to replicate the code required to fetch its items on every action of every controller that references it.

SOLUTION

Action filters are classes that inherit from the infrastructural `ActionFilterAttribute` class and provide entry points to inject logic during the execution of an action. Their base class exposes four virtual methods, listed in Table 9.1, which are automatically triggered by the ASP.NET MVC execution engine while processing a request.

Table 9.1   Overridable methods of the ActionFilterAttribute class

Name	Description
`OnActionExecuting`	Runs before the controller action is triggered.
`OnActionExecuted`	Runs just after the action concludes its execution, but before the `ActionResult` it returned starts up.
`OnResultExecuting`	This method is triggered just before the execution of the current `ActionResult`.
`OnResultExecuted`	The last method you can intercept. It runs after the result has been executed.

If you override these methods from within a custom filter class, you can inject personalized logic into one or more of the well-defined phases highlighted in figure 9.8. Then you can associate that filter with individual actions or with entire controllers—in which case it will be bound to every action it holds. The end result is a reusable component and no code duplication.

Figure 9.8   Entry points for action filters to inject code during the request flow

For our specific needs, our `LoadTagCloudAttribute` has to fetch the tag cloud data from the database (as you saw in chapter 8) and store it in the model. Because we want it to be applicable to many views, and, in turn, to the different models that those views will refer to, the idea is to create the `IHasTagCloud` interface to mark the models that provide a `TagCloudItems` property, as in the following listing.

Listing 9.7   IHasTagCloud and its implementation in HomepageModel

C#:
```
internal interface IHasTagCloud
{
```

```
    List<TagCloudItem> TagCloudItems { get; set; }
}

public class HomepageModel : IHasTagCloud
{
  public List<Post> Posts { get; set; }
  public List<TagCloudItem> TagCloudItems { get; set; }
}
```

VB:
```
Friend Interface IHasTagCloud
  Property TagCloudItems As List(Of TagCloudItem)
End Interface

Public Class HomepageModel
    Implements IHasTagCloud

    Public Property Posts As List(Of Post)
    Public Property TagCloudItems As List(Of TagCloudItem)
        Implements IHasTagCloud.TagCloudItems

End Class
```

Now it's time to turn our gaze to the actual action filter. We need to decide which of the four provided entry points better suits our needs. We want to integrate the model content, so we need a model instance that's already created and a filter that runs after the action executes. However, we have to do our job before the view is created; otherwise, it wouldn't have any data to render.

Guess what? Both OnActionExecuted and OnResultExecuting will work. For our needs, they're almost equivalent, so we can pick either one. We'll choose OnResult-Executing (the reason will be unveiled shortly). The following listing shows the filter's code.

Listing 9.8 Complete LoadTagCloudAttribute code

C#:
```
public class LoadTagCloudAttribute : ActionFilterAttribute
{
  public override void OnResultExecuting(
    ResultExecutingContext filterContext)
  {
    base.OnResultExecuting(filterContext);

    var view = filterContext.Result as ViewResult;
    if (view == null)
      return;

    var model = view.ViewData.Model as IHasTagCloud;
    if (model == null)
      return;

    using (var ctx = new BlogModelContainer())
    {
      var service = new TagCloudService(ctx);
      model.TagCloudItems = service.GetTagCloudItems();
```

 1 Fetch tag cloud data

```
      }
    }
  }
}
```

VB:

```
Public Class LoadTagCloudAttribute
  Inherits ActionFilterAttribute

  Public Overrides Sub OnResultExecuting(
      ByVal filterContext As ResultExecutingContext)
    MyBase.OnResultExecuting(filterContext)

    Dim view = TryCast(filterContext.Result, ViewResult)
    If view Is Nothing Then
      Return
    End If

    Dim model = TryCast(view.ViewData, IHasTagCloud)
    If model Is Nothing Then
      Return
    End If

    Using ctx As New BlogModelContainer
      Dim service = New TagCloudService(ctx)
      model.TagCloudItems = service.GetTagCloudItems
    End Using

  End Sub

End Class
```

❶ Fetch tag cloud data

The code we just showed you is pretty easy to understand. Our override of the OnResult-Executing method checks whether the result returned by the action is actually a view and whether the model implements the IHasTagCloud interface. If both those checks succeed, the service we built in chapter 8 loads the data from the database and then stores it into the model ❶.

> ### Why didn't we override OnActionExecuted instead?
> One feature of our filter is that it runs only if the result is a view. Limiting the result avoids unnecessary (and expensive, although we could probably cache all the stuff) roundtrips to the database in cases when the action, for example, returns a Redi-rectResult. The code we just wrote would have worked exactly the same way if we placed it in the OnActionExecuted method. But what if another action filter hooked that event and changed the result type? Doing our task after that phase keeps our code up-to-date, with the ultimate result returned by the action pipeline.

One key aspect we should point out is that we could've just stored the tag cloud items in the ViewData dictionary, without worrying about building an additional interface. But, with some negligible additional effort, we managed to keep our views and code strongly typed, while still being able to easily support this functionality for every model we need.

With our new `LoadTagCloudAttribute` action filter ready, all we have to do now to let an action load the tag cloud data is to decorate it. The code is shown in the following listing.

Listing 9.9 Homepage's Index action leveraging LoadTagCloudAttribute

C#:
```
[LoadTagCloud]
public ActionResult Index()
{
  using (var ctx = new BlogModelContainer())
  {
    var lastPosts = ctx
      .PostSet
      .OrderByDescending(p => p.DatePublished)
      .Take(3)
      .ToList();

    return View(new HomepageModel() { Posts = lastPosts });   ←①  No reference
  }                                                                  to tag cloud
}                                                                    logic
```

VB:
```
<LoadTagCloud()>
Public Function Index() As ActionResult
  Using ctx As New BlogModelContainer
    Dim lastPosts = ctx.PostSet.
      OrderBy(Function(p) p.DatePublished).
      Take(3).
      ToList()                                                      ①  No reference
                                                                       to tag cloud
    Return View(New HomepageModel With {.Posts = lastPosts})   ←        logic
  End Using
End Function
```

With the `LoadTagCloud` attribute in place, this new version of the action is a lot simpler and strictly involves just the homepage-specific code. The code loads the last three posts and assigns them to the model ❶; the custom filter takes care of everything that concerns the tag cloud data.

DISCUSSION

Action filters are an extremely powerful tool, not just because they allow you to avoid code duplication, but also because they contribute to keeping your action code simple and maintainable. Ending up with simple code is a key factor of developing good ASP.NET MVC applications. This outcome is so important that it's worth more discussion; let's focus for a moment on the result we've been able to achieve with the previous example.

We've built an action filter to fetch tag cloud data and used it to decorate the homepage's `Index` action. Doing that allowed us to have the code in the `Index` method, doing the specific task it was built for—fetching the most recent three posts. Displaying the tag cloud is a side requirement, potentially shared across multiple actions, which we isolated in a dedicated class and activated in a declarative manner when we decorated the action with an attribute. We did all that without polluting the action code with any logic related to the tag cloud.

Every time you're building a controller and you find that you're writing code that isn't specific to the particular request you're handling, you should evaluate the possibility of building an action filter for that situation. The same ASP.NET MVC framework exposes a lot of logic via action filters, like the controller's caching primitives you'll see in chapter 14.

In conclusion, keeping your action code simple is one of the most effective ways to write good applications. Besides what you just learned, ASP.NET MVC provides multiple entry points that you can customize to reach this ultimate goal—model binders are one of them. Let's look at those next.

9.2   User input handling made smart

So far in this chapter, you've seen how you can handle user input in an ASP.NET MVC application. ASP.NET MVC can translate everything that comes with the HTTP request into .NET objects, allowing you to work at a high level of abstraction without having to take care of the single items posted in an HTML form or coming as query string parameters.

Let's stay with our CoolMVCBlog application and take a look at figure 9.9; it shows a page we can use to edit blog posts.

As our application stands now, when it responds to a request for updating a blog post, it triggers an action similar to the one shown in the following listing.

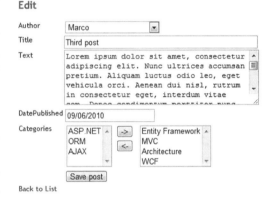

Figure 9.9   A screenshot from CoolMVCBlog's Backoffice. We can use this page to create and edit a post.

Listing 9.10   Action updating a Post

C#:

```csharp
[HttpPost]
public ActionResult Edit(Post post)
{
  if (this.ModelState.IsValid)                    ① Check for valid input
  {
    using (BlogModelContainer ctx = new BlogModelContainer())
    {
      var original = ctx.PostSet                  ② Fetching original Post
        .Where(p => p.Id == post.Id)
        .Single();
```

```
    if (this.TryUpdateModel(original))
    {
      ctx.SaveChanges();
      return this.RedirectToAction("Index");
    }
  }
}

  this.ViewData["Authors"] = AuthorsService.GetAuthors();
  this.ViewData["Categories"] = CategoriesService.GetCategories();

  return this.View(post);
}
```

❸ Updating original Post instance

❹ Saving changes to database

VB:

```
<HttpPost()>
Public Function Edit(ByVal post As Post) As ActionResult
  If Me.ModelState.IsValid Then
    Using ctx As New BlogModelContainer
      Dim original = ctx.PostSet.
        Where(Function(p) p.Id = post.Id).
        Single

      If Me.TryUpdateModel(original) Then
        ctx.SaveChanges()
        Return Me.RedirectToAction("Index")
      End If
    End Using
  End If

  Me.ViewData("Authors") = AuthorsService.GetAuthors()
  Me.ViewData("Categories") = CategoriesService.GetCategories()

  Return Me.View(post)
End Function
```

❶ Check for valid input

❷ Fetching original Post

❸ Updating original Post instance

❹ Saving changes to database

The code is rather easy to understand. If the model is valid ❶, it fetches the post from PostSet by using its Id ❷, and then applies the changes coming from the form using the TryUpdateModel helper ❸. The last step is to save it to the database ❹.

Although everything seems to be working in a straightforward way, the code in listing 9.10 suffers from two main problems:

- Every time we have an action that modifies an entity, we're going to replicate the same logic of loading the old version, updating it, and then saving it after checking for its correctness.
- Complex entities can't be automatically handled by the default infrastructure. The previous action, for example, can't actually understand the categories editor as we implemented it, so the collection won't be successfully populated.

In this section, you're going to learn how you can customize the logic ASP.NET MVC uses to handle the HTTP request to solve these two problems.

TECHNIQUE 55 **Custom model binders for domain entities**

When we wrote the Edit action in listing 9.10, we coded a method that accepts a Post object as an argument:

C#:

```
public ActionResult Edit(Post post)
```

VB:

```
Public Function Edit(ByVal post As Post) As ActionResult
```

Unfortunately, that `Post` object isn't an actual entity recognized by ADO.NET Entity Framework, and it can't be directly used to manage its lifecycle and persistence; it's just an instance of the same .NET type, which has never been part of an `EntitySet` and is unknown to any `ObjectContext`. For this reason, we had to write some code to refetch a post and update it.

Wouldn't it be awesome if we could put our hands onto a valid Entity Framework object at the beginning, one that's connected to an object context and already updated with the user input? To do this, we must customize the way ASP.NET MVC translates the HTTP form to a .NET object—more precisely, we must build our own model binder. Let's see how.

PROBLEM

Our application uses ADO.NET Entity Framework as a persistence layer. We want our actions parameters to be directly usable with an object context in order to save them to the database.

SOLUTION

When ASP.NET MVC transforms the HTTP request's content into a .NET instance, it leverages a particular object called a *model binder*. A model binder usually retrieves input data from the form and interprets it to instantiate objects. Figure 9.10 schematizes the whole process.

Building a model binder is just a matter of creating a new class that implements the `IModelBinder` interface and writing some code for its `BindModel` method:

C#:

```
public object BindModel(ControllerContext controllerContext,
  ModelBindingContext bindingContext)
```

VB:

```
Public Function BindModel(ByVal controllerContext As ControllerContext,
  ByVal bindingContext As ModelBindingContext) As Object
```

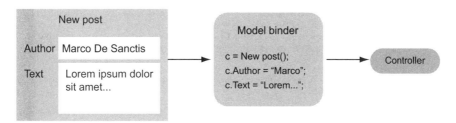

Figure 9.10   The model binder acts as a mediator between the HTML form and the controller, translating the input coming from the browser into a .NET object.

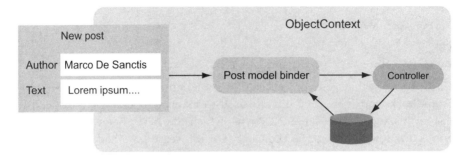

Figure 9.11   When ASP.NET MVC receives a form with a `Post`, it uses a custom model binder to get the original post from the database and update it with the data so the controller can easily persist it.

That method receives the following input parameters that represent the particular request context it's being executed into:

- A `ControllerContext` holds information related to the current request, like the `HttpContext`, the specific controller in charge of handling it or the routing data
- A `ModelBindingContext` is specific to the binding operation and allows access to the model being built or to the request data

The `BindModel` method returns an instance of `object`—no type is specified—which is forwarded to the executing action, in order to represent the input's alter-ego in the ASP.NET MVC world.

The idea is to customize the process by which this instance is built, creating a new model binder. The new model binder will be activated each time the action parameter involves a `Post` type and will use the form content to retrieve a `Post` entity from the database and update it before delivering it to the controller. Figure 9.11 shows the whole process.

The workflow in figure 9.11 is supposed to have both the model binder and the action sharing the same `ObjectContext` instance; that's the only way to let ADO. NET Entity Framework track all the changes both actors make to the post entity and to generate the correct `UPDATE` query when the action finally calls its `Save-Changes` method.

What we ultimately need is an object context to be active along the whole request. We can achieve this by using the HTTP module shown in the following listing.

Listing 9.11   ObjectContextModule takes care of creating an ObjectContext

C#:
```
public class ObjectContextModule : IHttpModule
{
  public void Init(HttpApplication context)
  {
```

```
  context.PostAcquireRequestState += (s, e) =>
  {
    CurrentContext = new BlogModelContainer();
  };
```
❶ Creates ObjectContext

```
  context.ReleaseRequestState += (s, e) =>
  {
    CurrentContext.Dispose();
    CurrentContext = null;
  };
}
```
❷ Disposes ObjectContext

```
public static BlogModelContainer CurrentContext
{
```
❸ Retrieves current context

```
  get
  {
    return (BlogModelContainer)
      HttpContext.Current.Session[sessionKey];
  }
  private set
  {
    HttpContext.Current.Session[sessionKey] = value;
  }
}
}
```

VB:
```
Public Class ObjectContextModule
  Implements IHttpModule

  Public Sub Init(ByVal context As HttpApplication)
      Implements IHttpModule.Init
    AddHandler context.PostAcquireRequestState,
      Sub(s, e)
        If Not HttpContext.Current Is Nothing AndAlso
          Not HttpContext.Current.Session Is Nothing Then
          CurrentContext = New BlogModelContainer()
        End If
      End Sub
```
❶ Creates ObjectContext

```
    AddHandler context.ReleaseRequestState,
      Sub(s, e)
        If Not HttpContext.Current Is Nothing AndAlso
          Not HttpContext.Current.Session Is Nothing Then
          CurrentContext.Dispose()
          CurrentContext = Nothing
        End If
      End Sub
  End Sub
```
❷ Disposes ObjectContext

```
  Public Shared Property CurrentContext As BlogModelContainer
    Get
```
❸ Retrieves current context

```
      Return TryCast(HttpContext.Current.Session(sessionKey),
        BlogModelContainer)
    End Get
    Set(ByVal value As BlogModelContainer)
      HttpContext.Current.Session(sessionKey) = value
```

```
    End Set
  End Property
End Class
```

ObjectContextModule's goal is to create a new BlogModelContainer instance when the request state is acquired and store it in a session variable ❶. Then, when the request terminates, ObjectContextModule releases the BlogModelContainer instance by calling its Dispose method ❷. With our HTTP module up and running, we don't have to worry anymore about building an object context when we're accessing the database: there's always one associated with each request, and we can retrieve it using the static CurrentContext property ❸:

C#:
```
var ctx = ObjectContextModule.CurrentContext;
```

VB:
```
Dim ctx = ObjectContextModule.CurrentContext
```

Now we have all we need to start building our custom model binder. ASP.NET MVC already provides a DefaultModelBinder that is so versatile it can map many default types:

- Native types, like string, double or DateTime
- .NET objects, including our Post class
- Collections of objects

Rather than starting from scratch, it might be worth leveraging all those DefaultModelBinder built-in features. What we're going to do is build a PostModelBinder that inherits from DefaultModelBinder and customizes its BindModel method, as in the next listing.

Listing 9.12   PostModelBinder's implementation of BindModel

C#:
```
public override object BindModel(ControllerContext controllerContext,
  ModelBindingContext bindingContext)
{
  if (bindingContext.Model == null)                    ⟵──── ❶ Checks whether to create
  {                                                              new Post instance
    var valueProviderResult =
      bindingContext.ValueProvider.GetValue("Id");

    if (!string.IsNullOrEmpty(                               ❷ Checks for Edit
        valueProviderResult.AttemptedValue))                   operation
    {
      int id = (int)valueProviderResult.ConvertTo(typeof(int));

      var original =
        ObjectContextModule.CurrentContext
          .PostSet.Include("Categories").Include("Author")
          .Where(p => p.Id == id).Single();
                                                          ❸ Associates Post with
      bindingContext.ModelMetadata.Model = original;   ⟵──  current context
```

```
    }
  }

  return base.BindModel(controllerContext, bindingContext);
}
```

VB:
```
Public Overrides Function BindModel(
    ByVal controllerContext As ControllerContext,
    ByVal bindingContext As ModelBindingContext) As Object

  If bindingContext.Model Is Nothing Then                    Checks whether to
    Dim valueProviderResult =                                create new Post
      bindingContext.ValueProvider.GetValue("Id")       ❶  instance

    If Not String.IsNullOrEmpty(                              ❷ Checks for Edit
            valueProviderResult.AttemptedValue) Then             operation
      Dim id = DirectCast(
        valueProviderResult.ConvertTo(GetType(Integer)), Integer)

      Dim original =
        ObjectContextModule.CurrentContext.
        PostSet.Include("Categories").Include("Author").
        Where(Function(p) p.Id = id).Single                ❸ Associates Post with
                                                              current context
      bindingContext.ModelMetadata.Model = original     ◁

    End If
  End If

  Return MyBase.BindModel(controllerContext, bindingContext)
End Function
```

Let's recall for a moment what we're aiming to do: we have an Edit action that accepts a Post object and we want that Post object to be retrieved from the database and populated. In other words, our custom logic must start up when there's a new Post instance to build ❶ and when a not null Id tells us we're in an edit context ❷. When that happens, we're going to go to the database and fetch the entity, setting it as the Model for the current BindingContext ❸. Then it's DefaultModelBinder's turn: in the last step, we invoke the original BindModel implementation, grabbing the values posted from the browser and putting them into the Post properties.

Thanks to all this work, our controller won't get a simple Post instance, but a real entity, already attached to the current Entity Framework's context. Our action will become much simpler—almost trivial—like the one in the following listing.

Listing 9.13   Edit action code after PostModelBinder

C#:
```
[HttpPost]
public ActionResult Edit(Post post)
{
  if (this.ModelState.IsValid)
  {
    ObjectContextModule.CurrentContext.SaveChanges();
    return this.RedirectToAction("Index");
```

```
  }
  // ... more code here ...
}
```

VB:
```
<HttpPost()>
Public Function Edit(ByVal post As Post) As ActionResult
  If Me.ModelState.IsValid Then
    ObjectContextModule.CurrentContext.SaveChanges()
    Return Me.RedirectToAction("Index")
  End If

  ' more code here
End Function
```

To get everything to work, there's one last step to do: register the new model binder and instruct ASP.NET MVC to use it every time it has to build a Post instance. We're doing this in the global.asax file with the following code.

C#:
```
ModelBinders.Binders[typeof(Post)] = new PostModelBinder();
```

VB:
```
ModelBinders.Binders(GetType(Post)) = New PostModelBinder()
```

DISCUSSION

In the example we just went through, we customized the logic according to which ASP.NET builds the parameters passed to our actions. Specifically, we provided a work-around for a big limitation that was forcing us to write a lot of code in the controller to persist changes with Entity Framework.

Thanks to the new PostModelBinder, our action has become simpler or, better said, it works at a higher level of abstraction. The infrastructure automatically takes care of realizing when there's an update in progress and a Post must be retrieved from the database.

The implementation we made is simple, and so suffers from some limitations:

- It's not wise to query the database so often. It would be better to cache the data, temporarily storing it elsewhere.
- The model binder is specific to the Post class, but with a little more effort, we can build a more general version that can work with all entity types.

> **Building a universal EntityModelBinder**
>
> ASP.NET MVC applies object inheritance rules to determine which model binder must execute. With this in mind, we could, for example, build an EntityModelBinder that can retrieve any known entity type from the database. If we then registered it for the EntityObject base class, the runtime would automatically execute it each time it encountered a class generated by Entity Framework, easily extending the behavior we discussed to all the entities in our application.

We didn't worry about these weak points in this example because they would've made the code pointlessly more complex, with the risk of losing sight of the main task: plug our custom logic into the ASP.NET MVC runtime when it comes to parse user input and translate it into .NET objects. We managed this superbly by reusing a lot of built-in code, thanks to the `DefaultModelBinder`.

Some cases are so specific that `DefaultModelBinder` can't correctly interpret the data, and we need to build a new model binder from scratch. The next section will show how you can accomplish even more, using this kind of customization.

TECHNIQUE 56 Building a new model binder from scratch

`DefaultModelBinder` does its job pretty well if data is coming from a standard form that includes only simple elements (like text boxes, drop-down lists, or check boxes) for editing the object properties. But if we move to something slightly more complex, like the category editor in figure 9.12, everything comes to a grinding halt.

Categories.ascx is a custom editor template for the `IEnumerable<Category>` type; it shows two list boxes and a couple of buttons to move the catego-

Figure 9.12 To modify the categories associated with a post, we use a custom editor that ASP.NET MVC cannot interpret with any built-in model binder.

ries from one list box to the other. Going into too much detail about how this template works would be a bit off-topic—you can check it out on the included samples and read its actual code. For our purposes, you just need to know that because list box content isn't posted with the HTML form, we wrote a bunch of JavaScript to populate a hidden field called `values` with the IDs of the categories the user selected:

```
function updateHiddenField() {
    var string = '';
    $('.target option').each(function (index, item) {
        if (string != '')
            string += ';';
        string += item.value;
    });

    $('.hidden').attr('value', string);
}
```

Once the form gets posted to the server, the selected categories are represented by a list of numbers separated by semicolons, which our application should interpret correctly:

```
1;2;5;7
```

ASP.NET MVC can't do this on its own (remember, we implemented customized logic for our categories editor), but we can once again leverage the model binders' infrastructure to hide all the details about how this kind of data travels back to the server from the browser. Let's see how.

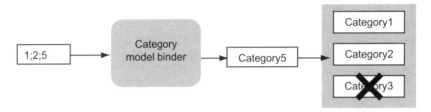

Figure 9.13 A custom category binder gathers the IDs coming from the request and uses them to populate an existing collection of categories accordingly.

PROBLEM

When we create or edit a `Post`, we want its `Categories` collection to be automatically populated with true Entity Framework entities, based on a list of IDs we receive from the request in a hidden field.

SOLUTION

For this kind of task, model binders will again be a great help in encapsulating the logic needed to translate a specific kind of input in a .NET object. Unfortunately, this time we can't re-use any infrastructural code like we did in technique 55 because we're using a customized way to encode the selected categories (which `DefaultModelBinder` obviously can't interpret). That means we have to build a new binder from scratch, with just the `IModelBinder` interface as a starting point for our `CategoriesModelBinder`:

C#:
```
public class CategoriesModelBinder : IModelBinder
{
  ...
}
```

VB:
```
Public Class CategoriesModelBinder
  Implements IModelBinder

  ...
End Class
```

This time, the implementation of the `BindModel` method works differently than it did in the previous example. As figure 9.13 shows, it works by taking an existing `Category` collection (probably coming from a given `Post` instance, but this isn't a requirement) and modifying its content by removing or adding instances of `Category` objects, according to a given list of IDs.

The next listing puts that logic into actual code.

Listing 9.14 Overview of BindModel code

C#:
```
public object BindModel(
  ControllerContext controllerContext,
```

```
    ModelBindingContext bindingContext)
{
  EntityCollection<Category> source =
    bindingContext.Model as EntityCollection<Category>;

  if (source != null)
  {
    IEnumerable<Category> fromRequest =
      this.GetPostedCategories(bindingContext);

    if (fromRequest != null)
    {
      this.UpdateOriginalCategories(source, fromRequest);
    }
  }

  return null;
}
```

❶ Gets reference to original model

VB:
```
Public Function BindModel(
    ByVal controllerContext As ControllerContext,
    ByVal bindingContext As ModelBindingContext) As Object
    Implements IModelBinder.BindModel

  Dim source As EntityCollection(Of Category) =
    TryCast(bindingContext.Model, EntityCollection(Of Category))

  If Not source Is Nothing Then
    Dim fromRequest As IEnumerable(Of Category) =
      Me.GetPostedCategories(bindingContext)

    If Not fromRequest Is Nothing Then
      Me.UpdateOriginalCategories(source, fromRequest)
    End If
  End If

  Return Nothing
End Function
```

❶ Gets reference to original model

We start by acquiring a reference to the existing model that we want to update ❶. In fact, CategoriesModelBinder can't create a new collection on its own. This isn't a limitation, though, because we're ultimately working on a Post instance, which always provides a not-null categories list.

Then we move our attention to the posted data, which we retrieve via a GetPosted-Categories method (more on this shortly) and use them to update the original collection. At this point, we've already updated the content of the original collection, so there's no need of a result; the last step is to return a null (Nothing in Visual Basic) value.

Now that you have an overall picture of how CategoriesModelBinder works, we can take a closer look at how we manage to retrieve the categories from the request in GetPostedCategories, whose code is shown in the following listing.

Listing 9.15 Retrieving Categories from the Request

C#:
```
private IEnumerable<Category> GetPostedCategories(
  ModelBindingContext bindingContext)
```

```
{
  var postedValue = bindingContext.ValueProvider.GetValue(
    bindingContext.ModelName + "." + "values");

  if (postedValue == null)
    return null;

  return GetCategoriesFromString(postedValue.AttemptedValue);
}
private IEnumerable<Category> GetCategoriesFromString(string stringValues)
{
  var values = stringValues.Split(';');

  foreach (var item in values)
  {
    int id = int.Parse(item);
    yield return ObjectContextModule.CurrentContext
      .CategorySet.Where(c => c.Id == id).Single();
  }
}
```

❶ Gets string of IDs from Request

❷ Translates list of IDs in actual categories

❸ Splits string into single

❹ Returns category given its ID

VB:

```
Private Function GetPostedCategories(
    ByVal bindingContext As ModelBindingContext)
    As IEnumerable(Of Category)
  Dim postedValue = bindingContext.ValueProvider.GetValue(
    bindingContext.ModelName + ".values")

  If postedValue Is Nothing Then
    Return Nothing
  End If

  Return GetCategoriesFromString(postedValue.AttemptedValue)
End Function

Private Function GetCategoriesFromString(
    ByVal stringValues As String) As IEnumerable(Of Category)
  Dim values = stringValues.Split(CChar(";"))

  Dim res As New List(Of Category)

  For Each item In values
    Dim id = Integer.Parse(item)
    res.Add(ObjectContextModule.CurrentContext.CategorySet.
        Where(Function(c) c.Id = id).Single)
  Next

  Return res
End Function
```

❶ Gets string of IDs from Request

❷ Translates list of IDs in actual categories

❸ Splits string into single

❹ Returns category given its ID

This code doesn't contain much that's strictly ASP.NET MVC; this framework comes up just to read the string of IDs from the request ❶. In fact, once we have the string, it's just a matter of translating it into actual `Category` instances ❷. GetCategoriesFrom-String accomplishes this task, splitting the sequence of IDs ❸ and, in turn, retrieving them using the current active Entity Framework context ❹.

One last step is still separating us from our ultimate goal—updating the original collection with the code shown in the following listing.

Why not read directly from the Request?

Although it might be possible to manually inspect the request content using the `HttpContext.Request` property, ASP.NET MVC value providers help to shield you from that dependency. For example, value providers theoretically allow the same code that's in listing 9.15 to work in a different context, where values are not coming from an `HttpRequest`.

Listing 9.16 Updating the original categories collection

C#:
```
private void UpdateOriginalCategories(EntityCollection<Category> source,
  IEnumerable<Category> fromRequest)
{
  var toRemove = source
    .Where(c => !fromRequest.Any(c1 => c1.Id == c.Id))     ❶ Items in source
    .ToList();                                                  and not in
                                                                fromRequest

  var toAdd = fromRequest                                   ❷ Items in
    .Where(c => !source.Any(c1 => c1.Id == c.Id))              fromRequest and
    .ToList();                                                  not in source

  toRemove.ForEach(c => source.Remove(c));                  ❸ Apply
  toAdd.ForEach(c => source.Add(c));                            changes
}
```

VB:
```
Private Sub UpdateOriginalCategories(
    ByVal source As EntityCollection(Of Category),
    ByVal fromRequest As IEnumerable(Of Category))

  Dim toRemove = source.                                    ❶ Items in source
    Where(Function(c) Not fromRequest.                         and not in
      Any(Function(c1) c1.Id = c.Id)).                         fromRequest
    ToList

  Dim toAdd = fromRequest.                                  ❷ Items in
    Where(Function(c) Not source.                              fromRequest and
      Any(Function(c1) c1.Id = c.Id)).                         not in source
    ToList

  toRemove.ForEach(Sub(c) source.Remove(c))                 ❸ Apply
  toAdd.ForEach(Sub(c) source.Add(c))                          changes
End Sub
```

Once again, no ASP.NET MVC here, but just some logic to find out which categories we have to remove ❶ and which ones we want to add ❷, and logic to apply the changes we calculated to the original collection ❸.

As in technique 55, for ASP.NET MVC to use our custom model binder when it comes across a collection of categories, we must register it in global.asax, whose `Application_start` method becomes like the one in the following listing.

Listing 9.17   Model binders setup in global.asax

C#:

```
protected void Application_Start()
{
    AreaRegistration.RegisterAllAreas();

    RegisterRoutes(RouteTable.Routes);

    ModelBinders.Binders [typeof(Post)] =
        new PostModelBinder();

    ModelBinders.Binders[typeof(EntityCollection<Category>)] =
        new CategoriesModelBinder();
}
```

VB:

```
Sub Application_Start()
  AreaRegistration.RegisterAllAreas()

  RegisterRoutes(RouteTable.Routes)

  ModelBinders.Binders(GetType(Post)) =
    New PostModelBinder

  ModelBinders.Binders(GetType(EntityCollection(Of Category))) =
    New CategoriesModelBinder

End Sub
```

From the controller's point of view, nothing changes and the code remains exactly the same as we've seen before:

C#:

```
[HttpPost]
public ActionResult Edit(Post post)
{
    if (this.ModelState.IsValid)
    {
        ObjectContextModule.CurrentContext.SaveChanges();
        return this.RedirectToAction("Index");
    }
    // ..a bit of more code here..
}
```

VB:

```
<HttpPost()>
Public Function Edit(ByVal post As Post) As ActionResult
  If Me.ModelState.IsValid Then
    ObjectContextModule.CurrentContext.SaveChanges()
    Return Me.RedirectToAction("Index")
  End If

  ' more code here
End Function
```

ASP.NET MVC will take care of invoking our new model binders while it's building the Post instance and, thanks to the new CategoriesModelBinder, its Categories collection will automatically be modified according to the user input.

DISCUSSION

What we've built in this last example, together with the one in the previous section, lets us handle the creation of a complex entity instance, plugging the whole logic into the ASP.NET MVC infrastructure. We managed to create re-usable and independent components. Thanks to them, we kept our actions code simple and focused on controllers' requirements (like checking whether the input is valid, redirecting to a particular view, or persisting changes to the database).

When you're working on a complex application, writing the logic in the correct place is important. With editor templates, you can define how an editor for a certain type looks, and with model binders you can bridge the gap between the request that editor produces and the actual .NET objects your controllers will receive.

Thanks to these notions, integrating an ASP.NET MVC application with ADO.NET Entity Framework (or another persistence layer) should be easier. Now, though we'll remain in the field of ASP.NET MVC customizations, we're definitely going to change topics. We'll explore how you can optimize the default routing infrastructure to improve search engine indexing of your web sites.

9.3   *Improving ASP.NET MVC routing*

We introduced routing in ASP.NET MVC in chapter 8. In that chapter, you discovered the central role it plays in this web development technology in mapping URLs to actions and controllers.

Routes are a great and effective way to improve URL readability, and ASP.NET MVC natively sets up a routing scheme that avoids query string parameters where possible, giving the application URLs a static look. Unfortunately, the standard functionality has a weak point, but we can correct it to significantly improve the search engine ranking of our pages. In this section, you'll discover how.

TECHNIQUE 57   **Routes with consistent URL termination**

ASP.NET routing is robust when it's parsing URLs to determine which controller will handle the request and what parameters it will receive. For example, it doesn't impose any rule for how the address has to be terminated. If we're using the default {controller}/{action}/{id} schema, it will successfully tokenize URLs like the following as if they were the same one:

- Home/Post/3
- Home/Post/3/

This feature makes it easy to avoid schema proliferation because both these URLs are valid and both need to be supported, but it raises a problem when it comes time to improve page rankings: they are different URLs, and this causes all the visits to be split among the two.

PROBLEM

You want to raise your web site search engine rank, so you have to avoid link duplication. You're going to add a trailing slash to your links and flag the ones that lack it as invalid.

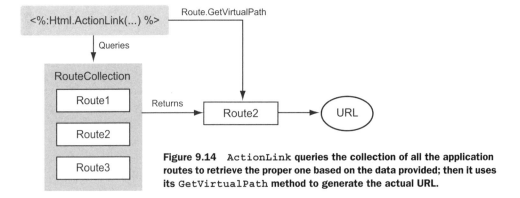

Figure 9.14   `ActionLink` queries the collection of all the application routes to retrieve the proper one based on the data provided; then it uses its `GetVirtualPath` method to generate the actual URL.

SOLUTION

The first point we're going to address is adding a trailing slash at the end of each URL. When we create a link using the `ActionLink` or `RouteLink` HTML helpers, as we did in the previous section, we generate links that don't terminate with a slash. We could consider building custom helpers to fix this, but it wouldn't be a wise choice because it would require manually modifying every view in our application to use our new helpers.

These methods are there to build links starting from the parameters on the routing settings and internally delegate to application routes the task of calculating the resulting path. Figure 9.14 shows this process.

The idea is to build a custom route that will be responsible for building the path with the trailing slash. The next listing shows its code.

Listing 9.18   Custom SEO-friendly routing

C#:
```
public class SEORoute : Route
{
  // ..some constructors here..

  public override VirtualPathData GetVirtualPath(        ❶ GetVirtualPath
    RequestContext requestContext,                          override
    RouteValueDictionary values)
  {
    VirtualPathData path = base.GetVirtualPath(requestContext, values);

    if (path != null)                                     ❷ Extension
      path.VirtualPath =                                    method for s
        path.VirtualPath.AppendTrailingSlash();             trailing slash

    return path;
  }
}

public static class RouteHelpers                          ❸ Routing extension
{                                                            methods
  // ..more code here..
```

```
  public static string AppendTrailingSlash(this string url)
  {
    int indexOfQueryString = url.IndexOf("?");
    if (indexOfQueryString != -1)
    {
      url = string.Concat(
        VirtualPathUtility.AppendTrailingSlash(
          url.Substring(0, indexOfQueryString)),
        url.Substring(indexOfQueryString));
    }
    else
    {
      url = VirtualPathUtility.AppendTrailingSlash(url);
    }

    return url;
  }
}
```

VB:
```
Public Class SEORoute
  Inherits Route

  ' ..some constructors here..

  Public Overrides Function GetVirtualPath(           GetVirtualPath
    ByVal requestContext As RequestContext,             override       ❶
    ByVal values As RouteValueDictionary) As VirtualPathData

    Dim path As VirtualPathData =
      MyBase.GetVirtualPath(requestContext, values)

    If Not path Is Nothing Then
      path.VirtualPath =                              ❷ Extension
        path.VirtualPath.AppendTrailingSlash()          method for s
    End If                                              trailing slash

    Return path
  End Function
End Class

Public Module RouteHelpers                    ◁── Routing extension
                                              ❸    methods
  <Extension()>
  Public Function AppendTrailingSlash(ByVal url As String) As String
    Dim indexOfQueryString As Integer = url.IndexOf("?")

    If indexOfQueryString <> -1 Then
      url = String.Concat(
        VirtualPathUtility.AppendTrailingSlash(
          url.Substring(0, indexOfQueryString)),
        url.Substring(indexOfQueryString))
    Else
      url = VirtualPathUtility.AppendTrailingSlash(url)
    End If

    Return url
  End Function

End Module
```

The SEORoute class inherits from the default ASP.NET Route class and overrides its GetVirtualPath method ❶. The new implementation is absolutely trivial and does nothing more than retrieve the default path and add the trailing slash where needed by using an extension method called AppendTrailingSlash ❷. This last method belongs to a static RouteHelpers class ❸ and leverages the VirtualPathUtility class to do its job after splitting the actual path from the query string.

We need to add this new route to the application's route collection in place of the default ASP.NET route. It can be useful to have a MapSEORoute extension method like the one in the following listing to help us in that task.

Listing 9.19   MapSEORoute extension method definition

C#:
```
public static class RouteHelpers
{
  // .. more code here ..

  public static Route MapSEORoute(this RouteCollection routes,
    string name,  string url, object defaults, object constraints)
  {
    var route = new SEORoute(
      url, new RouteValueDictionary(defaults),
      new RouteValueDictionary(constraints),
      new MvcRouteHandler());

    routes.Add(name, route);

    return route;
  }
}
```

VB:
```
Public Module RouteHelpers
  '.. more code here..

  <Extension()>
  Public Function MapSEORoute(
    ByVal routes As RouteCollection, ByVal name As String,
    ByVal url As String, ByVal defaults As Object,
    ByVal constraints As Object) As Route

    Dim route = New SEORoute(
      url, New RouteValueDictionary(defaults),
      New RouteValueDictionary(constraints),
      New MvcRouteHandler())

    routes.Add(name, route)

    Return route
  End Function
End Module
```

The method is simple: it builds an instance of SEORoute based on the routing parameter and then returns it. Even though it's simple, this method is useful because it lets us keep the code in global.asax similar to the code we typically use to declare routes, as you can see in the following listing.

Listing 9.20 Mapping the custom SEORoute

C#:
```
public static void RegisterRoutes(RouteCollection routes)
{
  // .. more code here ..

  routes.MapSEORoute(
    "Default", // Route name
    "{controller}/{action}/{id}", // URL with parameters
    new
    {
      controller = "Home", action = "Index", id = UrlParameter.Optional
    } // Parameter defaults
  );
}
```

VB:
```
Shared Sub RegisterRoutes(ByVal routes As RouteCollection)

  '.. more code here ..

  routes.MapSEORoute( _
    "Default", _
    "{controller}/{action}/{id}", _
    New With
    {
      .controller = "Home",
      .action = "Index",
      .id = UrlParameter.Optional
    }
  )

End Sub
```

What we've done up to now allows us to generate SEO-friendly URLs, but this solves just half the problem. If we're adding this optimization to a website that's already live, search engine bots might have already crawled our pages and stored the old URLs without the trailing slash. To solve this problem, we must permanently redirect them to the correct schema. If we want to do it transparently for every page, the right tool to leverage is the `HttpModule` shown in the following listing.

Listing 9.21 HttpModule that permanently redirects invalid URLs

C#:
```
public class SEORedirectModule : IHttpModule
{
  public void Dispose() {}

  public void Init(HttpApplication context)
  {
```

```
    context.BeginRequest +=
      new EventHandler(context_BeginRequest);
  }
```

1 Subscription of BeginRequest event

```
  private void context_BeginRequest(object sender, EventArgs e)
  {
    var context = HttpContext.Current;
    var url = context.Request.Url.AbsoluteUri;
```

2 Needed to exclude actual files

```
    if (!string.IsNullOrEmpty(url.GetExtension()))
      return;

    string newUrl = url.AppendTrailingSlash();

    if (newUrl != context.Request.Url.AbsoluteUri)
      context.Response.RedirectPermanent(newUrl);
  }
}
```

3 Permanent redirect to slash-trailed URL

VB:

```
Public Class SEORedirectModule
  Implements IHttpModule

  Public Sub Dispose() Implements IHttpModule.Dispose

  End Sub

  Public Sub Init(
    ByVal context As HttpApplication) Implements IHttpModule.Init

    AddHandler context.BeginRequest, _
      AddressOf context_BeginRequest
  End Sub
```

1 Subscription of BeginRequest event

```
  Private Sub context_BeginRequest(
    ByVal sender As Object, ByVal e As EventArgs)

    Dim context = HttpContext.Current
    Dim url = context.Request.Url.AbsoluteUri
```

2 Needed to exclude actual files

```
    If Not String.IsNullOrEmpty(url.GetExtension()) Then
      Return
    End If

    Dim newUrl As String = url.AppendTrailingSlash()

    If newUrl <> context.Request.Url.AbsoluteUri Then
      context.Response.RedirectPermanent(newUrl)
    End If
  End Sub
End Class
```

3 Permanent redirect to slash-trailed URL

This listing shows how SEORedirectModule is defined: it gets plugged into the runtime pipeline during the BeginRequest phase **1** and acts as a filter, checking whether a path is correctly terminated; if it's not, SEORedirectModule uses Redirect-Permanent **3** to return an HTTP 301 status code, which means Redirect Permanent. This kind of response, besides sending the browser to the correct address, is also correctly interpreted by a search engine, which will accordingly (and hopefully!) update its stored indexes. Obviously this logic makes sense only when a URL has a folder-like

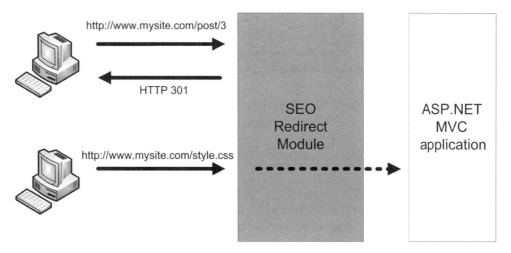

Figure 9.15 When a request comes from a URL that lacks the trailing slash, the SEO Redirect Module component issues an HTTP 301 status code to permanently redirect it to the correct URL. This outcome applies just to folders and not to filenames.

structure; redirecting http://www.mysite.com/style.css to http://www.mysite.com/style.css/ could be misinterpreted. SEORedirectModule does no processing at all if the request URL has an extension ❷ or contains a filename. Figure 9.15 summarizes how all this works.

DISCUSSION

One key point for optimizing your pages for search engine indexers is to have consistent URL terminations throughout the whole website. Having a trailing slash at the end of each path ensures that links aren't split between two equally valid addresses, which could dramatically improve your page rank. To that end, we fixed a couple of flaws in the default ASP.NET routing infrastructure.

First of all, we created a custom route class, called SEORoute, which produces correctly terminated paths when invoked by ActionLink or RouteLink HTML helpers. But this doesn't prevent manually generated URLs or other websites from having the wrong format. For this reason, we also built a custom HTTP module that catches these invalid requests and permanently redirects them to the correct URLs by issuing a 301 HTTP Status Code, allowing search engines to update their indexes.

9.4 *Summary*

When you develop real-world applications in ASP.NET MVC, you often have to deal with the same issues again and again. In this chapter, we tried to provide practical solutions for some of them. Although they're separate, distinct topics, they all highlight an extremely important and powerful feature of this web development technology: its expandability, thanks to which the framework can be customized to suit your specific needs.

Despite the fact that at a first sight ASP.NET MVC might seem more verbose than Web Forms, we showed how you can leverage, with a little effort, data templates and HTML helpers to minimize the amount of markup you manually write. You can build batteries of reusable components that result in websites with a more consistent look and feel.

At the same time, you want to keep your actions as simple as possible so that you have less code to maintain and debug. That means moving your own infrastructural or repetitive logic outside the controller. Action filters and model binders are a great help to meeting this requirement because they let you plug into the ASP.NET MVC response flow and customize it to your own will.

The last part of the chapter was about routing, which plays a key role in ASP.NET MVC. We showed how you can improve its URL generation logic so that your website is indexed more efficiently. Good indexing often results in a dramatically higher page rank.

This chapter concludes the third part of this book, which was entirely dedicated to ASP.NET MVC. The next chapters will change the topic, because we're going to look into security. Security is the main requirement your applications must meet to be ready for a production environment.

Part 4

Security

Part 1 showed you how ASP.NET works; parts 2 and 3 took a look at what features ASP.NET Web Forms and ASP.NET MVC give you when you're building the UI. Now in part 4, we'll take a look at one of the most important parts of every web application: how to protect your code and make it secure.

In chapter 10, we'll analyze the most common scenarios you'll encounter when you're dealing with security: how to build stronger applications, how to avoid common errors, and how to preserve the integrity of your applications. You'll find plenty of suggestions throughout the chapter.

Chapter 11 covers authentication and authorization in ASP.NET. This chapter will show you how to build a secure area, how to leverage ASP.NET's infrastructure, and how to build a custom provider to extend the existing features provided by ASP.NET's Membership and Roles APIs.

ASP.NET security 10

This chapter covers

- Analyzing security threats
- Handling untrusted user input
- Techniques to prevent SQL injection
- Cross-site scripting (XSS) in action
- Path canonicalization issues

In previous chapters, we covered both ASP.NET Web Forms and MVC, and how your application might benefit from new features available in version 4.0. Now it's time to take a look at security, which is a fundamental aspect of every well-realized application.

If you think that security is a secondary concern for your applications, you're wrong: an insecure application is an incomplete application. In fact, in a web application, security is more important than anything else because of the global availability of this kind of application and the large attack surface. Security is a pillar, and it has to be considered at every stage of the process, from the architectural stage right up to and including development itself.

Making an application secure is simple. You have to apply different techniques, though none of them are difficult to master. It's not black magic—it's common sense.

Security is often addressed in ASP.NET applications from two different angles:

- *In code*—You need to ensure that your applications are secure and protected from common types of attacks
- *By regulating access to features*—ASP.NET offers specific features to protect your applications with authentication and authorization, and to rapidly implement solutions. You can use these features to enable user access only to a specific set of pages, protecting your data from unwanted use.

To begin our discussion, let's try to create a picture of what security is and why you should care about it. This chapter will cover the first part of the problem, addressing specific scenarios related to writing more secure code and avoiding common pitfalls. Chapter 11 will fill in more details about authentication and authorization.

By implementing the techniques shown in this chapter, you'll have better applications. Remember: a secured application is a winning situation for both you and your customers. You can also apply these techniques to existing web applications to increase their security as well.

By the end of this chapter, you'll be able to build secure applications and identify the most common problems. Best of all, you'll be able to provide the correct solutions.

10.1 What is security in ASP.NET applications?

We're talking about security now because you understand the basics of ASP.NET and data access. You've been through the introductions, and now you're ready for the next important topic. We strongly believe that security deserves a high ranking in the topics chart every developer ideally uses.

Security is about best practices used the right way and about taking care of details in your application. Security is pervasive and affects every aspect of your software production cycle, from initial planning to architecture, development, and deployment. This book won't cover hardware or operating-system security, but you have to remember that these are important elements in your security strategy, too.

By not targeting security, you're exposing your application to a wide number of threats, the most likely of which are:

- *Data theft*—This situation is probably the one you least want to encounter because user data is like gold for every business
- *Server disk access*—Letting malicious users access your server disk might result in several problems, from data theft to code access or malicious file upload
- *Site defacement or alteration*—By manipulating your own code routine to store malicious markup and JavaScript in your database, someone can alter your site; the result can be anything from a simple alteration of the visual result to a complete defacement of your site.

An insecure web application is dangerous for both its developers and final users. As you might know, the code behind some of the business activities related to your application needs to be secret to avoid potential issues related to sensitive data; from the user's point of view, malicious code running via your site might help spread worms and viruses to their system.

Security is also a matter of brand image and trust. How can your users trust your business if you don't care about their data and safety while they're on your site?

As we've discussed, security is made up of a series of technology-independent principles that you must follow from the beginning to the end of your project to maximize quality. In the following sections, we'll discuss these principals in more detail. This discussion should help you remember your security goals every time you're beginning a new project.

SECURITY IS A FEATURE, NOT AN ADD-ON

It's quite frustrating to discover a serious vulnerability in your code. Vulnerabilities cost a lot, in terms of time, money, and developer respectability. Today, security is considered an inner feature of the application, and it's uncommon to consider it separately. As you plan usability, a nice UI, great performance, and scalability, you need to also plan for your application to be intrinsically secure. The potential problems you address in your applications might be the hardest part of your work toward making an application secure, but you'll save time and money in the long run.

FOLLOW THE PRINCIPAL OF LEAST PRIVILEGE

The fewer privileges you require for your application to run, the better. You need to run your web application under the least privilege you can. Don't run something exposed on the web with high privilege; if vulnerabilities exist, the code that could potentially be injected might run with unwanted consequences.

If part of your application requires higher privilege, try to isolate that part; an SOA is a great solution to this kind of problem.

DO NOT TRUST THE INPUT

Simply put, even if you're building an intranet, the input you receive is not to be trusted. In this case, the majority of attacks are going to come from the company employees, so don't think that because you're just running an intranet you don't need to seriously address security.

Generally speaking, don't trust any input. The input is going to come from different sources, most of which are beyond your control. Today it's common to have spiders trying to inject some code in your application or to bypass your protections.

Remember that the only secure input is what you yourself have written statically in your source code.

DO NOT DISCLOSE DETAILS

A personalized error page is way more professional than a default one, and it'll help you to protect sensitive data. Even though it's useful to know as much as you can about your environment while you're developing or debugging, an attacker can use this information to bypass your security check, to inspect your code, or, at worst, to arbitrarily execute some hidden functions.

DO NOT THINK THAT YOUR CODE IS BETTER

Make no mistake: software is always bugged. No software on the market is bug-free. The simple problem is that bugs do exist; the difficult part is to find them before someone else with bad intentions does. You'll have to deal with this problem, and the best you can do is react as soon as you can to these situations; to wait is to risk disaster.

USE YOUR HEAD

All software production has to be done using your head, but security deserves special treatment. The mantra of this chapter can't be repeated enough: *security is made of small things grouped together.* If you use your head and apply common sense principles—like the ones in this chapter—your application will be more secure.

Before we move on, we need to point out that a totally secure application doesn't exist, but you can aspire to the best, most secure application you can. This chapter is built around the following most common kinds of attack and shows you the related countermeasures you need to take:

- Malicious requests to alter the page flow and gain access to protected features of your application
- SQL injection to alter your SQL queries and execute malicious code, with the intent to delete data or to access protected information
- XSS to inject JavaScript code in your users' browsers to execute malicious code
- Path canonicalization to access blocked parts of the server disk or to upload unwanted files

We'll analyze every problem and the associated solution in more detail in the rest of this chapter. We'll use a typical web application as an example, so we'll include the most common scenarios. These scenarios will be related specifically to parsing and storing user input in a way that makes it as difficult as possible to present a threat to your application.

10.2 *Filtering and blocking incoming requests*

You shouldn't always trust user input. You have to filter every incoming request to make sure it's legitimate and that it doesn't aim to alter your flow. A thing as simple as using incorrect parameter values can force application behavior. By changing a parameter value to one not in the acceptable range, for example, an attacker can disclose information, bypassing some security checks.

Another attack type consists of passing an arbitrary value to gain access to protected information. Sometimes when designing an application, developers choose a globally unique identifier (GUID) as the format for the content key. Part of the reason for this choice is to protect themselves from this kind of attack: developers tend to think that a GUID is less spoofable than an integer. The truth is that this isn't a secure feature; it's like hiding your head in the sand.

Filtering a request, and blocking it if necessary, is a different approach. First of all, if the corresponding content is protected, you have to check that the current user identity has the right to access it. This requirement might seem obvious, but security is accomplished by carrying out relatively simple and obvious rules. In this section, we'll take a look at common attacks related to sending misleading information to a page and how you can handle and filter them to maintain a secure application.

TECHNIQUE 58   Handling improper parameter values

Even if you think that the browser is secure enough to rely on its sandboxed environment, the reality is that HTTP, the protocol behind the web, is simple, so building a tool to send specially crafted requests is not too difficult. By inspecting values coming with the request, you can add more security to your applications with little effort.

PROBLEM

Improper values are dangerous because they can alter the application behavior, generate runtime exceptions, and expose the error details to an attacker. You need a unified approach to sanitize these values and protect your application.

SOLUTION

Rule number 1 of security is use common sense. With that in mind, it's obvious that the first action you should perform is to check for data type consistency. If you know that a parameter can contain only integer values, it's a good practice to check that the passed value respects this requisite. Most primitive types (like `System.Integer`, `System.DataTime`, and `System.Boolean`) offer a useful `TryParse` static method. This method checks that the corresponding value is convertible to a given type. If the conversion takes place, the value is saved in the variable and used in conjunction with the original value. The following listing shows a simple example for parsing an `Integer` value from the query string.

Listing 10.1   Example of parameter type check

C#:
```
int id;
if (int.TryParse(Request.QueryString["ID"], out id))
{

}
```

VB:
```
Private Sub foo()
  Dim id As Integer
  If Integer.TryParse(Request.QueryString("ID"), id) Then

  End If
End Sub
```

This classic approach (not testing for a data type check) can lead to an error similar to the one shown in figure 10.1.

As you can see, the default error page when the app is in debug mode also shows a fragment of the source code. Lazy developers frequently leave an application in debug mode even when it's deployed; these developers have to be lucky enough to have no

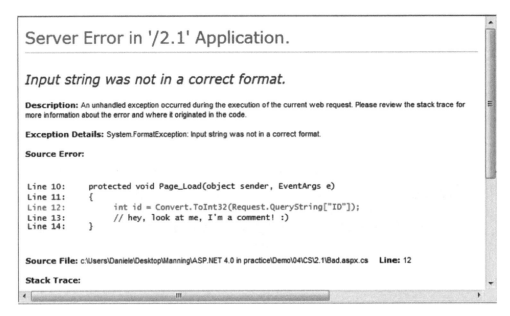

Figure 10.1   By not correctly checking your parameters, you can disclose too many details about your application.

sensitive information coming out with the default error message. (We're going to cover error page personalization and logging in more detail in chapter 15.)

DISCUSSION

This example is a basic one. When you're dealing with user input, you have to check for range consistency. For example, if you're expecting a birth date, you should check for a valid range; if you want an integer ID, you should check for that data type.

Don't trust your user input and always verify that the values are within the acceptable range; if you do, your application will be better and more secure. By implementing this technique proactively, you can also add a blocking mechanism to your applications, logging unwanted requests.

TECHNIQUE 59   **Monitoring and blocking bad requests**

Now that you can filter incoming requests, you're ready to build a blocking engine to handle and improve parameter values. To avoid problems, it's crucial to monitor bad requests. HTTP has its own request statuses. By using them, we're telling the browser (or, generally speaking, the client) that the request had some trouble and didn't execute correctly.

PROBLEM

We want to manage invalid requests and notify the client about any invalid parameters that were passed in. We'll leverage HTTP status codes to maintain great compatibility with intelligent clients (which search engine spiders certainly are) and to enable a forensic log analysis if we need it.

SOLUTION

When someone sends an invalid parameter, you should reply to the request using one of the specific error codes. For the common browser, this rule doesn't make any difference, but it'll help you when you have to deal with search engine spiders.

Every request could, in fact, be logged (via IIS) in the corresponding log files, so you can take further actions to analyze them and provide some kind of mechanism to report strange situations. This topic is more specific to the system administrator, so we're not going to cover it here.

Table 10.1 lists the principal HTTP error status codes. Each request produces a status code; if there are no errors, the default value is `200 OK`.

Table 10.1   Main HTTP status codes for errors

HTTP status code	Description
400	Bad request: Used to notify the browser that the request isn't considered valid.
404	Not found: The requested content isn't available.
500	Error: The request caused an error.

Analyze log files with LogParser

Microsoft's LogParser is a free tool that can analyze a lot of different log file formats, including the Microsoft IIS one.

LogParser uses a special version of a SQL dialect to submit queries against log files, retrieve the corresponding results, and put those results into different destinations, such as CSV files or a database.

You can download LogParser from the Microsoft website at http://www.mng.bz/5KrO. You can find more information about using LogParser in a Microsoft Knowledge Base (KB) article at http://www.mng.bz/slJe.

For example, when a parameter that's outside the scope is used, it's completely legitimate to reply using the `400 bad request` HTTP status code. You can get this result by throwing a new exception of type `HttpException`, using code similar to this:

C#:

```
if (string.IsNullOrEmpty(Request["ID"]))
    throw new HttpException(400, "Bad request");
```

VB:

```
If (String.IsNullOrEmpty(Request("ID"))) Then
    Throw New HttpException(400, "Bad request")
End If
```

To send a detailed response to the client, we're changing web.config settings to generate the response from a specific page, as shown in the following listing.

Listing 10.2   web.config configuration for a custom 400 error

```
<configuration>
  <system.web>
    <customErrors mode="On" defaultRedirect="GenericErrorPage.htm"
                             redirectMode="ResponseRewrite">
      <error statusCode="400" redirect="BadRequest.htm" />
      <error statusCode="404" redirect="FileNotFound.htm" />
    </customErrors>
  </system.web>
</configuration>
```

You can check the corresponding display in figure 10.2.

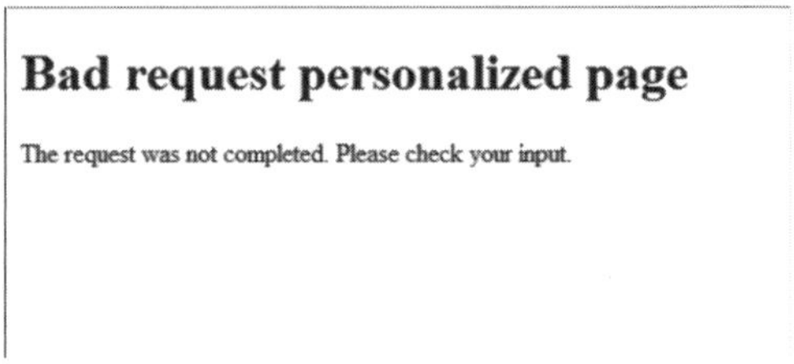

This technique is useful because we're achieving two results: we're notifying the client that there's a problem with the request, and we're storing the details in our log files so we can automate collecting and block unwanted IP addresses from doing additional requests if they exceed our threshold.

Bad request personalized page

The request was not completed. Please check your input.

Figure 10.2   A specific error page designed for bad requests. You can personalize the look and feel of the page and provide some guidelines for your users, like specifying allowed and disallowed characters.

DISCUSSION

HTTP status codes are here to help both client and server better serve each other. You definitely need to use them when you require non-ordinary responses; for example, a 404 response code is useful to inform a search engine spider that a resource doesn't exist. Use them safely, and both you and your clients will reap huge benefits.

The next part of this chapter is related to SQL injection. SQL injection is a specific vulnerability caused by incorrectly parsing user input and letting the value arrive directly to your SQL engine, without any block or filter.

10.3   *Protecting applications from SQL injection*

SQL injection is considered the worst attack for a web application. It's widely used as a way to gain control over an application by simply injecting some specially crafted SQL query via a parameter. This kind of attack is primarily caused by improper handling of *string concatenation*. Though the results can be devastating, the countermeasures are quite simple.

Given the availability of ORMs like Entity Framework, LINQ to SQL, and NHibernate, SQL injection is less common in modern applications. If you have some code based on ADO.NET Command, you'll probably find this part of the chapter extremely useful.

Figure 10.3 shows a typical problem related to SQL injection. Many variants of SQL injection strings exist, but the one displayed in this figure is one of the most common.

When the developer is using string concatenation, the special sequence -- can compose the resulting query to ignore the rest of the string. The result, in this example, is the ability to completely bypass a security login; a malicious user can authenticate themselves as the username specified.

SQL injection techniques

A malicious user can do literally dozens of things when a page is vulnerable to SQL injections. What that user decides to do depends on the database server type and your configuration. If a service isn't properly configured, that can be used as a vehicle for executing remote commands. For example, in SQL server an attacker could use the `xp_cmdshell` system stored procedure to arbitrarily execute an arbitrary command.

You'll find more information about these techniques at http://www.owasp.org/index.php/SQL_Injection.

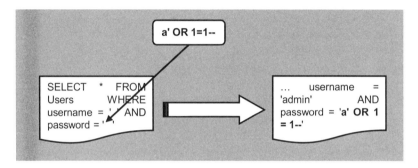

Figure 10.3   A simple problem related to SQL injection. String concatenation of user input occurs and the resulting query is executed without other filters.

TECHNIQUE 60   **Handling SQL queries using parameters**

SQL queries are potentially one of the biggest threats in a web application. So many scenarios need your attention when you're composing dynamically generated SQL strings that it's not easy to prevent them all if you're not using the right approach.

The most common scenario in which the danger can be high involves string values, where you have to deal with routines that help you safely compose your query.

PROBLEM

You want to write SQL queries the right way. You want to stay secure and avoid SQL injection, without losing functionalities.

SOLUTION

Let's try to resolve this problem step-by-step.

First of all, the simplest case is the one addressed in the introduction: dealing with routines that let you compose your queries by concatenating strings. You can rewrite the corresponding code by taking advantage of the `SqlParameter` class and using a parameterized query instead of string concatenation, as shown in the following listing.

Listing 10.3   The right way to compose a dynamic query

C#:

```
string sql = "SELECT * FROM Users WHERE Username = @Username" +
             " AND Password = @Password";

using (SqlConnection conn = new SqlConnection("..."))
{
  using (SqlCommand cmd = new SqlCommand(sql, conn))
  {
    SqlParameter p = new SqlParameter("@Username",              Parameter
                          SqlDbType.VarChar, 100);    ◁─┘       value
    p.Value = Username.Text;
    cmd.Parameters.Add(p);                               ◁─┐ Add to parameters
                                                           │ collection
    SqlParameter p2 = new SqlParameter("@Password",
                            SqlDbType.VarChar, 100);
    p2.Value = Password.Text;
    cmd.Parameters.Add(p2);

    using (SqlDataReader dr = cmd.ExecuteReader())
    {
      ...
    }
  }
}
```

VB:

```
Dim sql As String = "SELECT * FROM Users WHERE Username = @Username" &
                    " AND Password = @Password"

Using conn As New SqlConnection("...")
  Using cmd As New SqlCommand (sql, conn)
    Dim p As New SqlParameter ("@Username",                   Parameter
                          SqlDbType.VarChar, 100)    ◁─┘       value
    p.Value = Username.Text
    cmd.Parameters.Add(p)                                        ◁─┐

    Dim p2 As New SqlParameter("@Password", SqlDbType.VarChar, 100)
    P2.Value = Password.Text
    cmd.Parameters.Add(p2)                              Add to parameters
                                                             collection
    Using dr As SqlDataReader = cmd.ExecuteReader()
      ...
    End Using
  End Using
End Using
```

This code isn't difficult to understand or to implement. If you've used a stored procedure before, this approach is the same as that one. Parameterized queries are similar
in meaning to stored procedures: you pass the parameters explicitly, and their encoding is the responsibility of the underlying data access technology, not yours.

Parameterized queries with Access, Oracle, and MySQL

Even though the examples provided in this chapter are specific to SQL Server, you can
use the same techniques with Access, Oracle, and MySQL. The only difference is that

SQL Server supports the format @param, known as named parameter. Access (and OLE-db) uses the sequential order and a generic ? placeholder. Oracle uses the same approach as SQL Server, but the format is :param. MySQL uses the ?param format.

When you're using a parameterized query, the conversion and escape of the value is done by the engine itself; you're safe, and you don't need to take further action. You should always check for data type consistency, as we discussed earlier in this chapter, to avoid runtime errors and to execute only legitimate queries.

DISCUSSION

Simply escaping the apostrophe (or other potentially unsafe characters) is not enough. So many variations on the theme exist that the only secure way to handle these values is by using parameters. Just in case you're wondering whether your code is secure without parameters, the answer is simple: no, it's not. The only effective way of making a secure dynamic query is by using parameters. Again, don't trust the input and perform all the checks against the values, just like we've discussed previously.

The next step is to analyze a specific kind of SQL injection that's related to handling multiple values in a query. If you need to parse only a single value, the problem is much simpler than when you're dealing with multiple values.

TECHNIQUE 61   Dynamic queries with multiple values

Multiple values are often used in dynamically generated queries, for example, in combination with the IN SQL clause or when you need to filter by different words. This issue is separate from the other issues we're covering, and we need to address it specifically by using the correct approach.

PROBLEM

We want to apply the same technique we used in the previous example to a query composed of multiple values. We want to stay secure by continuing to use parameters, but we need to pass multiple values to the query.

SOLUTION

If you need to get every product in a given list of categories, you'll probably opt for a piece of code similar to this snippet:

C#:
```
string sql = "SELECT * FROM Products WHERE Category IN ({0})";
sql = string.Format(sql, Request["categories"]);
```

VB:
```
Dim sql As String = "SELECT * FROM Products WHERE Category IN ({0})"
sql = string.Format(sql, Request("categories"))
```

If you're using a <select /> HTML tag with multiple selection, the browser will automatically send the values, separated by a comma, which is the exact syntax used in SQL.

The problem is that if someone passes an evil string, like 0);DROP TABLE Products--, the result is the following query:

```
SELECT * FROM Products WHERE Category IN (0);DROP TABLE Products--)
```

The ; character is used to separate different queries, so this code can be used to arbitrarily execute a query. It's not uncommon to have tables named Users, Products, Categories, and so on. A malicious user can employ special techniques that aim at retrieving the database schema using a normal page created to visualize data. It's only a matter of time and attacker ability. For this reason, we need a mechanism to support these queries, but one that uses parameters. An example is shown in the following listing.

Listing 10.4   Dynamically composing a query with multiple values

C#:

```
StringBuilder sql =
    new StringBuilder("SELECT * FROM Products WHERE Category IN (");      ◄─┐  Compose
                                                                            base
string[] categories = Request["Categories"].Split(',');                    query

SqlParameter[] parameters = new SqlParameter[categories.Length];

for (int i = 0; i < categories.Length; i++)
{
  sql.AppendFormat("@p{0}, ", i);                                   ◄─┐  Set the
  parameters[i] = new SqlParameter(string.Format("@p{0}", i),         parameter
                                   categories[i]);                    value
}
sql.Append("0)");
```

VB:

```
Dim sql As New StringBuilder("SELECT * FROM Products " &        ┐  Compose
                        "WHERE Category IN (")          ◄─┘  base query
Dim categories As String() = Request("Categories").Split(",")

Dim parameters As SqlParameter() =
    New SqlParameter(categories.Length - 1)

For i As Integer = 0 To categories.Length - 1             ┐  Set the
    sql.AppendFormat("@p{0}, ", i)                 ◄─┘  parameter value
    parameters (i) = New SqlParameter(String.Format("@p{0}", i),
                                      categories(i))Next
sql.Append("0)")
```

This listing shows you the solution to our problem. We can dynamically generate the SQL string by safely adding the parameters, based on multiple values. It's perfectly possible to name parameters sequentially, so this is a good solution for our problem. Our solution doesn't rely on user input, and we can pass the values to the database engine, which will sanitize them for us.

The generated query will be similar to this one:

```
SELECT * FROM Products WHERE Category IN (@p0, @p1, @p2, 0)
```

The parameter is then added, using iteration, to the corresponding `SqlCommand` instance. Our query will be secured.

DISCUSSION

This code is similar to what you need when you're dealing with multiple LIKE clauses or when you're searching for many words. Using parameters provides more security to your queries even in more complex scenarios like the one we talked about here.

At this point, you've learned how SQL injection can be dangerous for your data and what the principal countermeasures to avoid potential data losses are. To complete our journey on the road of the typical problems related to security, it's time to take a look at XSS. By implementing a protection against XSS, we'll add more security to our application, avoid JavaScript injection, and maximize our users' security.

10.4 Dealing with XSS (cross-site scripting)

XSS is probably the most subtle kind of attack because it's quite often invisible at first glance. XSS is based on some code, usually markup or JavaScript, that's injected into your page. The most common problem is related to data that's saved in a database after user input and then loaded in a page. If not properly escaped, as in figure 10.4, the problem is that the user input is appended to the resulting HTML and the results are unexpected. For example, using JavaScript, it's quite easy to perform nasty actions, like *identity theft* and *session spoofing*.

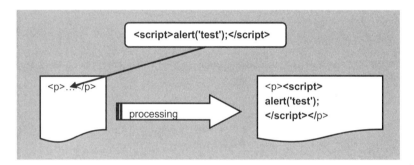

Figure 10.4   XSS is similar to SQL injection, but the code is inserted in the markup and isn't executed in a database query.

With identity theft, for example, an attacker could gain access to a website by simply cloning its identity cookie. For this reason, you have to avoid XSS in your applications.

TECHNIQUE 62   **Handling and displaying user input**

As we've stated previously, do not trust user input. This mantra applies to both SQL injection and XSS. In our next scenario, the countermeasures might vary, depending on how you need to treat (and store) user input.

PROBLEM

We want to avoid XSS and we want to let a user send different kinds of content: plain text and markup. We need a method to sanitize the user input before saving it in a database.

SOLUTION

ASP.NET, starting with version 1.1, is protected by default to malicious user input. If you try to insert some markup or JavaScript code via a GET or POST field, the runtime intercepts the input and produces an error similar to the one shown in figure 10.5.

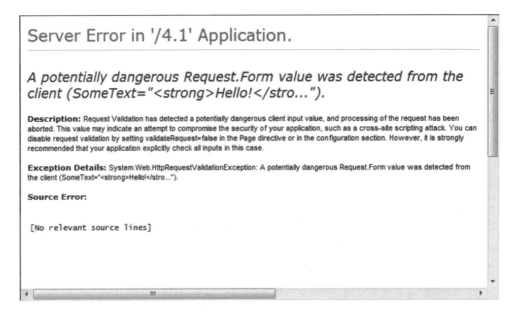

Figure 10.5 **ASP.NET has a default validation mechanism that can intercept potentially dangerous values and display a specific error page.**

If you need basic protection against common kinds of attacks, this default behavior is what will help you first. If you store your code to display it later in a page, it's better to encode it properly in the first place. Remember: do not trust user input!

You can implement this solution by using the `HtmlEncode` method from the `HttpServerUtility` or `HttpUtility` class in the `System.Web` namespace. You can also access it directly via the `Server` property on both `HttpContext` and `Page`.

You need to write the following code in your markup:

C#:
```
string text = HttpUtility.HtmlEncode (SomeText.Text);
```

VB:
```
Dim text as String = HttUtility.HtmlEncode(SomeText.Text)
```

New in version 4.0, this protection is applied to all requests (not just .aspx pages) because it's fired in the `BeginRequest` event of `HttpApplication`. If you need to revert to the old behavior, you can change it via web.config:

```
<httpRuntime requestValidationMode="2.0" />
```

In version 4.0, you can tweak the default validation mechanism by writing a new class that inherits from `System.Web.Util.RequestValidator` and specifying its name in web.config:

```
<httpRuntime
    requestValidationType="ASP4InPractice.MyValidator, ASP4InPractice" />
```

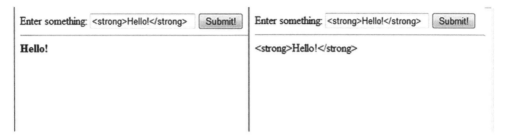

Figure 10.6   Without (on the left), and with (on the right) input encoding. In the first example, the markup is processed by the browser because it's not escaped.

Another way to allow blocked characters (like < or >, for example) is to set the ValidateRequest property on the @Page directive to false, which will help us in testing our new solution:

```
<%@ Page ValidateRequest="false" %>
```

Figure 10.6 shows you the result of using the encoding and of not using it.

Beginning in ASP.NET version 4.0, you can also use a handy shortcut and simply embed a value in the markup. This same syntax is available with ASP.NET MVC 2.0, shipped with ASP.NET 4.0.

C#:
```
<%: Request.Querystring["value"]%>
<%: new HtmlString("<i>Not encoded</i>")%>
```

VB:
```
<%: Request.Querystring("value")%>
<%: new HtmlString("<i>Not encoded</i>")%>
```

The syntax <%: is equivalent to <%=HttpUtility.HtmlEncode. A specific interface, IHtmlString, is also present for when you don't want to encode the value. The new HtmlString is created to preserve markup in such a situation and to avoid encoding.

If you need to support some markup, the only viable solution is to sanitize the text. It's not easy, so the best way to proceed is to allow only a subset of HTML tags or use some metalanguage. The metalanguage you'll find in most forum software out there is often referred to as Bulletin Board Code (or BBCode). BBCode is composed of tags indicated by [and], so you can remove the real HTML code and then convert the basic tag to the corresponding BBCode markup. Some sample code is shown in the following listing.

Listing 10.5   A simple BBCode routine

C#:
```
public static class SecurityUtility
{                                                        Remove
  public static string RemoveHtml(string text)          markup
  {
    return Regex.Replace(text, "<[^>]*>", String.Empty);
```

```
public static string BBCode(string text)                          Convert
{                                                                  metamarkup
  text = text.Replace("[b]", "<b>").Replace("[/b]", "</b>");
  text = text.Replace("[i]", "<i>").Replace("[/i]", "</i>");
  text = text.Replace("[u]", "<u>").Replace("[/u]", "</u>");
  return text;
}
}
```

VB:

```
Public Module SecurityUtility                                     Remove
  Public Function RemoveHtml(ByVal text As String) As String      markup
    Return Regex.Replace(text, "<[^>]*>", [String].Empty)
  End Function
                                                                  Convert
  Public Function BBCode(ByVal text As String) As String          metamarkup
    text = text.Replace("[b]", "<b>").Replace("[/b]", "</b>")
    text = text.Replace("[i]", "<i>").Replace("[/i]", "</i>")
    text = text.Replace("[u]", "<u>").Replace("[/u]", "</u>")
    Return text
  End Function
End Module
```

If you use BBCode, you'll have more control over the kinds of input your users are allowed to insert. Take a look at figure 10.7 to see the rendering produced by the text specified in the input area.

DISCUSSION

Encoding user input is the right choice to make if you're planning to store the information in a database and display it later to other users. With the examples in this section, you're ready to protect yourself and your users from malicious code injection.

XSS techniques are quite often subtle, so keep in mind that it's better to be aggressive toward user input, rather than be permissive and compromise your application security. You can always remove some restrictions later.

To let you concentrate on your business needs, some libraries simplify development by introducing a new set of ready-to-use libraries, such as the Microsoft Anti-XSS Library.

Figure 10.7   A BBCode-enabled page. This form will allow only a subset of markup and uses the [and] characters to totally avoid the use of tags.

Using Microsoft's Anti-XSS Library

Microsoft's Anti-XSS Library is a combination of functionalities that protect web applications. You can freely download it at http://wpl.codeplex.com/. At the time of this writing, Anti-XSS Library is available in version 4. Version 3 introduced new features, and it's been completely rewritten with performance in mind. A new Security Runtime Engine (SRE) HTTP module protects the applications, using an approach that's similar to the default validation mechanism offered by ASP.NET, but with more features.

PROBLEM

When you're dealing with XSS, the simple `HtmlEncode` won't be enough. Sometimes you'll have to deal with user input that's to be added to JavaScript code, tag attributes, XML, or a URL. You want to stay secure in these scenarios.

SOLUTION

The Anti-XSS Library offers more methods that are specifically targeted to different untrusted inputs. The methods used to encode the inputs are listed in table 10.2.

Table 10.2   The main encoding methods of the Anti-XSS Library

Method	Description
`HtmlAttributeEncode`	The input is used as an HTML attribute (like `<div class=" (input) ">`).
`HtmlEncode`	The input is used in HTML (but not on attributes).
`JavaScriptEncode`	The input is used in JavaScript code (`<script type="text/javascript"> alert('(input)');</script>`).
`VisualBasicScriptEncode`	The input is used in VBS code (`<script type="text/vbs"> somecode </script>`).
`UrlEncode`	The input is used in a URL parameter, such as a query string.
`XmlAttributeEncode`	The input is used as an XML attribute.
`XmlEncode`	The input is used in XML output, but not with attributes.

The SRE HTTP module will be useful when you want to add more security without touching your existing application. Its intention is to add more security, not to replace your current encoding strategies. SRE consists of a tool that analyzes an assembly and produces the corresponding configuration. Take a look at figure 10.8 for a peek at what it looks like.

The tool will create a list of controls and methods to be automatically encoded, and then it'll do everything else, too. The tool is a good starting point when you don't have time to consolidate your code security, but it's not a permanent security implementation.

Look at the next two examples of using the Anti-XSS Library within each set of code: the first one encodes a hypothetically unsafe value for HTML, and the second one does it for JavaScript:

C#:

```
Results.Text = AntiXss.HtmlEncode (SomeText.Text);
ClientScript.RegisterStartupScript(this.GetType(), "alert",
                     string.Format("alert({0});",
                         AntiXss.JavaScriptEncode (SomeText.Text)),
                     true);
```

VB:

```
Results.Text = AntiXss.HtmlEncode(SomeText.Text
ClientScript.RegisterStartupScript(Me.GetType(), "alert",
                     string.Format("alert({0});",
                         AntiXss.JavaScriptEncode(SomeText.Text)),

                                                            True
```

Generated code:

```
this is a test&#33; &#39; &#60;br &#47;&#62; wow&#33;
<script type="text/javascript">
//<![CDATA[
alert('this is a test\x21 \x27 \x3cbr \x2f\x3e wow\x21');//]]>
</script>
```

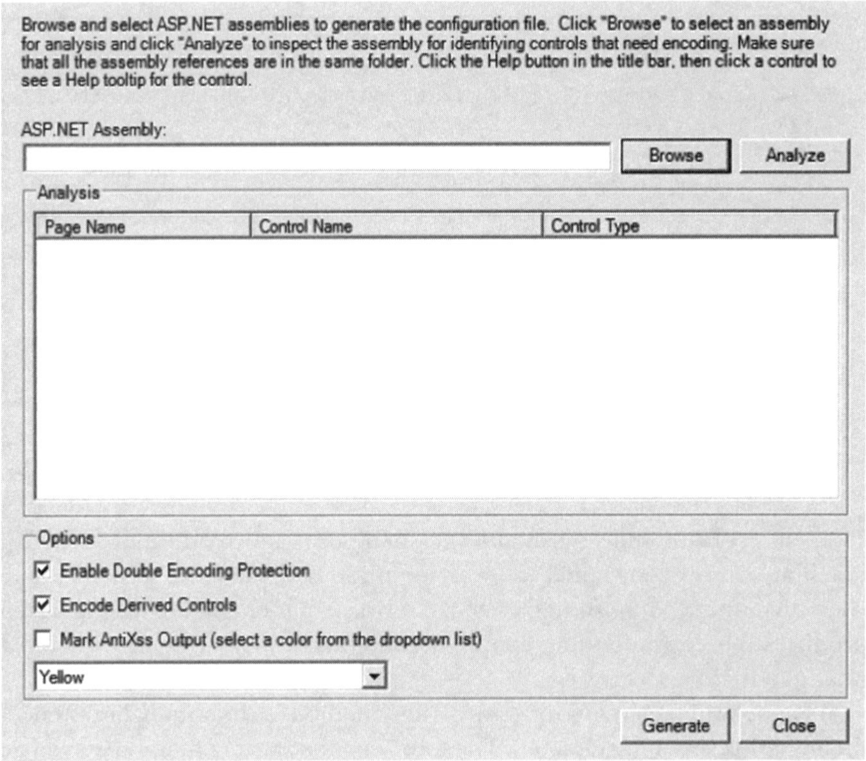

Figure 10.8 The SRE configuration tool. You can use this tool to perform a dynamic check against your already compiled ASP.NET applications.

As you can see, the generated code is properly escaped, so the untrusted user input became safe as well. If you need to handle a different scenario, be sure you choose the most appropriate method.

Starting with ASP.NET 4.0, you can also write a custom encoder. By deriving from `HttpEncoder` from `System.Web.Util`, you can change the default implementation and use your own. This means that you can use the AntiXSS Library feature without changing the reference to `HttpUtility.HtmlEncode` (or `HtmlDecode`). The following code shows a basic implementation:

C#:
```
public class AntiXssHttpEncoder : HttpEncoder
{
  public AntiXssHttpEncoder() { }
  protected override void HtmlAttributeEncode(string value,
                                              TextWriter output)
  {
    output.Write(AntiXss.HtmlAttributeEncode(value));       ◁─┐ Custom
  }                                                           │ implementation
}
```

VB:
```
Public Class AntiXssHttpEncoder
    Inherits HttpEncoder
    Public Sub New()
    End Sub

    Protected Overloads Overrides Sub HtmlEncode(
            ByVal value As String, ByVal output As TextWriter)
        output.Write(AntiXss.HtmlEncode(value))             ◁─┐ Custom
    End Sub                                                   │ implementation
End Class
```

To make this encoder work, you have to register it in web.config:

```
<configuration>
  <system.web>
    <httpRuntime encoderType="AntiXssHttpEncoder, App_Code"/>
  </system.web>
</configuration>
```

You don't need to change anything else, and even the new `<%:%>` syntax will automatically use the new specified provider.

DISCUSSION

The Anti-XSS Library is considered a must among ASP.NET developers due to its features. If you're planning to include user input in your application, especially in JavaScript fragments or to compose URLs, this library can save your life because it was developed to ensure great security in these areas. Our recommendation is to use the manual approach versus the SRE. When it comes to security, it's always better to analyze and decide, rather than rely on automatic features.

The next section will address a problem that's similar to two we've already addressed: path canonicalization. This problem is subtle to catch, but it can produce dangerous vulnerabilities. Let's take a look at how to prevent them.

10.5 *Controlling path composition: path canonicalization vulnerabilities*

Path canonicalization is the corresponding threat for file access, as SQL injection is for SQL queries. Canonicalization is, in general, a process for converting data into a canonical (or standard) form. With respect to the path, it refers to the action that builds a path in a safe form. This process is shown in figure 10.9.

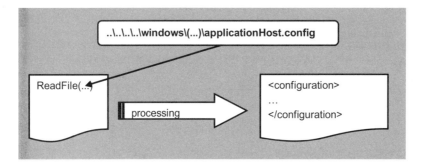

Figure 10.9   Path canonicalization in action. If a malicious user passes special characters, such as . . \ or . \, that user can alter the routine path and access files in other directories.

As with previous threats, the problem is in how string concatenations are performed. A web server is protected by default from this attack (also known as *directory traversal vulnerability*). If you have your code inside a physical directory named c:\inetpub\ mysite\ and you're requesting something like http://localhost/../../somefile.txt, the corresponding physical request won't be processed. The problem isn't in how the web server is processing these requests, but in how you dynamically compose a path. The path canonicalization issue surfaces in these scenarios.

TECHNIQUE 64   **Dynamically building a path**

It's common in web applications to compose a path using parameter values. This method is necessary in various situations: from a downloading system to user-generated files, dealing with dynamic path building is a common issue. The problem in these scenarios is that we can't trust user input, anymore than we can in other situations. All user input is potentially evil by default, so we need to take actions to sanitize it.

PROBLEM

Let's suppose we need to get a parameter via a query string, and we want to use it to access a file path composed by string concatenation. We want a safe system that composes a path dynamically and avoids path canonicalization vulnerabilities.

SOLUTION

In web applications, parameter values used to compose paths are important. If you need to build a local file path by using some user input, you'll probably end up with simple string concatenation, or you'll use the `Combine()` static method of the `Path` class from the `System.IO` namespace. This method is useful because it can handle leading and trailing slashes automatically, but unfortunately, it can't deal with directory traversal.

Let's suppose a malicious user passes c:\inetpub\mysite as the first part of the path and ..\..\windows\system32\cmd.exe as the second part. The result will be c:\window\system32\cmd.exe. This result isn't the one we want, and, depending on your application's behavior, the vulnerability might become quite dangerous.

> ## Dynamically executing an external program
>
> If you need to dynamically execute an external program originating from a web application, the best approach is to instrument it via an external service. In this situation, the service is responsible for creating the external program process that will run under its own security mechanism and won't be directly associated with the web application.
>
> Layering a complex application by using external services is the best deal when you're trying to achieve maximum security.

The best approach in this situation is to check for unwanted characters in the specified parameter. First, check for invalid characters in the parameter value by using the `GetInvalidFileNameChars()` method of the `Path` class. After that check, you can use the `Combine` method. Finally, you perform a last check on the results to make sure the resulting path starts with the base path. The following listing has the corresponding code to implement this check.

Listing 10.6   An anti-directory traversal routine

C#:

```
public static class PathExtensions
{
  public static string CanonicalCombine(string basePath, string path)
  {
    if (String.IsNullOrEmpty(basePath) || string.IsNullOrEmpty(path))
      throw new ArgumentNullException();

    basePath = HttpUtility.UrlDecode(basePath);      ❶ Check for
      path = HttpUtility.UrlDecode(path);                 invalid
                                                          chars
    if (path.IndexOfAny(Path.GetInvalidFileNameChars()) > -1)
      throw new FileNotFoundException("FileName not valid");
                                                     ❷ Use
    string filePath = Path.Combine(basePath, path);     Path.Combine
    if (!filePath.StartsWith(basePath))              Check the
      throw new FileNotFoundException("Path not valid");  ❸ composed path
```

```
        return filePath;
    }
}

string filPath = PathExtensions.CanonicalCombine(basePath, PathValue.Text);
```

VB:

```
Public Module PathExtensions
  Public Function CanonicalCombine(ByVal basePath As String,
                                   ByVal myPath As String) As String
    If String.IsNullOrEmpty(basePath)
       OrElse String.IsNullOrEmpty(myPath) Then
      Throw New ArgumentNullException()
    End If

    basePath = HttpUtility.UrlDecode(basePath)
    myPath = HttpUtility.UrlDecode(myPath)

    If myPath.IndexOfAny(Path.GetInvalidFileNameChars()) > -1 Then
      Throw New FileNotFoundException("FileName not valid")
    End If

    Dim filePath As String = Path.Combine(basePath, myPath)
    If Not filePath.StartsWith(basePath) Then
      Throw New FileNotFoundException("Path not valid")
    End If

    Return filePath
  End Function
End Module

Dim filePath as string =
            PathExtensions.CanonicalCombine(basePath, PathValue.Text)
```

Check for ❶
invalid chars

❷ **Use**
   Path.Combine

Check the
❸ **composed path**

This routine checks for invalid chars ❶ and then creates the path using the Combine method from the System.IO.Path class ❷. At the end, the composed path is checked ❸ to ensure that the generated path is still starting using the original path.

Let's build a new page to check this routine. We'll add a simple text box and a button to submit the value. The results are shown in figure 10.10.

Path canonicalization affects a lot of applications, and their developers likely don't understand the implications of such threats. Inadvertently giving users access to the server disk is bad in terms of security because often, along with code, the server has the configuration data. That data could be used to bypass other security defenses.

Insert a path value: ../test.txt   Generate!
File path not valid!

Figure 10.10   Path canonicalization is blocked by using our script in listing 10.6. This protection will ensure that malicious input is always blocked.

DISCUSSION

By using simple checks, you can ensure that dynamically built paths will be safe. When you're working with paths, you have to try to use, whenever possible, the minimum privilege necessary to access the file. A read-only Windows access control list (ACL) is ideal in this scenario to mitigate filesystem access issues. (You wouldn't put the execution permission on IIS, and the directory should be located outside the normal website path.)

With path canonicalization, our stay in the land of ASP.NET code security is near its end. This chapter hasn't included any black magic, just simple advice and code.

10.6 *Summary*

Security is an important topic. It's fundamental to every application, so this chapter has been dense with content, tips, recommendations, and examples.

Always keep in mind that security is especially key for web-based applications, so don't procrastinate on implementing it. It's better to be proactive in this field than to try to apply patches later. Security is one area of a web application where test-driven development (TDD) might add a lot of benefits; by implementing a test battery, you can automate critical scenarios that ensure that your code isn't targeted by the most common forms of security attacks.

Threats like SQL injection, XSS, or directory traversal are difficult to catch when your code is in production. It's much better to concentrate on the potential problems while you're planning and developing your application than to wait until the problems surface—and they will surface eventually.

Security isn't about difficult magic tricks; it involves simple things, but ones that you need to take care of. Keep your code simple, don't worry about performing a check, and never trust your user input. If you follow these simple rules, your application will be more secure!

Now that we've covered code security, it's time to move on to ASP.NET-specific features that address authentication and authorization in web applications. You need to know how to grant access to specific features of your application to only authorized users. Turn the page and find out how.

ASP.NET *authentication and authorization*

This chapter covers

- Authentication and authorization in ASP.NET
- `FormsAuthentication` and `WindowsAuthentication`
- `UrlAuthorization`
- The Membership and Roles APIs
- Building custom providers for the Membership and Roles APIs

The previous chapter was about code security and common threats in web applications. At this point, you have a clear understanding of what security is and how to avoid problems by analyzing user input. Now it's time to talk about two important and somewhat related topics—authentication and authorization.

ASP.NET has great flexibility in terms of authentication and authorization, which let you control access to web resources based on a different matrix of permissions by using usernames and roles. By protecting an application from unwanted access, you can add special features that designated users can use to maximize the usability of the site. An administrator, for example, can just log in and perform tasks like adding new content, modifying the site settings, or navigating the user list. On the other hand, a user can log in and participate more actively in the life of the site, adding comments, writing new posts in a forum, or giving feedback about the content. All these scenarios are regulated by authentication and authorization, which are fully integrated and supported by the ASP.NET infrastructure. Before moving on, you need to fully understand how ASP.NET implements their support so that you can gain control of and customize the default behavior to reflect your needs.

This chapter will focus on how to use authentication to perform common actions, like user registration, prompting for a password, or logging in. The bulk of the chapter is dedicated to authorization and authentication, which will help you protect special features for normal or anonymous users. A smaller part of the chapter is devoted to customizing the whole process, which involves replacing the default behavior with your own business rules.

The idea behind this chapter is to show you how to add a secure section to your website by following a simple list of steps. You'll be able to authorize the right users to have access to a reserved part of your website. The topics included in this chapter are valid for both Web Form- and MVC-based applications.

11.1 Authentication and authorization basics

ASP.NET has complete support for both authentication and authorization. We're going to start by clarifying what authentication and authorization are in the ASP.NET infrastructure. A clear definition will help you understand how to change the default mechanisms to better suite your needs.

The terms authentication and authorization do not represent the same concept. Authentication is the action associated with determining the identity of the user. Authorization is the step necessary to grant a user (who could also be anonymous) access to a requested resource. Both these features are implemented in ASP.NET with HTTP modules (described in chapter 1), using the events `AuthenticateRequest` and `AuthorizeRequest` from `HttpApplication`. ASP.NET provides great flexibility and allows you to fully change the default behavior. You'll find more information on extending ASP.NET in chapter 14, where we look at some more advanced scenarios.

Authentication and authorization are commonly associated with security because their function is to protect resources from unwanted access. You can find the options available in ASP.NET in tables 11.1 and 11.2.

Table 11.1 Authentication options in ASP.NET

Name	Description
FormsAuthentication	Authentication is performed using a form, and the identity is stored in a cookie or in the URL. This authentication type is the most common.
WindowsAuthentication	This option is used in intranets because it requires Windows. credentials to be sent by the browser.

Table 11.2   Authorization options in ASP.NET.

Name	Description
UrlAuthorization	Authorization is performed using `UrlAuthorizationModule`, which checks `web.config` for authorized users and checks roles against a specified set of URLs.
FileAuthorization	Authorization is performed using the `FileAuthorizationModule`, by checking the file ACLs of the requested file. The current thread identity is used.

You can use any combination of these options. Figure 11.1 shows how the options are integrated in the ASP.NET pipeline.

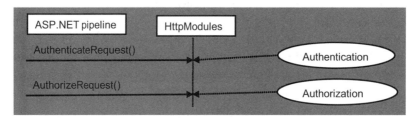

Figure 11.1   Authentication and authorization modules are integrated in the ASP.NET pipeline. This figure shows how they interact with the request and response flows.

In a public web site, the most common options that are used are `FormsAuthentication` and `UrlAuthorization`. `FormsAuthentication` has the advantage of being useful when `WindowsAuthentication` is not. The latter can be used only in intranets, where the Windows token can be sent by the browser and the need for another validation mechanism doesn't add anything to the application. The login is, in fact, performed when the user is logging in to the operating system, using centralized authentication storage like Active Directory (AD). `WindowsAuthentication` is useful only in an extremely limited set of situations, when the site is internal only.

On the other hand, `FormsAuthentication` is used when the authentication token from the operating system can't be sent across the boundaries, (which are what firewalls and the internet are). It's also much more flexible because the user storage can be changed, and you don't need to create a user in AD.

You don't use `FileAuthorization` unless you want to grant access to resources by simply using Windows ACLs (by setting permissions on users and groups on the disk). In 100% of the situations you'll encounter, you'll end up using `UrlAuthorization`, which lets you map users and roles to a URL inside the application.

Our next step is to analyze how you can use `FormsAuthentication` and `UrlAuthorization` in a common scenario to protect the application from unwanted access.

TECHNIQUE 65   Using FormsAuthentication and UrlAuthorization

When you're dealing with a secure section of your website, you need to authenticate the user with a corresponding pair of username and password inserted in a Web Form.

As we previously noted, FormsAuthentication gives its name to the corresponding class from the System.Web.Security namespace. This class has some helper methods that you use to initialize the corresponding elements. The best way to learn how to use FormsAuthentication is to set up a simple example. At the end of this section, you'll have mastered this kind of authentication.

PROBLEM

You want to build a system to let users authenticate themselves and access only a part of your website when they're logged in. This feature is a common one to implement and is available in the majority of websites. You also want to let the user sign out to complete the authentication flow.

SOLUTION

FormsAuthentication supports cookie-based authentication and cookieless authentication by embedding the token in the URL. The configuration is done via web.config, under the configuration\system.web\formsAuthentication section.

Before we move forward, we need to configure this section. The following listing shows a common configuration.

Listing 11.1   A common authorization configuration

```
<authentication mode="Forms">
  <forms
    cookieless="AutoDetect"
    defaultUrl="default.aspx"
    loginUrl="login.aspx"
    enableCrossAppRedirects="false"
    name="security"
    protection="All"
    timeout="60"                          Renewed at
    slidingExpiration="true" />      <--| every access
</authentication>
```

When the cookieless attribute is set to AutoDetect, ASP.NET decides whether to use cookie or cookieless support, based on the capabilities of the requesting client. The name attribute contains the name of the corresponding cookie. defaultUrl and loginUrl are used to specify the default page after the login and the login page itself. The timeout attribute, expressed in minutes, is used to control the timeout, and slidingExpiration lets you renew the ticket every time it's accessed if it's set to true.

When the authentication is performed, a *security ticket* is issued, using the FormsAuthenticationTicket class. In figure 11.2, you can see how the FormsAuthentication's HttpModule works.

The next step is to build a basic interface to collect the username and password. For now, we won't check for this combination in a database (which is a completely different topic that we'll address later in this chapter); right now, we want to focus on authentication, which is an architectural aspect of your application, not an implementation detail.

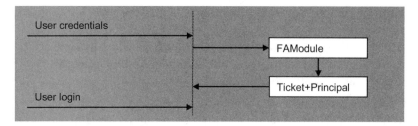

Figure 11.2 **The FormsAuthenticationModule issues a new ticket, plus a new principal with the correct user credentials. The ticket will be used for the rest of the requests.**

To start granting access to a given resource, we have to call the RedirectFromLoginPage method from the FormsAuthentication class. The configuration is read from web.config, so no other actions are required. The following snippet shows how to do this:

C#:

```
FormsAuthentication.RedirectFromLoginPage("username", false);
```

VB:

```
FormsAuthentication.RedirectFromLoginPage("username", False)
```

The first parameter represents the username, and the last one specifies whether the ticket must be created as persistent. If this value is set to true, you'll achieve the "remember me" feature available in most applications.

When a user is authenticated, ASP.NET associates an instance of the GenericPrincipal class to the corresponding User property on HttpContext. This instance is of type IPrincipal. IPrincipal is a special interface used to represent different identity types inside ASP.NET. It holds an IIdentity that represents the user identity plus its roles as an array of strings. In the case of FormsAuthentication, the identity is an instance of FormsIdentity, specifically created for this kind of authentication.

> **ACCESSING THE CURRENT PRINCIPAL** You can access the current principal, holding both the identity and roles, via the User property of the HttpContext singleton class (using the Current property), or directly via the User property on the Page class.

To display the current username, all you have to do is use code like this:

C#:

```
string username = HttpContext.Current.User.Identity.Name;
bool isAuth = HttpContext.Current.User.Identity.IsAuthenticated;
```

VB:

```
Dim username as String = HttpContext.Current.User.Identity.Name
Dim isAuth as Boolean = HttpContext.Current.User.Identity.IsAuthenticated
```

Now it's time to make our default page secure. To specify this rule, we have to add a special configuration fragment to our web.config because URL authorization will check the configuration\system.web\authorization section for the fragment. A sample configuration is available in the following listing.

Listing 11.2 The authorization configuration element

```
<authorization>
  <allow users="daniele,stefano,marco" />
  <deny roles="normaluser" />
  <deny verbs="POST" />
</authorization>
```

URL authorization supports allow or deny policies, plus the type of resource to be secured: users, roles, or HTTP verbs. By default, ASP.NET contains an allow policy for * users, and if the authorization isn't granted, a 401 HTTP status code is returned.

For users, * means every user, and ? represents an anonymous one. Note that the rules are applied using a short-circuiting mechanism: the first true rule will exit, and the others will not be evaluated.

To protect a single page or directory from anonymous user access, you have to use a configuration like the one in the following listing.

Listing 11.3 Configuration to prevent anonymous access from default.aspx

```
<configuration>
  <location path="default.aspx">
    <system.web>
      <authorization>
        <deny users="?" />
      </authorization>
        </system.web>
      </location>
</configuration>
```

Local rules will always be evaluated before the general ones, so be careful when you set them.

When a user accesses the default. aspx page as anonymous, the UrlAuthorizationModule intercepts the request and automatically redirects the user to the login page, passing the return URL via the ReturnUrl query-string parameter. After the login, the user is redirected to the requested page; if the parameter is empty, the defaultUrl attribute from web.config is used. You can see this mechanism in action in figure 11.3.

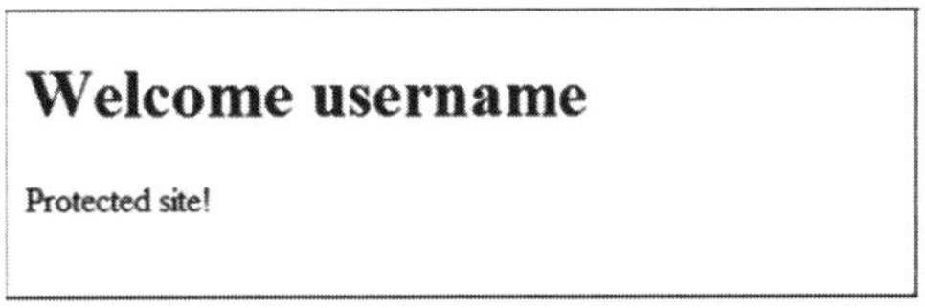

> # Welcome username
>
> Protected site!

Figure 11.3 The login page displays *username* as the current user after the user login. You can customize this page so the user can find the most relevant stuff when they're logged in.

> **MORE FLEXIBILITY IN AUTHENTICATION AND SIGNOUT** If you need more flexibility (you don't want to automatically redirect the user), you can use the SetAuthCookie () method on the FormsAuthentication class. Despite its name, it works with cookieless authentication, too.

To clear the authentication cookie and sign out the user, you can use the SignOut method.

By using `FormsAuthentication`, you don't need to take care of the code associated with creating a ticket, validating it, or destroying it. With `UrlAuthorization`, the entire infrastructure regulates access to available pages to designated groups of users only.

You need to understand that in an ASP.NET application it doesn't make sense to write your own authentication and authorization mechanism; you can customize the behavior of these building blocks for your own needs.

DISCUSSION

`FormsAuthentication` and `UrlAuthorization` are fundamental when you're dealing with application security in ASP.NET. The example shown in this section doesn't contain anything other than the core code necessary to handle authentication and authorization. In a typical application, you'll need to authenticate a user against a database, but this task is repetitive and can lead to code duplications, or worse, bugs.

When you need to authenticate against a database, the Membership API and Roles API come to the rescue so that you can focus on the application features. In the next section, you're going to learn about these APIs, using `FormsAuthentication` and `UrlAuthorization` as the pillars for your implementation.

11.2 Handling user authentication: introducing the Membership API

The Membership API is a set of programming APIs used to interact with membership features inside an ASP.NET application. The Membership API is based on the Provider Model design pattern.

Provider Model is a variant of the Strategy pattern, whereby the implementation details can be selected at runtime. As shown in figure 11.4, `Strategy` is an abstract type declaring a common interface, used by the `ConcreteStrategy` (the algorithm implementation). `Context` uses the common interface to execute the algorithm implementation given by `ConcreteStrategy` and holds a reference to this concrete object.

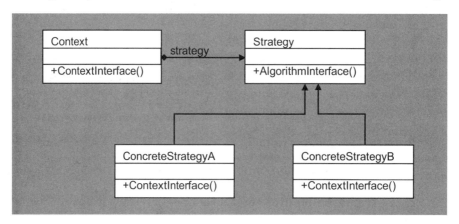

Figure 11.4 The Provider Model design pattern is based on the Strategy pattern, so their diagrams are similar. For each Strategy, one or more `ConcreteStrategies` exist.

In the Membership API, the `Membership` class from `System.Web.Security` corresponds to the Context, and the `MembershipProvider` class is the Strategy. Depending on the concrete implementation (the storage you want to query for membership information), you'll have a specific class for the `ConcreteStrategy`; for SQL Server, this class is `SqlMembershipProvider`.

The advantage of this approach is that the API will never change and neither will the provider-base class (the interface). You can swap concrete implementations (the providers themselves) without changing anything else. This approach is especially useful when you're building your application from scratch because it lets you concentrate on other aspects of your design. You'll have a building block ready to be used to implement a repetitive task.

Under the hood, the Membership API is built on the ASP.NET pipeline, so it leverages both `FormsAuthentication` and `UrlAuthorization`

To move on with our step-by-step guide to building a secure section in our website, we need to start implementing a simple application using the Membership API to grant access to a user who's logged in. We're going to implement two of the most common features in an application: registration and login. At the end of this section, you will have added a working, secure section to your website.

TECHNIQUE 66   Implementing a user login using the Membership API

The Membership API is what we need to use to add a login feature to our site. Because we're using the Provider Model design pattern, you just need to understand how to leverage this model to use the providers already available with ASP.NET and build a simple login system. The aim of the Membership API is to make you productive by letting you change the inner logic using a simple provider mechanism.

PROBLEM

We want to build a secured section on our site, using the Membership API to grant access to our reserved area to authenticated users only. We want to provide a complete experience, so we'll build user registration, password reminder/reset, and user login.

SOLUTION

Thanks to Provider Model, which was introduced in version 2.0, the login process in ASP.NET is easy to implement. The Membership API uses a dependency injection to read the configuration from the web.config configuration\system.web\membership\providers section, so you can change the provider without changing the code. If you need to change the implementation, all you need to do is change the default provider used in web.config. Neither the API nor the interface will change, and you don't need to alter any part of your code to reflect a different implementation.

This feature is important when you're building applications that target different customers. You can change the provider that's used from SQL Server to Oracle if your customer needs it, and you're done; you don't have to change anything else to implement this particular feature.

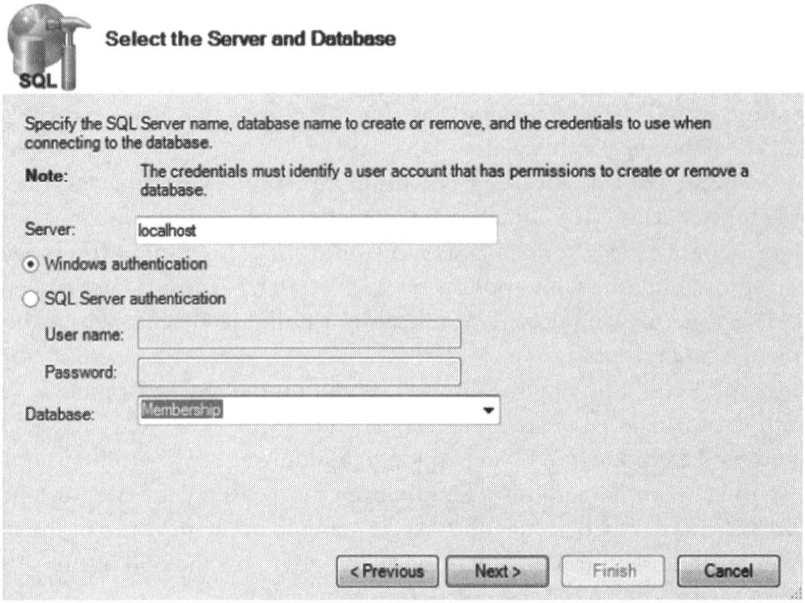

Select the Server and Database

Specify the SQL Server name, database name to create or remove, and the credentials to use when connecting to the database.

Note: The credentials must identify a user account that has permissions to create or remove a database.

Server: `localhost`

⦿ Windows authentication

◯ SQL Server authentication

User name:

Password:

Database: `Membership` ▾

[< Previous] [Next >] [Finish] [Cancel]

Figure 11.5 **The aspnet_regsql.exe tool, when launched without other parameters, has a graphical wizard for configuring the database. You can also launch it programmatically with parameters to create the schema in unattended mode.**

The Membership API ships in ASP.NET with two providers:

- `SqlMembershipProvider` supports SQL Server 7, 2000, 2005, and 2008 (even in Express/MSDE flavors)
- `ActiveDirectoryMembershipProvider` is specific for AD use in an intranet

For our example, we'll use `SqlMembershipProvider` to store the users in a SQL Server database because it's more common than using AD. Either way, the approach is identical because they both share the same base.

To start, you need to launch the aspnet_regsql.exe command-line tool under the .NET Framework directory (C:\Windows\Microsoft.NET\Framework\v4.0.30319\). This tool builds the database for you, so you can store the users in SQL Server. Figure 11.5 shows the wizard in action.

The typical user configuration in web.config that enables the SQL Server provider for the Membership API is shown in the following listing.

Listing 11.4 The SqlMembershipProvider web.config configuration

```
<membership defaultProvider="SqlServerMembership">
  <providers>
    <clear />
    <add name="SqlServerMembership"
      type="System.Web.Security.SqlMembershipProvider, System.Web,
            Version=4.0.0.0, Culture=neutral,
```

```
PublicKeyToken=b03f5f7f11d50a3a"          ⟵── Provider to be used
connectionStringName="SqlServer"                              ⟵─┐ Provider
enablePasswordRetrieval="false"                                 │ connection
enablePasswordReset="true"               ⟵── Password is hashed │ string
requiresQuestionAndAnswer="false"
applicationName="/"                      ⟵── Application name
requiresUniqueEmail="true"
passwordFormat="Hashed"
maxInvalidPasswordAttempts="5"
minRequiredPasswordLength="7"
minRequiredNonalphanumericCharacters="1"
passwordAttemptWindow="10"
passwordStrengthRegularExpression="" />
  </providers>
</membership>
```

The default Membership provider for SQL Server uses a custom set of stored procedures and tables. If you already have a database in place, you need to use a custom
provider, which is addressed later in this chapter.

The `applicationName` attribute is important because the default provider for SQL
Server supports multiple applications in the same database; this attribute indicates the
name of the current application. If you omit this value, the default virtual directory
path is used. Table 11.3 lists the methods that are most often used with the `Member-
ship` class.

Table 11.3 Methods most often used with the Membership class

Name	Description
ChangePassword	Changes the password of the specified user.
CreateUser	Creates a new `MembershipUser`.
DeleteUser	Deletes the specified user.
GetUser	Gets the specified `MembershipUser`, given the username.
ValidateUser	Validates the username and password with a Boolean response.

The class members in the Membership API are not directly called in your code;
because they're part of the Framework, they'll remain the same. They use the
defined Membership provider specified in web.config, so the code can be predetermined. For that reason, ASP.NET contains a number of custom controls that automate
the corresponding scenarios, so you can take advantage of them without explicitly
writing any code.

Let's take a look at some common scenarios with corresponding solutions that use
ASP.NET controls and Membership API features.

Registering a new user

If you need to create a new user, you can use the `CreateUserWizard` control, as in the
following listing.

Listing 11.5   Using the CreateUserWizard to create a new user

```
<asp:CreateUserWizard ID="CreateUserWizard1" runat="server">
  <WizardSteps>
    <asp:CreateUserWizardStep runat="server" />
    <asp:CompleteWizardStep runat="server" />
  </WizardSteps>
</asp:CreateUserWizard>
```

The `CreateUserWizard` control adds a simple wizard to create the user, as shown in figure 11.6.

THE MEMBERSHIP API IS JUST FOR... MEMBERSHIP! Membership information is about collecting a username, an email address, and a password. So the Membership API (and providers) supports only this kind of information. If you need to append more properties to a user, you don't need to extend the Membership API; instead, you use a new provider-based feature called the Profile API. We'll cover this API in detail in chapter 13.

Figure 11.6   The `CreateUserWizard` control displays a list of fields that let the user register in your application. You can customize this control using a template.

You literally don't need to write a single line of code to implement user registration; the magic is performed by the `CreateUserWizard` control, which automatically invokes the `CreateUser` method of the `Membership` class (that will use the corresponding concrete provider specified in web.config).

Implementing user login

As in the previous example, the login is performed by a specific control: the `Login` control. Behind the scenes, this control uses the authentication settings in web.config, which in this case is `FormsAuthentication`. The following snippet contains the corresponding markup used to display a login form:

```
<asp:Login ID="Login1" runat="server" />
```

This control is simple to use, and it's powerful—it automatically performs the associated action. A screenshot of the control is shown in figure 11.7.

In its simplicity and power, this control is probably the most tangible sign of the force of the Membership API: just write a single line of markup in your page, and it automatically takes care of tasks like validating user input, performing calls to the provider, and notifying the user.

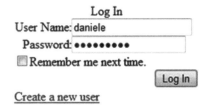

Figure 11.7   The `Login` control renders a simple pair of fields. The user enters a username and password; if they're correct, the user is logged in to the application.

Recovering or changing the user password

If you need to reset the user password, you use the `PasswordRecovery` control. To change the user password while the user is logged in, a `ChangePassword` control is available. The following snippet contains the markup necessary to implement the password recovery feature:

```
<asp:PasswordRecovery ID="PasswordRecovery1" runat="server" />
```

`PasswordRecovery` control supports body and subject personalization for the generated email. You'll find more information in the documentation on MSDN at http://www.mng.bz/NK3v.

DISCUSSION

The Membership API lets you take advantage of the controls that ASP.NET provides. The default providers will work in many situations, but even if you need to target different storage or a complex logic, the approach remains the same: thanks to Provider Model, all you need to do is change the concrete implementation (the provider) and not the rest of the code.

If you're comfortable with the default providers, you can insert this type of feature in your applications with little effort, and with no code at all, in just a couple of minutes. Not only that, this code is tested and developed by Microsoft to be safe, robust, and scalable. How cool is that?

Next up, we're going to look at some other controls to complete the picture we're making of ASP.NET security.

Other security controls

You can use other security controls to enhance the features related to authentication and authorization in ASP.NET, and increase your productivity at the same time. Table 11.4 contains a list of the security controls you can use in ASP.NET. Using these controls, you can write less code to implement the corresponding features.

Table 11.4 ASP.NET security controls

Name	Description
`ChangePassword`	Changes the password of the user who is currently logged in.
`CreateUserWizard`	Creates a new user.
`Login`	Provides the login form and authenticates the user.
`LoginName`	Displays the current username.
`LoginStatus`	Shows a login link when the user is anonymous, or a logout link when the user is logged in.
`LoginView`	Provides an alternate view for anonymous and logged-in users.
`PasswordRecovery`	Recovers a user password.

The Membership API lets you quickly implement all you need to use security in your application, but sometimes you just need to group users to simplify policy management. If this is what you need to do, the Roles API was invented for you.

11.3   *Adding support to roles using the Roles API*

In real-world applications, it's often useful—and necessary—to divide users into groups. By using groups, you specify a common set of rules to all users in the group and assign the group to roles. In this way, you can assign an entire group of users who perform similar actions to a particular role.

Using groups of users lets you easily define your security policy. You can specify, for example, that the Editor group is the one in which the users with editing permissions on your application will reside. You can protect your resources using a specific role. When someone needs to be added to this role, you don't need to specifically map this new user to the set of pages that implements this feature; instead, you simply add that user to the corresponding role. This process can greatly simplify your work, especially in large applications where it's difficult (if not impossible) to work with explicit permissions on individual users, but it's more pragmatic to work using groups.

Roles are fully supported in ASP.NET by the Roles API and Roles providers. Let's take a look at how to implement role-based authentication and authorization to our existing secured site section.

TECHNIQUE 67   **Implementing a role-enabled login using Roles API**

The Roles API is similar to the Membership API in terms of simplicity and power. To implement a role-enabled login, you need to leverage the Membership API; the Roles API is only about roles, not user management. This scenario is based on the login system we worked on in section 11.2. After you've completed the code, the user can log in, and you'll be able to assign users to roles.

PROBLEM

You need to grant only administrative users access to a given directory (named admin). You're going to configure the Roles API to use the SQL Server provider and specify the related authorization rules.

SOLUTION

Let's take a step back to technique 65. Just like every authentication mechanism in ASP.NET, FormsAuthentication is based on concrete IPrincipal and IIdentity implementations. As we've already discussed, the security principal is composed of the Identity and the user roles.

The Roles API is composed of the providers and the API itself, plus a special Http-Module: the RoleManagerModule in System.Web.Security. This module is responsible for handling the PostAuthenticateRequest event on HttpApplication and for generating a new RolePrincipal instance that's associated with the current thread principal. The result is the ability to use roles via the User property on HttpContext, which you saw in technique 65. The current Identity is preserved, so you can use the Roles API with all types of authentications, not just forms-based ones. Figure 11.8 shows how the RoleManager's HttpModule works.

Roles API features are handled by the RoleManager, which is disabled by default. You have to enable it and register a corresponding provider in the web.config file.

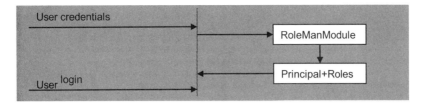

Figure 11.8   The RoleManager module changes the current principal to inject the user roles. The user ticket is renewed and the roles are added.

The Roles API uses the Provider Model design pattern, just like the Membership API does (see section 11.2 for more information about this design pattern). A typical configuration is shown in the following listing.

Listing 11.6   Roles API configuration

```
<roleManager enabled="true" defaultProvider="SqlServerRoles"
          cacheRolesInCookie="true" cookieProtection="All">
  <providers>
    <add name="SqlServerRoles"
        connectionStringName="SqlServer"
        applicationName="/"
        type="System.Web.Security.SqlRoleProvider, System.Web,
            Version=4.0.0.0, Culture=neutral,
        PublicKeyToken=b03f5f7f11d50a3a" />
  </providers>
</roleManager>
```

Similar to what we did to create a Membership provider, we need to declare a connection string. The attribute cacheRolesInCookie is useful here; when this attribute is set to true, the roles are cached in a cookie and a query isn't performed every time the roles associated with the user are requested.

Compared to the Membership API, the Roles API is quite invisible. No controls take direct advantage of its features (except for LoginView, which can provide different views based on roles).

A Role provider is based on the abstract class RoleProvider, from System. Web.Security. ASP.NET includes support for SQL Server via the SqlRoleProvider class and via WindowsTokenRoleProvider for Windows-based authentication. In table 11.5, you'll find the methods in the RoleProvider class that are used most often.

Table 11.5   Roles API most-used methods

Name	Description
AddUsersToRoles	Adds the specified usernames to the passed roles.
CreateRole	Creates a new role.
DeleteRole	Deletes an existing role.

Table 11.5 **Roles API most-used methods** *(continued)*

Name	Description
FindUsersInRole	Finds all users in a given role.
GetAllRoles	Retrieves the complete list of roles.
GetRolesForUser	Gets the roles for the specified username.
IsUserInRole	Determines whether the user is in the specified role.
RemoveUsersFromRoles	Removes the users from the passed roles.
RoleExists	Checks whether a role already exists.

Even though it's legitimate to check for user roles using `IPrincipal` and its `IsInRole` method (if you need to do that programmatically), it's more common to use `UrlAuthorization` to grant access to selected pages only. You can do this by using the configuration shown in the following listing.

Listing 11.7 Policy to allow only adminstrators to the admin directory

```
<location path="admin">
  <system.web>
    <authorization>
      <allow roles="administrators" />
      <deny users="*" />
      <deny users="?" />
    </authorization>
  </system.web>
</location>
```

To programmatically add a user to a given role, we have to implement a series of checks, as in the next listing.

Listing 11.8 Create a role and add a user to it

C#:
```
string roleName = "administrators";
if (!Roles.RoleExists(roleName))
  Roles.CreateRole(roleName);

if (!Roles.IsUserInRole(roleName))
  Roles.AddUserToRole(User.Identity.Name, roleName);
```

VB:
```
Dim roleName As String = "administrators"
If Not Roles.RoleExists(roleName) Then
  Roles.CreateRole(roleName)
End If

If Not Roles.IsUserInRole(roleName) Then
  Roles.AddUserToRole(User.Identity.Name, roleName)
End If
```

You have to check whether a role exists before you create it; otherwise, you'll get an exception. This same consideration applies to mapping a user to a role.

If a user without the requested role is accessing your protected page, that user will be redirected to the login page. To ensure that the user understands why they're being redirected to the login page even though they're logged in, you can show a specific message similar to that shown in figure 11.9 using the `LoginView` control, as in the following listing.

Listing 11.9 Message for why access is denied to a protected area

```
<asp:LoginView runat="server">
  <AnonymousTemplate>
    <asp:Login ID="Login1" runat="server" />
  </AnonymousTemplate>
  <LoggedInTemplate>
    We're sorry, the page you requested is not available to your role.
  </LoggedInTemplate>
</asp:LoginView>
```

You've implemented roles support, so your solution is ready. Contrary to the Membership API example, you had to write some code to accomplish your task. Roles API features are mostly used in administration pages, so you don't have to use any controls, except the `LoginView` control. You've added roles support to an existing application with few modifications; by doing so, you've gained more control over authorization.

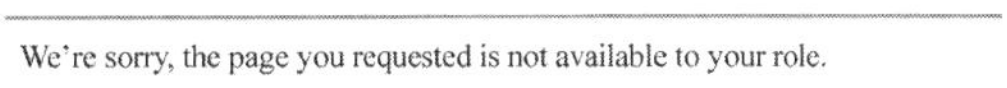

We're sorry, the page you requested is not available to your role.

Figure 11.9   You can display a personalized message when a user is denied access because their role doesn't permit it. You can further personalize this page to offer more instruction to your user.

DISCUSSION

With the Roles API in place, authentication is complete, and you can take full advantage of ASP.NET security mechanisms to grant or deny access to your resources.

A Roles provider doesn't need to work with the corresponding Membership provider. You can combine different strategies, even if you'll probably end up using the same storage. The same considerations apply to both the Membership API and the Roles API. The example we used in this section is based on the SQL Server provider, but given the nature of the Provider Model pattern, you only need to change the provider to make these features work with other forms of storage (database, XML, or whatever custom system you have).

The next section is about custom providers for authentication and roles. We'll cover everything from building them from scratch to using third-party providers. When you need to use a different database, or you simply want more control over the provider's inner data storage strategy, you need a custom provider.

11.4 *Custom providers for the Membership and Roles APIs*

When you're building an application from scratch, using the default schema provided by ASP.NET isn't a problem. If you need to take additional steps because you need to control your database schema, you have specific logic behind your users, or you simply want to target a different kind of storage, what you need is a custom provider.

Both the Membership and Roles APIs are built with extensibility in mind, so developing a provider is not terribly difficult: you just need to overwrite a couple of methods in the respective abstract base classes. Because this scenario is based on the example we used in the previous section, you can use the same code as before. And the results you'll get will be interesting.

> **TECHNIQUE 68**   **Other providers**

ASP.NET doesn't include providers other than the ones for SQL Server and AD. But in most scenarios, you'll want to provide the same functionalities using a different kind of storage. You'll be glad to hear that you can indeed have a provider ready for other kinds of storage. You can find them easily and quickly start building your application. In this section, you'll learn the most common solutions to this issue.

PROBLEM

Different kinds of storage need different providers. Because they're not distributed with ASP.NET, the following sections present the best providers for the most widely used authentication stores. You can freely download all of these from the internet.

SOLUTION 1: SQL SERVER

SQL Server providers are supported directly by the ASP.NET Class Library itself. The `SqlMembershipProvider` and `SqlRoleProvider` classes are in the `System.Web.Security` namespace. For more information, see technique 66.

Source code is available under a permissive license (for both commercial and noncommercial use) at http://www.mng.bz/uIY7. You'll find the source code useful if you need to alter the provider behavior but still want to use its database schema, or you just want to start using SQL Server with different tables for the storage.

SOLUTION 2: ACTIVE DIRECTORY

Support for AD is offered by the `ActiveDirectoryMembershipProvider` class in the `System.Web.Security` namespace. When developers use AD, they most often use Windows authentication; the `AspNetWindowsTokenRoleProvider` class provides support for the Roles API via the Windows authentication token, which is shown in the following listing.

Listing 11.10 Active Directory provider configuration

```
<connectionStrings>
  <add connectionString="LDAP://bochicchio.local/CN=Users,
                    DC=bochicchio,DC=local" name="ActiveDirectory"/>
</connectionStrings>
...
```

```
<membership defaultProvider="ActiveDirectory">
  <providers>
    <add name="ActiveDirectory"
      type="System.Web.Security.ActiveDirectoryMembershipProvider,
            System.Web, Version=2.0.3600.0, Culture=neutral,
            PublicKeyToken=b03f5f7f11d50a3a"
      attributeMapUsername="SAMAccountName"
      connectionStringName="ActiveDirectory"
      connectionUsername="bochicchio.local\SAUser"
      connectionPassword="password" />
  </providers>
</membership>

<roleManager enabled="true"
             defaultProvider="AspNetWindowsTokenRoleProvider" />
```

You don't need to modify anything else to use this provider; the configuration is done via the web.config file.

SOLUTION 3: ACCESS

Access is quite popular, especially in applications deployed to shared hosting, where SQL Server is not always available. You can download the Access provider from the Microsoft website at http://www.mng.bz/mEW7.

This provider is distributed with code (C# only), and needs to be compiled. Configuration information is provided in the download file. If you have a VB solution, you can compile the C# source code and reference the compiled version directly in your project.

SOLUTION 4: ORACLE

Oracle providers are created by Oracle Corporation, and they're available at http://www.mng.bz/1OD6. They're free and they support versions 9.2, 10.1, 10.2, and 11g.

SOLUTION 5: MYSQL

MySQL providers are available as part of MySQL Connector/Net 6.3.6 (or later) at http://www.mng.bz/54k7 (under a GPL license).

You need to add a reference to MySql.Web.dll, located under the installation path. You also need to set the `autogenerateschema` attribute on the provider configuration to `true` so that the provider builds the corresponding schema in your database the first time you run it.

SOLUTION 6: A GENERIC ODBC IMPLEMENTATION

If you need a generic Open Database Connectivity (ODBC) solution (one that works with any database that supports ODBC drivers), you can find one at http://www.mng.bz/0APS. You'll probably need to adapt the SQL queries to your engine dialect.

DISCUSSION

There are so many providers out there that you're sure to find one that meets your specific needs. The list we provided for you in this section includes the databases that are used the most. You'll probably find that one of these or one of the other ones that exist will serve you well, but just in case you can't find a provider ready for your authentication (and role) needs, take a look at the next section to learn how to build a custom provider. You'll be able to adapt your own logic to use in the standard ASP.NET flow for authentication and authorization. You'll use the same features, but you'll perform a customized set of actions.

TECHNIQUE 69   Building custom Membership and Role providers

The default schema used by the Membership and Role providers for SQL Server is flexible, but it's not designed for a specific purpose. These providers have redundant data to support globalization and a GUID key for the user table to support replication. They also support multiple applications in a single database, but that isn't necessarily useful in our scenario.

In everyday applications, you don't need this much flexibility because you generally know what your constraints are. More likely, you'll need a subset of the previous features, and by realizing a custom strategy, you can achieve better performance and totally control the database schema. Or, you might prefer to use something else to store you user credentials and roles; you're limited only by the code that you'll write in the providers.

It's easy to build a custom provider, so let's get down to business. This solution will better fit our needs, and you'll have a customized experience. At the end of this section, you'll be able to completely customize the actions related to authenticating and authorizing user access to your secure application.

PROBLEM

To gain flexibility and ease of use, we want to use the Entity Framework (see chapters 2 and 3 for more details) and map our tables in an easy way; we already have the users in a database table and we don't want to change our database schema. To accomplish this task, we need to build two custom providers: one for the Membership API and one for the Roles API.

SOLUTION

When you're building these kinds of custom providers, you're trying to apply your own rules to authenticate the users and load their roles. To start writing your own provider, you need to implement the base abstract classes `MembershipProvider` and `RoleProvider` from the `System.Web.Security` namespace.

Because both of these classes are abstract, you have to manually implement every single method and property to fully compile them. That doesn't mean that you have to explicitly provide working code in every method; if you don't need to perform a specific action, all you have to do is throw an exception to notify a third-party developer working on your project that the method they're trying to use isn't being implemented.

To make things easy, in this example we'll use a database similar to the one in figure 11.10.

The schema is simple and is composed of the following tables:

- *Users*—Contains the users
- *Roles*—Contains the roles
- *UsersInRoles*—Maps the users to the roles

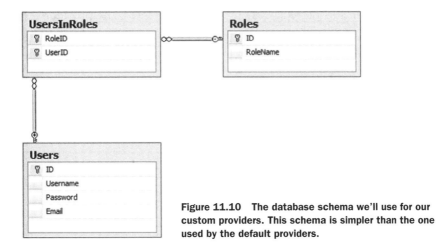

Figure 11.10 The database schema we'll use for our custom providers. This schema is simpler than the one used by the default providers.

To start, we can use the example from technique 66 and add two new classes: one implements the Membership provider and the other implements the Roles provider.

`MembershipProvider` has a lot of properties and methods. For our implementation, we'll provide a constant value for properties and implement only the method necessary to validate the user, create a new user, and get the user details. If you plan to use this provider for your own database schema, you'll need to read the configuration from the web.config file, which is a more flexible way to do it. For our simple starting example, we don't need to do that.

To speed up development, we're choosing the Entity Framework to map our tables to objects and to realize our object model. The results are shown in figure 11.11.

The Entity Framework is hiding the UsersInRoles table used for the relationships, so both the `User` and `Role` entities have a relationship to provide the associated roles to a user, or the associated users to a role, respectively.

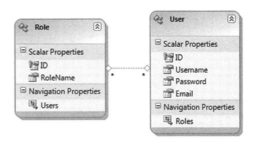

Figure 11.11 The object model in the Entity Framework is similar to the database schema, except for the UsersInRoles table; that table is used to map the many-to-many relationship.

The Membership provider

The schema we've used in this example is quite simple and lets us concentrate on the implementation. In a working solution, you'll probably need to add advanced features, such as account lockout or user registration date. The Membership API does support these features, but our provider doesn't implement them so we can concentrate on the main problem. You can add them by simply extending the database schema and writing the appropriate code.

With the schema in place and the mapping completed, the provider code will be similar to that shown in the following listing. (The code we've included isn't complete; only the relevant parts are included.)

Listing 11.11 The custom Membership provider code

C#:
```csharp
public class DBMembershipProvider: MembershipProvider
{
  public override string ApplicationName
  {
    get {return "/";}
    set {}
  }

  public override bool ValidateUser(string username, string password)
  {
    using (UsersEntities ctx = new UsersEntities())
    {
      return ctx.UserSet.Count(user =>
                  user.Username.Equals(username) &&
                  user.Password.Equals(password))==1;     ◁─── Login with
    }                                                          our model
  }
...
}
```

VB:
```vb
Public Class DBMembershipProvider
  Inherits MembershipProvider
  Public Overloads Overrides Property ApplicationName() As String
    Get
      Return "/"
    End Get
    Set(ByVal value As String)
    End Set
  End Property

  Public Overloads Overrides Function ValidateUser(
          ByVal username As String, ByVal password As String) As Boolean
    Using ctx As New UsersEntities()
      Return ctx.UserSet.Count(Function(user)
                        user.Username.Equals(username) AndAlso
                        user.Password.Equals(password)
                      ) = 1                              ◁─── Login with
    End Using                                                our model
  End Function
...
End Class
```

The code in this listing performs a basic step in the provider by logging in the user. The rest of the code is omitted, but you can appreciate how the custom provider will work. For example, if you need to control the user registration, you can use this code:

C#:

```csharp
public override MembershipUser CreateUser(string username,
           string password, string email, string passwordQuestion,
           string passwordAnswer, bool isApproved, object providerUserKey,
                            out MembershipCreateStatus status)
{
  using (UsersEntities ctx = new UsersEntities())
  {
    MembershipUser u = new MembershipUser(this.Name, username,
           username, email, passwordQuestion, string.Empty, true, false,
           DateTime.Now, DateTime.Now, DateTime.Now,
           DateTime.Now, DateTime.Now);

    User user = new User();
    user.Username = username;
    user.Password = password;
    user.Email = email;
    ctx.AddToUserSet(user);

    ...

    try
    {
      ctx.SaveChanges();
    }
    catch
    {
      status = MembershipCreateStatus.ProviderError; return null;
    }

    status = MembershipCreateStatus.Success;
    return u;
  }
}
```

◁── **Create Membership-User instance**

◁── **Check for conflicts**

◁── **If the user is created**

VB:

```vb
Public Overloads Overrides Function CreateUser(ByVal username As String,
                     ByVal password As String, ByVal email As String,
                     ByVal passwordQuestion As String,
                     ByVal passwordAnswer As String,
                     ByVal isApproved As Boolean,
                     ByVal providerUserKey As Object,
                     ByRef status As MembershipCreateStatus)
               As MembershipUser
  Using ctx As New UsersEntities()
    ' let's compose the user
    Dim u As New MembershipUser(Me.Name, username, username, email,
                       passwordQuestion, String.Empty, True,
                       False, DateTime.Now, DateTime.Now,
                       DateTime.Now, DateTime.Now,
                       DateTime.Now)

    Dim user As New User()
    user.Username = username
    user.Password = password
    user.Email = email
    ctx.AddToUserSet(user)
```

◁── **Create Membership-User instance**

```
    ...                                    ◁─── Check for
    ' updating...                               conflicts
    Try
      ctx.SaveChanges()
    Catch
      ' there was an error
      status = MembershipCreateStatus.ProviderError
      Return Nothing
    End Try

    ' successfully created                    │ If the user
    status = MembershipCreateStatus.Success  ◁─│ is created
    Return u
  End Using
End Function
```

Similarly, to retrieve the user information, you have to use the Entity Framework in the `GetUser` method of your provider:

C#:

```csharp
public override MembershipUser GetUser(string username, bool userIsOnline)
  {
    using (UsersEntities ctx = new UsersEntities())
    {
      User u = ctx.UserSet.FirstOrDefault(
                              x => x.Username.Equals(username));

      if (u == null)
        return null;

      return new MembershipUser(this.Name, username, username, u.Email,
                  string.Empty, string.Empty, true, false, DateTime.Now,
                  DateTime.Now, DateTime.Now, DateTime.Now,
                  DateTime.Now);                   ◁──│ Retrieved by Entity
    }                                                 │ Framework
  }
```

VB:

```vb
Public Overloads Overrides Function GetUser(ByVal username As String, ByVal
    userIsOnline As Boolean) As MembershipUser
  Using ctx As New UsersEntities()
    Dim u As User = ctx.UserSet.FirstOrDefault(
                            Function(x) x.Username.Equals(username)
                                             )
    If u Is Nothing Then
      Return Nothing
    End If

    Return New MembershipUser(Me.Name, username, username, u.Email,
                              String.Empty,
                              String.Empty,
                              True, False,
                              DateTime.Now,
                              DateTime.Now,
                              DateTime.Now,
                              DateTime.Now,      │ Retrieved by Entity
                              DateTime.Now)    ◁─│ Framework
  End Using
End Function
```

The rest of the code will implement the mandatory properties and methods. If you don't want to use a specific method, you can throw a `NotImplementException`. Doing so will notify the developer who will use the provider that only specific features are implemented. The following snippet contains an example:

C#:
```csharp
public override bool EnablePasswordReset
  {
    get { return false; }
  }

  ...

  public override bool RequiresUniqueEmail
  {
    get { return true; }
  }

  public override bool ChangePassword(string username,
                       string oldPassword, string newPassword)
  {
    throw new NotImplementedException();              ⟵⎯⎤ Specific
  }                                                       ⎦ exception
```

VB:
```vb
 Public Overloads Overrides ReadOnly Property RequiresUniqueEmail()
                                      As Boolean
  Get
    Return True
  End Get
 nd Property

 Public Overloads Overrides Function ChangePassword(
               ByVal username As String, ByVal oldPassword As String,
               ByVal newPassword As String) As Boolean
  Throw New NotImplementedException()                 ⟵⎯⎤ Specific
End Function                                              ⎦ exception
```

We can now use our custom code to authenticate the user by just changing the provider in web.config, without modifying the rest of the application.

To register the provider, you need to add this snippet to your `web.config`:

```xml
<membership defaultProvider="DBServerMembership">
  <providers>
    <clear />
    <add name="DBServerMembership" type="DBMembershipProvider, App_Code" />
  </providers>
</membership>
```

The Membership API is invoked by the controls, so you don't need to do anything else to change the implementation. This example highlights the true power of the Provider Model pattern in action!

The Role provider

To complete our task, we have to create the Role provider. The code is similar to the code for the Membership provider, but we need to implement the method related to creating a role, check for role availability, assign a user to a role, and check for a user in a given role. These features are the minimum requirements for experimenting with the Roles API.

The only difficult part to implement for the Role provider is the relation. To load the roles for a particular user, you have to use the `SelectMany` extension method. This method can generate a flat view from a relation like the one we used in our object model.

The next listing contains the code for the Roles API custom provider.

Listing 11.12   The custom Role provider code

C#:
```
public class DBRoleProvider: RoleProvider
{
  public override void AddUsersToRoles(string[] usernames, string[]
    roleNames)
  {
    using (UsersEntities ctx = new UsersEntities())
    {
      string username, roleName;
      for (int i = 0; i < usernames.Length; i++)
      {
        username = usernames[i];
        User u = ctx.UserSet.FirstOrDefault(            Check for
                  user => user.Username.Equals(username));     username
                                                               in array
        if (u != null)
        {
          for (int j = 0; j < roleNames.Length; j++)
          {
            roleName = roleNames[i];
            Role r = ctx.RoleSet.FirstOrDefault(
                    role => role.RoleName.Equals(roleName));
            u.Roles.Add(r);                                Add user
          }                                                to role
        }
      }

      ctx.SaveChanges();
    }
  }
...
}
```

VB:
```
Public Class DBRoleProvider
  Inherits RoleProvider

  Public Overloads Overrides Sub AddUsersToRoles(
                ByVal usernames As String(), ByVal roleNames As String())
    Using ctx As New UsersEntities()
      Dim username As String, roleName As String
      For i As Integer = 0 To usernames.Length - 1
        username = usernames(i)
        Dim u As User = ctx.UserSet.FirstOrDefault(
```

```
        Function(user) user.Username.Equals(username))      ◁─┐ Check for
                                                              │ username
      If u IsNot Nothing Then                                 │ in array
        For j As Integer = 0 To roleNames.Length - 1
          roleName = roleNames(i)
          Dim r As Role = ctx.RoleSet.FirstOrDefault(
            Function(role) role.RoleName.Equals(roleName))
          u.Roles.Add(r)                                   ◁─┐ Add user
        Next                                                 │ to role
      End If
    Next

    ctx.SaveChanges()
  End Using
End Sub
...
End Class
```

If you need to create a new role, the Entity Framework will come handy. You can use a snippet similar to this:

C#:

```
public override void CreateRole(string roleName)
{
  using (UsersEntities ctx = new UsersEntities())
  {
    ctx.AddToRoleSet(new Role() {                          ◁─┐ Create
                        RoleName = roleName });              │ new role
    ctx.SaveChanges();
  }
}
```

VB:

```
Public Overloads Overrides Sub CreateRole(ByVal roleName As String)
  Using ctx As New UsersEntities()
    Dim myRole as New Role
    myRole.RoleName = roleName                             ◁─┐ Create
    ctx.AddToRoleSet(myRole)                                 │ new role
    ctx.SaveChanges()
  End Using
End Sub
```

Similarly, to check whether a user is in a given role, we have to use the Entity Framework `SelectMany` extension method to make the resulting role list flat, starting with the users:

C#:

```
public override bool IsUserInRole(string username, string roleName)
{
  using (UsersEntities ctx = new UsersEntities())
  {
    return ctx.RoleSet.Include("Users").Where(
                  u => u.RoleName.Equals(roleName)
                ).SelectMany(x => x.Users).Count(          ◁─┐ Check for
                  x => x.Username.Equals(username)           │ user roles
                ) > 0;
```

```
    }
}
```

VB:

```
Public Overloads Overrides Function IsUserInRole(
    ByVal username As String, ByVal roleName As String) As Boolean
  Using ctx As New UsersEntities()
    Return ctx.RoleSet.Include("Users").Where(
            Function(u) u.RoleName.Equals(roleName)
          ).SelectMany(Function(x) x.Users).Count(
            Function(x) x.Username.Equals(username)) > 0
  End Using
End Function
```

Check for user roles

And, again, if you don't want to implement a particular feature (in this case, the Del-eteRole method), simply throw a new NotImplementException:

C#:

```
    public override bool DeleteRole(string roleName,
                                    bool throwOnPopulatedRole)
    {
      throw new NotImplementedException();
    }
...
```

VB:

```
Public Overloads Overrides Function DeleteRole(ByVal roleName As String,
                       ByVal throwOnPopulatedRole As Boolean) As Boolean
  Throw New NotImplementedException()
End Function
```

To register the provider, you have to add the following code to your web.config:

```
<roleManager enabled="true" defaultProvider="DBServerRoles" ...>
  <providers>
    <add name="DBServerRoles" type="DBRoleProvider, App_Code" />
  </providers>
</roleManager>
```

In this example, you can find all you need to implement a custom strategy for both membership and roles management, using the APIs from ASP.NET. To complete the steps and start using these providers if you already have an application using the Membership and Roles APIs, all you have to do is configure them in web.config, like we've shown you already.

Now our secure website can use a custom strategy to store and retrieve both users and roles.

DISCUSSION

A custom provider is useful when you want to preserve a cleaner database schema or when you already have a database to start with. It's not difficult to implement a provider, but you'll probably have to write some code for it to be fully in place.

By leveraging the Provider Model pattern, you can modify the inner details of your application without changing the code or the web controls used in the UI. This situation is ideal because you can concentrate on the implementation of the rules and let the ASP.NET infrastructure provide the support for the repetitive stuff.

You can easily use custom providers to implement different kinds of storage for your identities. In the next section, we'll take a look at a custom set of providers based on Windows Live ID, the popular authentication service from Microsoft. By implementing a custom provider with Live ID support, you can integrate one of the most popular systems with your application and attract more users.

TECHNIQUE 70 **Integrating Windows Live ID with your application**

Windows Live ID is the well-known, *federated* authentication service provided by Microsoft that's used by millions of people. Live ID accounts are everywhere and the authentication mechanism is well established. Best of all, you can use it in your applications at no cost.

Alternatives to Live ID: OpenID, Facebook Connect, and more!

A couple of alternatives exist to Live ID, even though Live ID remains the most popular authentication service in the world.

If you prefer to leverage the Facebook website, you can use Facebook Connect, which is still free. You can access information like the profile picture, data about friends, and much more. Facebook Connect is primarily based on JavaScript, and you can find more information at http://developers.facebook.com/

OpenID is an open alternative for providing a federated login. It's not based on a single vendor implementation, but everyone can be a provider, and the implementation details are the same and use a common format. OpenID is supported by Google, Yahoo, AOL, and others. You can find more information at http://openid.net/.

The average user tends to trust well-known brands, so Windows Live ID is a good choice. By adding support for this federated authentication service to your application, you can speed user authentication to your site, while continuing to keep your security bar high. Because your users are probably familiar with Live ID, they'll be able to log in with less effort and enjoy using your website that much more.

PROBLEM

You want to include Live ID as an alternate way for your users to log in, so they can use a well-known provider that they trust. Using Live ID will also simplify login for users.

SOLUTION

Windows Live ID authentication is based on token generation and a couple of redirects between the external application and Windows Live ID servers. An SDK is available at http://dev.live.com/liveid/. Specific Membership and Role providers are available, based on the SQL Server providers. You can find more technical information about the system when you download the SDK.

In figure 11.12, you can see a simple architectural schema of using Live ID.

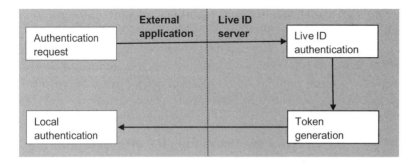

Figure 11.12   Windows Live ID architecture for federated authentication is based on a token exchange between Microsoft servers and the federating sites. Your application needs to store the unique token that the Live ID server generates for your user so that the user is recognized the next time they log in.

Even though the SDK provides some custom controls and providers for you to start with, the most common situation is the opposite one: you already have your custom providers (or the default ones) in place and you want to add this new authentication mechanism, not replace the ones you already have.

First, you have to apply for an account ID via the Azure Services Developer Portal at https://msm.live.com/app/manage.aspx. Like we said before, registration is free. You have to enter an application name, the return URL, and a server name. In return, you'll receive an application ID and a secret key.

Because Live ID uses redirects via the browser and not server-to-server requests, you can use a temporary domain name. Or, if you prefer, you can map your host via the hosts file in Windows.

Our implementation assumes the following scenario:

- The user is registered with a normal account on our site.
- Our site is using the Membership API and we want minimum impact.
- The user wants to log in without needing to remember another pair of credentials, but by simply using Live ID.

Unfortunately, the Membership API cannot be extended, so we need a different approach to include an alternate login mechanism. You can opt for a custom system, based on, for example, Entity Framework, and just query the database; or you can go for an alternative, trouble-free way and consider the Live ID account association as a special role for the user. This role will be unique because Live ID servers send a unique token for each registered user. Each option has its own pros and cons, but the second one is more flexible for an existing application. (Although, if you have a high-traffic website, a specific engine might work better and provide better performance.)

For more information about how to implement a Windows Live ID authentication, you'll find the correct token documentation at http://www.mng.bz/gToP. As noted in the documentation, the system supports the following actions:

- *SignIn*—When the user requests login
- *SignOut*—When the user explicitly requests logout
- *ClearCookie*—When the Live ID service is demanding transparent signout (remember, you can be signed in at multiple websites at the same time)

`SignIn` and `SignOut` can reply with anything you want (a page or a redirect), but `ClearCookie` has the mandatory reply of a 1x1 transparent GIF image.

To start coding, we can use the `WindowsLiveLogin` class, which is available as part of the SDK and is attached to this example. This class encapsulates the inner logic and is useful for implementing the code. First of all, set the key in web.config, as in this snippet:

```
<appSettings>
  <add key="wll_appid" value="your_key_here"/>
  <add key="wll_secret" value="01234567890123456789"/>
  <add key="wll_securityalgorithm" value="wsignin1.0"/>
</appSettings>
```

The login button presented on the login page is created by using an `iframe` and passing the corresponding application ID to it. Because the redirect is performed automatically and the token is encrypted using the secret key, this system is secure and cannot be used to illegally spoof a user account. The following listing shows the common markup that inserts the login/logout link using an `iframe`. When displayed in a web browser, the results are similar to what's shown in figure 11.13.

Listing 11.13   Listing 11.13 Windows Live ID code that generates the login URL

```
<iframe
  src="http://login.live.com/controls/WebAuth.htm?mkt=en-us&
➡ appid=<%=AppID%>&
context=<%=Server.UrlEncode(Request["ReturnUrl"])%>&
➡ style=font-size%3A+10pt%3B+
➡ font-family%3A+verdana%3B+background%3A+white%3B"
  width="80px"
  height="20px"
  marginwidth="0"
  marginheight="0"
  align="middle"
  frameborder="0"
  scrolling="no"
  style="border-style: hidden; border-width:
      0">
</iframe>
```

We have to configure our application to reply to Live ID servers on a page named live.aspx. This page will receive the data from Windows Live ID, use the `WindowsLiveLogin` class from the SDK to decrypt the value, and populate a new instance of the `WindowsLiveLogin.User` class.

Figure 11.13   The new login page has a new link for performing the login using Windows Live ID. Users can continue to perform a classic login if they want to.

The action to be performed is specified in the parameters, so the important part is in the association of the returned token to our database. As we mentioned before, we'll create a specific role if there's a need for one, or simply authenticate the user if the association is already performed. The code is shown in the following listing.

Listing 11.14   The login and user association code

C#:

```
string action = Request["action"] ?? "login";

WindowsLiveLogin wll = new WindowsLiveLogin(true);
WindowsLiveLogin.User user = wll.ProcessLogin(Request.Form);

switch (action)
{
...
 default:
  if (user == null &&
      Request.Cookies["LiveID"] != null &&
      !string.IsNullOrEmpty(Request.Cookies["LiveID"]["token"]))
  {
      string token = Request.Cookies["LiveID"]["token"];
      user = wll.ProcessToken(token);                          Remaining
  }                                                            logic
  if (user == null) {
    FormsAuthentication.RedirectToLoginPage("LiveID=1");
    return;
  }
...
}
```

VB:

```
Dim action As String = If(Request("action"), "login")

Dim wll As New WindowsLiveLogin(True)
Dim user As WindowsLiveLogin.User = wll.ProcessLogin(Request.Form)

Select Case action
...
  Case Else
    If user Is Nothing AndAlso
       Request.Cookies("LiveID") IsNot Nothing AndAlso
       Not String.IsNullOrEmpty(Request.Cookies("LiveID")("token"))
    Then
      Dim token As String = Request.Cookies("LiveID")("token")
      user = wll.ProcessToken(token)                          Remaining
    End If                                                    logic

    If user Is Nothing Then
      FormsAuthentication.RedirectToLoginPage("LiveID=1")
      Return
    End If
...
End Select
```

At this point, we need to check whether the user is authenticated, and, if he is, associate the Live ID with the account. The code is shown in the following listing.

Listing 11.15 The user is added to the specified role

C#:

```
string userID = user.Id;
string returnUrl = user.Context;
bool persistent = user.UsePersistentCookie;          │ UserID will compose
                                                     │ the rolename
string roleName = string.Concat("Live-", userID);   ◄─┘

if (Request.IsAuthenticated)
{
   if (!Roles.IsUserInRole(roleName))
   {
     if (!Roles.RoleExists(roleName))
       Roles.CreateRole(roleName);

     Roles.AddUserToRole(User.Identity.Name, roleName);
   }

   Response.Cookies.Remove("LiveID");
   Login(User.Identity.Name, persistent);            │ More code
}                                                    │ here
else...                                             ◄─┘
```

VB:

```
Dim userID As String = user.Id
Dim returnUrl As String = user.Context                │ UserID will
Dim persistent As Boolean = user.UsePersistentCookie  │ compose the
                                                      │ rolename
Dim roleName As String = String.Concat("Live-", userID)  ◄─┘

If Request.IsAuthenticated Then
  If Not Roles.IsUserInRole(roleName) Then
    If Not Roles.RoleExists(roleName) Then
      Roles.CreateRole(roleName)
    End If

    Roles.AddUserToRole(User.Identity.Name, roleName)
  End If

  Response.Cookies.Remove("LiveID")                   │ More code
  Login(User.Identity.Name, persistent)               │ here
Else...                                              ◄─┘
```

If the user isn't authenticated, we need to check whether the role exists; if it does, we grant access to the user:

C#:

```
else
{
  if (Roles.RoleExists(roleName))
  {
    string username = Roles.GetUsersInRole(roleName)[0];

    Login(username, persistent);
  }
  else
  {                                                   │ Save token
    Response.Cookies["LiveID"]["token"] = user.Token; │ in cookie
                                                     ◄─┘
```

```
        FormsAuthentication.RedirectToLoginPage(
                              string.Concat("LiveID=1&ReturnUrl=",
                              Request.Url.ToString()) );
    }
}
```

VB:

```
    Else
        ' retrieve the user via its role
        If Roles.RoleExists(roleName) Then
          Dim username As String = Roles.GetUsersInRole(roleName)(0)

          Login(username, persistent)
        Else
            Response.Cookies("LiveID")("token") = user.Token

          FormsAuthentication.RedirectToLoginPage(
                String.Concat("LiveID=1&ReturnUrl=", Request.Url.ToString()))

        End If
    End If
```

Save token in cookie

The `SignOut` and `ClearCookie` actions are omitted because both will perform the log-out using the `SignOut` method on the `FormsAuthentication` class.

The first time the user requests the login via Live ID, the page checks for the role in the database. If the role isn't found, a valid Live ID token is issued, the user is authenticated, the new role is created, and the user is associated with it. If the user isn't logged in and a Live ID user ID is sent, the user that corresponds to the role created by using the unique user ID is retrieved, and the `FormsAuthentication` class is used to perform the login. The flow is explained in figure 11.14.

Figure 11.14 shows the flow used to associate the Windows Live ID to your account. First of all, the Live ID credentials are required. Then the user is asked to associate the site user to the Live ID. Next time, the user can use Live ID to authenticate himself

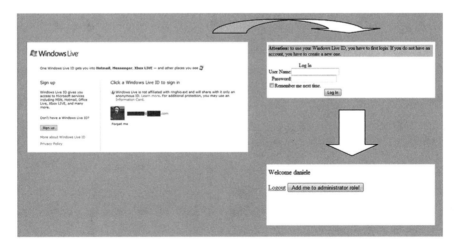

Figure 11.14   The authentication flow is modified when the user's Windows Live ID is associated for the first time. If the Live ID is associated, the user is automatically authenticated.

because the two accounts are now linked. This process is simple to implement and simple for the user to follow.

From our point of view, we're adding more features to our secure website without changing the inner workings of our security strategy. This is another advantage over using APIs instead of custom implementations.

DISCUSSION

Supporting Windows Live ID is advantageous, especially if you have a website with varied traffic, because the service is well known in both consumer and professional audiences.

Using the approach presented in this example, you can continue to use your own Membership and Roles providers. This integration page uses only the Roles API (but not the provider directly) and can be integrated with every application.

This example shows the power of using APIs instead of direct code. You can simply alter some behavior by adding code that leverages only the public face of that feature, and, thanks to Provider Model, you can use it in many situations because it's not linked to a particular implementation.

11.5   *Summary*

Security in the UI is so important that developers tend to spend a lot of their time fully implementing it. The effects of code security, as we discussed in this chapter, are invisible, but dangerous. Authentication and authorization are important for you to gain more control over application features. Often an application needs its user to be authenticated to access advanced features. You can provide different levels of power to different types of users, who are grouped together to simplify policy management.

ASP.NET implements support for authentication and authorization in its core. As you'll learn in the rest of this book with regard to other features, you can adapt these features to your needs by simply changing the default implementation provider.

The Membership and Roles APIs, on the other hand, use the Provider Model to provide an extremely powerful approach to repetitive tasks, which is what user and role management are. Thanks to the built-in security controls in ASP.NET, you can easily integrate this kind of solution in applications because all the work is performed behind the scenes. If you want more control over every aspect of your application, you can manually call Membership and Roles APIs methods, as we did in the last example of this chapter, by implementing a custom mechanism for letting users authenticate. The result is a secure and versatile website, built step-by-step by adding more features.

In the next chapter, we'll start to take a deeper look at ASP.NET, exploring advanced scenarios like state, caching, customization, and performance tuning.

Part 5

Advanced topics

Part 1 was about how ASP.NET works, and parts 2 and 3 provided a peek at the features that ASP.NET Web Forms and ASP.NET MVC have that you can use to build the UI. Then in part 4, we analyzed the scenarios to build more secure applications, and you learned how to protect them. This last part is dedicated to more advanced scenarios, which will combine most of the topics we've previously talked about in this book. These chapters cover both ASP.NET Web Forms and MVC.

Chapter 12 explains how to integrate ASP.NET applications into Ajax-enabled applications and Rich Internet Applications (RIAs). We'll take a look at how to leverage jQuery and ASP.NET Ajax.

In chapter 13, you'll learn how to handle state in ASP.NET: from cookies to ViewState to new features introduced in version 4, like the ability to compress the SessionState.

Chapter 14 is dedicated to caching. You'll find plenty of tips on how to achieve better scalability by implementing a good caching strategy. This chapter also covers how to build custom cache providers, and how Microsoft AppFabric caching works.

Chapter 15 contains miscellaneous topics related to fully extending ASP.NET, from HttpRuntime, to logging, to building a virtual path provider.

Finally, chapter 16 offers some tips on how to build applications that perform better. We'll talk about minifying content, multithreading, and ParallelFX.

Ajax and RIAs
with ASP.NET 4.0

This chapter covers

- Understanding Ajax
- Working with ASP.NET Ajax framework
- Understanding jQuery
- Understanding jQueryUI

In chapter 11, you learned how to take full control over the markup generated by your pages. Be sure you're comfortable with the contents of that chapter because it might affect the subjects in this chapter.

In this chapter, we're going to turn our attention to Ajax. Nowadays, everybody knows about it. Ajax stands for Asynchronous JavaScript and XML. The term was coined in 2005; since then, it's become the de facto standard for the web. With Ajax, also came new terms like RIA (Rich Internet Application) and the famous Web 2.0.

Though the term Web 2.0 is a marketing creation, Ajax and RIA are an authentic *revolution* in terms of user interface and usability. Even though Ajax doesn't introduce any new technology, it has established a pattern to better reuse the existing ones.

RIAs are a different beast. The term RIA identifies an application that enables a rich interface with fluent interaction. Although with Ajax it's perfectly possible to create an RIA, it would require a huge amount of work. A lot of JavaScript has been born to ease RIA development.

In this chapter, we'll start with a brief introduction to Ajax in general and then we'll move to the features embedded in ASP.NET Web Forms. Then we'll talk about jQuery, which is the JavaScript framework that Microsoft has embraced and integrated into ASP.NET templates. By the end of this chapter, you'll be able to combine the power of ASP.NET, Ajax technique, and JavaScript frameworks to create more appealing interfaces using a minimum of code.

12.1 Understanding Ajax

Ajax is a pattern that combines JavaScript and XMLHTTP components to invoke the server asynchronously without causing a reload of the page. Before delving into the details of how this works in ASP.NET, let's talk a bit about Ajax first.

12.1.1 How Ajax improves usability

Before the advent of Ajax, web applications had a simple flow:

1 The user requests a page.
2 The server replies with HTML interpreted by the browser.
3 The user performs an action on the page.
4 The page is posted back to the server.
5 The server processes user input and replies with a new HTML page, again interpreted by the browser.

Figure 12.1 visually explains these steps.

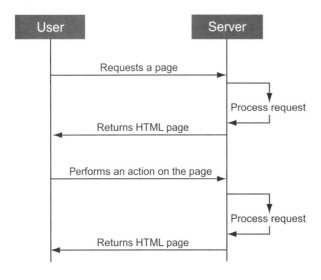

Figure 12.1   The interaction between the user and the server without Ajax. The user requests a page or performs an action on it, and the server replies with another HTML page.

This interaction model works perfectly, but suffers from a big problem. Each time the user needs data from the server, he needs to perform an action. This action causes the entire page to be posted to the server; the user has to wait for the server to reply with a brand new page.

Suppose you're using a page that shows a list of orders. For performance reasons, the amount isn't shown beside the order but must be requested using a link in the order row. If you have to check several orders, you'll click the link for the first one, wait for the server to respond, and then see the entire page refreshed—just for a number. Come on, we can do better than that.

With Ajax, the user-request/server-response model is still there. What's changed is the way requests and replies are sent. In Ajax, the request is sent in such a way that the page isn't halted during a request and a new page isn't reloaded when the server response arrives.

At the base of Ajax is the XMLHTTP component. This component actually performs the magic behind Ajax. It issues a call to the server and then asynchronously waits for its response.

Reprising the previous example, the server doesn't need to reprocess the entire page and resend HTML to the client just to see a number. You can simply send an *invisible* command to the server, which then calculates only the amount of the order and returns it to the client; the client then shows the amount beside the order. Figure 12.2 show this flow.

You obtain several advantages from this communication style. These advantages are described in table 12.1.

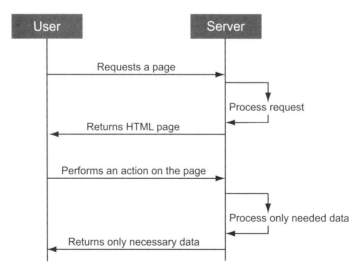

Figure 12.2   The interaction between the user and the server in Ajax style. The user requests a page and receives HTML. Then the user performs an action, and the browser sends only necessary data to the server. The server processes this data and then sends to the client only the information needed— not the entire page. It's the client's duty to show this data to the user.

Table 12.1   Advantages of adopting Ajax in your applications

Advantage	Description
Usability improvement	The page isn't reloaded at each user interaction. The user almost has the impression of working with a Windows application.
Bandwidth optimization	In an Ajax request pipeline, only necessary data goes over the wire. The client sends the minimal data the server needs, and the server replies with only the data needed by the client, rather than an entire page.
Faster server processing	Because the server doesn't have to process the whole page, it has less to do; it responds faster and, consequently, can accept more requests.

Ajax gives you a lot of advantages, doesn't it? They're the reason Ajax has rapidly become so popular. Now that you know the benefits of working with Ajax, we can move on and discover how Ajax works and the components that bring it to life.

12.1.2   *How Ajax works*

We've already mentioned that, technologically speaking, Ajax doesn't introduce anything new. It just introduces a new pattern to better reuse existing ones. Because Ajax is a client pattern, it's not surprising that the first technology it leverages is JavaScript.

Unfortunately, JavaScript can't communicate with the server; it can only post the page to it. To overcome this shortcoming, you can use the XMLHTTP component of Ajax. XMLHTTP enables invoking the server asynchronously without posting the page. It also enables executing arbitrary code when the response from the server has been received.

What's interesting about Ajax communication is the data exchange protocol. The x in the Ajax acronym might lead you to believe that XML is the protocol used. Although technically feasible, XML is verbose and slow to process. A more optimized protocol exists: JSON. JSON is a standard format for representing data and has the great advantage of being extremely concise and integrated with the JavaScript engine. Thanks to JSON, data going to and coming back from the server is highly optimized.

There are hundreds of Ajax frameworks out there. All of them abstract the little differences between browsers regarding XMLHTTP use. You'll always use one of these

History of the XMLHTTP Component

In long ago 1998, Microsoft introduced the XMLHTTP ActiveX control to improve Outlook Web Access application usability. After 1998, other browser vendors, understanding the immense power of XMLHTTP, began to introduce their version of this component in their browser. After a while, XMLHTTP became the de facto standard for all browsers.

Despite its power, XMLHTTP went unnoticed until Google began to use it in 2005 to create the autosuggestion feature in its search page. After Google began to use XMLHTTP, the component suddenly became popular; soon after that, the pattern Ajax was coined.

frameworks (ASP.NET Ajax, jQuery, MooTools, Prototype, and so on); you'll never use XMLHTTP directly, which is why we won't show it in action here. What we will show you is how to use ASP.NET Ajax. We'll also show you how to leverage Ajax using jQuery later in the chapter.

Now that you have an idea of what Ajax is and how it works, let's start analyzing the ASP.NET Ajax framework. This framework is the one realized by Microsoft to easily enable Ajax in ASP.NET applications.

12.2 Working with ASP.NET Ajax

When Microsoft realized the impact of the Ajax pattern on web applications, they started developing a framework that could easily add Ajax scenarios to new and existing applications. This framework is ASP.NET Ajax.

ASP.NET Ajax is separated into two main sections:

- *Server components*—Contain components to simplify development of Ajax behaviors using server-side code. The most important components in this section are the ScriptManager and UpdatePanel server controls, which you'll soon see.
- *Client components*—Contain a set of JavaScript classes that simplify Ajax calls and that interact with the server controls.

Server components are all about simplicity. If you develop an application using server controls, you can enable powerful Ajax interaction, without even writing a single line of JavaScript code. If that seems too good to be true, you're right. The drawback of using server controls is that although you optimize a lot compared with non-Ajax applications, you don't take full advantage of Ajax in terms of control over data and performance. When you need extreme performance and control, you can use the client-side components.

Now that you have an idea of how the ASP.NET Ajax framework is made, let's look more closely at its server part.

TECHNIQUE 71 Creating a classic page

Before we dig deep into the server components part, let's take a look at the sample we're going to build. We'll use this sample throughout the chapter.

PROBLEM

Suppose that you have a page where you have two drop-down lists. The first one contains all the regions in the Northwind database, and the second one contains the territories in the selected region. We need to populate the second drop-down list with the correct territories each time the item selected in the first one is changed.

SOLUTION

The following snippet shows the markup required to create the drop-down lists:

```
<asp:DropDownList runat="server"
  ID="Regions" AutoPostBack="true"
  OnSelectedIndexChanged="Regions_Changed"
  AppendDataBoundItems="true"
```

```
    DataTextField="RegionDescription"
    DataValueField="RegionId">
    <asp:ListItem  value="" Text="[Select a Territory]" />
</asp:DropDownList>
<asp:DropDownList ID="Territories" runat="server"
    DataTextField="TerritoryDescription"></asp:DropDownList>
```

The `Regions` list contains the vendors; the `Models` list is dynamically populated with the model of the selected vendor. The `AutoPostBack` property of the `Regions` list is set to `true` so that when the user changes the selected item, the page is automatically posted to the server and the event `SelectedIndexChanged` is raised. In the event handler (`Regions_Changed`), we retrieve the selected region and then load the territories. The code is a breeze, as you can see in the following listing.

Listing 12.1   Code needed to populate the second drop-down list

C#:
```
protected void Regions_Changed(object sender, EventArgs e)
{
  using (var ctx = new NorthwindEntities())
  {
    int id = Convert.ToInt32(Regions.SelectedValue);
    Territories.DataSource = ctx.Territories.Where(t => t.RegionID == id);
    Territories.DataBind();
  }
}
```

VB:
```
Protected Sub Regions_Changed(sender As Object, e As EventArgs)
  Using ctx = New NorthwindEntities()
    Dim id As Integer = Convert.ToInt32(Regions.SelectedValue)
    Territories.DataSource = _
      ctx.Territories.Where(Function(t) t.RegionID = id)
    Territories.DataBind()
  End Using
End Sub
```

That's all you need to do. We didn't show the code for populating the `Regions` drop-down list because that's not of real interest for our sample.

DISCUSSION

As you can see, creating such an interaction is quite simple. But now we need to introduce Ajax, which is basically a client-side technology. How can we introduce Ajax behavior without losing all that we've gained?

TECHNIQUE 72   **Ajaxize a page using the update panel**

One of the goals that drove the design of ASP.NET Ajax was the desire to be unobtrusive. The team didn't want you to have to rewrite an existing application only to introduce Ajax behaviors. They wanted you to be able to maintain the application and make only slight modifications. They achieved this goal pretty well.

PROBLEM

For this scenario, we're using the same page from the previous example. You need to update the territories list in the second drop-down list without causing a full PostBack of the page each time the region is changed.

SOLUTION

The solution to this problem is *partial rendering*. The idea behind partial rendering is pretty simple: you divide your page into different *parts* that are independently updated via Ajax. When a control inside a part causes page PostBack, JavaScript on the client intercepts it and transforms it into an Ajax call. When the call hits the server, it's processed as a classic full PostBack; you don't have to change a single line of code. When the processing is finished and the server generates HTML for the page, it sends to the client only the HTML code for the areas that have been updated.

The JavaScript on the page receives HTML for each updated area and uses it to update them. Because only some areas are refreshed, this technique is called partial rendering. Figure 12.3 illustrates partial rendering.

There's one little caveat you must be aware of: in addition to sending the HTML for an area, the server sends the `ViewState` to the client. This state of affairs explains why the PostBacks are executed normally.

At the base of partial rendering is the `UpdatePanel` control. It's the server control that delimits an area. `UpdatePanel` is pretty simple to use; it has a `ContentTemplate` property that contains the HTML of the area. In our sample, the `UpdatePanel` includes both drop-down lists, as shown in this snippet:

```
<asp:ScriptManager Id="sm" runat="server" />
<asp:UpdatePanel runat="server">
  <ContentTemplate>
    <asp:DropDownList runat="server" ID="Regions" ...> </asp:DropDownList>
    <asp:DropDownList ID="Territories" ...></asp:DropDownList>
  </ContentTemplate>
</asp:UpdatePanel>
```

We haven't included the complete markup of the drop-down lists, but it's the same as you saw in the previous section. The `ScriptManager` control is the center of ASP.NET

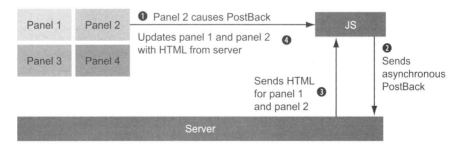

Figure 12.3   Panel 2 contains a button that causes a PostBack. The JavaScript on the page intercepts the PostBack and invokes the server, simulating a PostBack with an Ajax call. The server sends HTML for panels 1 and 2, and the JavaScript updates them.

Ajax. This control sends necessary JavaScript files to the page and enables the use of UpdatePanel. It also enables downloading JavaScript files from the content delivery network (CDN), and so on.

The markup changes slightly, and the server code doesn't change at all. With just this small change in the markup, we've enabled Ajax behavior. Isn't that awesome?

DISCUSSION

Using the update panel is a great choice when you need to do things fast and when you have to add Ajax behavior to existing applications. But it does pose some problems, especially with performance. The update panel optimizes performance when you compare it to the classic PostBack model, but you can optimize it even more. In the next section, you'll discover some additional tricks.

TECHNIQUE 73   Optimizing UpdatePanel using triggers

If you use an HTTP logger (for example, Fiddler2, Firebug for FireFox, Internet Explorer 9, or WebKit developer tools) to trace data that goes over the wire, you see that the server sends HTML for all controls in the UpdatePanel. This behavior is correct, but we need to update only the second drop-down list; sending HTML for both lists is a waste of resources.

PROBLEM

We need to optimize the traffic between the client and server when UpdatePanel is used. In particular, we need the server to send HTML to the client for only the first drop-down list.

SOLUTION

By default, the ASP.NET Ajax JavaScript intercepts the submit triggered by the controls inside the UpdatePanel. We can modify this behavior and cause an UpdatePanel to be updated even when an external control triggers the PostBack. The PostBack will be intercepted and transformed into an Ajax call, and everything works the same. Such a workflow is shown in figure 12.4.

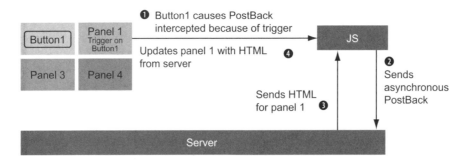

Figure 12.4   The button outside panel 1 causes a PostBack. The JavaScript on the page intercepts the PostBack (because panel 1 has a trigger on the button) and invokes the server, simulating a PostBack with an Ajax call. The server sends HTML for panel 1 (because of the trigger), and the JavaScript updates it.

We can strip the first drop-down list off the `UpdatePanel`, leaving only the second one. We can then instruct the `UpdatePanel` to refresh when the first list value is changed. This instruction is known as a *trigger* and is shown in the next snippet.

```
<asp:DropDownList runat="server" ID="Regions" ...> </asp:DropDownList>
<asp:UpdatePanel runat="server">
  <Triggers>
    <asp:AsyncPostBackTrigger ControlID="Regions"
      EventName="SelectedIndexChanged" />
  </Triggers>
  <ContentTemplate>
    <asp:DropDownList ID="Territories" ...></asp:DropDownList>
  </ContentTemplate>
</asp:UpdatePanel>
```

The `Triggers` property of the `UpdatePanel` contains the external controls that cause the panel to be updated. A trigger can be one of two types:

- `AsyncPostBackTrigger`—Causes the Ajax PostBack
- `PostBackTrigger`—Causes the classic PostBack

Each class has two properties:

- `ControlId`—Represents the name of the control that triggers PostBack
- `EventName`—The control event that triggers PostBack

After you've made this modification, run the page and look at the logger result. Now each time the `Regions` drop-down list is changed, the page is submitted asynchronously, and only the `Territories` drop-down list is sent to the client (along with ViewState and other minor information).

DISCUSSION

This modification is a little tweak that makes no difference in a demo. But, if you think about a real-world application, you'll understand that triggers can spare you a lot of vital resources, especially for a web application.

Using triggers isn't the only way to optimize performance. When you have multiple `UpdatePanels` in a page, you can granularly choose which panels you want to be updated after an asynchronous PostBack.

TECHNIQUE 74   Optimizing a page with multiple UpdatePanels

Let's do a little experiment: let's duplicate all controls so that now we have two `UpdatePanels` in the page. Then run the sample and change the drop-down list that causes the first panel to be updated. Now if you take a look at the HTTP logger, you'll notice that even if only the first `UpdatePanel` is changed, the server sends the HTML for the second panel to the client, too. This result is a useless waste of resources.

PROBLEM

Suppose that you have a page with multiple update panels. You need to figure out how to optimize it. When the server is invoked and only one `UpdatePanel` is updated, the server has to send to the client only the HTML for the modified panel, not for all of them.

SOLUTION

By default, the server sends the HTML for the all `UpdatePanels` in the page to the client. Why is this the outcome? Suppose that you have two `UpdatePanels`. When a button is clicked in the first one, a value in the second one is updated. If the server sent HTML for the first panel only, the second one would never be updated and you would end up showing stale data.

Sometimes this behavior is unnecessary and causes a significant performance slowdown. For those cases, you can set the `UpdateMode` property to `Conditional`. This setting instructs the `UpdatePanel` to be updated only when a control inside it or one specified in the `Triggers` collection causes a PostBack.

```
<asp:UpdatePanel runat="server" UpdateMode="Conditional">
```

Now, when a control in an `UpdatePanel` issues a PostBack, the server sends to the client the HTML code for that `UpdatePanel` only, and you get a big performance boost.

Depending on the runtime condition, you might need to update another panel. In these cases, you can programmatically cause the other panel to be updated by invoking the `Update` method of the `UpdatePanel` class:

C#:
```
otherPanelField.Text = "Value";
otherPanel.Update();
```

VB:
```
otherPanelField.Text = "Value"
otherPanel.Update()
```

The result of this code is that the first panel is updated because a control inside it caused the PostBack, and the second one is updated because it was explicitly marked via code.

DISCUSSION

When you're working with multiple `UpdatePanels` in a page, you have several options for increasing optimization. Doing nothing is the best way to do the worst thing. Always keep in mind the tricks you've learned in this section; they can make a big difference, especially if the page gets a lot of traffic.

So far we've been talking only about the server code. The ASP.NET Ajax JavaScript enables you to intercept the Ajax call pipeline and perform any arbitrary code before and after the call to the server. Let's look at that more closely.

| TECHNIQUE 75 | **Intercepting client-side pipeline** |

The ASP.NET Ajax framework has a server control named `UpdateProgress`. This control lets you define an HTML template that shows a wait message while the Ajax PostBack is being processed on the server. To do that, the control injects JavaScript code on the page that shows the HTML template before the call to the server and hides the HTML template after the response from server has been received. The pipeline isn't a black box; we can use it to inject our logic.

PROBLEM

Suppose you're working on orders. Each time you perform an action that causes a PostBack, you also have to check whether a new order has been added. If one has been added, you have to show a message to the user.

SOLUTION

You used the `UpdatePanel` to send HTML to modify the panels on the page. Now you're going to use the `ScriptManager` to send additional custom information that can be processed on the client. When a PostBack occurs, you can perform a query on the database to check for new orders and then send a boolean to the client. The client receives the data and shows a message if new orders have come in. Figure 12.5 shows the flow.

The method of the `ScriptManager` class that lets you add custom information is `RegisterDataItem`. This method accepts a `Control` instance and the value associated with it. The value can even be a class. The value will be serialized on the client in JSON format.

C#:

```
sm.RegisterDataItem(this, "true");
```

VB:

```
sm.RegisterDataItem(Me, "true")
```

When data returns on the client, you intercept it the moment the PostBack result is processed and inject your code. Intercepting the result of the client-side PostBack processing is pretty easy. When the page is initially loaded, you retrieve the `PageRequest-Manager` object through its static `getInstance` method, which is the component that intercepts the page PostBack and transforms them into Ajax calls. Then you use the `add_endRequest` method to pass a method that's invoked when the client has finished processing the server data:

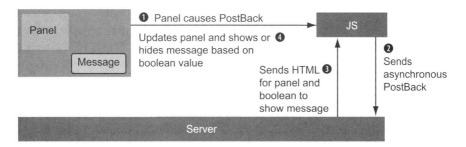

Figure 12.5   The panel contains a button that causes a PostBack. The JavaScript on the page intercepts the PostBack and invokes the server, simulating a PostBack with an Ajax call. The server sends HTML for the panel and a boolean that specifies whether the message should be shown. The JavaScript updates the panel and either shows or hides the message, depending on the value from the server.

```
<script type="text/javascript">
  Sys.Application.add_init(function () {
    var prm = Sys.WebForms.PageRequestManager.getInstance();
    prm.add_endRequest(function (form, handler) {
      (handler._dataItems.__Page);
    });
  });
</script>
```

The `Sys.Application` gives you access to page events. By using the `add_init` method, you can be sure that the function inside it is invoked as soon as the page is loaded. The main thing to notice is that you have to put this method at the bottom of the page and not in the `Head` section of the HTML.

DISCUSSION

By using this approach wisely, you can reduce `UpdatePanel` controls in your pages and highly optimize performance because only data, and not HTML, goes over the wire. Even if this approach is somewhat complicated because it requires you to write more JavaScript code, it's flexible and offers the best possible performance.

If you take this client-centric approach to the extreme, you can completely elimi-nate the `UpdatePanel`. The server just returns data and doesn't care about its HTML representation—that's client-side business. To remove the `UpdatePanel`, you have to radically change your approach and deal with tons of JavaScript code. But there is a better way.

ASP.NET Ajax has a rich client-side framework that enables you to simplify JavaScript coding. But jQuery is even more powerful and easier to use. Now you're going to discover how to follow the client-centric pattern to enable Ajax behavior in ASP.NET applications using jQuery instead of ASP.NET Ajax.

12.3   *Focusing on the client: jQuery*

Let's face it: developing JavaScript code is one of the most annoying things in the programming world. There's no compile-time checking, different browsers are sub-tly different, and editors offer limited features compared with what they offer for server-side code.

jQuery isn't a magic wand. It won't solve all your problems, but it can surely miti-gate them. It abstracts differences between browsers, has great support for autocom-plete in Visual Studio, and lets you write very little code (sometimes just one line) to create powerful features. It also has other advantages: it lets you query the page Docu-ment Object Model (DOM) using a correctly formatted string, has fluent APIs and, maybe most important, it's free!

Thanks to all these great features, Microsoft has made an agreement with the jQuery team, and now jQuery is integrated into Visual Studio templates. When you create a web application using Visual Studio, jQuery files are already in your applica-tion (this is true for both Web Forms and MVC applications)—you don't need any external files. Let's find out how to use jQuery.

12.3.1 jQuery Basics

Before delving into specific features of jQuery, let's cover the basics of this powerful framework. At the base of jQuery is the magic $ character. If you're not an experienced JavaScript developer, you might be surprised to know that this character is a *method*. The $ method is the entry point for all jQuery features. In this section, we're going to explore the most important features so that next sections will be easier to understand.

QUERYING THE DOM

When the browser receives HTML, the browser parses it and renders it on screen. During parsing, it also creates an internal representation of the controls and organizes them hierarchically. This internal representation is called the DOM.

When you have to refer to a control in JavaScript, you have to use the `GetElement-ById` method of the `Document` class. Doing this isn't hard, but it requires a long statement. jQuery makes things much faster. Take a look at the next snippet to get an idea of the power of jQuery:

Classic JavaScript:
```
document.getElementById("objId");
```

jQuery:
```
$("#objId");
```

In this case, the $ method accepts a string representing the object to retrieve. The fantastic part is that although `getElementById` lets you find only one object, jQuery offers a pattern to retrieve as many objects as you need in many ways. Here we used the # character to specify that we're searching for an object by its ID. If you're familiar with CSS, you know that the # character is used to identify an object by its ID. jQuery leverages CSS syntax to enable you to query the DOM by using just a string. In classic JavaScript, you would need *tons* of lines of code to do the same thing.

Now you can retrieve all objects of a given type using the next snippet:
```
$("span");
```

You can also apply additional filters. For example, if you have to search all `span` tags that have the `red` CSS class, you have to write the following snippet:
```
$("span.red");
```

Once again, if you're familiar with CSS, this syntax is clear to you; if you're not, this syntax is simple to understand, so fear not.

The searches we've performed so far have looked for an object in the whole DOM. Sometimes you need to start from a known object and then traverse the DOM to look for its immediate children, its indirect children, or its siblings. Let's see how that works.

Suppose that you have a form with a set of options. Each option is represented by a check box and a `span`, like in figure 12.6.

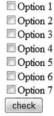

Figure 12.6   A form with several options. Each check box is followed by a span with the option label.

The following HTML renders the result shown in figure 12.6:

```
<div id="checkContainer">
  <input type="checkbox" /><span>Option 1</span><br />
  <input type="checkbox" /><span>Option 2</span><br />
  <input type="checkbox" /><span>Option 3</span><br />
  <input type="checkbox" /><span>Option 4</span><br />
  <input type="checkbox" /><span>Option 5</span><br />
  <input type="checkbox" /><span>Option 6</span><br />
  <input type="checkbox" /><span>Option 7</span><br />
  <input type="button" value="check" onclick="checkOptions()" />
</div>
```

If you want to retrieve the options that the user selects, issue the following query:

```
$(":checkbox:checked");
```

The :checkbox command is a shortcut to retrieve check boxes; :checked is another shortcut to retrieve only the checked items.

If you want to show a message to the user with selected options, you need to retrieve the span next to the check box; in other words, you need the siblings of the selected check boxes:

```
$(":checkbox:checked + span");
```

The + character instructs jQuery to retrieve span tags that are next to the check box. As before, you would have to write a lot of code to do this in classic JavaScript.

Now suppose that you have a treeview built using ul and li tags. The HTML of the treeview is represented by the code in the next snippet.

```
<ul id="tree">
  <li>Node1
    <ul>
      <li>Subnode1</li>
      <li>Subnode2</li>
    </ul>
  </li>
  <li>Node2
    <ul>
      <li>Subnode1</li>
      <li>Subnode2</li>
    </ul>
  </li>
</ul>
```

If you want to extract *all* nodes of the treeview, you need to issue this query:

```
$("#tree li");
```

The query simply retrieves the element with id tree and then takes all its direct and indirect children li tags. If you need only the direct children, you need to modify the query slightly:

```
$("#tree > li");
```

The > char does the trick of taking only the direct children. This query returns only the `Node1` and `Node2` elements of the HTML shown in previous snippet.

You can retrieve objects in other ways using jQuery. Discussing all of them is outside the scope of this book. If you're interested in deepening your knowledge, read *jQuery in Action* by Manning Publications or browse the online docs at www.jQuery.com.

Besides using a formatted string to query the DOM, jQuery lets you use methods, too. Read on.

QUERYING THE DOM USING METHODS

Many times you already have an instance of an object and you need to use it to find others. Revisiting the previous example about the treeview, you might have a method that receives the tree object and then needs to retrieve all its children. To do this, you need methods that work with the object you've received. Using strings is still feasible, but harder to work out; for that reason, we don't recommend that solution. jQuery methods are pretty easy to use and have a one-to-one mapping with characters in the string syntax.

Suppose that you receive an object and need to find all the spans inside it. The best way to find them is to wrap the object inside a jQuery object and then use the `find` method to pass in a string query:

```
$(obj).find("span");
```

If `obj` is the JavaScript `document` object, this statement retrieves all the spans in the page. Pretty easy, isn't it? If you need to find all the check boxes that have been selected in a list, you'll probably have to search inside their container element. In this case, nothing changes because you encapsulate the container element in a jQuery object and then use the same query we've used previously:

```
$(obj).$(":checkbox:checked");
```

If you need to find all the children of the treeview starting from the `tree` element, you can use the `find` method once again:

```
$(tree).find("li");
```

The `find` method searches recursively between the children; if you need only direct children, you have to use the `children` method:

```
$(tree).children("li");
```

jQuery has plenty of methods to traverse the DOM; showing all of them isn't possible for the sake of brevity. It's our experience that the `find` and `children` methods are the most used, along with the `parent` method (which returns the parent element of the object).

So far you've seen that if you pass a string to the $ method, you perform a query; if you pass an object, it's included in a jQuery object that you can then query using methods. Now let's discover what happens if you pass a method.

HANDLING THE PAGE LOADED EVENT

In ASP.NET Ajax, you use the `Application` object to execute some code when the page is loaded. In jQuery, you can write a method and then pass it to the $ method:

```
$(function () {
  alert("Page loaded");
});
```

You can put any logic you need inside the method. If you compare this code with the code required by ASP.NET Ajax, you'll realize that jQuery requires much less code to get the same result.

So far we've been querying the DOM. The last basic task we're going to face is modifying DOM objects that were retrieved using jQuery.

MANIPULATING THE DOM

When you manipulate the DOM, you're modifying an object of the page. You can modify objects in several ways. For instance, you can add or remove an element; add, modify, or remove an attribute; and so on.

Working with attributes is probably the easiest thing to do. Building on the previous example about check boxes, suppose that you have a button that checks or unchecks all of them. To select all check boxes, you can use the `attr` method:

```
$(":checkbox").attr("checked", "checked");
```

This method retrieves all check boxes and, for each of them, invokes the `attr` method. `attr` adds an attribute to the DOM element using the first parameter as the name and the second as the value. The result is that all check boxes will have the following HTML:

```
<input type="checkbox" checked="checked" />
```

What's great about this method is that if the attribute already exists, it doesn't write it again, but modifies the existing one. The result is that a single method can be used for both adding and modifying attributes.

Coming back to the example, to unselect all check boxes, we have to remove the `checked` attribute. You can do this by using the `removeAttr` method:

```
$(":checkbox").removeAttr("checked");
```

The `removeAttr` method is pretty simple because it accepts only the name of the attribute to remove.

Let's change the subject a bit and talk about adding elements. Again, going back to the treeview example, sometimes you need to add a new element to a node. To do that, you have to create a new element and then append it to the node. You'll be amazed by the simplicity of the jQuery code that does seemingly complicated stuff like this. Take a look:

```
$("#tree li:first > ul").append($("<li>").html("last node"));
```

The initial query retrieves the element to which the new element must be added. First, the query gets the `tree` element; then it takes the first `li` children and goes to the `ul` direct child. This example gives you a great idea of jQuery potential.

After retrieving the `treeview` node, we use the `append` method to add a DOM element. The `append` method accepts a parameter that contains a jQuery object containing one or more DOM elements. We build a new jQuery object with an `li` tag and set the inner HTML coding to `last node`.

> **NOTE**   The <tag> syntax is special syntax that tells the $ method that although we're passing a string, we don't need to issue a query; rather, we're just creating an object with that tag.

To solve this problem, we could have taken the opposite approach: create the new object and append it to the `treeview` element. In this case, we would use the `appendTo` method:

```
$("<li>").html("last node").appendTo($("#tree li:first > ul"));
```

Both methods work in the same way, so choosing one way or the other is just a matter of personal taste.

Suppose that now you want to remove the element you just added. You have to retrieve the element through a query and then invoke the `remove` element:

```
$("#tree li:first > ul > li:last").remove();
```

The query is similar to the one in the previous example. We've just added navigation to the node we added (`:last` is a query predicate that instructs jQuery to take only the last element). We then invoke `remove` to delete the item from the DOM.

Knowledge of DOM manipulation is vital when you're going the Ajax way. With jQuery, you don't use ASP.NET built-in behaviors. Instead, you manually fetch only data from the server and then update the interface using the jQuery manipulation methods we've talked about in this section.

Now we can move on to the last jQuery building block: event management.

MANAGING AN OBJECT'S EVENTS

With jQuery, you can dynamically add a handler to the events of a control on a page. You can add a handler that's triggered when a button is clicked, when a drop-down item is changed, or when the value of a text box is changed. You can also remove a handler in the same way and even trigger a specific event. The end result is that you can fully manage events.

Let's take a super-easy example. Suppose that you want to show a message when the user clicks a button. You generally write code like this:

HTML:
```
<input type="button" onclick="action();" />
```

JS:
```
function action(){ alert("you clicked the button"); }
```

The bad thing about this code is that you mix up JavaScript in the HTML code. HTML should contain only representational data, leaving to JavaScript the task of adding behavior. jQuery lets you strip out that ugly `onclick` from the HTML and lets you easily add a handler to the `onclick` event:

HTML:
```
<input type="button" id="btn"/>
```

JS:
```
$(function(){
  $("#btn").click(function(){
    alert("you ckicked the button");
  });
});
```

When the page is loaded, you retrieve the button and add the event handler through the `click` method. The code you need to write has increased, but the benefits are enormous because the clean separation of tasks you've gained between the HTML and JavaScript makes things easier to maintain.

jQuery has a method for each event type. For example, you can use the `change` method to attach a handler when a drop-down item is changed or when a text box value changes. `focus` and `blur` are used to attach an event when a control is in and out of focus, respectively. Other methods are also available; because we're not going to cover all of them here, you should take a look at *jQuery in Action* or use the online documentation to get a full reference to them.

Sometimes you might want to trigger an event programmatically. To do this, you just need to invoke the same methods you've already seen, without passing any parameters. For example, to trigger the `click` event of the button, you can write the following statement:

```
$("#btn").click();
```

Congratulations! You just went through a fast-paced introduction to the world of jQuery. We haven't told you everything you can do with jQuery, but now you have a clear idea of how jQuery simplifies development by making it easier to do and cutting out tons of lines of code. Now we can move on and explore how to use jQuery to enable Ajax in ASP.NET applications.

TECHNIQUE 76   Invoking REST web services with jQuery

jQuery lets you invoke the server in different ways. It has a low-level method named `ajax` that you can use to specify all call parameters; a set of specific high-level methods are built on it. You have a method to perform POST, another one for GET, and other ones for retrieving JSON data or a JavaScript file. You have a lot of choices, but the `ajax` method is the best way to go.

PROBLEM

Suppose you have a page that shows customer details. The user might want to know the total cost of the orders placed by a particular customer. Because the query might be heavy, it's performed only when the user explicitly requests it by clicking a button. You need to intercept the click, call the server to get the total amount of the orders for that customer, and then show it on the page.

SOLUTION

Creating this solution is pretty simple. First, you have to create a web service on the server that exposes the function via a REST call. To do that, add an item of type *Ajax-enabled WCF Service* to the project and name it `RestService`. Visual Studio automatically creates the plumbing to expose the web service via a REST. More precisely, it inserts in the web.config file all necessary WCF configurations, as shown in the following listing.

Listing 12.2 The web.config code needed to configure the REST service

```
<system.serviceModel>
  <behaviors>
    <endpointBehaviors>
      <behavior name="RestServiceAspNetAjaxBehavior">     Expose service
        <enableWebScript />                                to JavaScript
      </behavior>
    </endpointBehaviors>
  </behaviors>
  <serviceHostingEnvironment
    aspNetCompatibilityEnabled="true"                   Make service compatible
    multipleSiteBindingsEnabled="true" />               with ASP.NET
  <services>
    <service name="RestService">
      <endpoint address=""
        behaviorConfiguration=
          "RestServiceAspNetAjaxBehavior"                Expose
        binding="webHttpBinding"                         service
        contract="RestService" />
    </service>
  </services>
</system.serviceModel>
```

When web.config is ready, you need to create the method that exposes the total orders amount for the client. You have to put this method in the `RestService` class that's in the `RestService.cs|vb` file inside the `App_Code` directory. The code for the whole class is shown in the next listing.

Listing 12.3 The service class that exposes the total orders amount

C#:

```
[ServiceContract]
[AspNetCompatibilityRequirements(RequirementsMode =
AspNetCompatibilityRequirementsMode.Allowed)]
public class RestService
{
  [OperationContract]
  public decimal GetOrdersAmount(string CustomerId)
  {
    using (var ctx = new NorthwindEntities())
```

```
    {
      return ctx.Orders.Where(o => o.CustomerID == CustomerId).
        Sum(o => o.Order_Details.Sum(d => d.UnitPrice * d.Quantity));
    }
  }
}
```

VB:

```
<ServiceContract> _
<AspNetCompatibilityRequirements(_
  RequirementsMode := AspNetCompatibilityRequirementsMode.Allowed)> _
Public Class RestService
  <OperationContract> _
  Public Function GetOrdersAmount(CustomerId As String) As Decimal
    Using ctx = New NorthwindEntities()
      Return ctx.Orders.Where(Function(o) _
        o.CustomerID = CustomerId).Sum(Function(o) _
          o.Order_Details.Sum(Function(d) d.UnitPrice * d.Quantity))
    End Using
  End Function
End Class
```

The web service class is pretty simple. You just mark it with the `ServiceContract` (System.ServiceModel namespace) and `AspNetCompatibilityRequirements` (System.ServiceModel.Activation namespace) attributes. The methods to be exposed must be marked with the `OperationContract` attribute (System.ServiceModel namespace). The method itself just calculates the total amount for the input customer.

Now that the web service is created, we need to write the JavaScript code to invoke it. The method to use is `ajax`. It's a low-level method that lets us specify all the parameters of the call. Let's take a look at the code in the following listing.

Listing 12.4   Invoking the server using the jQuery API for Ajax

```
$.ajax({
  url: "RestService.svc/GetOrdersAmount",
  data: '{ "CustomerId": "ALFKI" }',
  type: "POST",
  contentType: "application/json",
  dataType: "json",
  success: function (result) {
    //code
  }
});
```

We've got a lot to talk about in this listing. First of all, the `ajax` method accepts just one parameter, which is a class containing all the real parameters. The first parameter of the class is `url`, which specifies the web service URL. The URL is made of the web service name (`RestService.svc`), plus the / character and the method name (`GetOrdersAmount`).

Next, the `data` parameter contains the method parameters. This class must be a *stringified* JSON class. This point is important; if this class isn't rendered correctly, the server won't be able to process the information.

The `type` parameter specifies how the request is submitted to the server. WCF REST services allow only POST calls (unless manually configured to accept GET), so you should force a POST. The `contentType` and `dataType` parameters inform the server about how data is serialized when they're sent from client to server and from server to client, respectively. In this case, data is both sent and received using the JSON format.

Finally, the `success` parameter specifies the callback to invoke when data is returned. Notice that the result is a class that contains several properties and the server result is exposed via the `d` property. Other than `success`, you can use `error` to specify the callback to execute when the server call generates an error.

Now that we have data from the server, we have to update the interface to show the orders amount. This process is almost trivial, thanks to the manipulation methods of jQuery. All you need to do is write the following statement in the `success` handler:

```
$("#amount").html(result.d);
```

This code retrieves the `span` tag, which shows the amount (the `span` tag that has the ID `amount`) and sets its content to the value returned by the server.

DISCUSSION

As you've learned in this section, manipulating the interface using server data isn't that difficult. In this example, the interaction has been overly simple because only one field had to be updated. When you have to update more complex widgets (a grid, for instance), then things get complicated. No matter what though, it's just a matter of retrieving the objects and setting their values—nothing more than that. More code might be necessary, but the technique doesn't change.

Sometimes you need a method only in a page. For these situations, placing it in a web service might be useless. What you can do instead is create a method in the page that requires it and then expose it to the client.

TECHNIQUE 77   Invoking page methods with jQuery

It's quite likely that you need the total orders amount calculation only in the page that shows the customer. Placing the method that calculates this amount in a web service is perfectly valid, but placing it only in the page that requires it might be a good idea, too. In ASP.NET terminology, such a method is called a *page method*.

PROBLEM

We need to create a method that calculates the total orders amount. Such a method must not live in a web service, but only in the page that uses it. This method must be available to the client.

SOLUTION

A page method is a method, just like all the others. It lives in the `page` class, and it *must* be static and marked with the `WebMethod` attribute (`System.Web.Services` namespace). The following listing shows the code for this method.

Listing 12.5   Invoking the server using jQuery API for Ajax

C#:

```csharp
[WebMethod]
public static decimal GetOrdersAmount(string CustomerId)
{
  using (var ctx = new NorthwindEntities())
  {
    return ctx.Orders.Where(o => o.CustomerID == CustomerId)
      .Sum(o => o.Order_Details.Sum(d => d.UnitPrice * d.Quantity));
  }
}
```

VB:

```vbnet
<WebMethod> _
Public Function GetOrdersAmount(CustomerId As String) As Decimal
  Using ctx = New NorthwindEntities()
    Return ctx.Orders.Where(Function(o) _
      o.CustomerID = CustomerId).Sum(Function(o) _
        o.Order_Details.Sum(Function(d) d.UnitPrice * d.Quantity))
  End Using
End Function
```

As you can see, the code in this method is identical to what you saw in the previous section. The only change is that the method is marked with the proper attribute and is static. The method is now available to the client and can be invoked using the same JavaScript code of the previous section; only the url parameter changes, as you can see in the next snippet:

```javascript
$.ajax({
  url: "page.aspx/GetOrdersAmount",
  data: '{ "CustomerId": "ALFKI" }',
  type: "POST",
  contentType: "application/json",
  dataType: "json",
  success: function (result) {
    //code
  }
});
```

The url parameter consists of the page name, plus the / character and the method name (it's similar to the web service URL); the rest remains identical. This code wasn't difficult at all!

DISCUSSION

The decision to place spare methods only where they belong is a good one. The problems occur when such a method must be used in other pages, too. The method can be duplicated in each page class, the client code for all pages can invoke the method in the original page, or you can move the method into a web service. The last choice is definitely our favorite because each time you have a *common* method, it's best to place it in a *common* place.

So far we've talked about how to use jQuery and the Web Form technique. Let's take a quick look at how to make jQuery query the server when you're using MVC.

TECHNIQUE 78 Invoking MVC actions with jQuery

In MVC, each action has a specific URL. Invoking a URL and passing parameters is what we've been doing so far with jQuery, so using it to call MVC actions should be pretty easy.

PROBLEM

We need to create an MVC action that retrieves the total orders amount and returns it to the client. We then need to invoke the action the Ajax way using jQuery.

SOLUTION

Creating the action is unbelievably simple. We just need to return the amount using the `Content` method, which is shown in the following listing.

Listing 12.6   The action that returns the total orders amount

C#:
```
public ActionResult GetOrdersAmount(string CustomerId)
{
  using (var ctx = new NorthwindEntities())
  {
    return Content(
      ctx.Orders.Where(o => o.CustomerID == CustomerId)
        .Sum(o => o.Order_Details.Sum(d => d.UnitPrice * d.Quantity)));
  }
}
```
VB:
```
Public Function GetOrdersAmount(CustomerId As String) As ActionResult
  Using ctx = New NorthwindEntities()
    Return Content(
      ctx.Orders.Where(Function(o) _
        o.CustomerID = CustomerId).Sum(Function(o) _
          o.Order_Details.Sum(Function(d) d.UnitPrice * d.Quantity))
  End Using

End Function
```
When we have the action, we can invoke it using the get method:

```
$.get(
  "/home/GetOrdersAmount",
  { CustomerId: "ALFKI" },
  function (data) {
    //code
  }
);
```

The first parameter of the get method is the URL of the action, the second one accepts the parameters of the action, and the last one represents the callback to be invoked when data is returned.

Using the `get` method is convenient because it requires less code. You can always use the `ajax` method if the `get` method doesn't fit your situation. If, instead of a simple number, you have more complex data, you can return it in JSON format. In that case, you'll have to use the `getJSON` method instead of `get`.

DISCUSSION

We've covered all of the ways ASP.NET exposes methods to the client and how to consume them using jQuery. Although you can use other ways to invoke the methods using jQuery, the `ajax`, `get`, and `getJSON` methods are, in our experience, the ones used the most.

We've been discussing some basic behavior of jQuery. Now it's time to talk about the library that made jQuery a real success: jQueryUI. jQueryUI is a set of ready-to-use jQuery plugins that enable you to enrich your interface with so little code that you won't believe it.

TECHNIQUE 79   **Enriching the interface via jQueryUI**

jQuery has a stable and robust core. When it was completed, jQuery was used to develop a set of widgets that have been included in a library named jQueryUI. This library includes widgets like a datepicker, an accordion, a tab control, a slider, an auto-complete, and others. These widgets are *not* included in ASP.NET templates, so you have to download them as a separate package. The package is small, and, believe me, you'll never regret the time it took to get it.

The library is freely downloadable from the http://www.jqueryui.com web site. You should also download the jQuery themes because they contain a ready-to-use CSS classes and images.

PROBLEM

Suppose that you're building a page to submit a new order. In this page, the user must enter the customer, the required shipping date, the shipping address, and the order details. The requirements state that the user must enter the customer name in a text box where autocomplete is enabled. Filling in the date must be eased by a calendar control, and customer and order details must be entered in a separate section. Finally, before the data is submitted to the server, a modal dialog box must be shown to the user for data confirmation.

SOLUTION

Wow, that's a lot of requirements. Even so, they're pretty common in many applications, so facing them now is going to help you in your everyday work. We're going to go over each of these requirements; let's start with the autocomplete requirement.

To attach autocomplete behavior to a text box, you simply have to retrieve it using a query and then invoke the `autocomplete` method. The best place to put such code is in the event JavaScript fires when the browser loads the page:

```
$(function(){
  $("#CustomerName").autocomplete();
});
```

By default, the `autocomplete` method takes the autocomplete items from a list that you can pass as a parameter. In this case, we want the behavior to go to the server. What we can do is add a method to the REST service we created in the previous section. This method returns the customer names that contain the value entered in the text box. This method takes a string parameter whose name *must* be `term` and that contains the value entered in the text box.

> **NOTE** We're not showing the code for this method because it's WCF related. You'll find it in the source code for the book.

When that's done, we can pass the `source` parameter to the `autocomplete` method, specifying the REST service method URL. The next snippet shows an example of this parameter:

```
$("#CustomerName").autocomplete({
    source: "RestService.svc/GetCustomers",
});
```

In addition to the `source` parameter, we can also set the number of characters that is necessary to issue a call to the server. By default, that value is 3, but we can modify it using the `minLength` parameter. The final result is visible in figure 12.7.

Figure 12.7   The autocomplete options are shown below the text box. By typing the letters "al", you can obtain a list of all customers whose name contains these letters.

Now that we have the autocomplete, it's time to add datepicker behavior to the text box that holds the required shipping date. To add a datepicker, you have to retrieve the text boxes using a query and then use the `datepicker` method:

```
$("#CustomerName").datepicker();
```

The `datepicker` method enables you to easily select a date, but naturally you don't want the user to select a date before today. To avoid such an error, we have to restrict the range of available dates from today to forever. Passing the `minDate` parameter to the `datePicker` method does just that. You can set this parameter to several values, but the best way to go is to pass a date. The `datepicker` method disables all days before that date. Because we don't want the user to select a date before today, we'll pass the current date:

```
$("#CustomerName").datepicker({ minDate: new Date() });
```

To make things complete, we also have a `maxDate` parameter, which works exactly like the `minDate` with the only difference being that it disables all days *after* the date you pass to it. If you want to prevent the user from selecting a date farther in the future than a certain number of days after the current date, you can create a new date instance, add the number of days (we're using 10 days), and then set the `maxDate` parameter. This solution will work, but there's a simpler way. You can simply set the `maxDate` parameter to the string `+10D` (10 days):

```
$("#CustomerName").datepicker({ minDate: new Date(), maxDate: "+10D" });
```

The result is that when the text box accepts the focus, a calendar is shown, like in figure 12.8.

You can also limit the years (Y) and months (M) that are shown by using the same syntax.

We can also set other properties like numberOfMonths, which specifies how many months are visible in the calendar; day-Names and dayNamesShort, to customize the names of the days (useful for localization); monthNames and monthNamesShort, to customize the name of the months (also useful for localization); and dateFormat, to specify the format of the date in the text box. These parameters are shown in the next snippet:

Figure 12.8   **By using the jQueryUI library, you can set the** maxDate **parameter so that only the current date and the next 10 days are available on the calendar.**

```
$("#CustomerName").datepicker({ minDate: new Date(), maxDate: "+10D",
  monthNames: ["Jan", "Feb", "Mar", "Apr", "May", "June", "July", "Aug",
    "Sept", "Oct", "Nov", "Dec"],
  dayNames: ["Sun", "Mon", "Tue", "Wed", "Thurs", "Fri", "Sat"],
  dateFormat: "mm/dd/yy"
});
```

Okay, we have the autocomplete for the customer name and the calendar for the required shipping date. Now it's time to separate the order information from the details. The best way to separate content in the same page is to group data into tabs. jQueryUI has a component that lets you do that easily. You produce the HTML code in a convenient way and jQuery takes care of the rest. The HTML is shown in the following listing.

Listing 12.7   Organizing a page using tabs

```
<div id="tabs">
  <ul>
    <li><a href="#orderData">order</a></li>
    <li><a href="#details">details</a></li>
  </ul>
  <div id="orderData">
    <!—Order data-->
  </div>
  <div id="details">
    <!—-Order details -->
  </div>
</div>
```

The HTML code is pretty simple. First, you need a container for the tabs (the div with ID tabs). After that, you use li tags to create a list of tab headings. Inside each

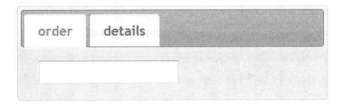

Figure 12.9   The figure shows
the result of the HTML in listing
12.7, after we invoke the `tabs`
method. A little bit of code for a
big gain in the user-friendliness
of your page.

header, you place the `a` tag and set its `href` property to the ID of the tab it refers to
(prefixed by the # character). Finally, you create a `div` for each tab and place the content inside them.

When you've got your HTML and it's correctly produced, use jQuery to show it as a
tabbed structure. You can do this easily by retrieving the main container and invoking
the `tabs` method:

```
$("#tabs").tabs();
```

If you don't believe it's that easy, take a look at figure 12.9, which shows the result of
this code.

The last requirement we need to meet is to show a confirmation dialog box where
the user confirms the data submission. The first step toward achieving this goal is to
create a `div` tag containing the confirmation message:

```
<div id="dialog">Are you sure you want to save?</div>
```

Now we need to use jQuery to transform this `div` into a modal dialog box and show it
when the user clicks the Save button. Retrieve the `div` and use the `dialog` method:

```
$("#dialog").dialog({ title: "confirmation", modal: true, autoOpen: false,
  buttons: { Yes: Yes_Click, No: No_Click} });
```

The `dialog` method has several parameters, but the ones used in this snippet are the
most important for our purposes. Let's see them in detail in table 12.2.

Table 12.2   Main properties of the dialog method

Property	Description
autoOpen	Specifies whether the dialog is shown immediately or only when the code explicitly requests it
buttons	Specifies the button in the bottom part of the dialog and the code to be invoked when it's clicked
modal	Instructs jQuery to create a modal dialog
title	The message that's shown in the header of the dialog message

Now that we have the confirmation dialog box ready, we have to open it when the user
clicks the Save button. To do that, we retrieve the button and, in its `click` event,
retrieve the `div` of the dialog box and invoke once again the `dialog` method, passing
in the `open` string:

```
$("#Save").click(function () {
  $("#dialog").dialog("open");
});
```

You can see the result of this method in figure 12.10.

As you probably know, at this point all we need to do is intercept the user answer and take the appropriate action. If the user clicks the Yes button, we close the dialog box and submit the page; if they click No, we simply close the dialog box. Closing the dialog box is pretty simple. We retrieve the dialog div and call the dialog method, passing the close string:

```
function Yes_Click(ev){
  //submitForm
  $("#dialog").dialog("close");
}

function No_Click(ev) {
  $("#dialog").dialog("close");
}
```

That's it! It took a while, but now you know how to use jQueryUI to add user-friendly behaviors to your page without writing a lot of extra code.

DISCUSSION

jQuery and jQueryUI are a must have in your toolbox. It's hard to imagine a modern web application that doesn't make use of these JavaScript frameworks. You probably feel the same way now, and we hope that you'll begin to use them in your everyday work.

Now that you're at the end of the chapter, you know how to create faster and more appealing applications using the Ajax technique. You know how to use UpdatePanel to easily introduce Ajax behaviors without even touching existing code and without writing a single line of JavaScript code. You also know how to take the opposite path, creating and exposing services on the server and consuming them the Ajax way, from JavaScript.

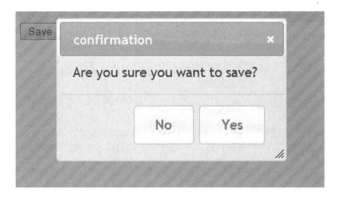

Figure 12.10
The confirmation dialog box is shown when the user clicks the Save button. The buttons specified in the buttons **property are placed at the bottom of the page and the** title **property is shown at the top of the dialog box.**

12.4 Summary

Ajax is a key technology for creating user-friendly web applications. Reducing full PostBacks to the server makes applications easier to use and more appealing to the user. This feature alone often transforms an adequate application into a real success.

Using update panels to transform the application into a success story is the fastest and easiest way because they let you add Ajax behavior using server-side code. In many cases, you don't need to write a single line of JavaScript code, which is why your productivity can be improved so much.

Although `UpdatePanel` control enables several optimizations, in scenarios where performance is critical, the best way to go is to invoke the server to retrieve only data and then use JavaScript code to update the interface. jQuery makes this pattern simple to follow. What's more, jQueryUI further simplifies building user-friendly interfaces, making it easier than ever to develop better applications.

You know enough about Ajax, so we can move on to another subject that in the stateless world of the web is vital: state management.

State

This chapter covers

- ViewState and new features in ASP.NET 4.0
- Session state
- Profile API
- Building a custom provider for the Profile API

Web applications are stateless by nature, which means that you don't have a native way to handle state. If you're familiar with desktop applications, you know that state plays a central role in a typical application. For example, you can save your users' preferences and let them find their preferences again next time they use the application. Even though no native way exists to handle state as per the HTTP protocol, modern application frameworks (like ASP.NET) provide a lot of features in this area. Depending on your needs, you can manage state at different levels—on the client or on the server. Generally, state handling is performed server side, where the data is stored.

The objectives of handling state are disparate: you can store user settings or save frequently requested objects to avoid the cost associated with fetching them every time. The objects can be stored with a lifetime that varies, depending on the approach that you choose, but typically, you have a lot of possibilities.

This chapter contains an overview of the most frequent scenarios, and the next one analyzes caching strategies, which are often treated as a special kind of state. We decided to separate these topics so that we can cover all these techniques in depth.

13.1   Handling state

The typical ASP.NET application contains different state management techniques that are related to different scopes. Some data needs to be volatile but available for the entire request lifecycle, on a single-user basis; other kinds of information need to be available to all users.

13.1.1   What is state?

To make things clear and to ensure that we approach the problems presented in this chapter with the right background, you need to understand some basic concepts. First of all, *state* is the ability to manage the lifetime of an object in a given interval. When we manage an object's state, we can make it persistent to gain speed. In fact, most of the time this object needs to be retrieved from a source (like a database); retrieving the data is the most expensive part of the process. On the other hand, modern hardware has a lot of memory, so it's possible to store these objects in memory, ready to be used. Storing objects in memory is the preferred way to store them, but they can also be stored on disk. Disk access has a more negative impact on performance than memory access does, but disk storage is useful in situations where the object materialization is expensive and an adequate amount of free memory isn't available.

Generally, we'll approach this problem by splitting state handling into three main scenarios, depending on how we want to span the object's lifetime. In this chapter, we're going to analyze the following kinds of state:

- Per-request
- Per-session
- Per-application

ASP.NET provides different answers to the questions related to these scenarios. We're going to take a look at each of them, but per-application state is analyzed in chapter 14, in the context of caching.

TECHNIQUE 80   **Per-request state**

Per-request state is the simplest form of state handling. The state of an object is saved across the entire request for a given page. You can share the instance of an object for the request and re-create it on subsequent requests.

Typically, you handle per-request state using ViewState, which we introduced in chapter 1. ViewState is important in ASP.NET Web Forms and acts as a bag in which to store information across the same group of requests performed on a page. It's not a true per-request state bag because it's available after the request itself, but neither is it a per-session bag because its scope is limited to a given page. If you need to store values that can be accessed in the same request, other options are available. Eventually, we'll talk about all of them.

PROBLEM

ViewState is both a joy and a pain for ASP.NET developers. You can use it to maintain the status across the different requests on a given page, but because it's saved in a hidden field, it consumes bandwidth if it's not used correctly. In this scenario, we'll take a look at how to save an object's state using ViewState and avoid re-creating the object.

SOLUTION

ASP.NET 4.0 introduces a new ViewState feature that minimizes the impact ViewState has. Before ASP.NET 4.0, the best practice in terms of ViewState was simple: disable it on every control that doesn't need it. Figure 13.1 shows the ViewState behavior.

The reality is that this best practice is quite often ignored, and a lot of bandwidth is wasted because developers don't follow it. Before ASP.NET 4.0, ViewState couldn't be disabled on a parent control because doing so would impact the children controls. This behavior wasn't flexible enough because each container control has to be handled carefully.

ViewState in ASP.NET 4.0

ASP.NET 4.0 introduces a new property called `ViewStateMode` that's defined in `System.Web.UI.Control`. The `ViewStateMode` property requires that the `ViewState` attribute be set to `true` to work; otherwise, its content is ignored. You can set this property to the following values:

- `Inherit`
- `Enabled`
- `Disabled`

The first option is the default and inherits the container setting, but the last two are more interesting. When the value is set to `Disabled`, the control stops using the `ViewState`, but its children can override this behavior and explicitly set it to `Enabled`. By doing so, the nested controls can have their own state, even if the container has it

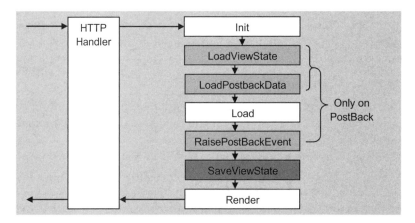

Figure 13.1   How ViewState works. `LoadViewState` and `SaveViewState` **events are raised between Init, Load, and Render states. This process is repeated by every control on the page (and by the page itself).**

disabled. Because the property is defined by `Control`, the page itself has this ability. You can define this property on the page and enable it only when it's used. Enabling the property only when you need it is a much better practice than having it on all the time.

As in previous versions, you can use a lot of controls without ViewState if you can get their value directly after a PostBack. Such controls include `TextBox`, `DropDownList`, and similar controls, when their value is accessed after the initial load of the page. The following snippet shows an example of this scenario:

```
<%@ Page ViewStateMode="Disabled" ... %>
<asp:Label runat="server" ID="DisabledText" />
<asp:Label runat="server" ID="EnabledText" ViewStateMode="Enabled" /  >
<asp:Button runat="server" ID="SubmitButton" Text="Submit" />
```

If you want to optimize your application, remember that ViewState can be your best friend if you use it correctly and your worst enemy if you abuse it.

Context.Items

Another useful container in per-request scenarios is `Context.Items`. This container is especially useful when you want to store information that can be accessed by all the actors in a typical request: `HttpHandlers`, `HttpModules`, the page, and its controls. It acts as a state bag that can be shared easily, by simply accessing `HttpContext`:

C#:
```
HttpContext.Current.Items["siteName"] = "My Site";
```

VB:
```
HttpContext.Current.Items("siteName") = "My Site"
```

`Context.Items` is often used to instantiate—and handle—an object per-request, like it does for the Entity Framework's object context, which we talked about in chapters 2 and 3. But it's also useful when you simply want to share a value along the entire request pipeline.

DISCUSSION

Per-request state has the limitation of being useful only in simpler scenarios where you need to store a value for the request (or a group of requests to the same page, as with ViewState and PostBack). This approach works for the typical flow of a data entry page, to save the objects' state across different requests.

In other cases, you'll find it more useful to save the state across a group of requests that are not linked to each other. In this kind of situation, per-session state is the answer to your questions.

TECHNIQUE 81   Per-session state

As its name suggests, per-session state can save the state across a session. Depending on what technique you use, the notion of session might vary. To be generic, a session starts with the first request made by a user and ends with his last one. Because we're in a stateless environment (HTTP as a protocol is, in fact, stateless), the last request can't be estimated so a timeout from the current request is used. If, after that amount of time, no other requests are made, the session is considered closed. In other situations, however, closing the browser has the same effect. Let's take a look at how ASP.NET supports these scenarios.

PROBLEM

Per-session state can be handled in different ways; your strategy will vary, depending on the data type used and its sensitivity. Per-session state can also be impacted by your application architecture. By handling per-session state, you'll be able to span the object's lifetime across multiple requests made by the same user.

SOLUTION

The most common form of per-session state is called *session state*. If you're not familiar with ASP.NET, the concept is simple: the state bag is available only to the same user, during that user's session. After the session closes, the state bag is automatically destroyed. The data in the state bag can't be stored automatically, but you can write code to perform this action if you need to. Figure 13.2 contains a schema that shows how this mechanism works.

Session can be accessed via `Page` or `HttpContext`, depending on the location of your code. By default, when the session starts, the `SessionStart` event is fired; at the end, the `SessionEnd` event is invoked. You can intercept them using a custom `HttpModule` or with the global.asax.

Session state implements the Provider Model design pattern, so you can write a custom provider to save it to a location other than memory. ASP.NET includes support for SQL Server and State Server.

> **SESSIONEND WITH OUT-OF-PROCESS PROVIDERS**   SQL Server, State Server, and custom out-of-process providers are designed to work in distributed scenarios where a cluster of two or more servers exist. In this kind of situation, the `SessionEnd` event won't fire because different requests can be executed by different servers, and a synchronization mechanism doesn't exist. To avoid multiple execution of this event, the event is simply not fired at all.

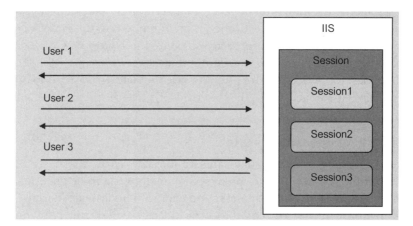

Figure 13.2 Session state works by saving different users' data into separated storage. The data is available for the user's entire session.

Generally, session state is maintained using a cookie that contains a special key called `ASP.NET_SessionID`. This cookie is sent between all the requests made by a given user. ASP.NET also supports a cookieless mode, in which browsers without cookie support receive the ID in the URL. If you configure your site using the `AutoDetect` option, ASP.NET tries to generate a cookie on the first request and, if that's not supported, it automatically switches to the cookieless mode. To take advantage of this feature, you need to enter this configuration in your web.config:

```
<configuration>
  <system.web>
    <sessionState cookieless="AutoDetect" />
  </system.web>
</configuration>
```

More generally, you can set additional properties in your web.config, like the cookie name, a custom timeout, and the providers (via the `mode` and `customProvider` attributes).

Values saved in session consume memory (if you use the default InProc provider, it consumes the server's memory). For this reason, you must use session state carefully. Because there's virtually no limit to object size, session state is often used in complex scenarios to make an object available across multiple requests. Session state can contain any serializable object and its content is secure because only the `SessionID` is sent to the client.

Session compression in ASP.NET 4.0

ASP.NET 4.0 has a new feature that minimizes the amount of space that the session state bag occupies. When you're dealing with a complex application and out-of-process providers, session state's global dimension can grow quickly and slow down your application. When you're using the two out-of-process providers (for SQL Server and State Server), you can enable the compression by setting the `compressionEnable` attribute in web.config to `true`.

Enabling compression will serialize (and deserialize) objects from session state and will compress (and decompress) them using the `System.IO.Compression.GZip-Stream` class, which applies a gzip algorithm. This feature will add a little overhead in terms of CPU cycles, but it will minimize the amount of space that the session state takes up, in terms of memory consumed. If you're using a custom provider, you can add the same behavior by using a similar approach.

Using Windows Server AppFabric session provider

When we were writing this book, Windows Server AppFabric was released in version 1. AppFabric is a distributed caching engine that consists of a set of features that can support cache sharing across multiple, different servers. Because session state is a form of cache, you can use AppFabric in this scenario, too. You can use it so that the same session state is synchronized across different web servers in the same cluster (even geographically, if you need to go that far).

You can download a provider for session state from http://www.mng.bz/oD7O. You can also use AppFabric Caching APIs directly if you need to (this provider is an implementation of these APIs).

We'll cover this aspect of Windows Server AppFabric, as well as the configuration needed to start, in the next chapter. For now, we're going to turn to cookies.

The alternative: cookies

If you don't want to impact your server's memory, or if you prefer to support a cluster, the only real alternative that you have is to store your data in cookies. A cookie can be made persistent by adding an explicit expire date or made valid until the browser is closed if the expire date is omitted.

Generally, using a cookie is a good idea if you just need to represent simple data: strings, objects, date, and so on. But, when you're dealing with complex objects, its size limitation (4096 bytes) can be an issue. Don't use cookies to store sensitive information unless you're encrypting them. Cookies can be accessed using the `Cookies` properties on the `HttpRequest` class. More information is available on MSDN at http://www.mng.bz/3Q0T.

Cookies represent a feasible alternative when the data can be represented in strings and you don't need to handle complex scenarios.

DISCUSSION

Per-session state is important because it lets you easily share the same state across different requests. You can use it to handle different needs: from storing user information to spanning the lifetime of an object instance. You can implement different techniques to support these different scenarios, each with pros and cons over the others. When you're dealing with session state, for example, the memory impact on the server and the need for synchronization over a cluster are important issues that you need to target specifically. ASP.NET supports different options for implementing per-session state, but most of them can't span across multiple sessions. In these scenarios, you've got to use a specific feature: the Profile API.

13.2 *Advanced user state*

Session state is considered the simplest form of per-session state handling. In advanced scenarios, you'll need more features, like the ability to store the state and have it available for different sessions performed by the same user. Session state is limited in this area, but ASP.NET has a specific feature that addresses this problem.

The Profile API was first introduced with ASP.NET version 2.0, as part of the Provider Model, which brings more extensibility to the platform. We took a look at the Provider Model in chapter 5, when we discussed the Membership and Roles APIs. The same concepts apply to the Profile API. This API is composed of two pieces:

- The API itself, which is called by the user
- A base class, used to implement the provider

Because all the providers share the same base class, the API can be safely used as a façade to access the real implementation.

The idea behind the Profile API is simple: it's a user-defined storage, which can be persisted across different sessions. Depending on the provider implementation, the storage might be a system-defined SQL Server database or a different container. By implementing a custom provider, you can decide how to store information in the database.

To use the Profile API, you need to first set up the environment. Let's do that now.

Using the Profile API

The Profile API is easy to use because, as for the Membership and Roles APIs, a default provider exists. This provider will work against a system-defined SQL Server schema, which you can't extend. Before we talk about customer providers, we're going to introduce the API itself and show you how to use it.

PROBLEM

You need to save information across multiple sessions, in complex forms, with less effort. We're talking about user properties, like full name, preferences, and so on. You also want to be able to change the provider easily, in order to have new storage ready to use, by leveraging the Provider Model.

SOLUTION

The Profile API is your best bet in this situation. To start with, the default provider, as outlined in chapter 5, you need to launch the aspnet_regsql.exe from C:\Windows\Microsoft.NET\Framework\v4.0.30319\. The wizard will create all the tables and stored procedures used by the Membership, Roles, and Profile APIs; if you've previously executed it (maybe you've already configured the Membership API), you're ready to start.

The next step is to configure the provider in web.config, as shown in the following listing (the node is located under configuration\system.web).

Listing 13.1   Profile API configuration is made in web.config

```
<profile defaultProvider="SqlServerProfile"                       ⊲┐
        enabled="true" automaticSaveEnabled="false">               │
  <providers>                                                    Provider
    <clear />                                                    name
    <add                                                           │
      name="SqlServerProfile"                                    ⊲┘
      type="System.Web.Profile.SqlProfileProvider,
          System.Web, Version= 4.0.0.0,
          Culture=neutral,                                       Provider
          PublicKeyToken=b03f5f7f11d50a3a"              ⊲┘       class
      connectionStringName="SqlServer"                 ⊲┐ Connection
      applicationName="/" />                              │ string
  </providers>
</profile>
```

Now that the provider is configured, you need to define the Profile properties.

Adding properties

The Profile API, in a nutshell, is a strongly typed interface where the properties must be specified before they can be used. You have two options for accomplishing this task:

- Define your properties in the web.config
- Create a class that inherits from `ProfileBase`, in the `System.Web.Profile` namespace

THE PROFILE API FOR ANONYMOUS USER　The Profile API can also be used with an anonymous user. This feature, called anonymous identification, is covered on MSDN at http://www.mng.bz/YD2e.

If you opt for the first option, you need to define the properties in web.config, using the syntax contained in the following listing.

Listing 13.2　Defining the profile's properties in web.config

```
<profile>
  <properties>
    <add name="FavoriteSkin" type="string" serializeAs="String" />
     <group name="UserProfile">
      <add name="FirstName"/>
      <add name="LastName"/>
      <add name="BirthDate" type="DateTime"/>
    </group>
  </properties>
</profile>
```

You can also use a custom type for your properties, but keep in mind that the types need to be serializable. You can control the serialization mechanism used by defining the `serializeAs` attribute, which you can set to `Binary`, `String`, `Xml`, or `ProviderSpecific`.

THE PROFILE API AND WEB PROJECTS　The definition of the properties in web.config can't be used with a web project, but only with a website. If you need to use the Profile API in a web project, you need to opt for the definition on a class that inherits from `ProfileBase`.

After you've configured the provider, Visual Studio will automatically let you access the properties, using the `Profile` class, while you're in `Page` or `UserControl`. If you take a look at `Page` properties, you might notice that a `Profile` property doesn't exist. It is, in fact, what is often referred to as syntactic sugar: the compiler (and Visual Studio) knows that, at runtime, a special class will be created, using the options defined in web.config.

If you opt for the base class, you need to define a class (as already noted) and register it with the `inherits` attribute under configuration\system.web\profile:

```
<profile ... inherits="ProfileAPI.MyProfile">
```

Now that you've added your properties, you need to learn how to access the user profile and save the related properties.

Retrieving and saving the properties

If you take a look at Visual Studio, the result at this point is quite interesting because IntelliSense shows the property, mapped with its defined type. You can take a look at figure 13.3 to understand what we're talking about.

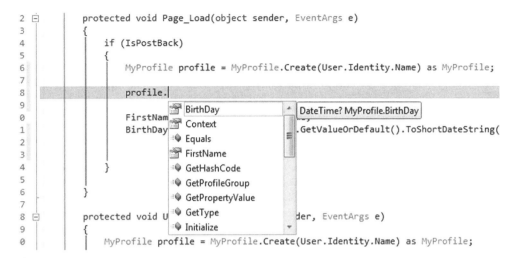

```
2      protected void Page_Load(object sender, EventArgs e)
3      {
4          if (IsPostBack)
5          {
6              MyProfile profile = MyProfile.Create(User.Identity.Name) as MyProfile;
7
8              profile.|
9                      ┌─────────────────────────────┐ ┌──────────────────────────────┐
0          FirstNam   │ 🔲 BirthDay              ▲   │ │ DateTime? MyProfile.BirthDay │
1          BirthDay   │ 🔲 Context                   │ └──────────────────────────────┘
2                     │ ◉ Equals                ▓   │ .GetValueOrDefault().ToShortDateString(
3                     │ 🔲 FirstName                 │
4          }          │ ◉ GetHashCode               │
5                     │ ◉ GetProfileGroup           │
6          }          │ ◉ GetPropertyValue          │
7                     │ ◉ GetType               ▼   │
8      protected void U│ ◉ Initialize                │der, EventArgs e)
9      {               └─────────────────────────────┘
0          MyProfile profile = MyProfile.Create(User.Identity.Name) as MyProfile;
```

Figure 13.3   The Profile API's properties are visible via IntelliSense. Because they're strongly typed, IntelliSense will show this information, too.

You'll be able to see the properties, whether you define your properties in web.config or create a class that inherits from ProfileBase.

To retrieve a value, you just need to write this simple and straightforward code:

C#:
```
string skin = Profile.FavoriteSkin;
string firstName = Profile.UserProfile.FirstName;
```

VB:
```
Dim skin as String = Profile.FavoriteSkin
Dim firstName as String = Profile.UserProfile.FirstName
```

If you previously defined a group property in your configuration, a complex type is automatically generated for you; the inner properties must be accessed using the specific syntax shown in the previous snippet.

If you need to save a value, the code isn't much different:

C#:
```
Profile.FavoriteSkin = "ocean";
Profile.UserProfile.FirstName = "Daniele";
Profile.Save();
```

VB:
```
Profile.FavoriteSkin = "ocean"
Profile.UserProfile.FirstName = "Daniele"
Profile.Save()
```

The result for a similar page, in which the user can enter the values, and then the Profile API saves them, is shown in figure 13.4.

Welcome Daniele

First Name: Daniele
Birth Day: 1/1/2001
[Update Profile]

Figure 13.4   Profile properties can be read and saved easily. They're persisted across future requests, so the user will find the properties when they return to the website.

By default, a property is saved when its value is assigned. You would do better to disable this behavior (as we did) by setting the `automaticSaveEnabled` property to `false`; you'll improve performance if you do. If you go this route, you need to manually call the `Save` method to ensure that all the properties are saved correctly. Be sure you remember to do so; otherwise, you won't save the data that's in the user profile.

Working with the Profile API and web projects

If you're using a web project instead of a website, or if you're outside a page, the previous code snippets won't work. In these scenarios, you need to directly reference the `Profile` property on `HttpContext.Current`. If you're using a custom class, you need to cast to that; otherwise, you can cast to `ProfileCommon`, which is a special type built for you by ASP.NET that also inherits from `ProfileBase`.

Let's imagine that we built a custom type for our profile, like the one in the next listing.

Listing 13.3   A custom profile implemented in code

C#:
```csharp
public class MyProfile : ProfileBase
{                                                    ◁── Anonymous
  [SettingsAllowAnonymous(true)]                          support is enabled
  public String FirstName
  {
    get
    {
      return base["FirstName"] as String;
    }
    set
    {
      base["FirstName"] = value;
    }
  }
}
```

VB:
```vb
Public Class MyProfile
  Inherits ProfileBase
  <SettingsAllowAnonymous(True)>                    ◁── Anonymous
  Public Property FirstName() As String                  support is enabled
    Get
      Return TryCast(MyBase.Item("FirstName"), [String])
    End Get
    Set
      MyBase.Item("FirstName") = value
    End Set
  End Property
End Class
```

To access its values, you just need to use this code:

C#:
```csharp
string firstName = ((MyProfile)HttpContext.Current.Profile).FirstName;
```

VB:

```
Dim firstName as string = DirectCast(HttpContext.Current.Profile,
                              MyProfile).FirstName
```

Except for the type we're using, this code is the same as what you need to use when you're using a website.

DISCUSSION

The Profile API is simple to use, but it's powerful. You can map the properties in web.config if you're using a website, or you can define a custom class (which is mandatory if you're using a web project). The power behind the Profile API makes using this approach interesting because you can easily integrate it into existing applications. A user profile takes a membership profile to the next level: it contains additional information about the user. This information isn't vital to the identification of the user, but it completes the user's navigation experience.

Although the default provider is configured to support any type of profile properties, it's of limited use in real-world scenarios. Because it uses a single column to contain all the properties, you'll run into problems if you need to perform statistics or use this information outside the web application. In such a situation, a custom provider is a better idea.

TECHNIQUE 83   A custom provider for the Profile API

We've already analyzed the implications of building a custom provider in chapter 5, when we introduced the Membership and Roles API. Because the Profile API is also implemented using the Provider Model pattern, you can easily change the implementation, without touching the rest of the code. In this scenario, we'll show you how to do that.

PROBLEM

The Profile API's default provider (called `SqlProfileProvider`), included in ASP.NET, has a table structure that isn't normalized. In fact, it uses two fields: one containing the property names and another with the corresponding values. This structure is flexible enough to be used in virtually any project without changing the database schema, but it has a major limitation: it mixes different properties together. This limitation makes it virtually impossible to query the data from outside the provider. We need to implement a provider that lets you do that.

SOLUTION

The Provider Model is useful because you can write all the code and then replace the implementation. When your site grows and you want to change the inner implementation, you'll find your life is a lot simpler. In the previous scenario, you learned how to use the API; this time, the scope is to change the storage implementation and save the information in a custom table, in which each property is mapped to a table column.

The table schema from the built-in provider and our custom table schema are shown in figure 13.5.

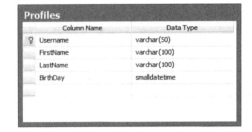

Figure 13.5   On the left is the default database schema. On the right is our custom one. Our provider is based on one column per property that's defined in the user profile. With this setup, we can query the data directly because it's normalized.

This provider, in contrast with our custom Membership and Roles providers, will use ADO.NET directly because the query will be generated dynamically. For brevity, the provider will use the SQL Server managed provider directly, often referred to as `SqlClient` (because its namespace is `System.Data.SqlCient`). If you need to target another database or write a generic implementation, you'll need to rewrite some parts of it.

The idea behind this provider is quite simple: given the properties specified by the profile, it will generate the best query to get the result from the database and then load it into the profile itself. When it's saved, the provider will check for modified properties via the `IsDirty` property exposed by the property itself and save only what's needed. To make everything ultra-secure, as you learned in chapter 10, we'll compose the query using a *parametric query*, avoiding SQL injection.

Loading a profile

To load a profile, you need to override the `GetPropertyValues` method from `ProfileProvider`, which is the base class used by the Profile API providers. This method gets the data from the database and loads it into an instance of the `SettingsPropertyValueCollection` class. This class represents a generic property container; the properties are represented by a string key and a generic object value. To ensure that the load is performed only one time per page, we'll implement the per-request pattern, which we've already described, using the `Context.Items` collection to cache the results. You can find the code in the following listing

Listing 13.4   Code for loading a user profile

C#:

```
public sealed class SqlProfileProvider : ProfileProvider
{
  public override SettingsPropertyValueCollection GetPropertyValues(
                  SettingsContext context,
                  SettingsPropertyCollection collection)
  {
    if (collection == null || collection.Count < 1 || context == null)
        return null;

    string username = GetUsername(context);
```

```
    string itemKey = string.Concat("profile-", username);

    if (HttpContext.Current.Items[itemKey] == null)          Save in context from
    {                                                            the database
      HttpContext.Current.Items[itemKey] =
                          GetProfileData(collection, username);   ◁──┘
    }

    return HttpContext.Current.Items[itemKey] as
                        SettingsPropertyValueCollection;      ◁───┐
  }                                                                │
}                                                              Get from
                                                              context
```

VB:
```
Public NotInheritable Class SqlProfileProvider
  Inherits ProfileProvider
  Public Overrides Function GetPropertyValues(
                  context As SettingsContext,
                  collection As SettingsPropertyCollection)
                          As SettingsPropertyValueCollection
    If collection Is Nothing OrElse
                  collection.Count < 1 OrElse
                  context Is Nothing Then
      Return Nothing
    End If

    Dim username As String = GetUsername(context)

    Dim itemKey As String = String.Concat("profile-",
                                          username)

    If HttpContext.Current.Items(itemKey) Is Nothing Then     Save in context
      HttpContext.Current.Items(itemKey) =                    from the  database
              GetProfileData(collection, username)   ◁──┘
    End If
                                                              Get from
    Return TryCast(HttpContext.Current.Items(itemKey),        context
              SettingsPropertyValueCollection)   ◁──┘
  End Function
End Class
```

The magic is performed by the GetProfileData method, which gets the information from the profile and dynamically composes the query. You can find the most important piece of code in the following listing.

Listing 13.5 The query that gets the user profile is composed dynamically

C#:
```
private SettingsPropertyValueCollection
              GetProfileData(SettingsPropertyCollection properties,
                              string username)
{
  SettingsPropertyValueCollection values =
                                  new SettingsPropertyValueCollection();

  StringBuilder commandText = new StringBuilder("SELECT t.Username");
  List<SettingsPropertyValue> columns = new List<SettingsPropertyValue>();
  int columnCount = 0;
```

```csharp
foreach (SettingsProperty prop in properties)          ◁──┐ Include
{                                                          │ each
  SettingsPropertyValue value = new SettingsPropertyValue(prop);  property
  values.Add(value);
  columns.Add(value);

  commandText.Append(", ");
  commandText.Append("t." + prop.Name);

  ++columnCount;
}

commandText.Append(" FROM " + _tableName + " t WHERE ");  ◁──┐ Filter by
commandText.Append("t.UserName = @Username");              │ username

SqlParameter param = new SqlParameter("@Username", username);

...                                                    ◁──┐ Query execution
                                                          │ omitted
  return values;
}
```

VB:

```vb
Private Function GetProfileData(properties As SettingsPropertyCollection,
                    username As String) As SettingsPropertyValueCollection
  Dim values As New SettingsPropertyValueCollection()

  Dim commandText As New StringBuilder("SELECT t.Username")
  Dim columns As New List(Of SettingsPropertyValue)()
  Dim columnCount As Integer = 0                     ◁──┐ Include each
                                                        │ property
  For Each prop As SettingsProperty In properties
    Dim value As New SettingsPropertyValue(prop)
    values.Add(value)
    columns.Add(value)

    commandText.Append(", ")
    commandText.Append("t." + prop.Name)

    columnCount += 1
  Next
                                                     ◁──┐ Filter by
  commandText.Append(" FROM " & _tableName & " t WHERE ")  │ username
  commandText.Append("t.UserName = @Username")

  Dim param As New SqlParameter("@Username", username)

...                                                  ◁──┐ Query execution
                                                        │ omitted
  Return values
End Function
```

The result is that the profile will be loaded from the specified table, and the generated query will fetch only the mapped properties, maximizing performance.

Saving a profile

If you understood how to load a profile, then saving it will be a piece of cake. The code is long because you have to check for null values and modified or read-only properties, but it's simple to analyze. We're basically cycling all the properties and assigning their values from the database.

The next listing contains the part where the single property is loaded, which is included in a foreach cycle. This snippet is similar to what's included in listing 13.5.

Listing 13.6   The most important part when saving a user profile

C#:

```
SqlDbType dbType = Utilities.ConvertFromCLRTypeToSqlDbType(
                        pp.Property.PropertyType);          ⟵──┐ Convert from
                                                               │ CRL to DBType
object value = null;

if (pp.Deserialized && pp.PropertyValue == null)          ⟵──┐ Check
  value = DBNull.Value;                                       │ for null
else
  value = pp.PropertyValue;

columnsQuery.Append(", ");
valuesQuery.Append(", ");
columnsQuery.Append(columnName);                             ┐ Create
string valueParam = "@Value" + count;                 ⟵──────┘ parameter
valuesQuery.Append(valueParam);

param = new SqlParameter(valueParam, dbType);             ────┐ Handle
                                                               │ DateTimes
if (param.DbType == DbType.DateTime)                      ⟵──┘
  if (DateTime.TryParse(value.ToString(), out dtParam))
    param.Value = Utilities.FormatDateTimeForDbType(dtParam);
  else
    param.Value = DBNull.Value;
else
  param.Value = value;

parameters.Add(param);

if (count > 0)
  setQuery.Append(",");                                     ┐ Create
                                                      ⟵──────┘ query
setQuery.Append(columnName);
setQuery.Append("=");
setQuery.Append(valueParam);
```

VB:

```
Dim dbType As SqlDbType =
      Utilities.ConvertFromCLRTypeToSqlDbType(
⟹ pp.Property.PropertyType)                                ⟵──┐ Convert from
                                                               │ CRL to DBType
Dim value As Object = Nothing

If pp.Deserialized AndAlso pp.PropertyValue Is Nothing Then ⟵──┐ Check
  value = DBNull.Value                                          │ for null
Else
  value = pp.PropertyValue
End If

columnsQuery.Append(", ")
valuesQuery.Append(", ")
columnsQuery.Append(columnName)                             ┐ Create
Dim valueParam As String = "@Value" & count           ⟵──────┘ parameter
valuesQuery.Append(valueParam)
```

```
param = New SqlParameter(valueParam, dbType)                          Handle
                                                                      DateTimes
If param.DbType = DbType.DateTime Then                          ◄─┘
  If DateTime.TryParse(value.ToString(), dtParam) Then
    param.Value = Utilities.FormatDateTimeForDbType(dtParam)
  Else
    param.Value = DBNull.Value
  End If
Else
  param.Value = value
End If

parameters.Add(param)

If count > 0 Then
  setQuery.Append(",")                                          Create
End If                                                    ◄─┘    query
setQuery.Append(columnName)
setQuery.Append("=")
setQuery.Append(valueParam)
```

The query will be executed, checking for the profile's existence. Depending on whether the profile exists, the query will issue an UPDATE or INSERT command. We're using a helper function (which is available in the downloadable samples) to convert from the CLR type to a SqlDbType enum value. This conversion will ensure that the database receives the correct data type and adds another layer of type safety check before the correct query executes.

Making it all work

Now that the provider is ready, we have to register it in our web.config (under configuration\system.web):

```
<profile … defaultProvider="SqlProfileProvider">
  <providers>
    <clear />
    <add name="SqlProfileProvider"
         type="ProfileAPI.CustomerProviders.SqlProfileProvider"
         tableName="Profiles"
         connectionStringName="Profiles" />
  </providers>
</profile>
```

The profile can be used from any page, just like the one we prepared with the default provider (see figure 13.3). The capability to use any page is one of the fundamental aspects of the Provider Model that lets you be more productive and re-use more code between projects.

DISCUSSION

The Profile API is the best way to implement your solution when you need to store user preferences. It's easy to use, simple to extend using the Provider Model, and can grow with your application's needs.

Even though it might seem difficult to create a custom provider, in reality it's not terribly complex, as we've shown you with this scenario. Keep in mind that, if you prefer, you can implement the same approach using a stored procedure. If you have different information stored in different tables, a stored procedure can encapsulate the logic to retrieve—and save—different properties to different tables, without working with multiple providers or implementing complex logic. The custom provider you built in this section is a first step in the right direction, though it will probably need a couple of additional features to be usable in every situation.

13.3 Summary

In this chapter, we analyzed different aspects of the most common patterns you'll use to handle state. First we presented the per-request solutions, then we moved on to per-session ones. We also took a look at common techniques: we analyzed how cookies and session state work and how to use them in different scenarios.

We looked closely at the Profile API, which is specifically designed to simplify actions related to a user profile. Creating and accessing a profile's information is easier, thanks to a common infrastructure and the Provider Model pattern. Each approach has its own pros and cons; you'll need to choose one based on what your application needs. The good news is that ASP.NET offers you a wide range of possibilities in this particular area.

Now that we've covered the most common techniques, you're ready to take a look at the most effective way to boost application performance: caching. You can easily use caching to save data for all the requests. Read on to find out how.

Caching in ASP.NET

This chapter covers

- Output caching techniques in ASP.NET Web Forms and ASP.NET MVC
- Leveraging ASP.NET Cache for storing data
- Integrating Windows Server AppFabric into your application

In chapter 13, you learned how state management in ASP.NET dramatically eases the process of building applications for a stateless context such as the World Wide Web. Now you're going to find out that state management is useful in other situations.

When your web application needs to serve a large number of concurrent requests per second, you need to scale. Scalability is the ability of your application to easily handle a growing amount of work, without needing to take drastic measures. If you need to handle more traffic in your web application, scalability means that you won't need to rewrite (or adapt) your application.

Scalability is an interesting point of debate, and lots of developers have different opinions about it. When you need to deal with scalability, you'll typically end up adding more hardware and adapting your application to work correctly. You'll find this task to be difficult to handle if you didn't design your application in the right way to begin with. By leveraging ASP.NET Cache, you can increase your application's scalability and serve multiple requests without needing to add more hardware. In ASP.NET applications, you can achieve scalability by adopting a special set of features, which we'll cover in this chapter.

Caching is something real applications can't live without: it's essential for getting around bottlenecks such as querying databases multiple times for the same data, or to keep in memory entire pages and let the server return them without any additional processing. In this chapter, we'll take a look at how you can plug ASP.NET 4.0 Cache into your code, and you'll learn how to build more scalable and responsive web sites.

14.1 Per-application state: Cache

When you need more scalability, per-application state is the way to go. By implementing this kind of state, you can boost performance because the objects are shared by all the requests to your pages.

You can handle per-application state in ASP.NET in two ways:

- *Output caching*—Caching the output (the HTML)
- *Data caching*—Caching objects

Both techniques have pros and cons. Because you're caching objects, data caching is more versatile, and you can display them in different forms using the same copy in memory. On the other hand, output caching removes the need to transform the data because the markup itself is cached; output caching is indicated whenever you need to increase performance by preventing the page from being instantiated. Figure 14.1 shows how each of these techniques work.

.NET Framework 4.0 introduces these new caching features:

- Data caching is now available in a separate assembly (System.Runtime.Caching) and can be safely used by any kind of application, not just ASP.NET ones
- ASP.NET Cache now has an object model that makes it easy to implement custom providers
- Distributed caching is now fully supported

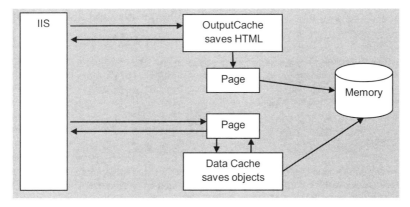

Figure 14.1 Data caching differs from output caching in terms of impact. The first caches an object, and the latter automatically saves the resulting HTML.

Because ASP.NET 4.0 is part of .NET Framework 4.0, you can benefit from these new features in your ASP.NET applications. Let's take a look at output caching to begin.

14.2   *Using OutputCache*

OutputCache is the simplest form of caching, in which the HTML produced by pages or controls can be automatically saved in memory. This kind of caching will help you save the cost of extracting the data and formatting the results.

TECHNIQUE 84   **Leveraging OutputCache to speed up your pages**

You can benefit from this technique in a lot of situations, but it isn't applicable to data that's specific to a user or that's needed in real-time. If, on the other hand, your data changes infrequently and can be cached already formatted, this technique can boost your application's performance.

PROBLEM

The scenario presented here is simple: we want to store the result of a page in memory and set it to expire after a given timeout. We'll explore how you can use all the features that ASP.NET 4.0 offers you for these situations.

SOLUTION

OutputCache works deep inside the ASP.NET runtime and is implemented as an `Http-Module` that intercepts the requests and caches them. You can see how it works in figure 14.2.

When the page is requested for the first time (or, in general, when a cached version doesn't exist), the page itself is executed normally. The `OuputCacheModule`, which is the `HttpModule` implementing this behavior, looks for the page to be cached and saves its results in the cache. Generally, the cache is in memory and works with a timeout-based expiration, but you can write a custom provider (in ASP.NET 4.0) and manage different dependencies (this feature already existed in previous versions of ASP.NET). On subsequent requests, the page class isn't instantiated at all, but the saved markup is instead sent directly.

To cache a page, you need to add the following specific directive at the top:

```
<%@OutputCache Location="server" Duration="60" VaryByParam="none" %>
```

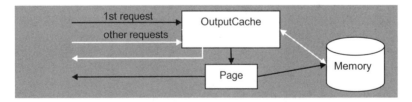

Figure 14.2   OutputCache is implemented as an `HttpModule` that intercepts the request, saves a copy of the resulting markup in memory, and, on subsequent requests, uses it instead of instantiating the page again.

This directive saves the output generated by the page for 60 seconds in the server's memory and doesn't vary, regardless of the parameter values. This configuration is the most simplified version and all the attributes are mandatory.

`VaryByParam` lets you save a different version for any of the different values specified in your parameters (via query string, form, or cookies). You can specify an asterisk (*) to support any combination of them, or you can specify a list of values separated by ; and that contains the parameters to watch. The last option is the best one because the first one can potentially be used as a security threat: any combination of the parameters will increase the memory consumed by your application, and you won't be able to control it.

OutputCache in a user control

OutputCache in a user control doesn't look much different from the page one. The directive you use is the same: you can't specify the `Location` attribute (it's implicit) and you can add an optional `Shared` attribute:

```
<%@OutputCache Shared="true" Duration="60" VaryByParam="none" %>
```

Specify the `Shared` attribute to use the same instance (in the cache) across multiple pages that reference the same control. If, on the other hand, you need different outputs for the same control to be stored in the cache depending on the page where it's declared, just set it to `false`. Other than this difference, pages and user controls work the same way. Remember that when using OutputCache in a user control, you can't reference it in your page because an instance of it effectively doesn't exist.

OutputCache dependencies

OutputCache can be linked to different types of dependencies that support different kinds of expiration notifications. These dependencies are grouped in table 14.1, which also contains a brief description of their features.

Table 14.1 OutputCache dependencies

Property	Description
`VaryByContentEncoding="encodings"`	You can specify a list of encodings, and a version per encoding will be created.
`VaryByControl="controlID"`	The OutputCache will be linked to a control and will expire when the control changes.
`VaryByCustom="browser|customstring"`	You can specify a custom implementation. See MSDN for more information at http://www.mng.bz/94Co.
`VaryByHeader="headers"`	Similar to `VaryByParam`, but only the request headers are used.
`VaryByParam="parameters"`	You can specify a list of parameters from query string, form, and cookie.
`SqlDependency`	You'll specify a dependency to SQL Server. When the data changes, the notification is triggered, and the OuputCache data is invalidated.

Note that the VaryByParam parameter is the only mandatory property; all the others are optional.

OutputCache via code

You can also configure OutputCache via code, using the Cache property of the HttpResponse class. You can use this option if the settings are related to conditions that must be evaluated at runtime.

To use this syntax, you have to write something like this:

C#:

```
Response.Cache.SetCacheability(HttpCacheability.Server);
Response.Cache.VaryByParams.IgnoreParams = true;
Response.Cache.SetExpires(DateTime.Now.AddMinutes(1))
```

VB:

```
Response.Cache.SetCacheability(HttpCacheability.Server)
Response.Cache.VaryByParams.IgnoreParams = True
Response.Cache.SetExpires(DateTime.Now.AddMinutes(1))
```

Using this approach, you can also specify dependencies from another object in the cache or from a file. Specifying a dependency from a file is useful to invalidate the markup when the file is used as the data source and has changed.

OutputCache profiles in web.config

When you have a group of pages—or controls—and you need to specify the same configuration, merely getting them in sync by hand isn't a feasible option: you probably couldn't remember how many pages need to be kept in sync, and it's not a task that can be shared by team members. For these reasons, ASP.NET supports cache profiles stored in web.config, and you can simply refer to them using the CacheProfile attribute on the aforementioned @OutputCache directive. You must include the following configuration under configuration\system.web\caching:

```
<outputCacheSettings>
  <outputCacheProfiles>
    <clear />
    <add name=""
         enabled="true"
         duration="-1"
         location=""
         sqlDependency=""
         varyByCustom=""
         varyByControl=""
         varyByHeader=""
         varyByParam=""
         noStore="false" />
  </outputCacheProfiles>
</outputCacheSettings>
```

The attributes used in this declaration are similar to the properties in table 14.1 (see table 13.1 for an explanation of the attributes). If you omit the name, as we did, you'll overwrite the default settings. If you specify a name instead, you can refer to this profile configuration in this way:

```
<%@ OutputCache CacheProfile="ProfileName" %>
```

By using a profile, you can centrally control the behavior for a group of resources and simplify its management.

DISCUSSION

OutputCache is useful, but it has a limitation: it can't be personalized easily after the markup has been generated. ASP.NET 2.0 introduced a control called `Substitution` that lets you insert some placeholders that can inject dynamic values at runtime. `Substitution` can be used to represents strings, like the username or a link that's available only to subscribers.

We've completed our look at OutputCache's features as far as it concerns Web Forms. Now it's time to take a look at how these same concepts apply to ASP.NET MVC.

14.3 *OutputCache in ASP.NET MVC*

ASP.NET MVC also has built-in support for OutputCache, which means you can effectively leverage it to handle similar requests without overcharging the server and achieve maximum scalability for your applications.

Unlike what you learned in the previous section about Web Forms, to activate this feature in ASP.NET MVC, you must decorate an action with the `OutputCacheAttribute`, as in the following code:

C#:
```
[OutputCache(Duration=10, VaryByParam="none")]
public ActionResult Index()
{
  // .. more code here ..
}
```

VB:
```
<OutputCache(Duration:=10, VaryByParam:="none")>
Public Function Index() As ActionResult
  ' .. more code here ..
End Function
```

If you need to, you can also decorate the whole controller so that every action is cached:

C#:
```
[OutputCache(Duration=10, VaryByParam="none")]
public class HomeController : Controller
{
  // ... more code here ...
}
```

VB:
```
<OutputCache(Duration:=10, VaryByParam:="none")>
Public Class HomeController
  Inherits Controller

  ' ... more code here ...
End Class
```

ASP.NET MVC's OutputCache also supports dependencies in a manner similar to the `@OutputCache` directive. `OutputCacheAttribute` provides a property for each one of the items in table 14.1 except `VaryByControl`.

> ### OutputCache in ASP.NET MVC smells like Web Forms
>
> OutputCache in ASP.NET MVC is tightly coupled to the specific view engine we're us-
> ing, which in our case derives from Web Forms. For that reason, `OutputCacheAt-`
> `tribute` internally is no more than a simple wrapper around the same functionality
> in Web Forms and can't be used with different view engines; the Spark view engine,
> for example, uses a different approach to caching, and Razor, which will be the new
> view engine adopted in ASP.NET MVC 3, still lacks official support for OutputCache.

Activating this feature seems to be trivial, but when we use it in a real application, the
default implementation suddenly shows two big limitations:

- If you decide that a page must be removed from the cache, you find that this
  feature isn't immediately available
- Sometimes you want to cache just some portions of a page, not necessarily the
  whole thing

We're going to cover these two problems in the following pages and provide solutions
for both of them.

TECHNIQUE 85   Deterministically removing items from OutputCache

The default implementation of OutputCache in ASP.NET MVC supports only a timeout-based expiration logic. For this reason, you can decide to keep a page in the cache
for a specific time span, for example, five minutes. The longer this timeout is, the better the performance gain will be, but at the same time your website will be less responsive to show up-do-date information. You can obviously tune the timeout to keep these
two aspects balanced, but you can't get control when a newer version of the page will
finally replace the cached one.

Unfortunately, in many situations, this result doesn't provide enough control, and
such website behavior can leave your visitors with a bad feeling. To better explain this
concept, let's recall for a moment CoolMVCBlog, the sample application we built in
chapters 8 and 9. Among all its great features, this application allows users to comment a blog post, thanks to the form in figure 14.3.

Now let's imagine that a user arrives at our web site and posts a comment. If we
blindly use OutputCache on that page, he won't see his new comment until the cache
timeout expires; he'll most likely try to resubmit it a couple of times, and then he'll
probably think our blog engine doesn't work.

Luckily for us, we can actually modify the default behavior of OutputCache in
ASP.NET MVC and provide it with better control over the expiration logic—we can tell
it to invalidate our cached pages whenever we need it to. Let's get started.

PROBLEM

We want to use ASP.NET MVC's OutputCache to improve performance of CoolMVCBlog's
Show Post page. At the same time, we want to be able to remove that page from the cache
when a user inserts a new comment so that the new page shows immediately.

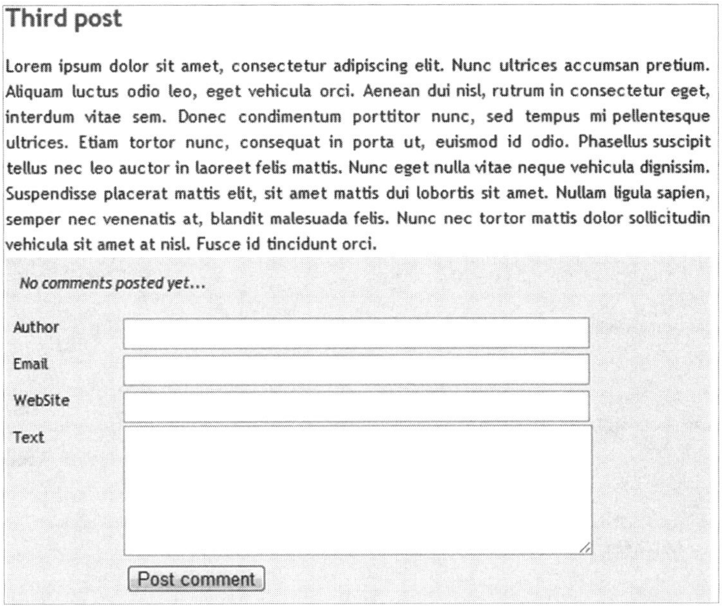

Third post
Lorem ipsum dolor sit amet, consectetur adipiscing elit. Nunc ultrices accumsan pretium. Aliquam luctus odio leo, eget vehicula orci. Aenean dui nisl, rutrum in consectetur eget, interdum vitae sem. Donec condimentum porttitor nunc, sed tempus mi pellentesque ultrices. Etiam tortor nunc, consequat in porta ut, euismod id odio. Phasellus suscipit tellus nec leo auctor in laoreet felis mattis. Nunc eget nulla vitae neque vehicula dignissim. Suspendisse placerat mattis elit, sit amet mattis dui lobortis sit amet. Nullam ligula sapien, semper nec venenatis at, blandit malesuada felis. Nunc nec tortor mattis dolor sollicitudin vehicula sit amet at nisl. Fusce id tincidunt orci.
No comments posted yet...
Author
Email
WebSite
Text
Post comment

Figure 14.3 **The user can fill in this form, which we built in chapter 8, to insert new comments. This page might behave in an ugly way if we blindly use ASP.NET MVC's OutputCache.**

SOLUTION

When we decorate an action with the `OutputCacheAttribute`, OutputCache stores its result into ASP.NET Cache and automatically recovers it when it must serve a subsequent analogous request. If we knew which cache key the page belongs to, we could easily remove it. Unfortunately, this isn't easily possible, and even if it were, we aren't supposed to know it because it resides in the internal logic of the caching infrastructure and might change without notice in future releases.

What we can do, though, is leverage the cache dependencies mechanism to achieve a similar result. This feature is similar to the change monitors we're going to talk about in section 14.4. Leveraging cache dependencies consists of tying one cache entry to another to automatically remove the first one when the latter is invalidated. Figure 14.4 schematizes the whole process.

The idea is to build a custom version of `OutputCacheAttribute`, similar to the one in listing 14.1. This version of `OutputCacheAttribute` will take care of inserting a second element in the cache, which will be the entry that we'll remove; this element will be our dependency item for the cached page, and we'll use it to deterministically invalidate the latter.

Cache
Item 1
Cache dependency
Item 2
Cache.Remove("Item 1")
Cache

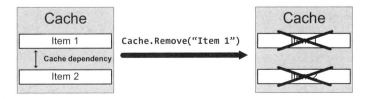

Figure 14.4 **How cache dependency works: if Item 2 has a dependency on Item 1, then when we remove the Item 1, Item 2 also becomes invalid.**

Listing 14.1   Code for DependencyOutputCacheAttribute

C#:

```csharp
public class DependencyOutputCacheAttribute :          ❶ Extend base
    OutputCacheAttribute                                  OutputCacheAttribute
{
  public string ParameterName { get; set; }
  public string BasePrefix { get; set; }

  public override void OnResultExecuting(              ❷ Override
    ResultExecutingContext filterContext)                 OnResultExecuting
  {
    base.OnResultExecuting(filterContext);

    string key =
      string.IsNullOrEmpty(BasePrefix) ?
      filterContext.RouteData.Values["action"].ToString() +       Calculate
      "_" +                                                       removal
      filterContext.RouteData.Values["controller"].ToString()     item's key ❸
      : BasePrefix;

    if (!string.IsNullOrEmpty(ParameterName))
      key += "_" + filterContext.RouteData.Values[ParameterName];

    filterContext.HttpContext.Cache.Insert(
      key,
      key,
      null,                                              ❹ Insert removal
      Cache.NoAbsoluteExpiration,                           item in cache
      Cache.NoSlidingExpiration);

    filterContext.HttpContext                           ❺ Set up cache
      .Response.AddCacheItemDependency(key);               dependency
  }
}
```

VB:

```vbnet
Public Class DependencyOutputCacheAttribute            ❶ Extend base
  Inherits OutputCacheAttribute                           OutputCacheAttribute

  Public Property ParameterName As String
  Public Property BasePrefix As String

  Public Overrides Sub OnResultExecuting(              ❷ Override
    ByVal filterContext As ResultExecutingContext)        OnResultExecuting

    MyBase.OnResultExecuting(filterContext)

    Dim key As String
    If String.IsNullOrEmpty(BasePrefix) Then
      key = filterContext.RouteData.Values("action").ToString + "_" +
              filterContext.RouteData.Values("controller").ToString
    Else
      key = BasePrefix                                   Calculate removal
    End If                                               item's key ❸

    If Not String.IsNullOrEmpty(ParameterName) Then
      key += "_" +
```

```
                    filterContext.RouteData.Values(ParameterName).ToString
     End If

     filterContext.HttpContext.Cache.Insert(
        key, key, Nothing,                                    ❹ Insert removal
        Cache.NoAbsoluteExpiration,                              item in cache
        Cache.NoSlidingExpiration)

     filterContext.HttpContext.                                ❺ Set up cache
        Response.AddCacheItemDependency(key)                      dependency
  End Sub

End Class
```

Our custom `DependencyOutputCacheAttribute` inherits from the standard `Output-CacheAttribute` ❶ and modifies its `OnResultExecuting` method ❷, by which the base class inserts the current page into the cache. Our task is to insert a second element into the cache ❹, whose key is automatically determined and links the controller and the action names. We'll also insert another optional parameter if it's contained within the request ❸. The last step is to set up a dependency between the OutputCache entry and this new one, which will be our removal item ❺. The entire logic is shown in figure 14.5.

Figure 14.5 Thanks to the removal item and the cache dependency that we set up, we're finally able to evict the cached page when we need to.

Now we can take care of the removal logic. Once again, the action filter's infrastructure proves to be an extremely smart way to declaratively inject our custom logic where we want. The following listing shows `RemoveCachedAttribute`'s code.

Listing 14.2 Implementation of RemoveCachedAttribute

C#:
```
public class RemoveCachedAttribute : ActionFilterAttribute
{
  public string ParameterName { get; set; }
  public string BasePrefix { get; set; }

  public override void OnResultExecuting(
     ResultExecutingContext filterContext)
  {                                                              ❶ Calculate
    base.OnResultExecuting(filterContext);                          removal
                                                                    item's key
    string key = string.IsNullOrEmpty(BasePrefix) ?
       filterContext.RouteData.Values["action"].ToString() + "_" +
       filterContext.RouteData.Values["controller"].ToString() : BasePrefix;

    if (!string.IsNullOrEmpty(ParameterName))
       key += filterContext.RouteData.Values[ParameterName];
```

```
        filterContext.HttpContext.Cache.Remove(key);
    }
}
```
①➋ Invalidate
removal item

VB:
```
Public Class RemoveCachedAttribute
    Inherits ActionFilterAttribute

  Public Property ParameterName As String
  Public Property BasePrefix As String

  Public Overrides Sub OnResultExecuting(
      ByVal filterContext As ResultExecutingContext)
    MyBase.OnResultExecuting(filterContext)

    Dim key As String
    If String.IsNullOrEmpty(BasePrefix) Then
      key = filterContext.RouteData.Values("action").ToString + "_" +
              filterContext.RouteData.Values("controller").ToString
    Else
      key = BasePrefix
    End If

    If Not String.IsNullOrEmpty(ParameterName) Then
      key += "_" +
              filterContext.RouteData.Values(ParameterName).ToString
    End If

    filterContext.HttpContext.Cache.Remove(key)
  End Sub
End Class
```
❶ Calculate
removal
item's key

❷ Invalidate
removal item

This new filter represents the counterpart of DependencyOutputCacheAttribute and uses the same logic to redetermine the same key ❶ and use it to evict the removal item from the cache ❷. Based on how ASP.NET Cache dependency works, the result is the timely invalidation of the page from the OutputCache.

At last, we managed to build everything we need to achieve our ultimate goal: to cache the Show Post page and remove it whenever a new comment is inserted. We can do it by simply decorating the corresponding two actions, as shown in the following listing.

Listing 14.3   Deterministically removing the page from the cache

C#:
```
[DependencyOutputCache(Duration = 30,
    Location=OutputCacheLocation.Server,
    VaryByParam="None",
    ParameterName="id")]
public ActionResult Post(int id)
{
  // post load logic here
}

[HttpPost]
[RemoveCached(ParameterName = "id")]
```
❶ OutputCache
with dependency

❷ Page removed
from cache

```
public ActionResult Post(int id, Comment newComment)
{
  // comment save logic
}
```

VB:

```
<DependencyOutputCache(Duration := 30,
    Location:=OutputCacheLocation.Server,
    VaryByParam:="None",
    ParameterName:="id")>
Public Function Post(ByVal id as Integer) as ActionResult
  ' post load logic here
End Function

<HttpPost>
<RemoveCached(ParameterName := "id")>
Public Function Post(ByVal id as Integer,
    ByVal newComment as Comment) as ActionResult
  ' comment save logic
End Function
```

❶ **OutputCache with dependency**

❷ **Page removed from cache**

This code contains the two actions involved in the process of showing a post and inserting a new comment. The first one caches the page by using `DependencyOutput-CacheAttribute` ❶, discriminating the removal item's key with the `id` parameter. We need to use the ID because we want to be able to have as many removal items as we have cached posts. The second action, using the same parameter, invalidates the page by using `RemoveCacheAttribute` ❷.

What if the two actions had different names?

`DependencyOutputCacheAttribute` and `RemoveCachedAttribute` build the removal-item key by using the controller and the action names. This state of affairs works fine until the two actions involved in the process have the same name, as in listing 14.3. In the more typical case in which this isn't necessarily true, a `Base-Prefix` property is provided for both attributes to set up a common key.

DISCUSSION

OutputCache is one of the best ways to limit the computational load on the server, although the standard implementation in ASP.NET MVC isn't exempt from limitations; the inability to deterministically remove pages from the cache forces us to base our invalidation logic on timeout only. Unfortunately, you won't always be able to accept this compromise. When your website offers a certain degree of interactivity, users always expect to see the results of their inputs on the page immediately.

Thanks to ASP.NET MVC's high level of expandability, you can have the best of both worlds with a simple customization. In this section, we built an extended version of OutputCache support that allowed us to signal to the framework when an action must cause a page to disappear from the cache. We did this by using action filters or, in other words, by writing declarative code in ASP.NET MVC fashion. The advantage of this solution is not only stylistic—it's much less invasive and can easily be plugged into an existing project.

TECHNIQUE 86   OutputCache and partial views

When you're building an application, it's quite uncommon to cache the whole page; usually only portions of it are customizable on a per-user basis. Take a look at figure 14.6, which shows CoolMVCBlog's homepage.

The page shown in figure 14.6 has a welcome message that's shown only when it's served to an authenticated user. The message itself changes from user to user, and it's customized with their name. These characteristics make it unfeasible to cache this whole page. On the other hand, the list of posts is a good candidate for being cached because it remains unchanged each time the page is returned, unless someone writes a new post.

> **COULDN'T WE USE VARYBYCUSTOM FOR THIS?** To get around this issue and keep showing to each user the correct welcome message, we could use a `VaryByCustom` parameter on the `OutputCache` attribute to differentiate the cache entries based on the session ID. Although everything would work as expected, this isn't a solution to the problem of scalability because it won't be shared among users; we'll end up having a cached page for each user, raising the memory pressure without almost any performance gain. Doing things this way would be like saving pages in session storage.

We need something that allows us to cache only portions of a page. Even though this solution isn't immediately available in ASP.NET MVC, you can still leverage it on your websites by referencing the MvcContrib external library. Let's see how.

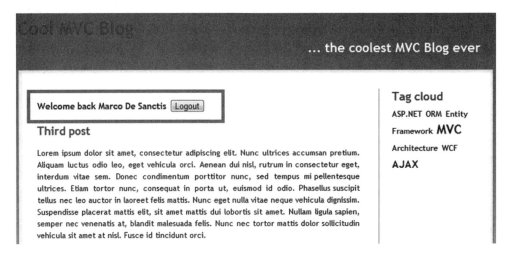

Figure 14.6   CoolMVCBlog provides a welcome message for the authenticated user. If we cached this whole page, the same message would be shown to everyone who visits our website.

PROBLEM

We do like OutputCache, but we want to apply it to only some portions of the page instead of the whole page.

SOLUTION

As far as we know, when a request to an ASP.NET MVC application returns a web page, it can be the result of one view and some partial views, but on the controller side the process is orchestrated by a single action. This process flow isn't always true; we can effectively render a portion of a page using different actions via the `RenderAction` HTML helper. When you use actions in this way they're called child actions and are another way to build reusable components, in addition to the ones you saw in chapter 9. Let's imagine we have an action that returns the server time, like the one in the following listing.

Listing 14.4   Action and view to show the server time

C#:
```
public ActionResult CurrentServerTime()
{
  ViewData["time"] = DateTime.Now.ToLongTimeString();

  return this.View();
}

<%@ Control Language="C#"
  Inherits="System.Web.Mvc.ViewUserControl" %>
Hi from CurrentServerTime: <%: ViewData["time"] %>
```

VB:
```
Public Function CurrentServerTime() As ActionResult
  ViewData("time") = DateTime.Now.ToLongTimeString

  return this.View
End Function

<%@ Control Language="VB"
  Inherits="System.Web.Mvc.ViewUserControl" %>
Hi from CurrentServerTime: <%: ViewData("time") %>
```

We can insert the output it produces within another view, referencing it with the `RenderAction` HTML helper:

```
<% Html.RenderAction("CurrentServerTime"); %>
```

If we could leverage OutputCache for just this child action, we could effectively achieve our goal of caching portions of pages. Unfortunately, the standard `OutputCacheAttribute` doesn't work with child actions. So what happens if we decorate `CurrentServerTime` with the attribute, as in the following code?

C#:
```
[OutputCache(Duration=30, VaryByParam="none")]
public ActionResult CurrentServerTime()
{
  // ...
}
```

VB:
```
<OutputCache(Duration:=30, VaryByParam:="none")>
Public Function CurrentServerTime() As ActionResult
    ' ...
End Function
```

What happens is you don't get any results: the caching feature isn't triggered and the action gets executed at every request. You can easily verify this by adding this child action to a parent non-cached one, which produces the output in figure 14.7. Then you can experiment to determine that the two times are perfectly in sync.

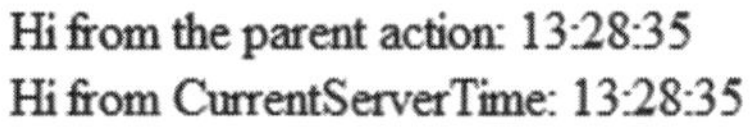

To activate OutputCache for child actions, you need an additional feature that's available in ASP.NET MVC only as a separate download. It's part of the MvcContrib project and you can download it at http://mvccontrib.codeplex.com/.

Hi from the parent action: 13:28:35
Hi from CurrentServerTime: 13:28:35

Figure 14.7 Although `CurrentServerTime` is OutputCache-enabled, this feature doesn't affect the child action. As a result, both the non-cached parent and the cached child show the same time.

MvcContrib what?

MvcContrib is an open source project that involves some of the best ASP.NET gurus on the planet. MvcContrib aims to extend ASP.NET MVC by providing features that aren't part of the original release. Its code is released under the Apache 2.0 license, so you can use it for both proprietary and open source projects. ASP.NET MVC 3 will hopefully feature built-in support for partial caching.

After you've downloaded MvcContrib's bin file and referenced it in your project, activating partial caching is a breeze. All you have to do is decorate the child action with `ChildActionCacheAttribute`:

C#:
```
[ChildActionCache(Duration=30)]
public ActionResult CurrentServerTime()
{
    // ...
}
```

VB:
```
<ChildActionCache(Duration:=30)>
Public Function CurrentServerTime() As ActionResult
    ' ...
End Function
```

With this attribute in place on the child action, if you rerun and refresh the previous page, you'll get the result shown in figure 14.8—the caching is actually working!

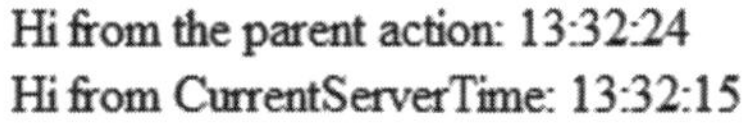

Hi from the parent action: 13:32:24
Hi from CurrentServerTime: 13:32:15

Figure 14.8 Parent and child action times are not in sync anymore because the child `CurrentServerTime` action has been successfully cached and refreshes only every 30 seconds.

Notice that the current implementation is far simpler than the "official" Output-Cache; all it provides is a `Duration`-based expiration logic. A `Key` property is also provided; you can specify the cache key you want to use so that you can manually remove the cached entry when you need to.

DISCUSSION

In an application, you won't usually keep the whole page in memory. Think about per-user customized content, such as welcome messages and login forms, or consider what happens when you provide dynamic advertising, banners, or data that must be up-to-date at each response. In these situations, the ability to cache only some portions of a web page, without affecting others, is dramatically useful. Even though ASP.NET MVC doesn't provide a built-in mechanism to accomplish such a result, you don't have to build your own implementation; instead, consider using the one provided with the MVCContrib open source project, which makes achieving your goals a breeze.

Until now, we've used ASP.NET Cache to keep some HTML output in memory so that we can reuse it when similar and subsequent requests occur. Because ASP.NET Cache is primarily general-purpose storage, you can leverage it to keep objects of any type. Our next step is to analyze what ASP.NET 4.0 can offer in terms of data caching and how this feature can meet your needs for scaling.

14.4   *Data caching techniques*

OutputCache isn't flexible enough when you have different representations of the same data that differ only in terms of the markup generated. If you use OutputCache, you're saving the cost associated with generating the markup (which is minimal, after all), but you'll continue to make different queries to the same data just to save its different representation in memory. OutputCache has other limitations, so in distributed applications you should opt for data caching (often simply referred to as caching). By saving an object in memory, you can use it whenever you like, without limits, and transform it into different shapes.

TECHNIQUE 87   **Implementing data caching in ASP.NET**

Because ASP.NET 4.0 is based on .NET Framework 4.0, you get a set of new caching features that are useful and interesting. In this scenario, we'll explore what you can do with these features.

PROBLEM

If the amount of work that the pages are sending to the database is growing, the problem is that you need to be parsimonious. Remember, external calls (to a database, or, in distributed environments, to services) have a high cost. In most cases, the requests made by different pages are identical and so is the response. You can dramatically improve the performance and scalability of your application with some caching.

SOLUTION

We're comfortable with the axiom that our page will be faster if we don't invoke a query—or perform a call to a service—each time the page is requested. Caching tries to apply this axiom, using an API that we can program against.

As previously outlined, .NET Framework 4.0 has a new set of APIs that are built from scratch and can be used independently from ASP.NET. If you have old applications that you're migrating from previous versions, don't worry: the old calls will automatically be redirected to the new implementation, so you won't need to do it manually. Technically speaking, the new caching features are implemented in classes located under System.Runtime.Caching and custom providers are supported (we'll talk about all this in more detail later in this chapter).

The base abstract class is called ObjectCache and represents a generic cache implementation that's not specifically limited to in-memory. The default (and only) provider shipped with .NET Framework 4.0 is called MemoryCache and works in memory, but, thanks to the base abstract class, you can directly work against ObjectCache in your business layer. The base abstract class will help you be prepared to change the implementation based on your future needs, without rewriting the code.

ObjectCache has an interface that supports cache region (useful when you're dealing with out-of-process caching services) and change monitors (the equivalent of cache dependencies from previous versions), and has a richer API—it's more mature and more useful in modern applications.

MemoryCache doesn't support regions, but has new methods to query the cache store, which are used in the following listing.

Listing 14.5   MemoryCache can be used to save and retrieve data from cache

C#:

```
string key = "lastUpdate";

if (!MemoryCache.Default.Contains(key, null))
  MemoryCache.Default[key] = DateTime.Now;

DateTime value = (DateTime)MemoryCache.Default[key];

DateTime value2 = (DateTime)MemoryCache.Default.AddOrGetExisting(key,
                  DateTime.Now, ObjectCache.InfiniteAbsoluteExpiration,
                  null);
```

VB:

```
Dim key as String = "lastUpdate"

If Not MemoryCache.Default.Contains(key, Nothing) is Nothing Then
  MemoryCache.Default(key) = DateTime.Now
End If

Dim value as DateTime = (DateTime)MemoryCache.Default(key)

Dim value2 as DateTime =
        (DateTime)MemoryCache.Default.AddOrGetExisting(key,
                  DateTime.Now, ObjectCache.InfiniteAbsoluteExpiration,
                  null)
```

ObjectCache provides a full API that lets you add, replace, remove, and enumerate objects from the cache store. The previous code is the same even if you use another provider. You can simply refer to ObjectCache to represent the correct provider's instance to refer to it.

CACHE: ADD VERSUS INSERT   Although adding and inserting elements into the cash might seem to be similar tasks, they're actually different. If you add an object to the cache and another object already exists for the given key, an exception is thrown. If you just want to replace an object (if it's present), you need to use the insert methods.

Change monitors are an important aspect of .NET Framework 4.0's cache implementation; they're used to provide an expiration policy that isn't only based on timeout, but can also be linked to particular events, like a file modification or another cache object's expiration. Let's take a closer look at change monitors.

Using change monitors

ASP.NET 4.0 supports the following change monitors, which are all based on the `Chan-geMonitor` class in `System.Runtime.Caching`:

- `CacheEntryChangeMonitor`—Monitors another cache entry
- `FileChangeMonitor`—Links to a list of files
- `SqlChangeMonitor`—Uses SQL Server's cache dependency

The change monitor classes implement the corresponding features that were previously provided by cache dependencies and are similar to them.

Figure 14.9 is a basic schema of how a change monitor works.

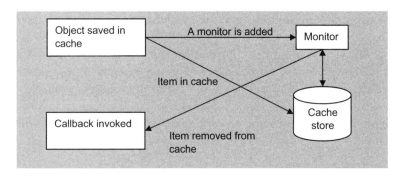

Figure 14.9   Change monitors are used to monitor an external resource. When their monitored resources change, a callback to the application is invoked and the related cache entry is removed.

With change monitors, you have more granular control over the expiration policy, and they're simpler to combine together than cache dependencies are. The following listing contains an example of how the new API works.

Listing 14.6   Explicitly specifying a CacheItemPolicy with ChangeMonitor

C#:
```
CacheItemPolicy policy = new CacheItemPolicy {
  AbsoluteExpiration = DateTime.Now.AddHours(1),
  SlidingExpiration = ObjectCache.NoSlidingExpiration,
  Priority = CacheItemPriority.Default,
  ChangeMonitors = {
```

```
      new HostFileChangeMonitor(new List<String> {
        "c:\\pathto\\myfile.ext"
      })
    }
  }
};
MemoryCache.Default.Add("cacheKey", DateTime.Now, policy, null);
```

VB:

```
Dim policy As New CacheItemPolicy With {
    .AbsoluteExpiration = DateTime.Now.AddHours(1),
    .SlidingExpiration = ObjectCache.NoSlidingExpiration,
    .Priority = CacheItemPriority.Default }

policy.ChangeMonitors.Add(New HostFileChangeMonitor({"c:\path"}))

MemoryCache.Default.Add("cacheKey", DateTime.Now, policy, Nothing)
```

In this example, a new `HostFileChangeMonitor` is added to the collection of change monitors in the current `CacheItemPolicy`, which monitors the specified files and, if any of them is modified, triggers the invalidation. Using callbacks, you can associate your own logic with removal and updating using the `RemovedCallback` and `Update-Callback` properties.

DISCUSSION

Caching features in .NET Framework 4.0 are now mature, and you can use them not only for your web applications, but also for non-web ones. Even though caching was possible with previous versions, now that the classes reside in a separate assembly, you don't need to reference System.Web, which simplifies the deployment.

Cache in ASP.NET 4.0 might benefit from these new features, which will add more granular control over an item's expiration policy and support custom providers, like the one you use when you have to share the cache items across multiple, different servers. Before moving on to the topics related to building custom cache providers, listen up while we tell you about some tips and tricks that are useful when you're working with caching.

14.4.1 *Cache tips and tricks*

This section consists of a list of tips and tricks that we've learned from our own experience of working with caching in everyday applications. Use this information as a guide to enhance your cache strategy and get some great advice from us!

DO NOT DIRECTLY USE CACHE

It's always a good choice to wrap your cache in your business logic so that you don't directly reference the cache in your pages. Wrapping your cache in this way will help you to granularly control its behavior and keep everything organized. Caching is a responsibility that is demanded of the business logic, which can centrally apply the requested behavior.

USE LOCKS TO AVOID RACE CONDITIONS

Typically, Cache is accessed in a multithreading environment, which means that you're subject to deadlocks and race conditions. When this happens, it's possible that a call to an instruction is performed at the same time from different threads, and then an unwanted situation occurs.

Depending on your code, you might execute the code multiple times or not at all. To keep that from happening, you need to write code that will use locking and avoid concurrency. Of course, you only need to do this when items are being added to the cache, because reading is thread-safe by design. In reality, `MemoryCache` is thread-safe, but because race conditions can occur while reading, a lock is required to ensure data integrity. The following listing contains the implementation of the solution.

Listing 14.7   A thread-safe cache pattern

C#:
```csharp
private static object lockObject = new object();

public List<Customer> GetCustomers()
{
  string cacheKey = "customers";
  List<Customer> customers = ObjectCache[cacheKey] as List<Customer>;

  if(customers == null)
  {
    lock (lockObject)
    {
      customers = ObjectCache[cacheKey] as List<Customer>;
      if (customers == null)
      {
   ...
        ObjectCache[cacheKey] = customers;
      }
    }
  }
  return customers;
}
```

VB:
```vb
Private Shared lockObject As New Object()

Public Function GetCustomers() As List(Of Customer)
  Dim cacheKey As String = "customers"
  Dim customers As List(Of Customer) =
               TryCast(ObjectCache(cacheKey), List(Of Customer))

  If customers Is Nothing Then
    SyncLock lockObject
      customer = TryCast(ObjectCache(cacheKey), List(Of Customer))
      If customers Is Nothing Then
        ...
        ObjectCache(cacheKey) = customers
      End If
    End SyncLock
  End If
  Return customers
End Function
```

Locking the items will let you control the phase and avoid race conditions. As for multithreading techniques, we're going to explain them in more detail in chapter 16.

DO NOT USE HIGH TIMEOUTS

High timeouts aren't always a good option. If you need to persist your objects for a long time, it might be the right choice. On the other hand, if you already know that the objects aren't going to be used very often, are going to change frequently, or aren't crucial to your application, a policy with a lower timeout is a better choice. Always remember that you're consuming your server's memory, so it's not ideal to cache objects for a long time; they probably won't be used effectively for a long period.

DO NOT USE REMOVEDCALLBACKS TO INSERT ITEMS IN THE CACHE

If you need to ensure that a copy exists in the cache every time a particular object is requested, you don't need to use `RemovedCallbacks` to implement this behavior. `RemovedCallbacks` are, in fact, useful for associating custom logic with removal (to remove other objects, based on some conditions). If you simply insert an item into the cache again just after it's removed (after a memory pressure from the server occurred), *you decrease your scalability*. The best pattern to use to ensure that a fresh item is inserted in the cache every time it's accessed (if it's not already present) is shown in listing 14.7.

DO NOT ALTER COLLECTIONS IN MEMORY

This point is related to the first one about not using caching directly. When you're dealing with a cached object, you're dealing with multithreading, and race conditions might occur. To avoid this problem, *avoid altering collections in memory*; if you need to, use a lock, like we showed you in listing 14.7. Accessing an item by key is quicker than retrieving a collection from memory and finding the item inside it.

PREPARE YOUR OBJECTS TO BE SERIALIZABLE

This tip is important for dealing with out-of-process providers, when an item saved in cache must be serializable. A serializable item can not only be copied in memory, but can also be transmitted across the wire. If you're planning to switch sometime to an out-of-process provider, you'll want to remember this advice. Because you can choose the caching provider at the runtime stage in ASP.NET 4.0, serializable items let you transparently move from an in-process strategy, such as the standard ASP.NET Cache, to an enterprise cache server, like AppFabric, by building your own provider.

We just provided you with a wealth of tips that you can use to make your applications the best they can be. Now let's talk about custom cache providers and what they can do for you.

14.5 *Building custom cache providers*

If you're lucky enough to work on big projects, you'll probably have needs that are different from those of the average developer. Big projects don't come around often, but they need non-trivial techniques.

In previous versions of ASP.NET, support for cache providers was nonexistent, so you had to write the implementation and basic infrastructure code if you needed to support different strategies and switch them without rewriting the code. For these situations, you couldn't even use OutputCache. It's so tied to the ASP.NET infrastructure that the only way to implement a custom approach is to be part of the ASP.NET team itself.

Version 4.0 introduces a new set of APIs specifically targeted to developing a custom provider, so your work is simplified. Before we get into it, we need to analyze the reasons behind writing custom providers and how you can benefit from existing solutions on the market.

14.5.1 Do I need a provider?

When you have a high number of concurrent requests, caching might help you avoid calls to external resources, like a database or a service. In these scenarios, you'll typically be using more than one server in a cluster configuration. Clusters are powerful because you can reply to a huge amount of requests in a short amount of time, depending on how many nodes you add to it. Clusters let you scale quickly by adding more hardware.

In a distributed architecture like this one, the problem with ASP.NET memory cache is that it's limited to a single server and can't be synchronized across them. You can write code that does this for you (by using a set of services that will work under the hood), but doing it that way will add a lot of complexity in terms of code to be written, and it will have an impact on deployment, too.

> **CACHE LIFETIME IN OUT-OF-PROCESS ENGINES**   When you use an out-of-process engine for caching, the items are saved outside the ASP.NET process and serialized (and deserialized) on request. This means that the class must be marked as `Serializable`. The items aren't tied to a specific AppDomain, so when one of the web applications recycles, the items aren't removed from the cache. To clear the cache, you have to follow the engine rules.

To handle this situation, you need to change your implementation from an in-memory one to an out-of-process one. The best option is to use a *distributed caching engine*, which can automatically synchronize cache items across several servers, without requiring you to do any additional work. It's a good idea to follow this route when you're working with clusters, but you can also use it as a way to share the same objects across different AppDomains. The typical scenario is an application that has more than one web site (www., forum., and so on). Generally, each site will have its own copy of cached objects, which will consume more memory and introduce problems with consistency of data across the different AppDomains. Out-of-process caching will help in this situation, too.

The next topic we'll cover is how to simply achieve out-of-process caching by taking advantage of the features offered by Microsoft Windows Server AppFabric, a new application framework recently introduced by Microsoft.

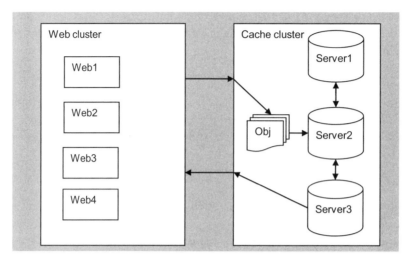

Figure 14.10   When an item is added to the cache, AppFabric caching automatically balances it across the cluster's nodes. When retrieved, the object can be sent from any server in the cluster.

14.5.2 *Windows Server AppFabric caching*

Plenty of cache engines work out-of-process, from MemCached to NCache to Scale-Out. A new player that was released just a month after .NET Framework 4.0 is Microsoft Windows Server AppFabric caching, previously known by the code name Velocity .

AppFabric caching is a fully distributed cache engine that supports cache regions, balancing items across the nodes, and so on. Read more about AppFabric caching on http://www.mng.bz/sxza. You can install it on Windows Vista, Windows 7, Windows Server 2008, and Windows Server 2008 R2. Best of all, it's free of charge. You can see how it works in figure 14.10.

We're going to use AppFabric caching in this section because it's gaining a lot in popularity. If you don't have it installed already, you can do so quickly from Microsoft Web Platform Installer. AppFabric caching works as a single node cluster, which is useful for you to test its behavior before moving to production. Unfortunately, its administration is possible only via a command prompt (based on PowerShell) or API. An official graphical interface doesn't exist, but the commands to start and query the engine status are simple and are highlighted in MSDN.

Our first provider based on AppFabric caching will be a custom cache provider.

TECHNIQUE 88   **Custom cache provider**

You can write a custom cache provider in ASP.NET 4.0 by simply implementing a class that inherits from `ObjectCache`, which is the base abstract class that's used by the only provider already implemented in ASP.NET, the aforementioned `MemoryCache`.

Writing a custom provider isn't difficult. In this example, we'll use Windows Server AppFabric, which we assume is configured and running locally. You can obviously use this as a base to implement additional option or to target a different caching engine.

PROBLEM

We need to share the cache objects in a cluster and make the cached items synchronized across the different servers. AppFabric caching will make this possible.

Our custom provider will be based on `ObjectCache`, and we'll show you how to build a simple cache factory. You'll be able to change the provider by changing the configuration. This ability fills a gap present in ASP.NET, where a full Provider Model (like the one for the Membership, Roles, or Profile APIs) doesn't exist for caching.

SOLUTION

The API for AppFabric caching is located in the `Microsoft.ApplicationServer.Caching.Client` and `Microsoft.ApplicationServer.Caching.Core` assemblies. You need to add a reference to them in your application before you start. Our solution will offer a new caching provider for .NET Framework 4.0, which we'll use in our ASP.NET application.

Configure AppFabric

First of all, you need to configure the caching servers. You can be this via code or in web.config. Using web.config is a better idea because you can control this setting more easily.

```
<configSections>
  <section name="dataCacheClient"
        type="Microsoft.ApplicationServer.Caching.DataCacheClientSection,
             Microsoft.ApplicationServer.Caching.Core, Version=1.0.0.0,
             Culture=neutral, PublicKeyToken=31bf3856ad364e35" />
</configSections>

<dataCacheClient>
  <hosts>
    <host name="localhost" cachePort="22233" />
  </hosts>
  <securityProperties mode="None" protectionLevel="None"/>
</dataCacheClient>
```

Now that the provider is configured, you can write the code necessary to implement the provider.

DataCache and DataCacheFactory

The class that's responsible for accessing AppFabric caching is `DataCache`, which can be created via the `DataCacheFactory` class. Because creating this instance is expensive, it needs to be created and shared across multiple requests. To implement this behavior, we chose a static property; the code is shown in the following listing.

Listing 14.8 DataCache factory initialization

C#:
```
private static DataCache factory;

private static DataCache CacheFactory
{
  get
```

```
    {
      if (factory == null)
      {
        lock (syncObj)
        {
          if (factory == null)
          {
            DataCacheFactory cacheFactory = new DataCacheFactory();
            factory = cacheFactory.GetDefaultCache();
          }
        }
      }

      return factory;
    }
}
```

VB:
```
Private Shared factory As DataCache

Private Shared ReadOnly Property CacheFactory() As DataCache
  Get
    If factory Is Nothing Then
      SyncLock syncObj
        If factory Is Nothing Then
          Dim cacheFactory As New DataCacheFactory()
          factory = cacheFactory.GetDefaultCache()
        End If
      End SyncLock
    End If

    Return factory
  End Get
End Property
```

By using this code, we're reading the configuration from the application configuration file, which in our case is web.config.

Saving items in the cache

The cache instance is ready, but we need to access it. ObjectCache provides a lot of overloads, which are mandatory and must be implemented. You can find the complete listing in the downloadable code samples for this book. The following listing shows the most interesting part. The other overloads will simply call this method.

Listing 14.9   Saving items in cache using Windows Server AppFabric

C#:
```
public override void Set(CacheItem item, CacheItemPolicy policy)
{
  if (item == null || item.Value == null)
    return;

  if (policy != null && policy.ChangeMonitors != null
      && policy.ChangeMonitors.Count>0)
    throw new NotSupportedException("Change monitors are not supported");
```

```
    item.Key = item.Key.ToLowerInvariant();        ⟵── Keys are case sensitive
    CreateRegionIfNeeded();                              ⟵

    TimeSpan expire = (policy.AbsoluteExpiration.Equals(null)) ?
      policy.SlidingExpiration :
      (policy.AbsoluteExpiration - DateTimeOffset.Now);    ⟵

    if (string.IsNullOrEmpty(item.RegionName))
      CacheFactory.Put(item.Key, item.Value, expire);
    else
      CacheFactory.Put(item.Key, item.Value,
                       expire, item.RegionName);
}
```

Keys are case sensitive

Region created if needed

Absolute or sliding expiration check

VB:
```
Public Overrides Sub [Set](item As CacheItem,
                          policy As CacheItemPolicy)
  If item Is Nothing OrElse item.Value Is Nothing Then
    Return
  End If

  If policy IsNot Nothing
     AndAlso policy.ChangeMonitors IsNot Nothing
     AndAlso policy.ChangeMonitors.Count > 0 Then
    Throw New NotSupportedException("Change monitors are not supported")
  End If

  item.Key = item.Key.ToLowerInvariant()        ⟵── Keys are case sensitive
  CreateRegionIfNeeded()                              ⟵

  Dim expire As TimeSpan =
      If((policy.AbsoluteExpiration.Equals(Nothing)),
        policy.SlidingExpiration,
        (policy.AbsoluteExpiration - DateTimeOffset.Now))    ⟵
  If String.IsNullOrEmpty(item.RegionName) Then
    CacheFactory.Put(item.Key, item.Value, expire)
  Else
    CacheFactory.Put(item.Key, item.Value, expire, item.RegionName)
  End If
End Sub
```

Keys are case sensitive

Region created if needed

Absolute or sliding expiration check

Remember that to be cached in AppFabric caching, the objects need to be serializable. The only other important point to keep in mind is that AppFabric's API provides explicit calls for default or explicit regions, and you must address this fact in your code. Regions are used to separate the items, which are contained in the same area, to be divided by multiple applications. You don't have to use regions, but using them enables you to differentiate your cache policy. AppFabric caching also supports named caches, which is another option that groups together a set of regions.

To create the region, you need to use the CreateRegion method provided by DataCache. The following listing contains the code.

Listing 14.10   Create or check for a cache region

C#:
```
private void CreateRegionIfNeeded()
{
```

```
  try                                                    ⌐  Create
  {                                                      ◄─┘ region
    CacheFactory.CreateRegion(DefaultRegionName);
  }
  catch (DataCacheException ex)
  {
    if (!ex.ErrorCode.Equals(                               Ignore
        DataCacheErrorCode.RegionAlreadyExists))            exception
      throw ex;
  }
}
```

VB:

```
Private Sub CreateRegionIfNeeded()
  Try                                                    ⌐  Create
    CacheFactory.CreateRegion(DefaultRegionName)         ◄─┘ region
  Catch ex As DataCacheException
    If Not ex.ErrorCode.                                    Ignore
      Equals( _                                            exception
        DataCacheErrorCode.RegionAlreadyExists) Then
      Throw ex
    End If
  End Try
End Sub
```

As you can see, you need to explicitly create the region every time because it's removed when the service restarts (it's saved in memory). Unfortunately, there isn't a specific API to check for the existence of a region, and a specific exception is provided instead. This is by design and can't be changed.

Retrieving items from the cache

To retrieve an item previously cached by AppFabric, you have to use the Get method. As you can see in the following listing, the code is straightforward.

Listing 14.11   Retrieving items from cache using AppFabric

C#:

```
public override object Get(string key, string regionName = null)
{
  key = key.ToLower()Invariant;
  CreateRegionIfNeeded();

  return (regionName == null) ?
    CacheFactory.Get(key) :
    CacheFactory.Get(key, regionName);
}
```

VB:

```
Public Overrides Function Get(key As String,
    regionName As String = Nothing) As Object
  key = key.ToLowerInvariant()
  CreateRegionIfNeeded()

  If regionName Is Nothing Then
    Return CacheFactory.Get(key)
```

```
   Else
     Return CacheFactory.Get(key, regionName)
   End If
End Function
```

You don't need to know anything else to start working with AppFabric. You can test your provider directly, or, as you'll learn in the next section, write a simple set of classes to implement a Provider Model.

Using a Provider Model

To support a Provider Model, you need to implement a custom interface:

C#:
```
public interface ICacheBuilder
{
  ObjectCache GetInstance();
}
```

VB:
```
Public Interface ICacheBuilder
  Function GetInstance() As ObjectCache
End Interface
```

You need this interface because `MemoryCache` doesn't have a public parameterless constructor, but its instance needs to be accessed using its `Default` property.

To speed up development, we used an Inversion of Control (IoC) container, specifically Unity from Microsoft patterns & practices. Take a look at the previous snippet, which exposes a static property of type `ObjectCache`. Using this approach, you can simply refer to this class, called `CacheFactory`, which will instantiate the provider defined in web.config.

DISCUSSION

Custom providers are a new and exciting feature in ASP.NET 4.0. If you write a custom provider, you're no longer forced to store your objects in local memory—you can also go out-of-process. Windows Server AppFabric caching is the solution offered by Microsoft to easily manage out-of-process and distributed caching. By implementing a custom provider using its API and putting forth a small amount of effort to produce a cache factory, we made ASP.NET fully support a true Provider Model; we specified the configured provider in web.config and automatically injected it using an IoC container.

TECHNIQUE 89   ## Custom OutputCache provider

To complete our examination of cache providers, we need to take a look at Output-Cache. In this scenario, we'll write a custom provider using the same API that we presented before, so that we can save the items directly in Windows Server AppFabric's caching store.

PROBLEM

When OutputCache items are saved out-of-process in a distributed cache store, they can be synchronized across multiple servers, and you can keep them updated with less effort. ASP.NET 4.0 supports custom providers, and we want to use AppFabric caching as the designated storage.

SOLUTION

To implement a custom OutputCache provider, you need to inherit from the base class `OutputCacheProvider`, which has a single implementation already available that saves the items in memory. This class provides three methods to insert, get, and remove items; we're not providing them in this book because they're simple (and will basically implement code similar to the code in section 14.5.2).

The interesting thing about this case is that you can also specify the provider programmatically, by overriding the `GetOutputCacheProviderName` method in global.asax:

C#:
```csharp
public override string GetOutputCacheProviderName(HttpContext context)
{
  if (context.Request.Path.EndsWith("outputcache.aspx",
                        StringComparison.InvariantCultureIgnoreCase))
    return "AppFabricCache";
  else
    return base.GetOutputCacheProviderName(context);
}
```

VB:
```vb
Public Overrides Function GetOutputCacheProviderName(context As
                                              HttpContext) As String
  If context.Request.Path.EndsWith("outputcache.aspx",
                        StringComparison.InvariantCultureIgnoreCase) Then
    Return "AppFabricCache"
  Else
    Return MyBase.GetOutputCacheProviderName(context)
  End If
End Function
```

Or, you can globally register the provider in web.config:

```xml
<caching>
  <outputCache>
    <providers>
      <add name="AppFabricCache" type="AppFabricCacheProvider, App_Code"/>
    </providers>
  </outputCache>
</caching>
```

When a page with the `@OutputCache` directive that matches our requirements is found (a page that has outputcache.aspx as its path), our new provider will be used.

DISCUSSION

ASP.NET 4.0 fully supports caching, thanks to an extensible model that enables custom providers to be implemented. Data caching or output caching serve different needs, but can work together to support your caching strategies. When these different caching strategies are used correctly, they can give your existing applications new life, without any additional investments in hardware.

14.6 *Summary*

This chapter analyzed in depth the different options available in ASP.NET when it comes time to give a serious boost to your applications. If your website is performing slowly, or you're experiencing overloads on the server, caching is the key to effective scaling.

Cache is especially useful in high traffic sites because it shields the database (or the services, if an SOA architecture is used) from a high number of calls. In turn, your application's throughput will increase, without investments in more hardware.

In this chapter, we went through different, practical issues you might face in real-world scenarios, all of which had a common solution: always keep the most used items (whether .NET objects or entire pages) in separate storage, so that you can easily and quickly reuse them.

After exploring many features of data caching and output caching, valid for both ASP.NET Web Forms and MVC applications, we moved on to the new features in .NET Framework 4.0 for building custom cache providers. When you need to keep the cache synchronized across different servers, this is the way to go. Using an out-of-process engine, like Microsoft Windows Server AppFabric caching, you can further enhance your performance and gain even more scalability.

Now that most of the picture is clear, the next chapter will cover some extreme customizations and concepts you can put into practice to build even smarter applications.

Extreme ASP.NET 4.0

This chapter covers

- `HttpModules`
- Logging and error handling
- Extending `HttpRuntime`
- How to build a virtual path provider

Extensibility is a driving force of ASP.NET, and this chapter is composed of different techniques used to implement advanced—and probably extreme—ASP.NET-based features.

We described `HttpModules` and `HttpHandlers` in chapter 1 from an architectural point of view. In this chapter, we'll use them to implement common strategies in websites; for example, we'll look at error handling, which is fundamental for both security and troubleshooting. We'll use multithreading techniques to increase performance in specific scenarios. Finally, we'll talk about how `HttpRuntime` extensibility can address your remaining needs, letting you store your own source in any non-conventional storage, such as a database or even remote servers.

This chapter and the next are the last in the book, and we've already covered everything you'll see from now on, to some degree, in the previous chapters. This chapter, in particular, is organized to show you advanced topics related to

`HttpRuntime` and multithreading. If you need out-of-the-ordinary techniques in your application, this chapter is for you.

15.1 Using HttpModules

As we mentioned in chapter 1, `HttpModules` are a special kind of class used to intercept mainly `HttpApplication` events (but you can handle events from any object if you need to). An `HttpModule` implements the `IHttpModule` interface from the `System.Web` namespace and is loaded at runtime. Generally, `HttpModules` are stateless with regard to the current request, so they don't contain state related to the current request, but they do use `HttpContext` (a singleton class) as their state context.

`HttpContext` offers access to both `HttpRequest` and `HttpResponse`, enabling state to be used across request and response. You also have the ability to use session state, caching, and application state.

Each `HttpApplication` has only one instance of a given `HttpModule`. Remember that you can have different instances of `HttpApplication` in a given web application, depending on the ASP.NET `HttpApplication` pool configuration (not to be confused with IIS ones), or in case ASP.NET demands more. (For a complete rundown of the details of this topic, see chapter 1.) This single-instance behavior is reflected by `IHttpModule` interface members, which are composed of a simple `Init()` member, used to initialize elements, and a `Dispose()` member, optionally used to clean up resources if you need to do that.

Migrating HttpHandlers and HttpModules to the IIS 7.0 integrated pipeline

To enable `HttpHandlers` and `HttpModules` in the IIS 7.0 integrated pipeline, you need to move the data under the `system.WebServer` node, instead of under `system.web`. You can automatically do this with the following command-line tool:

```
%windir%\system32\inetsrv\APPCMD.EXE migrate config <Application Path>
```

To avoid a runtime error when the legacy `httpModules` section is present (for example, if you need to deploy this application to both IIS 6.0/7.0 in classic pipeline and IIS 7.0 in integrated pipeline), you can set `validateIntegratedModeConfiguration` under `system.webServer\validation`.

You can also use a shortcut to enable all managed modules to run for all requests in your application, regardless of the `preCondition` attribute (to be set to `managedHandler`), by setting the `runAllManagedModulesForAllRequests` property in the `system.webServer\modules` section.

To build an `HttpModule`, you need to register it in the web.config file. Depending on your IIS version, you can make an `HttpModule` globally available and use it across all kinds of requests. For information about this specific feature, available on IIS 7.0 and 7.5, see chapter 1.

NOTE HttpApplication has different events, giving you full control over which ASP.NET state you need to capture, either request or response. You can find all the events in the documentation, which is also available on MSDN at http://www.mng.bz/SeWM.

HttpModules are considered the heart of ASP.NET because common features are implemented with it: OutputCache, SessionState, authorization, and authentication, to name a few. Extensibility in ASP.NET often depends on HttpModules because they enable you to modify virtually anything related to the response and request flows. This section is dedicated to leveraging HttpApplication.

TECHNIQUE 90   **Modifying the response flow with HttpModules**

HttpModules can modify every single aspect of ASP.NET, so you can use them to manipulate the response flow before you send the output straight to the browser. This technique can be useful in a lot of scenarios: you can add specific headers to specific kinds of content or simply modify the flow and redirect the user to a specific page. When you use HttpModules creatively, you can deeply influence the way ASP.NET handles the response flow, as we'll show you in this example.

PROBLEM

We want to write a module to handle a custom authorization mechanism for our application. We want to provide a new authorization feature, with our custom logic inside. ASP.NET includes UrlAuthorizationModule by default, which is useful for mapping access, via web.config, to a given set of URLs. This custom module will let you dynamically specify authorization rules, so you don't have to rely on static specification with the web.config rules.

SOLUTION

Generally, BeginRequest or EndRequest events of HttpApplication are used the most because you usually need to modify the output either before the corresponding HttpHandler begins its work or right after the output is ready to be sent.

The AuthorizeRequest and AuthenticateRequest events are also useful. They're respectively related to authorization and authentication requests from ASP.NET. They both enable you to customize those mechanisms, as outlined in figure 15.1.

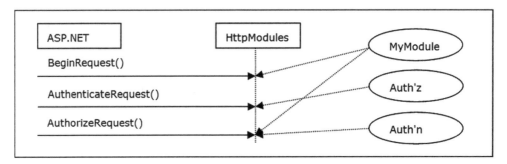

Figure 15.1   The ASP.NET request flow in action. HttpApplication **events are intercepted by custom modules, so the flow can be changed. In this figure,** MyModule **is a custom module that will intercept** BeginRequest **and** AuthorizeRequest **events.**

These events are strictly synchronous, but you can also use their asynchronous equivalents in a fire-and-forget way. Using them asynchronously is handy when you have to deal with data loading or intensive processing routines, where you don't need to modify the request or response status.

For our specific problem, we need to intercept and handle the `AuthorizeRequest` event of the `HttpApplication` class. This event occurs after `BeginRequest` and `AuthenticateRequest` to ensure that the request will be authorized before any handler or module is processed any further.

For our simple example, we're going to intercept the event, and, if the current time is after 5 PM, we'll set the `StatusCode` property of `HttpResponse` to 401, which means that the request isn't authorized. The result is that ASP.NET will stop the request, and, depending on the authentication configuration, the user will be redirected to the login page; in the case of Windows Authentication, the user will be asked for a valid account.

Obviously, you can use a better-fitting dynamic routine, but this solution is a good way for you to get the point regarding authorization customization. The code in the following listing shows how to achieve the result.

Listing 15.1   A custom authorization module to modify the response flow

C#:
```csharp
public class AuthorizationModule : IHttpModule
{
  ...
  public void Init(HttpApplication context)
  {
    context.AuthorizeRequest += new EventHandler(OnAuthorizeRequest);
  }

  void OnAuthorizeRequest (object sender, EventArgs e)
  {
    HttpApplication app = (HttpApplication)sender;

    if (DateTime.Now.Hour >= 17)
      app.Context.Response.StatusCode = 401;
  }
}
```

VB:
```vbnet
Public Class AuthorizationModule
    Implements IHttpModule
  ...
  Public Sub Init(ByVal context As HttpApplication)
        Implements IHttpModule.Init
    AddHandler context.AuthorizeRequest, AddressOf OnAuthorizeRequest
  End Sub

  Private Sub OnAuthorizeRequest(ByVal sender As Object,
                          ByVal e As EventArgs)
    Dim app As HttpApplication = DirectCast(sender, HttpApplication)

    If DateTime.Now.Hour >= 17 Then
      app.Context.Response.StatusCode = 401
```

```
      End If
   End Sub

End Class
```

The code is self-explanatory: we're intercepting the authorization request and changing the request flow by setting a specific HTTP response code.

As we already mentioned, the `HttpModule` needs to be registered in web.config. It will work on every request coming to ASP.NET (not only those coming to .aspx pages), so if you have special content, like images or style sheet, you should exclude them from its range.

DISCUSSION

Customizing the ASP.NET response flow isn't so difficult: you have to intercept and handle `HttpApplication` events and provide your own custom code in response. This approach could lead to some interesting personalization, using a clean and centralized solution.

Even though the code presented in this example is simple, you can add your own rules to validate the current request authentication, and consequently authorize the response based on your needs. You can get even more creative in your use of `HttpModules`, as you'll see in the next example in which we'll intercept and handle a mobile-device-specific skin.

TECHNIQUE 91   **Intercepting and handling mobile device requests**

Mobile devices are extremely popular today, but they require a special kind of UI. They have smaller screens, less power, and different screen resolutions than other devices. They can also have different screen orientations: square screen, portrait, or landscape. They need special treatment to use a website to its maximum potential. This example addresses this problem with a solution applied in the heart of the application.

PROBLEM

We want to write a custom action to intercept and manage requests coming from mobile devices. We're going to apply a specific master page because we don't want to let non-mobile users navigate in our specific low-band version; we want to reserve it for the exclusive use of mobile users.

SOLUTION

The solution is simple and is based partially on browser capabilities (see section 7.2). The magic behind this script is in how ASP.NET intercepts and handles our request. The result will be similar to the screenshot shown in figure 15.2.

Figure 15.2   The website, as it will be displayed in its mobile-specific layout. By using a specific version for specific devices, you'll achieve better usability.

Let's suppose that we have the browser definitions updated (or a custom provider in place); all we need to do is check the `IsMobileDevice` property of the `Http-BrowserCapabilities` instance, which we can access through `HttpRequest`.

To indicate that a mobile version is running, we're injecting a special value into `HttpContext.Items` so that we can access it later in our controls. Listing 15.2 contains the code that will help us identify mobile requests and produce the corresponding output in the inner components (for example, it will change the page size for lists or simply provide less content for some specific views).

Listing 15.2 A custom HttpModule to handle mobile devices

C#:
```csharp
public void Init(HttpApplication context)
{
  context.PreRequestHandlerExecute += new EventHandler(CheckMobileRequest);
}

void CheckMobileRequest(object sender, EventArgs e)
{
  HttpApplication app = sender as HttpApplication;              ⟵ For mobiles
                                                                   only
  if (app.Request.Browser.IsMobileDevice)
  {
    app.Context.Items["isMobile"] = true;
    ModifyMasterPage(app);
  }
}

private void ModifyMasterPage(HttpApplication app)             ⟵ Check for page
{                                                                request
  if (app.Context.Handler is Page)
  {
    ((Page)app.Context.Handler).PreInit +=
                      new EventHandler(ApplyMasterPage);
  }
}

private void ApplyMasterPage(object sender, EventArgs e)       ⟵ Change
{                                                                to mobile
  ((Page)sender).MasterPageFile = "~/Masters/Mobile.master";
}
```

VB:
```vb
Public Sub Init(ByVal context As HttpApplication) Implements IHttpModule.Init
  AddHandler context.PreRequestHandlerExecute, AddressOf CheckMobileRequest
End Sub

Private Sub CheckMobileRequest(ByVal sender As Object,
                               ByVal e As EventArgs)
  Dim app As HttpApplication = TryCast(sender, HttpApplication)

  If app.Request.Browser.IsMobileDevice Then                  ⟵ For mobiles
    app.Context.Items("isMobile") = True                         only
    ModifyMasterPage(app)
  End If
End Sub

Private Sub ModifyMasterPage(ByVal app As HttpApplication)    ⟵ Check for
  If TypeOf app.Context.Handler Is Page Then                      page request
```

```
     AddHandler DirectCast(app.Context.Handler, Page).PreInit,
                  AddressOf ApplyMasterPage
  End If
End Sub

Private Sub ApplyMasterPage(ByVal sender As Object, ByVal e As EventArgs)
  DirectCast(sender, Page).MasterPageFile =
                       "~/Masters/Mobile.master"           ◁─┐ Change
End Sub                                                      │ to mobile
```

The code is simple and consists of a series of checks that ensure that we're modifying only requests directed to pages and only those made by mobile devices. The result will look similar to figure 15.2.

DISCUSSION

Instead of a classic example based on HttpApplication events, this one is the best way to demonstrate the potential offered by HttpModules: you can change every single aspect of the pipeline and plug your code where it's functional for your needs.

The important technique shown in this example is the ability to, from a central point, add an event handler for every page requested. You can do this by using the Handler property of HttpContext, which contains the current handler assigned to the response. The remaining code is self-explanatory: we changed the master page to Mobile.master, which is how the magic of changing the layout occurs.

We created three master pages: one to act as a master for the others (Main.master), one for the normal version (Full.master), and one for the mobile one (Mobile. master). Pages will reference only Full.master, which is based on Main.master (nested master pages are fully supported); this module will change—on the fly—the value of the Page.MasterPageFile property to the corresponding path for our mobile-enabled master page.

The result is truly amazing because it clearly shows you the potential of HttpModules. You might arrive at a similar result using a base common class for pages, but the approach we've described here is more versatile because you can apply your own rules to existing applications, or you can apply them granularly to a specific set of pages. All this is possible because you can easily plug HttpModules into the pipeline.

The next part is dedicated to another important topic: how to deal with errors, log them, and handle them properly.

15.2   *Logging and handling errors*

Logging exceptions is important for controlling your applications when they're deployed. You can opt for your own way of storing this information, using a variation of the code shown in listing 15.1 and intercepting the Error event of HttpApplication, or by using one of the libraries available on the market. Both solutions have their own pros and cons: writing your own code is probably a win/win situation if you don't want to include references to gigantic libraries in order to use only a small portion of their features; using third-part code lets you implement the task in less time.

No matter which method you choose, handling errors the right way is crucial from a security point of view: the less your attacker can see, the more secure your application is. In this section, you'll learn how to protect your errors from others' eyes, and, at the same time, log them for tracing purposes.

15.2.1 *Error logging with Enterprise Library and log4net*

If you decide to use custom libraries to handle logs, you'll probably choose between Microsoft Enterprise Library and Apache Software Foundation's (ASF) log4net.

Microsoft Enterprise Library (at the time we were writing this book) is available in version 5.0 at http://www.mng.bz/T85o. This library is free and contains a lot of functionalities, of which logging is only a small part. It's widely used among enterprise applications; even though it's not part of the .NET Framework BCL, developers tend to trust external class libraries that come from Microsoft. log4net is a project from Apache Software Foundation and is available under the Apache License at http://www.mng.bz/0OX6. Both libraries provide great flexibility: you can log information (and errors) to a file, a database, a message queue, the event log, or just generate an email. If you're trying to choose between the two, consider these points:

- Enterprise Library has a GUI tool for configuring its Logging Application Block
- log4net supports hierarchical log maintenance

The choice is based mainly on features you need to address because, from a performance point of view, they're similar. Enterprise Library is often used because of its capabilities. If you're using it already in your project (for example, because you're using the Cache Application Block), it might seem familiar to you; in this case, using the Enterprise Library is the right choice because you already have a dependency on the main library. On the other hand, log4net is preferred by developers who are searching for a simple and complete library to perform this task, and nothing more.

If you prefer to write code, and your logging needs are relative only to exceptions, you'll probably find it easier to handle errors and store this information with your own custom code.

TECHNIQUE 92   Intercepting, and handling errors with a custom module

Exposing errors to end users isn't a good idea, from both a usability and a security point of view. Error handling implemented the right way will help administrators to inspect the complete error, and will provide the casual user with a more useful courtesy page.

PROBLEM

You want to avoid full error disclosure to normal users but display the full error to administrators. Your application will be secure, and administrators will be able to inspect errors, without accessing the error logging tool, while they're running the page that caused the error. You also want to provide an entry point to add more powerful exception logging capabilities in the future.

SOLUTION

As we discussed in chapter 4 when we talked about security, it's important not to show sensitive information to users: you should always consider errors to be dangerous. ASP.NET gives you control over errors, letting you choose from three options:

- Always show errors
- Never show errors
- Show errors only when the request is coming from the same machine that's running the application

Following code comes from a typical web.config and demonstrates each of these options:

```
<configuration>
  <system.web>
    <customErrors mode="On|Off|RemoteOnly"
                  defaultRedirect="CustomPage.htm" />
  </system.web>
</configuration>
```

These settings are flexible enough to cover your needs while you're developing the application. The reality is that when you put your application in production, you probably won't make requests from the same machine running the page, and so you need to be the only one accessing error details.

`HttpApplication` has a useful `Error` event, used to intercept exceptions that aren't blocked at a higher level, such as in a try/catch block. This event can be handled to combine authorization and authentication from ASP.NET—you can show the error to only a specific group of people, thanks to the Roles API that's available on ASP.NET (see chapter 5 for more information about the Roles API). The code is simple: you just have to handle the event, verify user permissions given the current roles, and then show a personalized error page—or just let ASP.NET do the magic, using the values specified in web.config.

We need to configure web.config to register our module, just like we did in listing 15.1. When an error occurs, the exception will be handled by our event handler, and we'll display an error message similar to the one shown in figure 15.3.

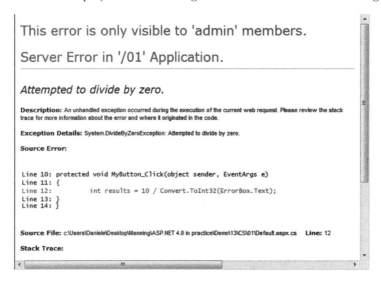

Figure 15.3
Using our custom error system, we can add additional information to the error page or decide to show the error to specific clients.

To implement such a personalized view, we need to write a custom `HttpModule` like the one shown in the following listing.

Listing 15.3 A custom error logging module

C#:

```
namespace ASPNET4InPractice.
{
  public class ErrorModule: IHttpModule
  {
    ...
    public void Init(HttpApplication context)
    {                                                    ◁──── Register for Error event
      context.Error+=new EventHandler(OnError);                on HttpApplication
    }

    void OnError(object sender, EventArgs e)
    {
      HttpApplication app = (HttpApplication)sender;
      HttpException ex = app.Server.GetLastError() as HttpException;

      if (app.User.IsInRole(AdministrativeRole))          ◁──┐ Display error
      {                                                       │ details
        app.Response.Clear();
        app.Response.TrySkipIisCustomErrors = true;
        app.Response.Write(
            string.Format("<h1>This error is only visible" +
                          " to '{0}' members.</h1>", AdministrativeRole));
        app.Response.Write(ex.GetHtmlErrorMessage());
        app.Context.ApplicationInstance.CompleteRequest();       }
    }
  }
}
```

VB:

```
Namespace ASPNET4InPractice
  Public Class ErrorModule
    Implements IHttpModule
    ...
    Public Sub Init(ByVal context As HttpApplication)    Register for Error event
        Implements IHttpModule.Init                      on HttpApplication
      AddHandler context.Error, AddressOf OnError     ◁────
    End Sub

    Private Sub OnError(ByVal sender As Object, ByVal e As EventArgs)
      Dim app As HttpApplication = DirectCast(sender, HttpApplication)
      Dim ex As HttpException = TryCast(app.Server.GetLastError(),
                                        HttpException)

      If app.User.IsInRole(AdministrativeRole) Then      ◁──┐ Display error
        app.Response.Clear()                                 │ details
        app.Response.TrySkipIisCustomErrors = True

        app.Response.Write(String.Format("<h1>This error is only visible" &
                          " to '{0}' members.</h1>", AdministrativeRole))
        app.Response.Write(ex.GetHtmlErrorMessage())
        app.Context.ApplicationInstance.CompleteRequest()        End If
```

```
      End Sub
    End Class
End Namespace
```

You can easily adapt this code to integrate more logging instrumentations, like form variables or application status. To register the module, you have to place this configuration in your web.config:

```
<configuration>
  <appSettings>
    <add key="admnistrativeRole" value="admin"/>
  </appSettings>
  <system.web>
    <httpModules>
      <add name="CustomErrorModule"
           type="ASPNET4InPractice.Chapter15.ErrorModule, App_Code"/>
    </httpModules>

    <customErrors mode="On" defaultRedirect="ErrorPage.htm" />
  </system.web>
</configuration>
```

Sending error message details via email

If you want to send every error via email, the `Error` event handler is the right place to add your code. You can use the `MailMessage` class from `System.Net.Mail` to compose a notification email and send it to your address. If you want to use something already available, take a look at Health Monitoring in the MSDN documentation at http://www.mng.bz/8p51. If you want to store the error log in a database table or in a file, see the corresponding topics in chapters 2 and 3.

Use the `TrySkipIisCustomErrors` property from the `HttpResponse` class to modify the default behavior of IIS 7.x when you're dealing with custom errors. By default, IIS 7 bypasses local error handling and, instead, uses the configuration applied in the `system.webServer` section. By setting this property, you can control IIS 7.x behavior, too; the behavior of IIS 6.0 isn't affected by this change.

DISCUSSION

`HttpModules` enable global event handling and are useful whenever you have that kind of situation. This approach is simple, centralized, open to additional improvements, and shows you how easy it is to tweak ASP.NET behavior and avoid security concerns at the same time. You can handle error logging with many different approaches, as well as with the libraries we mentioned earlier. The methods we've described here are a starting point. The main thing to keep in mind no matter how you decide to deal with the problem is that the less an attacker sees, the better your application security is.

Our journey through ASP.NET advanced techniques will continue now with a topic that's bound to be of interest to you: how to extend ASP.NET `HttpRuntime` and gain more control over ASP.NET page compilation.

15.3 Extending ASP.NET HttpRuntime

ASP.NET HttpRuntime provides great flexibility. If you need to tweak something related to ASP.NET, you'll probably end up with HttpRuntime. Both HttpHandlers and HttpModules are considered part of HttpRuntime, but you can leverage other things to modify ASP.NET.

VirtualPathProvider is a feature that was introduced with ASP.NET 2.0. You can use it to dynamically load resources from a source that's different from that of the file-system and to build them as if they were normal resources. VirtualPathProvider is intended for browsable resources (.aspx, .ascx, master pages, and themes). If you want to virtualize other kinds of resources, you need to implement a BuildProvider.

VirtualPathProvider must be registered at application startup, usually in the AppInitialize static method with global.asax or in the constructor of an HttpModule. Unfortunately, VirtualPathProvider won't work with a precompiled web site, unless you try some of the hacks that use reflection to invoke a private method. That scenario isn't tested, so try it at your own risk.

| TECHNIQUE 93 | **Running your site from the database** |

Running your code from the database is easy using VirtualPathProvider. You can define special kinds of requests to be served from a database, so maintenance will be simpler and won't require FTP access. Microsoft Office SharePoint Server (MOSS) is built on that assumption, so you'll probably find this technique useful in your projects, too.

PROBLEM

Saving the page source on disk is feasible for many of the situations you'll face. But in some cases, you might need to store it at other locations, such as a database, without any loss of features. This solution might be useful when you have multiple servers and you need to keep the source in sync among different servers, without using network shares or something similar.

SOLUTION

VirtualPathProvider is built on top of three fundamental classes that come from the System.Web.Hosting namespace:

- VirtualPathProvider—Used as a base class for the implementation
- VirtualDirectory—Represents a directory
- VirtualFile—Represents a file

NOTE Custom implementations for the VirtualPathProvider, Virtual-Directory, and VirtualFile classes need to run under full trust permissions. If you're using another trust level, you can't run this example. For more information on trust levels, see http://mng.bz/cuH6.

First of all, we need to implement a new class that derives from VirtualPathProvider and overrides the FileExists and DirectoryExists methods. These methods are used to determine whether the requested file or directory exists. The `GetFile` and `GetDirectory` methods are implemented to serve an instance of `VirtualFile` and `VirtualDirectory`, respectively. These classes represent the files and directories, and you use them even with normal files and directories coming from the filesystem. You'll get the same experience, but your code will be loaded from the database. The difference in this scenario is that we need to implement these classes to represent our concepts of both directories and files.

Our custom `VirtualDirectory` implementation isn't difficult: we simply need to implement a class similar to the one shown in the following listing.

Listing 15.4   Our VirtualDirectory implementation

C#:
```
namespace ASPNET4InPractice
{
  public class DatabaseDirectory : VirtualDirectory
  {
    private List<string> _directories = new List<string>();
    private List<string> _files = new List<string>();
    private List<string> _children = new List<string>();

    public DatabaseDirectory(string virtualPath) : base(virtualPath) {}

    public override IEnumerable Children
    {
      get
      {
        return _children;
      }
    }

    public override IEnumerable Directories          ← Directories
    {                                                    in path
      get
      {
        return _directories;
      }
    }

    public override IEnumerable Files                ← Files in
    {                                                    path
      get
      {
        return _files;
      }
    }
  }
}
```

VB:
```
Namespace ASPNET4InPractice
  Public Class DatabaseDirectory
    Inherits VirtualDirectory
    Private _directories As New List(Of String)()
```

```vb
    Private _files As New List(Of String)()
    Private _children As New List(Of String)()

    Public Sub New(ByVal virtualPath As String)
      MyBase.New(virtualPath)
    End Sub

    Public Overloads Overrides ReadOnly Property Children() As IEnumerable
      Get
        Return _children
      End Get
    End Property

    Public Overloads Overrides ReadOnly Property Directories()
          As IEnumerable
      Get
        Return _directories
      End Get
    End Property

    Public Overloads Overrides ReadOnly Property Files()
          As IEnumerable
      Get
        Return _files
      End Get
    End Property
  End Class
End Namespace
```

A `VirtualFile` implementation is more difficult to pull off because we need to get the file content from the database. We'll use a table like the one in figure 15.4 to represent our virtual filesystem. We'll use Entity Framework to map our table to an object model and query it using LINQ extensions methods.

Figure 15.4   The database model used to represent our virtual filesystem is simple and consists of three columns to identify the page path, its content, and the last modified date.

The core of this system is shown in the following listing, which contains a snippet from the `VirtualFile` implementation details.

Listing 15.5   VirtualFile implementation to load content from a database

C#:
```
namespace ASPNET4InPractice
{
  public class DatabaseFile : VirtualFile
  {
    public DatabaseFile(string virtualPath) : base(virtualPath) { }

    public override Stream Open()
    {
      // get file contents and write to the stream
      string fileContents = Utility.GetFileContents(        ◄─┐ Retrieve file
            VirtualPathUtility.ToAppRelative(VirtualPath));   ◄─┘ contents

      Stream stream = new MemoryStream();
      if (!string.IsNullOrEmpty(fileContents))                   Read content
      {                                                     ◄── in memory
        StreamWriter writer = new StreamWriter(stream);
        writer.Write(fileContents);
        writer.Flush();
        stream.Seek(0, SeekOrigin.Begin);
      }
      return stream;
    }
  }
}
```

VB:
```
Namespace ASPNET4InPractice
    Public Class DatabaseFile
        Inherits VirtualFile
        Public Sub New(ByVal virtualPath As String)
            MyBase.New(virtualPath)
        End Sub

        Public Overloads Overrides Function Open() As Stream
            ' get file contents and write to the stream
            Dim fileContents As String = Utility.GetFileContents(   ◄─┐ Retrieve file
                VirtualPathUtility.ToAppRelative(VirtualPath))       ◄─┘ contents

            Dim stream As Stream = New MemoryStream()                  Read content
            If Not String.IsNullOrEmpty(fileContents) Then        ◄── in memory
                Dim writer As New StreamWriter(stream)
                writer.Write(fileContents)
                writer.Flush()
                stream.Seek(0, SeekOrigin.Begin)
            End If
            Return stream
        End Function
    End Class
End Namespace
```

To check whether a file is modified, we'll add a new method that contains this code:

C#:
```
public byte[] LastModifiedTimeStamp
{
  get
  {
    return Utility.GetLastModifiedTimeStamp(
              VirtualPathUtility.ToAppRelative(VirtualPath));
  }
}
```
VB:
```
Public ReadOnly Property LastModifiedTimeStamp() As Byte()
  Get
    Return Utility.GetLastModifiedTimeStamp(
          VirtualPathUtility.ToAppRelative(VirtualPath))
  End Get
End Property
```

The last thing to implement is the real `VirtualPathProvider` custom class. We need to derive from this class and override a couple of methods:

- `GetCacheDependency` and `GetFileHash`—Implemented to provide a custom mechanism for cache dependency. ASP.NET uses a simple method to determine whether a given resource needs to be recompiled or the current one can be used. Our custom implementation has no `CacheDependency` but does provide a custom-computed `HashCode`, using a timestamp column in the database

- `FileExists` and `DirectoryExists`—These methods are used to determine whether a file or directory exists. For directories, we simply return `true` if the path is inside our scope. For files, we check the existence of the virtual path using our Entity Framework model.

- `GetFile` and `GetDirectory`—Get the corresponding `VirtualFile` and `VirtualDirectory` custom implementations, which are included in the downloadable code.

The code in the following listing contains the main methods used to retrieve the file and directory content.

Listing 15.6 The VirtualPathProvider implementation

C#:
```
namespace ASPNET4InPractice
{
  public class DatabasePathProvider : VirtualPathProvider
  {
    public DatabasePathProvider() : base()
    {

    public override VirtualFile GetFile(string virtualPath)
    {
      if (IsVirtualPath(virtualPath))
        return new DatabaseFile(virtualPath);         Load content
                                                      from database
```

```
      else
        return Previous.GetFile(virtualPath);          ◁──┐ Use previous
    }                                                      │ provider

    public override VirtualDirectory GetDirectory(string virtualDir)
    {                                                             Load content
      if (IsVirtualPath(virtualDir))                         ◁──┐ from database
        return new DatabaseDirectory(virtualDir);
      else
        return Previous.GetDirectory(virtualDir);      ◁──┐ Use previous
    }                                                      │ provider

  }
}
```

VB:
```
Namespace ASPNET4InPractice
  Public Class DatabasePathProvider
    Inherits VirtualPathProvider
    Public Sub New()
      MyBase.New()
    End Sub

    Public Overloads Overrides Function GetFile(
        ByVal virtualPath As String) As VirtualFile
      If IsVirtualPath(virtualPath) Then                     Load content
        Return New DatabaseFile(virtualPath)            ◁──┐ from database
      Else
        Return Previous.GetFile(virtualPath)       ◁──┐ Use previous
      End If                                          │ provider
    End Function

    Public Overloads Overrides Function GetDirectory(
        ByVal virtualDir As String) As VirtualDirectory
      If IsVirtualPath(virtualDir) Then                      Load content
        Return New DatabaseDirectory(virtualDir)       ◁──┐ from database
        Return Previous.GetDirectory(virtualDir)   ◁──┐ Use previous
      End If                                          │ provider
    End Function
  End Class
End Namespace
```

To verify that a file or directory exists, you have to implement the FileExists and DirectoryExists methods. The VirtualPathUtility.ToAppRelative method is used to convert the absolute path to an application-relative one (for example, /myroot/Virtual/test2.aspx to ~/Virtual/test2.aspx), as in the following listing.

Listing 15.7   FileExists and DirectoryExists implementation

C#:
```
public override bool FileExists(string virtualPath)
{
  if (IsVirtualPath(virtualPath) &&
        Utility.FileExists(
                    VirtualPathUtility.ToAppRelative(virtualPath)))
    return true;
```

```
    return Previous.FileExists(virtualPath);
}

public override bool DirectoryExists(string virtualDir)
{
  if (IsVirtualPath(virtualDir))
    return true;

  return Previous.DirectoryExists(virtualDir);
}
```

VB:
```
 Private Function IsVirtualPath(ByVal virtualPath As String) As Boolean
      Return VirtualPathUtility.ToAppRelative(virtualPath).
                            StartsWith(Utility.BasePath,
                              StringComparison.InvariantCultureIgnoreCase)
    End Function

Public Overloads Overrides Function FileExists(
                ByVal virtualPath As String) As Boolean
      If IsVirtualPath(virtualPath) AndAlso
          Utility.FileExists(VirtualPathUtility.ToAppRelative(virtualPath))
      Then
        Return True
      End If

      Return Previous.FileExists(virtualPath)
    End Function

    Public Overloads Overrides Function DirectoryExists(
                ByVal virtualDir As String) As Boolean
      If IsVirtualPath(virtualDir) Then
        Return True
      End If

      Return Previous.DirectoryExists(virtualDir)
    End Function
```

Last, but not least, to avoid performance loss, you must cache the compilation. VirtualPathProvider has two methods that control caching behavior, as implemented in the following listing.

Listing 15.8   Controlling page compilation in VirtualPathProvider

C#:
```
public override CacheDependency GetCacheDependency(string virtualPath,
                IEnumerable virtualPathDependencies, DateTime utcStart)
{
  if (IsVirtualPath(virtualPath))
    return null;

  return base.GetCacheDependency(virtualPath,          ◁── Implementation
                  virtualPathDependencies, utcStart);       default
}

public override string GetFileHash(string virtualPath,    Invalidate
          IEnumerable virtualPathDependencies)        ◁── compilation
```

```
{
  HashCodeCombiner hashCodeCombiner = new HashCodeCombiner();

  List<string> unrecognizedDependencies = new List<string>();

  foreach (string virtualDependency in virtualPathDependencies)
  {
    if (IsVirtualPath(virtualDependency))
    {
      DatabaseFile file = (DatabaseFile)GetFile(virtualDependency);
      hashCodeCombiner.AddObject(file.LastModifiedTimeStamp);
    }
    else
    {
      unrecognizedDependencies.Add(virtualDependency);
    }
  }

  string result = hashCodeCombiner.CombinedHashString;

  if (unrecognizedDependencies.Count > 0)
  {
    result += Previous.GetFileHash(virtualPath, unrecognizedDependencies);
  }

  return result;
}
```

VB:

```
Public Overloads Overrides Function GetCacheDependency(
                                    ByVal virtualPath As String,
                 ByVal virtualPathDependencies As IEnumerable,
                 ByVal utcStart As DateTime) As CacheDependency
  If IsVirtualPath(virtualPath) Then
    Return Nothing
  End If

  Return MyBase.GetCacheDependency(
                   virtualPath,
                   virtualPathDependencies,          |  Implementation
                   utcStart)                     <───|  default
End Function

Public Overloads Overrides Function GetFileHash(
                                    ByVal virtualPath As String,
              ByVal virtualPathDependencies As IEnumerable) As String
  Dim hashCodeCombiner As New HashCodeCombiner()      <───|  Invalidate
                                                          |  compilation
  Dim unrecognizedDependencies As New List(Of String)()

  For Each virtualDependency As String In virtualPathDependencies
    If IsVirtualPath(virtualDependency) Then
      Dim file As DatabaseFile = DirectCast(
                     GetFile(virtualDependency), DatabaseFile)
      hashCodeCombiner.AddObject(file.LastModifiedTimeStamp)
    Else
      unrecognizedDependencies.Add(virtualDependency)
    End If
  Next

  Dim result As String = hashCodeCombiner.CombinedHashString
```

```
  If unrecognizedDependencies.Count > 0 Then
    result += Previous.GetFileHash(virtualPath, unrecognizedDependencies)
  End If

  Return result
End Function
```

The code used in this solution isn't hard to understand, but it is a bit verbose; `VirtualPathProvider` and its relative classes are general purpose and need a lot of plumbing code to be implemented. As we've shown you in this example, you don't need to fully implement all of them, but only the one that's useful in your scenario.

DISCUSSION

The scenario addressed in this section provided a good lesson in how extensible ASP.NET is. The code isn't difficult to understand and it uses some of the inner details of `HttpRuntime`. You can apply this code in multiple ways, beginning with using a different store for the file source to enable better administration and to simplify code distribution across load-balanced web servers. As you can see in figure 15.5, the result will look as if the page was stored on a disk and then traditionally executed.

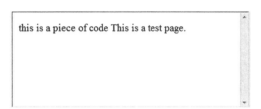

If you plan to use this code in production, you'll probably need to add some caching to improve performance and save your database from a few calls. We've attached a simple page (admin.aspx) to let you experiment easily by administering the virtual file-system content.

Figure 15.5 The resulting page is served from the database that was previously created. When the database content is changed, the new version is automatically used.

This example is the last one in the chapter because it deals with compilation, the Page Parser, and the inner details of ASP.NET engine. We hope it's useful to you and has shown you how easily you can enhance ASP.NET to suit your needs.

15.4 Summary

This chapter contained special techniques to address specific scenarios. Remember that ASP.NET is built for flexibility; this characteristic reflects how many incredible things you can do by using extreme techniques.

`HttpRuntime` offers the right entry points to add your own custom mechanisms to implement simple things like intercepting (and logging) exceptions and more complex things like modifying page behavior using an `HttpModule`, or implementing a `VirtualPathProvider` to load code from a database. ASP.NET is so powerful that you can literally do anything you need to: you just have to write code and express your imagination!

The next chapter, which is the last one in the book, will continue on this path and introduce you to useful tips that will increase the performance of your ASP.NET applications.

16

Performance and optimizations

This chapter covers

- Compressing and minifying your markup, CSS, and JavaScript files
- Using multithreading techniques to boost performance
- Writing parallel code using ParallelFX
- Optimizing web.config

This chapter is the last one of our book, and we're approaching the end of our exploration of ASP.NET. What better way to end our voyage than with performance.

Performance is a driving factor for web applications. You never know how crucial it is until you have a problem. Performance is often confused with scalability, but they aren't the same thing. You can achieve better performance by scaling, and you can optimize your user experience by following a simple set of rules—and by employing some tricks. Depending on the context, the word *performance* can assume different meanings: for our purposes, it's the possibility of performing the same work in less time. Minifying JavaScript, CSS, or markup, for example, can speed up page load on the browser side. Sometimes performance is just a matter of doing little things the right way.

On the other hand, multithreading techniques can boost the performance of your application on the server side by using multiple threads to span the work across them. Modern hardware capabilities let you build a new kind of application because multicore architecture is well established.

This chapter will guide you through the different aspects of gaining better performance in a typical ASP.NET application. You don't need to write a high-traffic application in order to enjoy the benefits of these techniques!

16.1   *Increasing download performance by minifying*

Minifying is a special technique that compresses markup, CSS, and JavaScript by removing unwanted characters to improve download speed. In a real-world scenario, imagine trying to run with a lot of extra weight attached to you—this is what your application feels like. It would be easier to just get rid of everything that's not necessary.

Should I dynamically compress the generated data or let IIS do the magic?

Because modern browsers can decompress content on the fly, without significant overhead, compression can be your friend.

You can certainly dynamically compress the markup (or, generally speaking, the content) using the gzip/deflate implementation inside the BCL provided by .NET Framework, but that's not the best deal in terms of performance.

Starting with version 6.0, IIS can compress both static and dynamic content, resulting in better performance than you could achieve writing your own module. You can find related information on Windows Server SDK on Technet.com. Information for IIS 6 is at http://www.mng.bz/b49a; IIS 7 is at http://www.mng.bz/9C1A.

HTML, JavaScript, and CSS usually contain a lot of unnecessary weight; tabs, spaces, and lines are useful to improve readability while you're developing, but they're a waste for the browser. This section will address removing unwanted characters from markup, CSS, and JavaScript. Each of these is characterized by different needs, so we'll introduce different strategies. You'll be able to remove tabs and line feeds from markup, and comments from JavaScript external files. To address these different strategies, we'll use `HttpModule` and `HttpHandler`, as well as other advanced techniques.

▰ TECHNIQUE 94   **Building a request filter to minify HTML**

You can apply minifying techniques to markup to reduce response size. With modern internet speeds, moving your data might not be a problem, but minifying will affect how fast a browser can render the page. Compressing and minifying markup helps to reduce size and speed rendering time for browsers. In most pages, size can be reduced by 60% or more.

PROBLEM

We want to modify page output to control ASP.NET rendering or to replace some placeholder on our page. We don't want to touch existing pages, so we need to apply this filter from a central and unique point. The result will be a minified HTML markup page, with unuseful (for the browser) return carriage characters and tabs removed.

SOLUTION

In this example, we'll build a response filter to modify ASP.NET output. The term response filter is based on the `Filter` property of the `HttpResponse` class in the `System.Web` namespace. The response filter consists of a class deriving from `Stream` in the `System.IO` namespace. We're going to modify the output to remove tab characters and carriage returns. You can use this technique to minify markup, too. You can also add substitution patterns (like replacing more than two spaces with one space, or something similar).

The flow of the proposed solution is a little bit complicated: first of all, we need to create an `HttpModule` and then intercept the `PreRequestHandlerExecute` event of `HttpApplication`. Then we'll check for the `CurrentHandler` property of `HttpContext` to verify that the request is made from a class deriving from `Page`, and then finally we'll set our filter. Performing the check will help to avoid the interception of non-HTML requests that won't benefit from our manipulation.

The filter class will also receive the current `OutputStream` property value of the `HttpResponse` object, which holds the `Stream` related to the generated response output. We'll be able to substitute the default filter with our custom implementation. To write the filter, we need to implement a class deriving from `Stream`, so that the real logic is inside its `Write` method—we need to append the content to a buffer, to replace it in the `Flush` method. Next, the magic happens: we search for an `</html>` string, to make sure that the writing is complete and that we can perform our replacements. The result is a shrinked page, as you can see by exploring the resulting markup. The module code is shown in the following listing.

Listing 16.1 The HttpModule responsible for changing the response filter

C#:
```
public class CustomResponseModule : IHttpModule
{
  ...

  public void Init(HttpApplication context)
  {
    context.PreRequestHandlerExecute +=                      Add
                  new EventHandler(AddFilter);               filter
  }

  void AddFilter(object sender, EventArgs e)
  {
    HttpApplication app = (HttpApplication)sender;           Ignore
                                                             non-page
    if (!(app.Context.CurrentHandler is Page) ||             and Ajax
        !string.IsNullOrEmpty(                               requests
                app.Request["HTTP_X_MICROSOFTAJAX"]))
```

```
        return;                                                    ❶ Handle
                                                                     bug
    Stream filter = app.Response.Filter;

    app.Response.Filter = new ResponseFilter(
                            app.Response.OutputStream);            Add custom
                                                                   filter
    }

}
```

VB:
```
Public Class CustomResponseModule
  Implements IHttpModule
  ...

  Public Sub Init(ByVal context As HttpApplication)
        Implements IHttpModule.Init
    AddHandler context.PreRequestHandlerExecute,              Add
              AddressOf AddFilter                             filter
  End Sub

  Private Sub AddFilter(ByVal sender As Object, ByVal e As EventArgs)
    Dim app As HttpApplication = DirectCast(sender, HttpApplication)

    If Not (
        TypeOf app.Context.CurrentHandler Is Page) OrElse
        Not String.IsNullOrEmpty(app.Request("HTTP_X_MICROSOFTAJAX")
          ) Then                                         Ignore non-page
      Exit Sub                                           and Ajax requests
    End If

    Dim filter As Stream = app.Response.Filter           Handle
                                                       ❶ bug
    app.Response.Filter =
        New ResponseFilter(app.Response.OutputStream)    Add custom
  End Sub                                                 filter

End Class
```

We need to mention one thing in this code. Due to a bug introduced in ASP.NET 3.5, you need to query the `Filter` property before assigning a value to it ❶; otherwise, you'll get an exception and your code won't work.

This module works with a specific response filter, which analyzes the markup and removes the unwanted characters from the output. The following listing contains the filter code.

Listing 16.2 The response filter implementation for minifying markup

C#:
```
public class ResponseFilter : Stream
{
  private Stream responseStream;
  private StringBuilder markup;
  private string resultingHtml;

  public ResponseFilter(Stream inputStream)
  {
```

```csharp
    if (inputStream == null)
      throw new ArgumentNullException("inputStream");

    markup = new StringBuilder();
    resultingHtml = String.Empty;
    responseStream = inputStream;
  }

  public override void Write(byte[] byteBuffer,            ◄─── Compose
                      int offset, int count)                    buffer
  {
    string buffer = Encoding.Default.GetString(byteBuffer, offset, count);
    markup.Append(buffer);
  }

  public override void Flush()
  {
    resultingHtml = markup.ToString();

    if (resultingHtml.IndexOf("</html>",                   ◄─── Allow only
     StringComparison.InvariantCultureIgnoreCase) > -1)         HTML content
    {
      resultingHtml = Regex.Replace(resultingHtml, "\t", " ");
      resultingHtml = Regex.Replace(resultingHtml, "\r\n", " ");
      resultingHtml = Regex.Replace(resultingHtml, "\r", " ");
      resultingHtml = Regex.Replace(resultingHtml, "\n", " ");

      resultingHtml = resultingHtml.Trim();
    }

    byte[] data = Encoding.Default.GetBytes(resultingHtml);     Send
    responseStream.Write(data, 0, data.Length);            ◄─── data

    responseStream.Flush();
  }
  ...
}
```

VB:

```vb
Public Class ResponseFilter
  Inherits Stream
  Private responseStream As Stream
  Private markup As StringBuilder
  Private resultingHtml As String

  Public Sub New(ByVal inputStream As Stream)
    If inputStream Is Nothing Then
      Throw New ArgumentNullException("inputStream")
    End If

    markup = New StringBuilder()
    resultingHtml = [String].Empty
    responseStream = inputStream
  End Sub

  Public Overloads Overrides Sub Write(
          ByVal byteBuffer As Byte(),
          ByVal offset As Integer,                         ◄─── Compose
          ByVal count As Integer                                buffer
```

```
    Dim buffer As String = Encoding.Default.GetString(byteBuffer, offset,
                                                                   count)
    markup.Append(buffer)
  End Sub

  Public Overloads Overrides Sub Flush()
    resultingHtml = markup.ToString()                            Allow only
                                                                 HTML content
    If resultingHtml.IndexOf("</html>",
       StringComparison.InvariantCultureIgnoreCase) > -1 Then
      ' in this example, we will remove tab and \r\n from markup
      resultingHtml = Regex.Replace(resultingHtml, vbTab, " ")
      resultingHtml = Regex.Replace(resultingHtml, vbCr & vbLf, " ")
      resultingHtml = Regex.Replace(resultingHtml, vbCr, " ")
      resultingHtml = Regex.Replace(resultingHtml, vbLf, " ")

      resultingHtml = resultingHtml.Trim()
    End If

    ' send data out to response buffer                           Send
    Dim data As Byte() = Encoding.Default.GetBytes(resultingHtml)  data
    responseStream.Write(data, 0, data.Length)

    responseStream.Flush()
  End Sub
  ...
End Class
```

The code in listing 16.2 will reduce the markup size, using a mechanism similar to the
one shown in figure 16.1.

By combining the classes we created in this scenario, you can totally compress the
resulting text to include only the necessary characters, eliminating less important
ones. Keep in mind that if you need to preserve whitespaces (for example, when
you're using the pre tag), this technique could require some extra effort: you need to
use a regular expression to make sure that these blocks are excluded and their
whitespaces preserved.

DISCUSSION

This example is the most powerful one you'll find for pipeline manipulation. It shows
how flexible ASP.NET is and that it's built with personalization in mind. Using a simple
approach, we just replaced the default rendering mechanism with a custom one and
then changed the content on the fly.

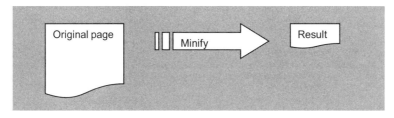

**Figure 16.1 The mechanism associated with minifying: the original page is modified,
and its minified content is sent to the browser.**

You have to keep in mind, though, that strings are immutable in .NET Framework, so playing with these too much can actually cause performance degradation—and trouble. We encourage you to use this technique in moderation (it's widely used in production applications). Remember also that this specific example will mess up JavaScript inline code, and you'll need to apply the right formatting, avoiding carriage return replacements in proximity to this kind of code.

Our next examples are dedicated to CSS and JavaScript.

TECHNIQUE 95   Building an HTTPHandler to minify CSS

CSS minifying is the simplest possible task because all we need to do is replace tabs, line feeds, and double spaces. CSS style sheets are easy to address because comment blocks (/*..*/) are the only things present; you don't need to consider special characters or sequences.

PROBLEM

We want to reduce the size of the style sheet for a page dynamically but also preserve performance. Because you don't often modify style sheets, we'll cache the result in memory so that we can improve performance. The modification of the original file will result in the invalidation of the current compressed request and produce a new one; in this way, the content is always up-to-date.

SOLUTION

This solution is based on a custom `HttpHandler`, mapped to the .css extension. You'll need to map this extension, via IIS, to the common ASP.NET engine. You won't have to do this if you're running an integrated pipeline via IIS 7.x. If you want to use this code in hosting, you can simply use the same code in a page, which is used as a gateway to the real file. Figure 16.2 shows a minified and unminified version of the same file.

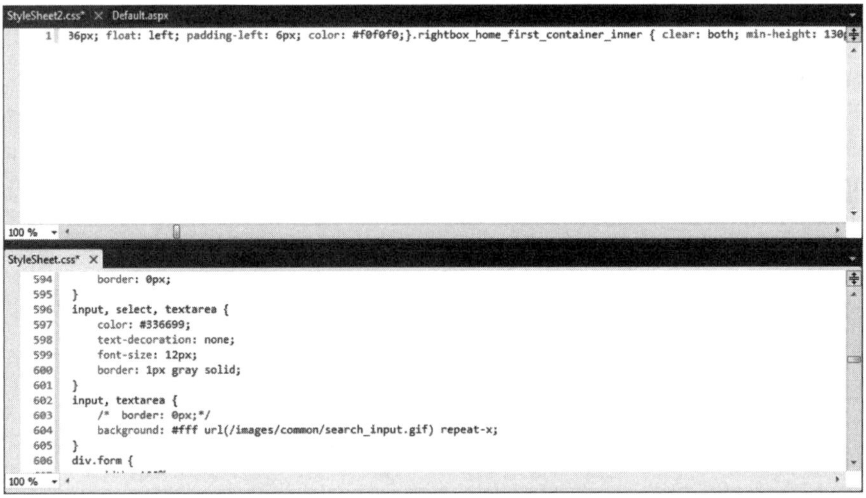

Figure 16.2   The minified version of a file (top) is composed of a single line, without spaces and tabs. The usual version contains a lot of unwanted characters.

First of all, let's create the `HttpHandler` class. The file path is loaded using the `PhysicalPath` property of the `HttpRequest` object, available via the current `HttpContext`.

The remaining code is about replacements and caching. We're taking advantage of the cache dependency feature available in ASP.NET to relate a specific cache entry to a path. Now, every time we modify the physical file, the cache entry will be invalidated automatically, and it will be populated again with fresh content at the next useful request. The results are shown in the following listing.

Listing 16.3   The HttpHandler to minify .css style sheet files

C#:

```csharp
public class CssHandler : IHttpHandler
{

  public bool IsReusable
  {
    get { return true; }
  }

  public void ProcessRequest(HttpContext context)
  {
    string fileContent = string.Empty;
    string filePath = context.Request.PhysicalPath;        // ❶ Cache key
    string cacheKey = string.Concat("css-", filePath);
    object cacheValue = context.Cache[cacheKey];

    if (cacheValue == null)                                // ❷ Save content in cache
      fileContent = AddInCache(filePath, cacheKey);
    else
      fileContent = cacheValue as string;

    context.Response.ContentType = "text/css";
    context.Response.Write(fileContent);
  }

  private static string AddInCache(string filePath, string cacheKey)
  {
    string fileContent = File.ReadAllText(filePath);
    fileContent = string.Concat("/* minifyed at ", DateTime.Now, "*/ ",
                                fileContent);

    fileContent = Regex.Replace(fileContent, "\t", string.Empty);
    fileContent = Regex.Replace(fileContent, "\r\n", string.Empty);
    fileContent = Regex.Replace(fileContent, "\r", string.Empty);
    fileContent = Regex.Replace(fileContent, "\n", string.Empty);

    fileContent = Regex.Replace(fileContent,                    // ❸ Replace more than two spaces
                  "[ ]{2,}", string.Empty);

    HttpContext.Current.Cache.Insert(cacheKey, fileContent,
                        new CacheDependency(filePath),          // ❹ Cache text for two hours
                        DateTime.Now.AddHours(2),
                        TimeSpan.Zero);

    return fileContent;
  }

}
```

VB:

```vb
Public Class CssHandler
  Implements IHttpHandler

  Public ReadOnly Property IsReusable() As Boolean
        Implements IHttpHandler.IsReusable
    Get
      Return True
    End Get
  End Property

  Public Sub ProcessRequest(ByVal context As HttpContext)
        Implements IHttpHandler.ProcessRequest
    Dim fileContent As String = String.Empty
    Dim filePath As String = context.Request.PhysicalPath
    Dim cacheKey As String =
                  String.Concat("css-", filePath)
    Dim cacheValue As Object = context.Cache(cacheKey)

    If cacheValue Is Nothing Then
      fileContent = AddInCache(filePath, cacheKey)
    Else
      fileContent = TryCast(cacheValue, String)
    End If

    context.Response.ContentType = "text/css"
    context.Response.Write(fileContent)
  End Sub

  Private Shared Function AddInCache(ByVal filePath As String,
                ByVal cacheKey As String) As String
    ' write the file and replace values
    Dim fileContent As String = File.ReadAllText(filePath)
    fileContent = String.Concat("/* minifyed at ", DateTime.Now, "*/ ",
                              fileContent)

    fileContent = Regex.Replace(fileContent, vbTab, string.Empty)
    fileContent = Regex.Replace(fileContent, vbCr & vbLf, String.Empty)
    fileContent = Regex.Replace(fileContent, vbCr, String.Empty)
    fileContent = Regex.Replace(fileContent, vbLf, String.Empty)

    fileContent = Regex.Replace(fileContent,
                  "[ ]{2,}", String.Empty)

    HttpContext.Current.Cache.Insert(cacheKey, fileContent,
                              New CacheDependency(filePath),
                              DateTime.Now.AddHours(2),
                              TimeSpan.Zero)

    Return fileContent
  End Function

End Class
```

❶ **Cache key**

❷ **Save content in cache**

❸ **Replace more than two spaces**

❹ **Cache text for two hours**

web.config:

```xml
<configuration>
  <system.web>
    <httpHandlers>
      <add verb="*" path="*.css" validate="false"
          type="ASPNET4InPractice.Chapter16.CssHandler"/>
```

```
    </httpHandlers>
  </system.web>
</configuration>
```

`IsReusable` is generally set to `true` to reuse the same instance of the class across differ-ent requests. To achieve scalability, items are saved in the cache ❶ ❷ ❹. The content type and the content are sent to the browser, after the replacements are performed ❸.

By associating this content with .css files, we're modifying the output of these files. You can apply the same techniques to similar content, when you need to perform the same replacements.

DISCUSSION

Typical CSS files aren't big in size, so caching them in memory is acceptable and—of course—fast. Just like the previous technique, this one uses string manipulation, so the same caveats apply. The results of this simple handler are pretty amazing: you can considerably reduce the size of a CSS file. Given the nature of style sheets, which are composed of lots of line feeds, spaces, and tabs, minification can greatly improve the speed of your application.

TECHNIQUE 96   Building an HTTPHandler to minify JavaScript

This example is similar to the one we presented in technique 95. The real difference is in the algorithm associated with the minifying. In this scenario, to minify JavaScript exter-nal files, we'll also remove comments from code, both inline (/*…*/) and per line (//…).

PROBLEM

JavaScript files are full of tabs, comments, and spaces. These characters are useful while you're in the throes of developing, but they're less useful to browsers (the same considerations for the example in technique 95 apply here, too). We want to build a system that minifies JavaScript content on the fly, without modifying files before deployment. As always, we're also keeping great performance in mind.

SOLUTION

The solution is similar to the one we used in technique 95—the only real difference is in the content type response header and the regular expression that does the magic to strip out comments.

You have to map the resulting `HttpHandler` to the .js extension in IIS (if you aren't using IIS 7.x integrated mode) and register it in web.config. As we've said before, you can reuse this code in a bridge page if you need to use it in a hosting scenario where you can't map custom extensions.

The core piece of this class is the regular expression used to catch comments in the following code:

C#:
```
fileContent = Regex.Replace(fileContent,
        @"(?mi)(/\*[\d\D]*?\*/)|(//.*$)", string.Empty);
```

VB:
```
fileContent = Regex.Replace(fileContent,
        "(?mi)(/\*[\d\D]*?\*/)|(//.*$)", string.Empty)
```

The rest of the code is similar to listing 16.3; the only difference is that we first need to remove comments and then remove line feeds and tabs.

This solution isn't the only option available to you. Let's look at another possibility.

Another option: Microsoft Ajax Minifier

To carry out our solution, you could also use a new tool called the Microsoft Ajax Minifier, available at http://ajaxmin.codeplex.com/. The Ajax Minifier consists of a command-line tool, an MSBuild task to minify JavaScript files at compile time, and a library to do it at runtime, just like we're doing in this example. You might be able to further compress JavaScript that's already been compressed by using the Minifier's hypercrunching mode, which renames variables to reduce file size.

For real-world scenarios, the Minifier is the best choice. We've provided the last two examples so that you can understand different approaches to the same problem if you need to provide your own rules in terms of personalizations.

DISCUSSION

Even though the outcome isn't quite perfect, the solutions offered here will work for most situations. Keep in mind that complex comments sequences might modify this script output, so, as always, you'll need to test this technique with your files before going into production. Performance increases are guaranteed by caching and compressing content, and size reductions of 70% and more are possible.

Similarly, multithreading techniques can impact your server performance because you can span the work across multiple threads. The next section of this chapter will expose you to that option, starting with a technique not entirely new to ASP.NET 4.0, and continuing with ParallelFX, a new technology that uses the parallelism that was introduced in .NET Framework 4.0.

16.2 *Reducing computing time with multithreading*

With so many multicore CPUs on the market, multithreading and parallel execution are becoming more popular topics among developers. Both multithreading and parallel execution aim to reduce computing time, which improves performance.

Let's define our terms:

- Multithreading is the ability to execute multiple tasks at the same time, using different threads. Figure 16.3 shows an example of a multithread architecture.
- Parallel execution is the ability to span a single task across multiple CPUs to use the power of all of them to execute a computing task in the fastest possible way.

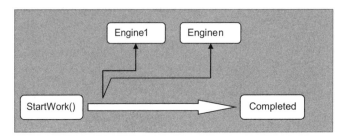

**Figure 16.3
In the multithreading architecture shown here, the StartWork method will instantiate different engines at the same time to execute multiple requests at one time.**

Process, thread, and execution

When a program is executed, the operating system creates a particular object called a *process* and gives isolated memory space to it. A process contains *threads*, which are used to execute the code. A process doesn't have the ability to execute anything. A process contains at least one thread (the primary one). When the primary thread is terminated, the process itself is terminated and the memory is unloaded.

From a performance point of view, creating a thread is easier than creating a process because you aren't required to allocate memory.

When a piece of code is executed, the thread is blocked and waits for the response. If you have a single thread responding to your code execution needs, the problem is simple: you'll have a waiting list for code to be executed. For most applications, this method isn't going to work. Let's imagine that while you're in a production program like the ones in Microsoft Office, you have to wait for every single operation you do to complete before you can move on to another one. Under these circumstances, it would be impossible to have a background spell checker or to start printing while you're still editing a document.

This example highlights the importance of multithreading. ASP.NET supports multiple threads, as we discussed in chapter 1. Using multithreads, one request doesn't stop the others, and multiple requests can be served at the same time. More important is the ability to create new threads and assign a specific code to them, so that part of the work can be executed in a different thread. To be clear, we're talking about generating multiple threads from a single request to increase response time. When you need to make calls to external resources, like databases or web services, you'll find this approach to be quite useful.

Vigorous debate is going on about whether generating multiple threads in a web application is a best practice. Remember, the working threads are shared by all the requests. In this kind of situation, if you can afford better application componentization, you can achieve the same results by simply moving thread generation to a different layer and using the application as a controller and method of display only. Even though the jury is still out, the technique shown in the next example should be useful to you in scenarios where you don't need this kind of componentization or it's just not possible.

TECHNIQUE 97 **Increasing performance with multithreading**

Applying multithreading techniques is a good idea when you have to deal with multiple requests and you don't want to slow the process while you're waiting for results. A typical example is a system made of many requests to different web services. If you need to implement something similar, you'll probably end up using a simple `for` iteration and calling each web service in this block. That technique might work with a few requests, but to speed up execution, you need to use multithreading.

PROBLEM

Let's suppose you have to gather some data using different web services and then display the results on the page, just like a flight comparison engine does. You want to avoid latency and provide a better experience for users while they're waiting for different external services to respond to their requests. Usually, if you opt to execute a single task at a time, the total time will be the sum of the entire operation. You can dramatically improve speed by executing the tasks in parallel, and you'll gain in total response time.

SOLUTION

In heavy-load scenarios where you need to execute different tasks at the same time, you might be able to use a worker thread to reduce the total execution time. A worker thread is a secondary thread created by the primary one to accomplish a specific task.

The .NET Framework has a specific namespace, called `System.Threading`, to support threads, and a specific class, named `Thread`, to represent the concept of a thread in managed code. `Thread` has a special constructor that receives the code to be executed and a `Start` method to begin execution. When the thread is created, there's a *fork* in the execution flow: the primary thread continues its normal execution, and the secondary starts its work.

To provide a true multithreading experience, we're going to execute every request on a separate thread. Using this approach, the total time for the complete request to be executed isn't the amount of time it takes to execute all the different requests, but the longest amount of time that it takes to execute any one of them (plus the overhead of creating, destroying, and joining threads).

Even if it's possible, it's not a good idea to directly instantiate threads; for this specific scenario, a specialized class called `ThreadPool` exists. This class represents a pool of threads managed by the CLR itself, and can be used to coordinate them.

When you're using a technique like this one, you need thread synchronization: each call to the `QueueUserWorkItem` method immediately returns, so you need a way to notify your class that each thread has completed its work and that the results are ready to show. To accomplish this task, you need to use a `WaitHandle` class manually, as shown in figure 16.4.

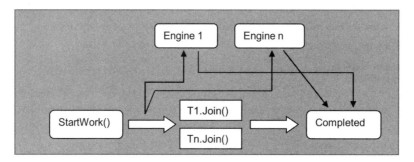

Figure 16.4   Thread generation and synchronization need to be handled manually to work correctly with threads. When completed, a single thread will notify the `ThreadPool`.

The problem at this point is that while accessing the List<T> to add our results, there's no guarantee that there won't be collisions resulting from different threads trying to modify the same collection at the same time. List<T> isn't thread-safe, so we need to synchronize the modifications using the lock keyword (in C#) or the Monitor class. All the code is shown in the following listing.

Listing 16.4 The engine for initializing the multithreading requests

C#:
```
public class PriceEngine
{
  public PriceEngine(string flightNumber)
  {
    FlightNumber = flightNumber;
    FlightResults = new List<FlightPriceResult>();
  }

  public void GetFlightPrices()
  {
    StartTime = DateTime.Now;
    try
    {
      List<WaitHandle> handles = new List<WaitHandle>();          ◄─ WaitHandle tasks

      foreach (IFlightPriceProvider provider in GetProviders())   ◄─ Retrieve providers list
      {
        ManualResetEvent handle = new ManualResetEvent(false);
        handles.Add(handle);
        Tuple<IFlightPriceProvider, ManualResetEvent> currentState =
          new Tuple<IFlightPriceProvider, ManualResetEvent>
                              (provider, handle);                  ◄─ Create and register handle

        ThreadPool.QueueUserWorkItem(
          delegate(object state)
          {
    ...     // Engine implementation in listing 16.5
          }, currentState
        );
      }
      WaitHandle.WaitAll(handles.ToArray());

    }                                                              ◄─ Set completed flags
    finally
    {
      EndTime = DateTime.Now;
      Completed = true;
    }
  }
}
```

VB:
```
Public Class PriceEngine
  Public Sub New(ByVal number As String)
    FlightNumber = number
    FlightResults = New List(Of FlightPriceResult)()
```

```
    End Sub

    Public Sub GetFlightPrices()
      StartTime = DateTime.Now
      Try                                                         ┐ WaitHandle
        Dim handleList As New List(Of WaitHandle)()          ◄──┘ tasks

        For Each provider As IFlightPriceProvider In GetProviders()  ◄┐ Retrieve
          Dim handle As New ManualResetEvent(False)                    │ providers list
          handleList.Add(handle)                                  ◄──┐ Create and
          Dim currentState As                                         │ register handle
              New Tuple(Of IFlightPriceProvider, ManualResetEvent)
                                                          (provider, handle)
          ThreadPool.QueueUserWorkItem(AddressOf ExecuteProvider,
                                  currentState)
        Next

        WaitHandle.WaitAll(handleList.ToArray())            ◄──┐ Set completed
      Finally                                                   ┘ flags
        EndTime = DateTime.Now
        Completed = True
      End Try   End Sub
End Class
```

In this listing, you can see the general structure of the engine, but its inner workings are contained in the code in the following listing. Each result is retrieved from the different providers and added to the results collection using a thread-safe approach.

Listing 16.5   The engine implementation

C#:
```
delegate(object state)
{
  Tuple<IFlightPriceProvider, ManualResetEvent> invokeState =
  (Tuple<IFlightPriceProvider, ManualResetEvent>)state;

  FlightPriceResult result = null;
  IFlightPriceProvider currentProvider = invokeState.Item1;
  result = currentProvider.GetFlightPrice(FlightNumber);

  bool lockTaken = false;
  Monitor.Enter(Sync, ref lockTaken);                ◄── Using lock to
  try                                                     be thread-safe
  {
    FlightResults.Add(result);   }
  finally
  {
   if (lockTaken)
      Monitor.Exit(Sync);
  }

  ManualResetEvent resetHandle = invokeState.Item2;
  resetHandle.Set();                                 ◄── Rejoining the
}                                                        thread
```
VB:

```
  Private Sub ExecuteProvider(ByVal state As Object)
    Dim invokeState As Tuple(Of IFlightPriceProvider, ManualResetEvent) =
      DirectCast(state, Tuple(Of IFlightPriceProvider, ManualResetEvent))

    Dim result As FlightPriceResult = Nothing
    Dim currentProvider As IFlightPriceProvider = invokeState.Item1
    result = currentProvider.GetFlightPrice(FlightNumber)

    Dim lockTaken As Boolean = False
    Monitor.Enter(Sync, lockTaken)                    ◁─┐ Using lock to
    Try                                                 │ be thread-safe
      FlightResults.Add(result)
    Finally
      IF lockTaken Then
        Monitor.Exit(Sync)         End If
    End Try

    Dim resetHandle As ManualResetEvent = invokeState.Item2
    resetHandle.Set()                                 ◁─┐ Rejoining the
  End Sub                                               │ thread
End Class
```

The `IFlightPriceProvider` interface guarantees that every provider has the `Get-FlightPrice` method to load results. It's part of our design strategy, often referred to as the Provider Model. The providers attached to this example are just for testing purposes, and in order to simulate latency, they have a call to `Thread.Sleep` to freeze execution for a couple of seconds. A simple implementation is shown in the following listing.

Listing 16.6 A simple provider implementation

C#:
```csharp
public class SecondProvider: IFlightPriceProvider
{
  public FlightPriceResult GetFlightPrice(string FlightNumber)
  {
    Thread.Sleep(3000);                               ◁─┐ Simulate
                                                        │ latency
    return new FlightPriceResult() {
            FlightNumber = FlightNumber,
            Price = 260 };                            ◁─┐ Return fixed
  }                                                     │ value
}
```

VB:
```vb
Public Class SecondProvider
  Implements IFlightPriceProvider
  Public Function GetFlightPrice(
      ByVal FlightNumber As String) As FlightPriceResult
    Thread.Sleep(3000)                                ◁─┐ Simulate
                                                        │ latency
    Dim result as New FlightPriceResult()
    result.FlightNumber = FlightNumber
    result.Price = 260
    Return result                                     ◁─┐ Return fixed
  End Function                                          │ value
End Class
```

In real-life scenarios, you'll insert your code in this method and populate a new instance of the `FlightPriceResult` class to return the corresponding flight price.

To effectively start the work, we need to create a page with a `Textbox` in which to enter the flight number and a `Button` to execute the code, as shown in the following listing.

Listing 16.7   The page containing the code to start the work

C#:
```
protected void StartWork_Click(object sender, EventArgs e)
{
  PriceEngine engine =                               ◁── Start new
        new PriceEngine(FlightNumber.Text);                instance

  Session["engine"] = engine;                    ◁── Execute next
                                                     statement
  ThreadPool.QueueUserWorkItem(
    delegate(object state)
    {
      PriceEngine priceEngine = (PriceEngine)state;
      priceEngine.GetFlightPrices();
    }, engine);                                  ◁── Redirect on
                                                     waiting page
  Response.Redirect("results.aspx");
}
```

VB:
```
Protected Sub StartWork_Click(ByVal sender As Object, ByVal e As EventArgs)
  Dim engine As New PriceEngine(FlightNumber.Text)      ◁── Start new
                                                             instance
  Session("engine") = engine
                                                 ◁── Execute next
  ThreadPool.QueueUserWorkItem(AddressOf Execute,     statement
                          engine)

  Response.Redirect("results.aspx")              ◁── Redirect on
End Sub                                              waiting page

Protected Sub Execute(ByVal state As Object)
  Dim priceEngine As PriceEngine = DirectCast(state, PriceEngine)
  priceEngine.GetFlightPrices()
End Sub
```

The code in this listing is simple: the engine will start, saving its instance in `Session` so that we can access it later.

The results.aspx page includes code that checks in `Session` for the instance of the `PriceEngine` class that originates the threads, checking at intervals for the execution to be completed. By using a simple reload of the page, as shown in the following listing, we can check the state of the job, and, if it's done, display only the results to the user.

Listing 16.8   The results.aspx page contains both the waiting panel and the results

Markup:
```
<asp:PlaceHolder ID="WaitingPanel"                 ◁── Show waiting
                 runat="server" Visible="false">       panel
```

```
  Please wait...
</asp:PlaceHolder>

<asp:PlaceHolder ID="ResultsPanel"
                 runat="server" Visible="false">

  <h1>Results</h1>

  <asp:literal ID="Feedback" runat="server" />

  <asp:GridView ID="ResultList" runat="server" />
</asp:PlaceHolder>
```

Show results panel ◁

C#:
```
protected void Page_Load(object sender, EventArgs e)
{
  PriceEngine engine =
              Session["engine"] as PriceEngine;
  if (engine == null)
    Response.Redirect("./");

  if (engine.Completed)
  {
    ResultsPanel.Visible = true;
    ResultList.DataSource = engine.FlightResults;
    ResultList.DataBind();

    Feedback.Text = string.Format("Elapsed time: {0}",
            engine.EndTime.Subtract(engine.StartTime));

  }
  else
  {
    WaitingPanel.Visible = true;

    Header.Controls.Add(new HtmlMeta() {
                        HttpEquiv = "refresh",
                        Content = "2" });
  }
}
```

Get engine from session ◁

Complete work ◁

Refresh page and check again ◁

VB:
```
Protected Sub Page_Load(ByVal sender As Object, ByVal e As EventArgs)
  Dim engine As PriceEngine =
              TryCast(Session("engine"), PriceEngine)
  If engine Is Nothing Then
    Response.Redirect("./")
  End If

  If engine.Completed Then
    ResultsPanel.Visible = True
    ResultList.DataSource = engine.FlightResults
    ResultList.DataBind()

    Feedback.Text = String.Format("Elapsed time: {0}",
                  engine.EndTime.Subtract(engine.StartTime))
  Else
    WaitingPanel.Visible = True

    ' programmatically add a refresh meta tag
```

Get engine from session ◁

Complete work ◁

```
    Dim meta as New HtmlMeta()
    meta.HttpEquiv = "refresh"
    meta.Content = "2"
    Header.Controls.Add(meta)
  End If
End Sub
```

Refresh page
and check again

he sequence of the entire workflow is shown in figure 16.5. It's similar to what flight comparison engines do to speed up their execution while you're waiting for the results to display in the web page.

Dealing with multithreading isn't simple because, as we've discussed, you have to take care of details and be sure to use thread-safe collections. But if you use a solution like this one, the performance boost you can achieve by letting different threads simultaneously execute different tasks will be obvious to both you and your customers.

DISCUSSION

Multithreading can boost specific applications, like the one in this scenario, by leveraging the ability to span the work on different threads. It's not intended to be used by every application because you do have to consider some drawbacks.

ASP.NET uses a thread pool, which we talked about in chapter 1. The pool size includes both ASP.NET-generated threads and the ones generated in your code. Remember: if you use this technique in high-traffic applications, the entire pool size can be consumed, and you'll need to increase it accordingly if you notice that its size is low.

TIP   You can monitor current threads in the Control Panel, under Performance Monitor.

Even with that limitation, using threads to execute multiple tasks separately is a good design decision that increases performance dramatically and leverages ASP.NET's multithread nature.

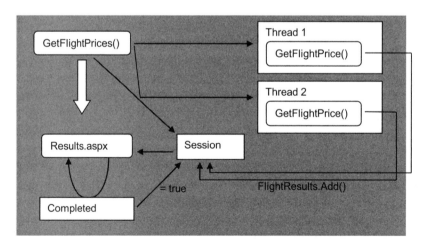

Figure 16.5   The sequence of our multithreading system: first, the providers are initialized and their work is executed. When all the providers are done, the engine is notified so the results can be displayed.

Another possibility that might work for you is to employ parallel computing. Let's talk about that next.

TECHNIQUE 98   Using ParallelFX

ParallelFX is debuting with .NET Framework 4.0. It's a framework specifically designed to build applications that need parallelism. Parallel computing is a new trend among developers because it's clear that it will be difficult to increase CPU power (in GHz), but in the future it will be fairly common to have multicore CPUs everywhere. Right now, the most common server hardware architecture is multicore enabled, but applications aren't. Parallel computing isn't easy to master unless you're lucky—like we are—to have a framework to develop on.

PROBLEM

The problem is the same as in technique 97. We want to execute multiple tasks in parallel to make a gain in total computation time. This time, though, we want to use ParallelFX, a new feature in .NET Framework 4.0.

SOLUTION

Parallel task execution isn't easy to implement. You have to take care of concurrent access from multiple threads, thread joining, and other problems we addressed in technique 97. NET Framework 4.0 introduces new high-level APIs, collectively called ParallelFX, so that you can easily use parallelism in your applications. The difference between ParallelFX and manual thread allocation is shown in figure 16.6.

The example we'll use in this section is the same one we used in the previous scenario: we want to provide a flight search system that can query multiple providers in order to obtain the best price on a specified fictitious flight number.

The ParallelFX Task Parallel Library (TPL) is designed to be optimized against the direct use of `ThreadPool`, which is what we did in technique 97. To scale well on multiple processors, TPL uses an algorithm to dynamically adapt work items over the threads and distribute them accordingly. By default, one single thread per process is created, to avoid thread switching otherwise performed by the underlying operating system. A specific task manager is responsible for this action.

Each worker thread has a local task queue, representing the actions to be completed. Usually, the worker threads use a simple push/pop mechanism to queue and

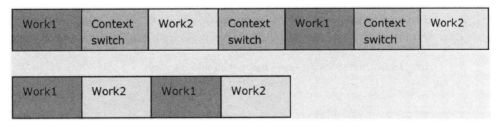

Figure 16.6   The upper part of this figure shows how manual thread allocation works; as you can see, there's a context switch between threads. ParallelFX avoids this problem by using a new architecture, which in this example uses two cores.

enqueue the tasks. To optimize the computing time, when a local queue is empty, the TPL looks for a queue handled by other worker threads so that they can perform the work associated with a task and then removes the thread from the corresponding queue. TPL has a distinct advantage over manual `ThreadPool` use: because the queues are distributed, it doesn't use synchronization between worker threads to join them. This distinction is important because it enables you to achieve true scalability.

> **MORE INFORMATION ABOUT PARALLELFX**   ParallelFX isn't limited to tasks; you can use it with queries (with Parallel LINQ), iterations, and collections. You can find more information on ParallelFX on MSDN at http://www.mng.bz/6w9g.

.NET Framework 4.0 includes new classes specifically designed to execute parallel tasks, under the `System.Threading.Tasks` namespace. You can use the `Task` class when, just like in this scenario, you want more control over the task—controlling when it ends, appending execution of other tasks, and managing extension. In simple scenarios, you can also directly use the `Parallel.Invoke` method. These new APIs are so simple to use that to parallelize a task, you write something like this:

C#:
```
Task.Factory.StartNew(() => ...);
```

VB:
```
Task.Factory.StartNew(Sub ()
...
End Sub)
```

Using `Task`, you can write more concise code and you don't need to directly handle thread creation and its lifecycle. You have the `Wait`, `WaitAll`, and `WaitAny` methods to respectively wait for a single task, all the tasks, or any task in the array to complete.

To simplify exception management, when any exception is raised in a task, it's saved by the task scheduler and then raised when all tasks are completed. TPL creates an `AggregatedException` that has an `InnerExceptions` property, which contains all the exceptions generated by your tasks—exceptions can be managed centrally. The exceptions are raised only if you call one of the `Wait` methods; otherwise, you'll never receive any.

Both a single task and an array of tasks can use the `ContinueWith` or `Continue-WhenAll` methods to associate code to be executed after the tasks are completed. In the following listing, you'll find the first part of the code, where the providers are instantiated and executed in parallel.

Listing 16.9   Instantiating tasks using a simple iteration

C#:
```
...
IFlightPriceProvider[] providers = GetProviders().ToArray();
Task[] tasks = new Task[providers.Length];

for (int i = 0; i<providers.Length; i++)
```

```
{
  tasks [i] = Task.Factory.StartNew(currentProvider =>
      {
        return ((IFlightPriceProvider)currentProvider).
                         GetFlightPrice(FlightNumber);
      },
    providers[i]
  );
}
```

VB:

```
...
Dim providers As IFlightPriceProvider() = GetProviders().ToArray()
Dim tasks As Task() = New Task(providers.Length - 1)

For i As Integer = 0 To providers.Length - 1
  tasks(i) = Task.Factory.StartNew(Function(currentProvider)
      Return DirectCast(currentProvider, IFlightPriceProvider).
                         GetFlightPrice(FlightNumber)
    End Function,
  providers(i)
)
Next
```

This method is interesting because the tasks are loaded in an array. Because this is a typical *fire-and-forget* situation, we can use the ContinueWhenAll method, instead of the typical WaitAll. ContinueWhenAll waits for all the tasks to be completed and then asynchronously runs the corresponding code. The code is shown in the following listing.

Listing 16.10   Results from the providers are aggregated when all work is done

C#:
```
Task.Factory.ContinueWhenAll(tasks.ToArray(), tasks =>
  {
    foreach (Task<FlightPriceResult> task in tasks)
      FlightResults.Enqueue(task.Result);

    EndTime = DateTime.Now;
    Completed = true;
  }
);
```

VB:
```
Task.Factory.ContinueWhenAll(tasks.ToArray(), Sub(currentTasks)
  For Each task As Task(Of FlightPriceResult) In currentTasks
    FlightResults.Enqueue(task.Result)
  Next
  EndTime = DateTime.Now
  Completed = True
End Sub)
```

The code in this listing will queue the tasks and wait for all the tasks to be completed. Finally, a flag is set so we can notify the engine (and then the user) that the tasks are completed. If you execute this code in debug, you can verify that the code is executed after the providers have completed their corresponding work. In the meantime, you aren't blocking any threads to wait for the tasks to be completed. You can accomplish all this easily because ParallelFX simplifies the use of these techniques.

In the `System.Collections.Concurrent` namespace, you'll find specific thread-safe collections that you can use in these scenarios. In listing 16.9, we used `ConcurrentQueue` to queue the results as they arrive. We don't need to take care of concurrent threads accessing the collection in write. This feature is fantastic if you think of all the code you would need to write to do the same thing manually, as we did in the previous example!

The rest of the code is similar to that in technique 97, so we're not going to discuss it here. As you can see, with TPL you can simplify your code, take care of multithreading access to collections, handle exceptions in an easier way, and increase performance, thanks to the minimal thread switching that it provides.

DISCUSSION

ParallelFX is a new feature introduced in .NET Framework 4.0 that you probably won't use directly in an ASP.NET page, as we did in our example. More likely, you'll wrap it in a middle tier or something similar. ParallelFX can certainly help your routines perform faster. If you've had trouble in the past using `ThreadPool`, it's a giant step forward in accessing the operating system's multicore inner features.

16.3 Optimize your web.config

ASP.NET 4.0 introduces a new web.config version, which contains less markup than in previous versions. If you look at a web.config file from an ASP.NET 3.5 application, you'll notice the difference: a lot of the new features are baked into the core, so you don't have to do a new registration for them. This section presents a short list of what you can do to optimize your web.config.

TECHNIQUE 99 **Tips for your web.config**

The web.config file contains the configuration of your application and plays a central role in ASP.NET. It's commonly used to register features, which in many cases aren't used and waste resources.

PROBLEM

The web.config file contains a lot of different sections, so it's not always easy to master. The typical approach is to just leave all the features on by default, to support the highest number of different configurations. But if you're willing to spend five minutes, you can optimize your application without writing any code.

SOLUTION

The following sections describe the actions you can take to optimize your configuration. We're not providing these actions in any order; you can use each one independently of the others.

Always avoid debugging in production

Debugging during production will severely affect your site performance as a result of the artifacts that are added to support debugging. If you want to use different configurations for the environments that you support, take a look at Visual Studio 2010 web.config transformation at http://www.mng.bz/DEq3.

Remove unnecessary HttpModules

You'll never use a bunch of the `HttpModules`. If you take a look at C:\Windows\ Microsoft.NET\Framework\v4.0.30319\Config\web.config, under configuration\system. web\httpModules, you'll find the ones that are built-in.

The following modules are the ones you're least likely to use:

- `Session` (if you don't use session state)
- `WindowsAuthentication` (if you don't use Windows authentication)
- `FormsAuthentication` (if you don't use forms authentication)
- `PassportAuthentication` (deprecated)
- `FileAuthorization`
- `AnonymousIdentification` (if you don't use anonymous profiles)
- `ErrorHandlerModule` (deprecated)

You can remove these modules from web.config by inserting a `<remove />` tag under the configuration\system.web\httpModules section. Removing session state is a special case; let's deal with that separately.

Remove session state

If you don't use session state, you can remove the appropriate `HttpModule` (the afore-mentioned `Session`) and disable it:

```
<configuration>
  <system.web>
    <sessionState mode="Off" />
  </system.web>
</configuration>
```

You can apply this same code to other features you aren't using.

DISCUSSION

This section contained a short list, but we've packed in some useful advice. Optimizing your web.config is important—when you remove unwanted features, you keep them from consuming resources.

And now, our journey exploring the techniques related to performance and optimization is complete.

16.4 Summary

Things like minifying markup, CSS, and JavaScript can decrease load time, and multi-threading techniques have a high impact on response time in applications with intensive I/O requests. This chapter has shown how you can increase the performance of your applications from several different angles, not only by optimizing server-side code, but also by decreasing file size, compressing markup, or using more threads to process the work. ASP.NET is so powerful that you can literally do anything—you just have to write code and express your imagination!

We hope that you've found this book exciting and full of great inspiration. All the techniques we've demonstrated are the result of our day-to-day experiences using ASP.NET. Our aim was to help you build your future applications with a much deeper understanding of how things work under the hood. Have a great development experience!

appendix A:
ASP.NET and IIS 7.x

Starting with IIS 7.0, which is included in Windows Server 2008 and Windows Vista, .NET Framework became part of the web server, using a new architecture that enables direct execution of managed code. IIS 7.0 introduced a new pipeline called an integrated pipeline, which treats ASP.NET modules the same way IIS 6.0 treats native ones. You can write your own extensions to web server request and response handling using the same model that ASP.NET uses for `HttpModules`, and you can apply them to all kinds of requests, not only ASP.NET ones.

This appendix will analyze how to extend IIS and how to integrate it with ASP.NET.

A.1 What's new in IIS 7.5

IIS 7.5 is available on top of Windows Server 2008 R2 and Windows 7 (because they share the same base kernel). As in version 7.0, IIS 7.5 can host services in addition to web applications. In fact, you can host WCF services natively using another binding protocol, just like direct TCP support lets you do.

Starting with this version, IIS can use ASP.NET in Windows Server Core, a specific version of Windows Server, using versions 2.0, 3.0 (WCF), 3.5 SP 1, and, of course, 4.0. Now you can finally host applications with different ASP.NET versions (like 2.0 and 4.0) in the same application pool.

IIS 7.5 introduces support for PowerShell 2.0, a technology that uses managed code to perform administrative tasks from the command line. PowerShell has a better administration UI than did previous versions, supports Visual Studio one-click publishing to deploy web sites, and has configuration tracking capabilities. Last but not least, a lot of the extensions previously available at http://www.iis.net/extensions/ are now integrated. Those modules are still valid if you're using IIS 7.0.

In this section, we'll take a look at how you can modify IIS behavior in both ASP.NET and non-ASP.NET applications. You can do that by writing special modules that come directly from ASP.NET and that are now extended to be part of IIS, too.

Windows Server Core

Server Core is a specific version of Windows Server that doesn't have a UI. This setup is ideal in scenarios where you want to avoid wasting resources. You can configure and administrate Server Core only via scripting. You don't get a GUI, and you can't even connect using a Terminal Session graphical interface.

Server Core is lightweight. Because of its features, it's used in environments where configuration can be injected via scripting, such as in cluster scenario where a web server is similar to others in the node for both hardware characteristics and software configuration.

A.2   *Building extensions*

You can build the same functionality offered by ISAPI modules when you use IIS 7.x in integrated pipeline mode. ISAPI modules are built using native code (mainly C++) and are quite difficult to master.

For compatibility with ASP.NET, you have to write a class that implements the IHttpModule interface (from the System.Web namespace). This interface provides a simple Init method that's used to initialize its behavior: you'll generally add an Http-Application event handler in the Init method, but you can also use this method to initialize some application-specific data because this method is called when the application starts.

The new option offered by the integrated pipeline is useful in integration scenarios when you have to deal with different applications that were written using different technologies and you want to apply the same approach to them from a single and centralized point. In integrated mode, the events related to both request and response are dispatched for every kind of content, not only ASP.NET pages. You can use some ASP.NET features, such as authorization and authentication, in ASP, PHP, or even JSP applications with little effort. Figure A.1 shows the new integrated pipeline in detail.

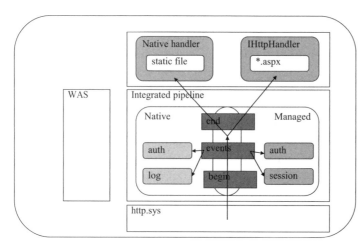

Figure A.1   IIS 7.x integrated pipeline mode enables a useful integration between ASP.NET and the web server. You can write managed modules to intercept events and provide the same results as you can with unmanaged ones.

The separation of the component outlines shown in figure A.1, where WAS, http.sys, and application pools run in separate processes, ensures that when a problem occurs, every single component can be recycled and, using the Application Pools features, isolated from the others. We talk about extensibility techniques for `HttpModules` in detail in chapter 15.

Using the same technique to build an `HttpModule`, you can modify IIS behavior with managed modules. You can implement features previously implemented only with native code, like changing the default document behavior or intercepting every single request. Let's take a look at how you can easily accomplish these tasks with IIS 7.x.

TECHNIQUE 100   Modifying IIS behavior with managed modules

IIS 7.x gives you the possibility to write extensions using managed code and lets you extend every single piece of its infrastructure.

PROBLEM

We want to modify IIS default behavior when we're accessing a directory with no default page inside. IIS generates a default message saying that you can't browse directory content, and we want to change this behavior.

SOLUTION

With IIS 7.x, you can modify this behavior by creating a simple `HttpModule` and registering it under web.config. Our aim is to create an alternative message to be displayed when a default content page isn't present. To start using a managed module, the first step is to register it in web.config, as shown in the following listing.

Listing A.1   Registering HttpModule in web.config

```
<configuration>
  <system.webServer>
    <modules>
     <remove name="DirectoryListingModule"/>
     <add name="DirectoryListingModuleManaged"
        type="MyFirstModule"/>
    </modules>
  </system.webServer>
</configuration>
```

This configuration works only with IIS 7.x and when the application is in an integrated pipeline Application Pool. We removed the default module, called `DirectoryListingModule`, and registered a new one. When you browse a directory that doesn't have a default page defined with this module in place, you'll end with a page similar to the one in figure A.2.

> This is a custom default page. Add your custom login here.

Figure A.2   A new default page associated with our application running on IIS 7.x. You can easily customize content to include special behavior; for example, you can automatically show the thumbnails associated with images in the current directory.

Our module is a simple class that implements the IHttpModule interface, so in the Init method we registered the EndRequest event of the HttpApplication class. The code is shown in the following listing.

Listing A.2   Our custom HttpModule code

C#:
```csharp
using System;
using System.Web;
using System.IO;

public class DirectoryListingModuleManaged : IHttpModule
{
  public void Init(HttpApplication application)
  {
    application.EndRequest +=
              new EventHandler(application_EndRequest);      ◁─── Register EndRequest event
  }

  void application_EndRequest(object sender, EventArgs e)
  {
    HttpContext context = ((HttpApplication)sender).Context;
    {
      if
        (Path.GetFileName(context.Request.Url.AbsolutePath).Length == 0 ||
            Path.GetFileName(context.Request.Url.AbsolutePath)
              .Equals(Path.GetFileNameWithoutExtension(
                     context.Request.Url.AbsolutePath),
            StringComparison.InvariantCultureIgnoreCase)     ◁─── No specific page requested
        )
      {
        context.Response.Clear();
        context.Response.Write("<p>This is a " +
                           "custom default page.</p>");       ◁─── Write to the response stream
        context.Response.End();
      }
    }
  }

  public void Dispose() {/*nothing */}
}
```

VB:
```vb
Imports System
Imports System.Web
Imports System.IO

Public Class DirectoryListingModuleManaged
    Implements IHttpModule
    Public Sub Init(ByVal application As HttpApplication)
      Implements IHttpModule.Init                             ◁─── Register EndRequest event
        AddHandler application.EndRequest,
         AddressOf application_EndRequest
    End Sub
```

```vbnet
Private Sub application_EndRequest(ByVal sender As Object,
                                   ByVal e As EventArgs)
    Dim context As HttpContext = DirectCast(sender,
                                     HttpApplication).Context

    If True Then
        If Path.GetFileName(
               context.Request.Url.AbsolutePath).Length = 0
           OrElse
             Path.GetFileName(context.Request.Url.AbsolutePath)
                 .Equals(Path.GetFileNameWithoutExtension(
                          context.Request.Url.AbsolutePath),
               StringComparison.InvariantCultureIgnoreCase) Then
               context.Response.Clear()
               context.Response.Write("<p>This is a custom " +
                                  "default page.</p>")
               context.Response.End()
        End If
    End If
End Sub

Public Sub Dispose() Implements IHttpModule.Dispose
    'nothing
End Sub
End Class
```

No specific page requested ◁— (annotation pointing to the `StringComparison.InvariantCultureIgnoreCase) Then` line)

Write to the response stream ◁— (annotation pointing to the `context.Response.Write` line)

Starting from this simple example, you can further expand this module to better suit your needs. You can modify every single default behavior of IIS using managed modules. In specific scenarios when you need to use additional features, you can also use native modules like the ones written in C++. There are no real differences between managed and native modules, but managed ones need .NET Framework to be initialized, so you take a small overhead hit when they're used for the first time in the application lifetime.

DISCUSSION

At this point, it must be clear that you can modify every single aspect of the server using the IIS 7.x integrated pipeline, and we're not just talking about the ones related to ASP.NET itself. You still need to create a classic `HttpModule`, but it will be used by the entire pipeline. Remember that when you're using integrated pipeline mode, you need to remove ASP.NET `HttpModules` and register them under the specific web.config node related to IIS (configuration\system.webServer\modules).

ASP.NET and IIS 7.x are so tightly integrated that when you run IIS modules, you're leveraging the ASP.NET `HttpModule` infrastructure and controlling the request and response for all resources, not only ASP.NET ones.

TECHNIQUE 101   ### Configuring application warm-up in IIS 7.5

IIS 7.5 includes a unique feature called application warm-up. ASP.NET application compilation and startup are performed on demand; in many situations, the first request might take a lot of time.

PROBLEM

You need to pre-load an application with data-intensive routines. Or, you want to synchronize access in load balancing scenarios. Either way, the following solution will work for you.

SOLUTION

ASP.NET uses an on-demand compilation model, so when you restart the application pool or the web server, the first request causes a compilation. Depending on what you're doing in your application startup routines, this compilation might require a lot of time, leaving the user with the feeling that your code is running slowly. The new warm-up feature helps you mitigate this behavior and makes it possible to add, at startup, intensive data loading to your application.

To enable this feature, the first thing you have to do is modify the application-Host.config file, which contains general IIS configuration policies. The following listing contains an example.

Listing A.3   applicationHosting.config to enable warm-up

```
<applicationPools>
    <add name="MyApplicationPool" startMode="AlwaysRunning"/>
</applicationPools>
...
<sites>
  <site name="MySite" id="1">
    <application path="/"
        serviceAutoStartEnabled="true"              ◁──┐ Enable
        serviceAutoStartProvider="MyWarmUpProvider">  ◁──┐ autostart
        ...
    </application>
  </site>
</sites>
...
<serviceAutoStartProviders>
    <add name="MyWarmUpProvider"                       ◁──
        type="MyApp.MyWarmUpProvider,MyAssembly" />
</serviceAutoStartProviders>
```

(annotations: "Enable autostart", "Configure Provider")

Next, you need to create a specific class in the example named MyWarmUpProvider, implementing IProcessHostPreloadClient interface from the System.Web.Hosting namespace. You'll see a basic example in the following listing.

Listing A.4   Code to be implemented for warm-up

C#:
```
public class MyWarmUpProvider: System.Web.Hosting.IProcessHostPreloadClient
{
  public void Preload(string[] parameters)
  {
...                                          ◁──┐ Initialization
  }                                              │ code
}
```

VB:
```
Public Class MyWarmUpProvider
  Implements System.Web.Hosting.IProcessHostPreloadClient
  Public Sub Preload(ByVal parameters As String())
```

```
. . .
   End Sub
End Class
```

Initialization
code

The only limitation is that in this context, you don't have access to the application context.

DISCUSSION

This feature gives you a unified approach to data loading during an application cold start. It's particularly useful when you have to deal with intensive data loading at startup. Note that ASP.NET won't respond to any HTTP request prior to the end of the `PreLoad` method execution, so this method is useful in a load-balancing scenario—you can inform the balancer that the node is ready to serve requests.

A.3　Summary

ASP.NET can be easily plugged into IIS 7.x, with benefits for both. Using IIS's extensions, you can change the default behavior and gain granularity in the configuration. You can easily control the behavior of the web server by using managed code (C# or VB) and adding the same capabilities to non-ASP.NET applications. You can also use a new warm-up feature in IIS 7.5 that might be useful in clustered applications, where you need to control the behavior associated with the application's load state.

You can use IIS and ASP.NET together to produce interesting solutions. It's important for an ASP.NET developer to understand the advantages of these solutions when they're used correctly.

The next appendix will cover how to deal with data access when you're using ADO.NET or getting data from XML sources. This topic is quite common, even though it's not considered trendy among developers; as you learned in chapters 2 and 3, new approaches continue to emerge.

appendix B:
Data access fundamentals

Throughout this book, we've used Entity Framework to access data stored in a database. Although it's recommended, Entity Framework isn't the only choice for retrieving data. A good alternative is to use ADO.NET. Entity Framework itself leverages this component. ADO.NET is easy to use, but you have to manually handle the connection to the database, the command to execute queries, and the transaction to execute multiple update commands. Finally, data isn't returned as objects but as a generic-purpose container. All these features make ADO.NET simple but extremely code intensive. That's why Entity Framework is the recommended approach.

Another alternative for managing data is to use XML. Although you can't use XML as a database in medium to big real-world applications, it's still perfectly valid for other purposes. It's a great format for data exchange through messages or files and is perfectly suitable for storing configuration information (the web.config file is an XML file) or small pieces of data. For these reasons, it's important for you to know about XML.

Let's start this appendix by discussing how to use ADO.NET to retrieve and update data. As usual, we're going to use the Northwind database so that you can compare the code in this chapter to the one in chapter 2. The code examples are similar, but you'll discover how much more code is required with ADO.NET.

B.1   Using ADO.NET to access data

ADO.NET is a technology that enables physical interaction with a database. Internally, it leverages Component Object Model (COM) providers, but it exposes functionalities through .NET classes. Most of the complexity of communicating with the database is stripped away, and you only have to deal with ADO.NET classes.

Even if working with classes is somewhat hard, you can do lots of things to simplify the process of retrieving data and pouring it into objects. The reverse process has the same issue; persisting entities data into a database is code expensive. You have to create and open a connection to the database, issue the commands, process the result, and close the connection. This flow is shown in figure B.1.

Another problem is that if you need to issue multiple commands that change data, you have to deal with the transaction, too. Let's put all this stuff in practice.

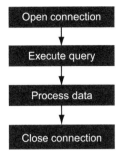

Figure B.1   The query execution workflow. First, a connection is created and opened. Later, the query is executed and the result is processed by our code. Finally, the connection is closed.

TECHNIQUE 102   Querying the database using ADO.NET

As we said before, querying the database involves many steps. In this section, we're going to look at them so that you can understand how to issue a query to the database and get back objects that you can work with.

PROBLEM

Suppose you have to create a web form that shows orders. Because the Northwind database has hundreds of orders, you can't show them all at once and you have to page them. This scenario is common in most web applications that need to show lists of data. The page doesn't have to access the database directly but must rely on the business layer or the domain model (we talked about these two layers in chapter 2) to retrieve data. They must abstract persistence from UI.

SOLUTION

For this particular example, the UI problem isn't what matters so let's focus on the code that interacts with the database. What we have to do is create a method that opens a connection, sends the query to the database, iterates over the result, and, for each record, creates an object that fills its properties with database data. Finally, we have to close the connection and return the objects to the UI. Sounds easy, doesn't it?

Connecting to the database is just a matter of instantiating the `SqlConnection` class located in the `System.Data.SqlClient` namespace, passing in the connection string and invoking the `Open` method.

> **NOTE** The connection string contains information about the database location plus other additional information that can be different across different platforms. `SqlConnection` passes it to the COM infrastructure to physically connect to the database. The application configuration file contains a section where you can place any connection string, and the .NET Framework class library contains APIs to retrieve them. We'll use such APIs in this appendix instead of always rewriting the connection string.

Because the connection implements the `IDisposable` interface, we can wrap it inside a `using` block, as in the following listing, so that it's automatically disposed (and closed) at the end of the block.

Listing B.1   Connecting to a database

C#:
```
var connString = ConfigurationManager.
  ConnectionStrings["conn"].ConnectionString;
using (var conn = new SqlConnection(connString))
{
  conn.Open();
  ...
}
```

VB:
```
Dim connString = ConfigurationManager.
  ConnectionStrings("conn").ConnectionString
Using conn = New SqlConnection(connString)
 conn.Open()
  ...
End Using
```

Okay, we've completed the first step. Now we need to create the Order class and put data inside it. For brevity's sake, we won't show the Order code here. It's a simple class that has a property for each column in the Orders table with the addition of only the Customer and Order_Details properties (which reference the customer who placed the order and the details of the order).

After the class is created, we can issue a SELECT command to the server using the SqlCommand class, as shown in Listing B.2. This class is responsible for issuing any type of command to the database. Because we have to retrieve a set of records, we'll use the ExecuteReader method, which returns an SqlDataReader instance. This instance is a read-only and forward-only kind of cursor.

Listing B.2   Issuing a command

C#:
```
string sql = "WITH cte AS " +
  "(SELECT *, ROW_NUMBER() OVER(ORDER BY orderid) AS RowNumber " +
  "FROM orders) " +
  "SELECT * FROM cte " +
  "WHERE RowNumber >= @startIndex AND RowNumber <= @endIndex ";
using (var comm = new SqlCommand(sql, conn))
{
  comm.Parameters.AddWithValue("startIndex", ((pageIndex-1) * pageCount));
  comm.Parameters.AddWithValue("endIndex", (pageIndex * pageCount));
  var result = new List<Order>();
  conn.Open();
  using (var reader = comm.ExecuteReader())
  {
    while (reader.Read())
    {
      ...
    }
  }
}
```

VB:

```
Dim sql As String = "WITH cte AS " & _
  "(SELECT *, ROW_NUMBER() OVER(ORDER BY orderid) AS RowNumber " & _
  "FROM orders) " & _
  "SELECT * FROM cte " & _
  "WHERE RowNumber >= @startIndex AND RowNumber <= @endIndex "
Using comm = New SqlCommand(sql, conn)
  comm.Parameters.AddWithValue("startIndex", ((pageIndex - 1) * pageCount))
  comm.Parameters.AddWithValue("endIndex", (pageIndex * pageCount))
  Dim result = New List(Of Order)()
  conn.Open()
  Using reader = comm.ExecuteReader()
    While reader.Read()
      ...
    End While
  End Using
End Using
```

Now we have to create objects from the data reader. Once again, it's simple. You just iterate over the records create an object for each one. Then, you pour data from record columns into object properties. This technique is shown in listing B.3. Keep in mind that the `Get` and `GetNullable` methods aren't `SqlDataReader` methods but convenient extension methods we've created to cut down on some lines of code. You'll find these in the downloadable code for the book.

Listing B.3   Creating objects from a data reader

C#:

```
Order o = new Order()
{
  EmployeeID = reader.Get<int>("EmployeeID"),
  Freight = reader.GetNullable<decimal>("Freight"),
  OrderDate = reader.Get<DateTime>("OrderDate"),
  OrderID = reader.Get<int>("OrderID"),
  RequiredDate = reader.GetNullable<DateTime>("RequiredDate"),
  ShipAddress = reader.Get<string>("ShipAddress"),
  ShipCity = reader.Get<string>("ShipCity"),
  ShipCountry = reader.Get<string>("ShipCountry"),
  ShipName = reader.Get<string>("ShipName"),
  ShippedDate = reader.GetNullable<DateTime>("ShippedDate"),
  ShipPostalCode = reader.Get<string>("ShipPostalCode"),
  ShipRegion = reader.Get<string>("ShipRegion"),
  ShipVia = reader.GetNullable<int>("ShipVia")
};
result.Add(o);
```

VB:

```
Dim o As New Order() With { _
  .EmployeeID = reader.[Get](Of Integer)("EmployeeID"), _
  .Freight = reader.GetNullable(Of Decimal)("Freight"), _
  .OrderDate = reader.[Get](Of DateTime)("OrderDate"), _
  .OrderID = reader.[Get](Of Integer)("OrderID"), _
  .RequiredDate = reader.GetNullable(Of DateTime)("RequiredDate"), _
```

```
  .ShipAddress = reader.[Get](Of String)("ShipAddress"), _
  .ShipCity = reader.[Get](Of String)("ShipCity"), _
  .ShipCountry = reader.[Get](Of String)("ShipCountry"), _
  .ShipName = reader.[Get](Of String)("ShipName"), _
  .ShippedDate = reader.GetNullable(Of DateTime)("ShippedDate"), _
  .ShipPostalCode = reader.[Get](Of String)("ShipPostalCode"), _
  .ShipRegion = reader.[Get](Of String)("ShipRegion"), _
  .ShipVia = reader.GetNullable(Of Integer)("ShipVia") _
}
result.Add(o)
```

Congratulations! You've successfully connected to a database, issued a query, and created objects from it.

DISCUSSION

The code for this example wasn't difficult to write, but embedding queries inside the code is something that's not appealing for database administrators. They always prefer that you use stored procedures because these can be controlled.

TECHNIQUE 103   Using stored procedures to query the database

Stored procedures offer a big advantage. They enable a high level of isolation between the code and the database. If you need to optimize or change a query, you can do it without recompiling the application.

PROBLEM

Suppose that you have to modify the problem in the previous section to use a stored procedure instead of the embedded SQL statement. This scenario is common when you have a DBA who wants full control over SQL statements issued to the database and you want to raise isolation between code and database.

SOLUTION

Invoking a stored procedure is extremely simple. The code differs only slightly from what we created previously. In fact, invoking a stored procedure is just a matter of using its name instead of the full SQL statement and setting the CommandType property of the SqlCommand class. The following listing shows the necessary code.

Listing B.4   Invoking a stored procedure

C#:

```
string sql = "GetOrders";
using (var comm = new SqlCommand(sql, conn))
{
  comm.CommandType = CommandType.StoredProcedure;
  ...
}
```

VB:

```
Dim sql As String = "GetOrders"
Using comm = New SqlCommand(sql, conn)
  comm.CommandType = CommandType.StoredProcedure
  ...
End Using
```

Believe it or not, that's all you need to do. With a tiny change you get lots of benefits.

DISCUSSION

Using a stored procedure is a must in many applications. Fortunately ADO.NET was designed to enable this feature, too. Thanks to this design, invoking stored procedures is easy.

So far, you've seen only how to query the database. We're still missing the other side of the coin: saving data in an object into the database.

TECHNIQUE 104   **Persisting data into the database**

When you need to save data into the database, the process is identical to what we did before. You open a connection, execute the command, and close the connection. The only optional variation is that if you have to send more than one command, you have to use a transaction to ensure an all-or-nothing update. If a command goes wrong, you can roll back the transaction and invalidate all previous commands; if everything works fine, you can commit the transaction so that all changes made by the commands become persistent. Figure B.2 shows this workflow.

Now let's see how we can write code that represents the workflow shown in figure B.2.

PROBLEM

Suppose you have a form in which the user can update the order information. He can change the shipping address, as well as the shipping date or the shipment method. He can also add a new detail, modify an existing one (for instance, change the quantity or the discount), and remove one or more of them. What we have to do is create a data access code to handle all these modifications.

SOLUTION

To resolve this problem, you can create a method that accepts the order, and three parameters that represent the details that were added, modified, or removed. In that method you can then launch a command to update the order and launch other commands for each of the details.

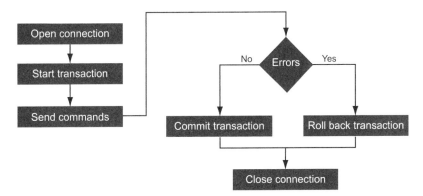

Figure B.2   The database update workflow. First, we open the connection and start the transaction. Next, we send commands to the database. If all the commands are executed correctly, we commit the transaction; otherwise, we roll it back.

Because we have to issue multiple commands, we have to wrap them inside a transaction and manually commit or roll it back, depending on errors. If the user was able to update only the order, the transaction doesn't need to be completed.

Sending a command to update the database requires you to use another method of the SqlCommand class: ExecuteNonQuery. It doesn't accept any parameter, but it returns an Int32 representing the number of rows that were affected by the command.

To start a transaction, you have to call the BeginTransaction method of the Sql-Connection class. That method returns a SqlTransaction object that you later have to pass to the SqlCommand object, along with the connection. To commit or roll back a transaction, you have to call the Commit or Rollback methods respectively, as in the following listing.

Listing B.5 Persisting data using a transaction

C#:

```
using (var conn = new SqlConnection(connString))          Open
{                                                          connection
  using (var tr = conn.BeginTransaction())                Start
  {                                                        transaction
    try
    {
      string sql = "UpdateOrder";
      using (var comm = new SqlCommand(sql, conn, tr))
      {
        comm.CommandType = CommandType.StoredProcedure;
        comm.Parameters.AddWithValue("ShipAddress", order.ShipAddress);
        comm.Parameters.AddWithValue("ShipCity", order.ShipCity);
        comm.Parameters.AddWithValue("ShipCountry", order.ShipCountry);
        comm.Parameters.AddWithValue("ShipName", order.ShipName);
        comm.Parameters.AddWithValue("ShipPC", order.ShipPostalCode);
        comm.Parameters.AddWithValue("ShipRegion", order.ShipRegion);
        comm.Parameters.AddWithValue("ShipVia", order.ShipVia);
        comm.Parameters.AddWithValue("OrderId", order.ShipVia);
        comm.ExecuteNonQuery();                            Execute
      }                                                    command
      foreach (var detail in addedDetails)
      {
        ...
      }
      foreach (var detail in modifiedDetails)
      {
        ...
      }
      foreach (var detail in deletedDetails)
      {
        ...
      }                                                    Commit if no
      tr.Commit();                                         exception
    }
    catch
    {                                                      Rollback if
      tr.Rollback();                                       exception
```

```
        }
    }
}
```

VB:

```
Using conn = New SqlConnection(connString)
  Using tr = conn.BeginTransaction()
    Try
      Dim sql As String = "UpdateOrder"
      Using comm = New SqlCommand(sql, conn, tr)
        comm.CommandType = CommandType.StoredProcedure
        comm.Parameters.AddWithValue("ShipAddress", order.ShipAddress)
        comm.Parameters.AddWithValue("ShipCity", order.ShipCity)
        comm.Parameters.AddWithValue("ShipCountry", order.ShipCountry)
        comm.Parameters.AddWithValue("ShipName", order.ShipName)
        comm.Parameters.AddWithValue("ShipPC", order.ShipPostalCode)
        comm.Parameters.AddWithValue("ShipRegion", order.ShipRegion)
        comm.Parameters.AddWithValue("ShipVia", order.ShipVia)
        comm.Parameters.AddWithValue("OrderId", order.ShipVia)
        comm.ExecuteNonQuery()
      End Using
      For Each detail As var In addedDetails
        ...
      Next
      For Each detail As var In modifiedDetails
        ...
      Next
      For Each detail As var In deletedDetails
        ...
      Next
      tr.Commit()
    Catch
      tr.Rollback()
    End Try
  End Using
End Using
```

Open connection → (points to `Using conn = New SqlConnection(connString)`)

Start transaction → (points to `Using tr = conn.BeginTransaction()`)

Execute command → (points to `comm.ExecuteNonQuery()`)

Commit if no exception → (points to `tr.Commit()`)

Rollback if exception → (points to `tr.Rollback()`)

The code inside the loop has been omitted because it simply invokes the stored procedures that add, modify, and delete details. That's not at all different from the code used to update the order.

What's interesting in this code is the transaction management. All code is inside a `try`/`catch` block. The last statement of the `try` block is the `Commit` method, and the only statement of the `catch` block is the `Rollback` method, which invalidates all the commands executed in the `try` block.

DISCUSSION

In the end, modifying data is similar to reading it. In the first case, you read it and create a set of classes and in the other one, you read classes and pour their values inside the database.

All the code we've written so far involves only the `Order` class (and the `Order_Details` class, in the last example), but the complete scenario requires more. Are you thinking about how much code you would have to write to query all the classes? In a real-world project, you would end up writing thousands of lines of code.

But there's more. Suppose that in another page, you have to show orders and their related customers. That means that the code we've seen so far is somewhat limited because it treats only one table and one class. You have to write new code to handle both the Order and Customer classes in a single query. As complexity grows, so do the lines of code.

And what about this problem: the objects paradigm is completely different from the database paradigm. Databases don't have the concept of inheritance, they keep relationships using foreign keys (objects use references to other objects), and they organize data in rows and columns (objects organize data in properties that can contain a scalar value or other objects). Handling such differences in code is trivial in some scenarios but painful in others.

Working with pure ADO.NET classes represents the most basic way of writing data access code. You can use third-party libraries, like the Microsoft Enterprise Library, but that's just a way to eliminate lots of lines of code. Now you know why Entity Framework greatly simplifies development.

B.2   *Reading and writing XML*

In this section, you'll learn how to create and read an XML file using LINQ to XML. We decided not to use the System.Xml APIs because they're obsolete and are maintained in .NET Framework 4.0 for compatibility reasons only.

TECHNIQUE 105   **Writing XML**

When LINQ to XML was designed, one of the goals was to make it simpler by using fewer classes and less code to create and read a file. The result was the set of classes shown in figure B.3.

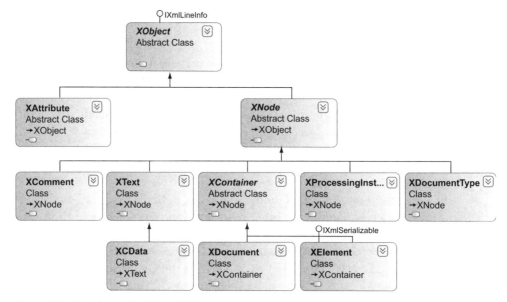

Figure B.3   The classes in LINQ to XML

Without going into each class in detail, you need to know that each of them is included in the System.Xml.Linq namespace and that the following ones are the most important:

- XDocument—Represents the XML
- XElement—Represents a node in the XML
- XComment—Represents a comment
- XAttribute—Represents an attribute
- XDeclaration—Represents the XML declaration

You will surely use the other classes, but in our experience, 90% of the time these are the ones you'll use the most.

PROBLEM

You need to create an XML file that contains the ID and the name of a given customer. This file must be saved on the server machine for further processing.

SOLUTION

Creating an XML file using LINQ to XML is pretty easy. You have to create an XDocument instance and, in its constructor, pass the XElement instances that create the root node. In turn, the XElement constructor takes a list of XElement instances that represent the children. Thanks to this design, you can create the whole XML in a single statement, nesting XElement instances. If it's well indented, such code is extremely easy to understand, as you can see in the next listing.

Listing B.6 Creating an XML structure

C#:
```
XDocument doc = new XDocument(
  new XDeclaration("1.0", "utf-8", "true"),
  new XComment("comment"),
  new XElement("Customers",
    new XElement("Customer",
      new XAttribute("Id", "ALFKI"),
      new XElement("Name", "NAME")
    )
  )
);
```

VB:
```
Dim doc As New XDocument(
  New XDeclaration("1.0", "utf-8", "true"),
  New XComment("comment"),
  New XElement("Customers",
    New XElement("Customer",
      New XAttribute("Id", "ALFKI"),
      New XElement("Name", "NAME")
    )
  )
)
```

First, you create an XDocument instance and then nest an XDeclaration element and an XComment element. Next, you nest an XElement (Customers) inside XDocument.

Inside the XElement, you put another XElement (Customer) to which you add an Attribute (Id) and another XElement (Name). The result is the following:

```
<?xml version="1.0" encoding="utf-8"?>
<!—comment-->
<Customers>
  <Customer Id="ALFKI">
    <Name>Name</Name>
  </Customer>
</Customers>
```

After you have the XDocument instance with the XML shown in the previous snippet, you can use the Save method to save the XML string in a file placed wherever you want:

C#:
```
doc.Save(path);
```

VB:
```
doc.Save(path)
```

If you compare the code needed to write an XML file using LINQ to XML with the code using System.Xml classes, you'll understand that there's no contest: LINQ to XML is better.

DISCUSSION

This sample has clearly demonstrated that LINQ to XML is well designed and easy to use. However, the benefits of such technology don't end here—there's more to learn. Creating a simple XML structure on the fly with LINQ to XML is easy, but the real power comes when you have to create a structure starting with a set of data.

TECHNIQUE 106   Generating XML from a data source

Have you ever happened to have a list of classes coming from a query or any other source, and you need to transform its data into XML? Well, we have. Once again, System.Xml classes make this task a real nightmare because lots of code is needed, but LINQ to XML keeps things small and easy.

PROBLEM

You have a page where the user submits a file containing the ID of all the customers they need information about. You have to retrieve these customers and create an XML file with the name and the full address for each of them.

SOLUTION

The solution here is split in two phases: the first one retrieves the customers from the database, and the second one creates the XML. We'll skip the first one and concentrate on the second.

In the previous section, you learned that you can pass a list of elements to the XElement constructor. By exploiting this feature, you can use a LINQ query to pass child elements and nest data. The following listing shows this technique.

Listing B.7   Creating an XML structure from a list of objects

C#:

```csharp
var customers = CustomersFromAQuery();
var doc =
  new XDocument(
    new XElement("Customers",
      from c in customers
      select new XElement("Customer",
        new XElement("Name", c.CompanyName),
        new XElement("Address", c.Address),
        new XElement("PostalCode", c.PostalCode),
        new XElement("City", c.City),
        new XElement("Country", c.Country)
      )
    )
  );
```

VB:

```vb
Dim customers = CustomersFromAQuery()
Dim doc =
  New XDocument(
    New XElement("Customers",
      From c In customers
      Select New XElement("Customer",
        New XElement("Name", c.CompanyName),
        New XElement("Address", c.Address),
        New XElement("PostalCode", c.PostalCode),
        New XElement("City", c.City),
        New XElement("Country", c.Country)
      )
    )
  )
```

The nested LINQ query contains the structure of each `Customer` node. We don't know what you think, but the first time we wrote code like this, we almost cried thinking about the power and simplicity of it.

DISCUSSION

The capability and extreme simplicity of creating simple structures (and complex ones) and the readability of the code make LINQ to XML one of the wonderful gems of the .NET Framework. Now that you know how to create an XML structure, let's turn to how to read it.

TECHNIQUE 107   **Reading XML**

As the name says, LINQ to XML enables you to execute LINQ queries over the XML structure. In this case, you don't have a set of classes, so you don't have type safety. This issue isn't a significant problem because you can still perform queries in an untyped way.

PROBLEM

Suppose that you have to read the XML file you already generated. You need to extract all customers in France for special processing, and after that you have to process all customers in alphabetic order.

SOLUTION

To retrieve the customers in France, you have to follow these steps:

1 Create the XDocument using the XML.

2 Navigate the XElement elements to reach the Customer ones.

3 Take the XElement instances that have a child XElement whose name is Country and whose value is France.

The next listing translates these actions into code.

Listing B.8   Reading customers located in France

C#:

```
var doc = XDocument.Load(path);
var france = doc.Root.Elements("Customer")          ❶ Perform
  .Where(c => c.Element("Country").Value == "France")      filter
  .Select(c =>
    new
    {
      Name = c.Element("Name").Value,
      Country = c.Element("Country").Value
    }
  );
```

VB:

```
Dim doc = XDocument.Load(path)
Dim france = doc.Root.Elements("Customer").           ❶ Perform
  Where(Function(c) c.Element("Country").Value = "France").   filter
  Select(Function(c) _
    New With { _
    .Name = c.Element("Name").Value, _
    .Country = c.Element("Country").Value _
    }
  )
```

The Root property of the XDocument object represents the root node, and the Elements property gives access to the children of the root (Customer). You then filter them using a lambda expression ❶. Unfortunately, the lambda expression code isn't strongly typed because you're working with XML, which is a loose-typed data format.

Naturally, we can use any LINQ method in LINQ to XML syntax. For this reason, we can use the OrderBy method to sort the customers by their name, as required in the Problem section. The following listing shows the required code.

Listing B.9   Sorting customers by name

C#:

```
var sorted = doc.Root.Elements("Customer")
  .OrderBy(c => c.Element("Name").Value)
```

```
  .Select(c =>
    new
    {
      Name = c.Element("Name").Value,
      Country = c.Element("Country").Value
    }
  );
```

VB:
```
Dim sorted = doc.Root.Elements("Customer").
  OrderBy(Function(c) c.Element("Name").Value).
  Select(Function(c) New With { _
    .Name = c.Element("Name").Value, _
    .Country = c.Element("Country").Value _
})
```

Using the same mechanism, you can write any query you like. You're not obliged to pour data into objects; you can do whatever you want—even leave original queried elements as XElement objects.

DISCUSSION

Reading an XML file using LINQ isn't as easy as reading data from a list of objects, but it's far better than manually iterating over elements or using an XPath expression (which is supported by LINQ to XML). If you've already worked with System.Xml classes, you'll surely agree.

You've learned that LINQ to XML is a great technology for both reading and writing data. One day you're going to find yourself struggling against XML; we hope that you'll remember that LINQ to XML is the best tool in your toolbox.

B.3   Summary

Now you know two alternative techniques for reading and writing data. ADO.NET requires lots of code compared with Entity Framework, but don't underestimate it. Remember that Entity Framework is based on ADO.NET and that ADO.NET has evolved in each release of .NET Framework. What's more, Entity Framework doesn't offer all the power of ADO.NET. For instance, Entity Framework doesn't support stored procedures that return multiple result sets. This is why you always have to keep an eye on ADO.NET.

On the other hand, LINQ to XML has totally overcome the classes in the System.Xml namespace. We've shown you only basic examples, but they unveiled the great potential LINQ to XML enables in both reading and writing XML. If you're starting to develop an application from scratch, we strongly recommend that you use LINQ to XML.

index